William Shakespeare's

King Lear

for Leaving Certificate

with annotations, analysis and commentary by
Patrick Murray

Edco
The Educational Company of Ireland

First published 2014

The Educational Company of Ireland
Ballymount Road
Walkinstown
Dublin 12
www.edco.ie

A member of the Smurfit Kappa Group plc

ISBN: 978-1-84536-594-3

The paper used in this book comes from Managed Forests in Northern Europe For every tree felled, at least one new tree is planted

Editor: Jennifer Armstrong

Design, layout and cover: Liz White Designs

Cover photography: Karl Hugh, courtesy of the Utah Shakespeare Festival, 2007.

Photograph acknowledgements: Pages iv, 5, 6, 21, 33, 42, 73, 76, 85, 96, 102, 105, 125, 135, 140, 141, 153, 160, 167, 174, 182, 198, 205, 276, 277, 285: photos by Karl Hugh, courtesy of the Utah Shakespeare Festival, 2007.

Pages 15, 30, 47, 50, 55, 63, 92, 118, 148, 156, 219, 256, 288, 289: Rex Features.

Pages 19, 54, 91, 115, 133, 134, 180, 181, 188, 211, 212, 214, 222, 262, 263, 264, 265, 273: Shutterstock.

Pages 74, 112, 218: TopFoto.

Pages 147, 191, 210, 215, 216, 221, 224, 226, 227, 228, 230, 231, 233, 234, 235, 236, 237, 238, 239, 240, 242, 244, 246, 248, 249, 254, 255, 257, 258, 259, 260, 261, 266, 268, 271, 275, 287, 290: photos by Anthony Woods, courtesy of the Abbey Theatre.

Page 213: Alamy.

Preface

ALL MODERN STUDENTS OF Shakespeare's plays struggle with the difference between his language, particularly his diction, and present-day English. Some of the words in *King Lear* are no longer in common use and some have different meanings from those they had when the play was written over four hundred years ago. On top of that, the syntax, or ordering of words, can be complex, even puzzling.

In response, this edition of *King Lear* seeks to enlighten the reader by providing useful explanatory notes in the margins of the text, summaries for each scene and detailed commentary on the play. These features will ensure that students fully understand the text.

To appreciate a play, we must think about what is happening to and within the characters, as revealed by their actions, dialogue, soliloquies and asides. The questions at the end of each scene and the activities at the end of each Act stimulate such thinking. They are designed to suit both Ordinary and Higher Level students. Detailed accounts of the characters are provided at the back of the book.

It is also important to be aware of the kind of world in which *King Lear* was written (early seventeenth-century England). This book therefore includes contextual information on the type of theatre and audience for which Shakespeare wrote the play.

All the major areas prescribed for study in the Leaving Certificate syllabus in relation to *King Lear* are extensively covered. These include literary genre (i.e. tragedy); themes; imagery; general vision and viewpoint; roles of hero, heroine and villain; character change and development; and relationships between characters.

Colour photographs from various theatre and film productions of *King Lear* are displayed throughout the book. These images remind students that they are reading a play and provide a chance to consider different casting and staging decisions.

To assist with revision and exam preparation, the book identifies the key moments in the play and highlights useful quotations. It also sets out the parallels between the play's main plot and its sub-plot. A final section is devoted to typical exam questions, accompanied by some tips and sample answers.

The approach taken to *King Lear* in this edition will help students to:

- develop an appreciation of Shakespeare's use of language
- acquire a sound knowledge of the meaning of the text
- understand the workings of the plot and sub-plot
- recognise the play's tragic elements, themes, imagery and use of irony
- study the characters, their motives and their interactions with each other
- learn about the social, cultural and intellectual background to the play
- remember that *King Lear* was written for performance rather than reading
- learn about the early seventeenth-century stage and Shakespeare's audience
- consider how the play might be performed and produced today.

Teachers can access the *King Lear* e-book at **www.edcodigital.ie**.

Contents

Introduction

About William Shakespeare

LITTLE IS KNOWN FOR certain about William Shakespeare. His father, John, moved to Stratford-upon-Avon in Warwickshire in the 1550s, practised a variety of trades, achieved prosperity, owned property and became a leading citizen of the town, which then had a population of about 1,000. William Shakespeare was christened in the parish church in Stratford on 26 April 1564.

It seems likely that Shakespeare went to the local grammar school until he was aged sixteen. However, the attendance records of the school have not been preserved. At that time a grammar school education focused on the study of the Latin language, its grammar and its literature, and on rhetoric, the art of public speaking. Such training is evident in Shakespeare's plays.

In 1582 Shakespeare married Anne Hathaway. She was twenty-six years of age; he was eighteen. They had three children: Susanna and twins, Judith and Hamnet. Hamnet died in 1596, aged eleven. No record of Anne exists between the baptism of her children and the drafting of her husband's will in 1616, when he left her his second-best bed.

By the 1590s Shakespeare was an established actor and a promising dramatist, based in London. We do not know how he became a man of the theatre or when he left Stratford.

By 1595 he was a shareholder in an acting company. Two years later he was able to buy New Place, the second largest property in Stratford. He retired to Stratford in 1611, and died there in 1616.

Shakespeare combined his supreme creative ability with an impressive business sense. He wrote at least thirty-seven plays, including five tragic masterpieces: *Hamlet*, *Othello*, *King Lear*, *Macbeth* and *Anthony and Cleopatra*. He also wrote poetry and he contributed thousands of new words and phrases to the English language.

Records show him acquiring considerable property and shrewdly protecting his legal interests. He also purchased farmland and an interest in tithes, which guaranteed a substantial income. When debts owing to him remained unpaid, he was quick to sue the defaulters, even in petty cases.

About *King Lear*

SHAKESPEARE DID NOT OVERSEE the printing of those editions of his plays published during his lifetime. Much of his work was still in manuscript form when he died, and remained so until two of his friends and colleagues published his plays in 1623 in an edition now known as the First Folio.

King Lear was written between 1605 and 1606. It was performed before James I on 26 December 1606 at Whitehall. A Quarto edition was published in 1608. A revised version of *King Lear* is included in the First Folio (1623), and is shorter than the Quarto text.

King Lear did not prove popular: there were only a couple of recorded performances up to 1675, and then none for more than 160 years. Its unpopularity was largely due to the fact that audiences found the deaths of Lear and Cordelia too distressing. In 1681 Nahum Tate, an Irishman educated at Trinity College,

Dublin, produced a revised version of the play, in which the Fool is omitted and all ends happily with Lear restored to his throne and Cordelia marrying Edgar. Tate's version was the only one performed on the English stage until the actor Edmund Kean restored the tragic ending in 1823. Shakespeare's play was further restored in 1838 by William Charles Macready, actor and theatre manager.

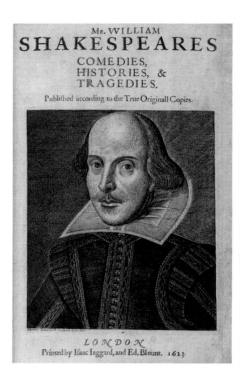

About Shakespeare's theatre

THE THEATRES THAT HOSTED most of the early performances of Shakespeare's plays were public ones, such as the Globe theatre. Shakespeare was a shareholder in the Globe, which was situated close to the River Thames in Southwark, London. It opened in 1599.

A Dutch traveller called Johannes de Witt made a drawing around 1596 of London's Swan theatre. A copy of de Witt's drawing is shown here. It is the only surviving sketch of the interior of the kind of playhouse in which Shakespeare's plays were first performed. The Swan was quite a large theatre and de Witt estimated that it could hold 3,000 spectators.

The drawing, labelled in Latin, shows a round, open-air playhouse. The main feature is the large stage (*proscaenium*) with its overhead canopy known as 'the heavens'. The stage extends into an open yard, described as level ground without sand (*planities sine arena*).

For the price of a penny, spectators (called 'groundlings') stood in the yard looking up at the actors. There were also three tiers of galleries, where, for an extra penny or two, people could sit and avail of some shelter under the roof (*tectum*).

The wealthiest members of the audience wanted to see and also to be seen and therefore availed of a private box in a gallery above the stage. This gallery was part of the tiring-house (*mimorum ades*) building at the back of the stage. It housed a dressing area where actors changed their costumes or attire (hence the term 'tiring-house') and stored props.

The tiring-house was topped by a storage loft and a flagpole. A banner was hoisted to indicate that a play would be performed that afternoon.

Different flags may have been used for different types of play, for example comedy or tragedy. The man shown outside the loft in the drawing appears to be sounding a trumpet.

Actors entered and exited the stage through two sets of large doors in the tiring-house façade. There was no painted scenery to indicate where the action was taking place. The audience members suspended their disbelief and understood the stage to be any place required by the action.

Women were not permitted to take part in dramatic performances and therefore female characters were played by specially trained boy-actors.

Dramatists were experts in using language to set a scene. For example, the storm scenes in *King Lear* are night scenes, but their performances in the playhouse took place in daylight. To overcome this problem, the language spoken by the actors creates an illusion of darkness. In Act 3, Scene 2, the word 'night' is freely used: 'Here's a night … things that love night … such nights as these … this is a brave night'.

Sometimes Shakespeare drew attention to the permanent structure of the theatre. For example, the underside of 'the heavens' was painted to represent the sky and the heavenly bodies. *King Lear* has numerous references to the stars and the heavens, indicating not

Sketch of the interior of the Swan Theatre, by Johannes de Witt,
as copied by Aernout van Buchel, c. 1596.

KEY

1. Playhouse flag
2. Storage loft
3. The heavens
4. Gallery over stage
5. Tiring-house
6. Stage doors
7. Upper gallery
8. Middle gallery
9. Entrance to lower gallery
10. Stage
11. Hell (under stage)
12. Yard

only the sky that curves over the world, or astrological forces believed to determine human destiny, but also the painted 'heavens' of the theatre at which the actors gestured as they spoke. For example, the actor playing Kent may have done this as he declared, 'It is the stars, the stars above us govern our conditions' (Act 4, Scene 3, lines 32–3).

Audience members were trained listeners, and much better equipped than modern audiences to cope with Shakespeare's blank (unrhymed) verse and complex word order. For example, the majority enjoyed listening to and learning from very long church sermons. Such sermons featured magnificent passages of rhetoric, subtle argument and splendid imagery.

KING LEAR

Dramatis personae

LEAR	King of Britain
GONERIL	Lear's eldest daughter
REGAN	Lear's middle daughter
CORDELIA	Lear's youngest daughter
DUKE OF ALBANY	Goneril's husband
DUKE OF CORNWALL	Regan's husband
KING OF FRANCE	suitor (and later husband) to Cordelia
DUKE OF BURGUNDY	suitor to Cordelia
EARL OF KENT	
EARL OF GLOUCESTER	
EDGAR	Gloucester's son
EDMUND	Gloucester's illegitimate son
OSWALD	Goneril's steward
LEAR'S FOOL	
CURAN	a courtier
OLD MAN	Gloucester's tenant

HERALD, CAPTAIN, GENTLEMEN, KNIGHTS, OFFICERS, MESSENGERS, SOLDIERS, ATTENDANTS, SERVANTS

Note on the text: There are three separate and quite distinct versions of the play commonly known as Shakespeare's *King Lear*. An early version, consisting of 3,500 lines, was published in 1608 and is known as the First Quarto (Q1). A second version (approximately 3,300 lines) appeared in 1623 in the First Folio (F1), which was the first collected edition of Shakespeare's plays. A third version (about 3,600 lines), first produced in 1733, contains everything in Q1 not found in F1, and everything in F1 not found in Q1.

Based on the belief that the F1 version represents Shakespeare's second thoughts and is a better theatrical work, the present edition provides the text of F1. The Q1 passages not found in F1 are included in a **blue** font.

ACT 1 ✝ Scene 1

Plot summary

The scene can be divided into four defined parts. In the first (lines 1–31) the Earls of Gloucester and Kent discuss King Lear's decision to divide the kingdom of Britain among his daughters. Gloucester introduces his illegitimate son, Edmund, to Kent, noting that Edmund was born a year after his legitimate son (Edgar).

In the second part (lines 32–183) Lear announces his intention to retire from royal duties (due to his age) and to divide the kingdom into three parts. He wants to give a larger share to the daughter who says that she loves him most. Goneril and Regan play along, declaring their love for Lear in elaborate terms. When Cordelia refuses to outdo her older sisters in empty praise of their father, Lear disowns her and deprives her of her share of the kingdom. He also banishes Kent when he tries to defend her. He divides the kingdom into two parts, assigning these to his elder daughters' husbands, the Dukes of Albany and Cornwall. Lear and his entourage will spend alternate months living with each of them.

In the third part (lines 184–278) the Duke of Burgundy, who was willing to marry Cordelia if she had one-third of Britain for her dowry, rejects her. However, the King of France, who admires her integrity, chooses to make her his queen.

In the final part (lines 279–300) Goneril and Regan discuss the recent odd behaviour of their father: his poor judgement, lack of self-knowledge and changeable nature. Their cynical but shrewd comments are greatly at odds with the flattering remarks they made to his face earlier in the scene.

Sir, I love you more than word can wield the matter

GONERIL, Act 1, Scene 1, 51

King Lear's palace.

Enter KENT, GLOUCESTER and EDMUND.

KENT

I thought the King had more affected the Duke of Albany than Cornwall.

GLOUCESTER

It did always seem so to us: but now, in the division of the kingdom, it appears not which of the dukes he values most; for qualities are so weighed that curiosity in neither can make choice of either's moiety.

KENT

Is not this your son, my lord?

GLOUCESTER

His breeding, sir, hath been at my charge; I have so often blushed to acknowledge him that now I am brazed to't.

KENT

I cannot conceive you.

GLOUCESTER

Sir, this young fellow's mother could; whereupon she grew round-wombed, and had, indeed, sir, a son for her cradle ere she had a husband for her bed. Do you smell a fault?

KENT

I cannot wish the fault undone, the issue of it being so proper.

GLOUCESTER

But I have a son, sir, by order of law, some year elder than this, who yet is no dearer in my account. Though this knave came something saucily into the world before he was sent for, yet was his mother fair; there was good sport at his making, and the whoreson must be acknowledged. Do you know this noble gentleman, Edmund?

EDMUND

No, my lord.

GLOUCESTER

My lord of Kent.

Remember him hereafter as my honourable friend.

---

1. *more affected:* more affection for, favoured

4. *appears not:* is not clear

5–6. *so weighed . . . moiety:* so evenly balanced that careful scrutiny ('curiosity') cannot determine which is the better share ('moiety'), the result being that neither Albany nor Cornwall can reasonably prefer the other's part of the kingdom to his own

8. *breeding:* upbringing
   hath . . . charge: has been at my expense
9. *brazed to't:* hardened to it, unashamed

10. *cannot conceive:* do not understand. The use of 'conceive', which also means 'to become pregnant', provides Gloucester with an opening for the pun that follows
11. *could:* could conceive (she conceived Edmund)
    whereupon: at which point
12. *round-wombed:* pregnant
13. *ere:* before
    smell: detect, find
    fault: sin, offence

14. *issue:* both 'result' and 'child'

15. *proper:* handsome

16. *by order of law:* legitimate
    some year elder: about a year older. This suggests that Edmund may have been conceived during an adulterous encounter
17. *account:* opinion, estimation
18. *knave:* fellow
    something saucily: somewhat rudely or lustfully
19. *fair:* beautiful
    sport: amusement
20. *whoreson:* literally, 'son of a whore'; also, bastard or fellow. Gloucester is not using the word as a term of abuse

24. *hereafter:* after this

25 *services:* respects, duty

26 *sue:* beg

27 *study deserving:* do all I can to earn your good opinion

28 *hath been out:* has been away (perhaps meaning abroad)
29 *within:* from off stage; behind the stage façade

Sennet: trumpet call signalling a procession

30 *Attend:* accompany, escort

32 *Meantime:* meanwhile
we: Lear refers to himself as 'we' rather than 'I'; this is known as the royal plural or 'royal we'. Note also that the text has switched from prose to verse, as befits the more formal occasion
darker purpose: secret intention
34 *'tis ... intent:* it is my fixed intention
35–7 *To shake ... death:* Lear hopes to transfer the worries and tasks of the monarch to the next generation and live a carefree retirement
37 *son:* son-in-law
39 *constant will:* firm purpose
publish: announce publicly
40 *several dowers:* individual dowries (marriage settlements)
40–1 *future ... now:* by dividing his kingdom now, Lear hopes to remove the possibility of future conflict between his successors
42 *Great:* powerful, noble
43 *amorous sojourn:* visit to win Cordelia's love
44 *answered:* given a decision

45 *divest us:* rid myself

46 *Interest:* legal possession

47–9 *Which ... challenge:* Lear is offering the largest portion of the kingdom to the daughter whose natural affection (love for him) and inner worth ('merit') entitle her to lay claim to ('challenge') his generosity ('bounty')

51 *I ... matter:* my love for you is too great to be expressed in mere words

---

EDMUND

25 My services to your lordship.

KENT

I must love you, and sue to know you better.

EDMUND

Sir, I shall study deserving.

GLOUCESTER

He hath been out nine years, and away he shall again.

[*trumpets sound within*] The King is coming.

Sennet. Enter KING LEAR, CORNWALL, ALBANY, GONERIL, REGAN, CORDELIA, and ATTENDANTS.

LEAR

30 Attend the lords of France and Burgundy, Gloucester.

GLOUCESTER

I shall, my lord.

Exit.

LEAR the love test. → the 1st error

Meantime we shall express our darker purpose.

Give me the map there. Know that we have divided

In three our kingdom; and 'tis our fast intent

35 To shake all cares and business from our age,

Conferring them on younger strengths, while we *retire*

Unburdened crawl toward death. Our son of Cornwall,

And you, our no less loving son of Albany,

We have this hour a constant will to publish

40 Our daughters' several dowers, that future strife

May be prevented now. The princes, France and Burgundy,

Great rivals in our youngest daughter's love,

Long in our court have made their amorous sojourn,

And here are to be answered. Tell me, my daughters —

45 Since now we will divest us both of rule,

Interest of territory, cares of state —

Which of you shall we say doth love us most?

That we our largest bounty may extend

Where nature doth with merit challenge. Goneril,

50 Our eldest-born, speak first.

GONERIL

Sir, I love you more than word can wield the matter,

*Lear wants a peaceful retirnment.

Dearer than eye-sight, space and liberty,

Beyond what can be valued rich or rare,

No less than life, with grace, health, beauty, honour,

As much as child e'er loved or father found;   55

A love that makes breath poor and speech unable;

Beyond all manner of so much I love you.

CORDELIA [*aside*]

What shall Cordelia speak? Love, and be silent.

LEAR

Of all these bounds, even from this line to this,

With shadowy forests and with champains rich'd,   60

With plenteous rivers and wide-skirted meads,

We make thee lady. To thine and Albany's issues

Be this perpetual. What says our second daughter?

Our dearest Regan, wife of Cornwall? Speak.

REGAN

I am made of that self metal as my sister,   65

And prize me at her worth. In my true heart

I find she names my very deed of love;   *sibling rivalry*

Only she comes too short: that I profess   *double meaning?*

Myself an enemy to all other joys

Which the most precious square of sense possesses,   70

And find I am alone felicitate

In your dear highness's love.

CORDELIA [*aside*]

                                        Then poor Cordelia!

And yet not so, since I am sure my love's

More ponderous than my tongue.

LEAR

[*to REGAN*] To thee and thine hereditary ever   75

Remain this ample third of our fair kingdom,

No less in space, validity and pleasure

Than that conferred on Goneril. [*to CORDELIA*] Now our joy,

Although our last and least, to whose young love

The vines of France and milk of Burgundy   80

Strive to be interess'd, what can you say to draw

A third more opulent than your sisters? Speak.

---

52 *space and liberty:* freedom and property

53 *valued:* estimated, considered as being

55 *As ... found:* the love you experience from me is as great as that experienced by any father from a child
e'er: ever

56 *A ... unable:* language ('breath' and 'speech') is incapable of expressing my love

57 *Beyond ... you:* I love you beyond every kind of comparison ('so much') I've made
aside: a speech that is not heard by the other characters on stage

58 *What ... silent:* What will I say? I must show my love by remaining silent about it (i.e. by not taking part in this display of hypocrisy and vanity)

59 *bounds:* boundaries. Lear is referring to the map mentioned at line 33 – it appears that the divisions are already decided and therefore the love-test is simply an exercise in vanity

60 *shadowy:* shady
champains rich'd: rich, fertile plains

61 *wide-skirted meads:* broad meadows

62 *issues:* children, heirs

63 *Be this perpetual:* the division of the kingdom is to be permanent

64 *Speak:* text in blue comes from the Quarto version of the play

65 *self metal:* same substance or temperament

66 *prize ... worth:* I value myself as equal to her; or I ask you [Lear] to value me as her equal

67 *she ... love:* Goneril has spoken the very words of love that are written on my own heart as though on a legal document ('deed')

68 *comes too short:* does not adequately describe the nature of my love for you

68–72 *I ... love:* I declare myself opposed to all kinds of happiness that the most balanced person might enjoy; my only happiness is found in your [Lear's] love

71 *alone felicitate:* only made happy

72–4 *Then ... tongue:* Cordelia is 'poor' because she cannot match her sisters' sentiments, but she is 'not so' poor because her love for her father is more substantial ('ponderous') than the mere words ('tongue') of her sisters

75 *To ... ever:* to you and your heirs for all time

76 *Remain:* live in
ample: complete

77 *validity:* value

79 *least:* perhaps 'youngest' or 'smallest'

80 *the vines ... Burgundy:* the King of France (represented by its vineyards) and the Duke of Burgundy (represented by its grazing pastures)

81 *Strive ... interess'd:* compete to gain a legal right (i.e. to be bound to Cordelia by marriage)

82 *more opulent:* richer. This suggests that Cordelia's third is better than those given to her sisters

CORDELIA

Nothing, my lord.

LEAR

Nothing?

[margin: stubborn]

CORDELIA

85 Nothing.

[margin notes: flaw - vanity, pride | mistake | wants to be flattered in front of an audience 'which of you love me the most']

LEAR *[note: vain, pride.]*

Nothing will come of nothing. Speak again.

CORDELIA *[note: stubborn / honest, has integraly]*

Unhappy that I am, I cannot heave *[note: she cannot express her love in words]*

My heart into my mouth. I love your majesty *[note: (figurativly + physically)]*

According to my bond; no more nor less.

[note: I love you like a daughter should love her father.]

LEAR *[note: (legal language)]*

90 How, how, Cordelia? Mend your speech a little,

Lest you may mar your fortunes.

CORDELIA *[note: logical]*

                Good my lord,

You have begot me, bred me, loved me; I

Return those duties back as are right fit,

Obey you, love you, and most honour you.

95 Why have my sisters husbands, if they say *[note: logical]*

They love you all? Happily when I shall wed,

That lord whose hand must take my plight shall carry

Half my love with him, half my care and duty.

Sure I shall never marry like my sisters.

100 To love my father all.

LEAR

But goes thy heart with this?

CORDELIA

                Ay, my good lord.

LEAR

So young, and so untender?

CORDELIA

So young, my lord, and true.

LEAR *[note: her truth was not good enough]*

Let it be so. Thy truth then be thy dower;

105 For by the sacred radiance of the sun,

[Left margin glossary:]

86 *Nothing . . . nothing:* you will get nothing from me for saying nothing

89 *bond:* obligation as a child

91 *Lest . . . fortunes:* in case you destroy your worldly prospects

92 *begot:* fathered
bred: raised

93 *are right fit:* is appropriate

96 *love you all:* love nobody but you

97 *take my plight:* accept my marriage vows

101 *But . . . this?* Do these words express your deepest feelings?

102 *untender:* unkind. Cordelia's youth (her tender years) does not make her as tender towards her father as it should

103 *true:* honest, loyal

[handwritten margin note near lines 93–100: × her sisters must either love Lear or their husbands → liars either way | half love to dad not to husband]

The mysteries of Hecate and the night,

By all the operation of the orbs

From whom we do exist and cease to be,

Here I disclaim all my paternal care,

Propinquity and property of blood, 110

And as a stranger to my heart and me

Hold thee from this for ever. The barbarous Scythian,

Or he that makes his generation messes

To gorge his appetite, shall to my bosom

Be as well neighboured, pitied and relieved, 115

As thou my sometime daughter.

KENT

[handwritten: Lear's best friend.]

Good my liege—

LEAR

Peace, Kent!

[NB] Come not between the dragon and his wrath.

I loved her most, and thought to set my rest

On her kind nursery. [*to CORDELIA*] Hence, and avoid my
        sight! 120

So be my grave my peace, as here I give

Her father's heart from her! — Call France. — Who stirs?

Call Burgundy. [*ATTENDANTS hurry out*] Cornwall and Albany

With my two daughters' dowers digest the third.

Let pride, which she calls plainness, marry her. 125

I do invest you jointly with my power,

Pre-eminence and all the large effects

That troop with majesty. Ourself, by monthly course,

With reservation of an hundred knights

By you to be sustained, shall our abode 130

Make with you by due turn. Only we shall retain

The name and all th' addition to a king;

The sway, revenue, execution of the rest,

Beloved sons, be yours; which to confirm,

This coronet part between you.

KENT

Royal Lear, 135

Whom I have ever honoured as my king,

Loved as my father, as my master followed,

As my great patron thought on in my prayers—

[Handwritten annotations:]
I am no longer your father.
× never going to love her
Cordelia is proud
• no dowry
give ½ ½ to other daughter

106 *mysteries ... night:* secret rites of the goddess of the underworld, witchcraft and the night

107–8 *operation ... be:* influence exerted by the planets and stars ('orbs') over human existence and fate

109–10 *disclaim ... blood:* renounce my fatherly regard and protection, kinship and blood relationship [with Cordelia]

111–12 *And ... ever:* I regard you from this time forth as a stranger to myself and my love

112 *Scythian:* the Scythians occupied a territory in (roughly) southern Russia from approximately the eighth to the third centuries BC, and were regarded by the Romans as savage and unnatural

113 *generation:* children
messes: portions or dishes of food

114 *gorge:* satisfy

114–16 *shall ... daughter:* Lear is telling Cordelia that in future he will extend no more kindness, pity or help to her than he would to a cannibal

116 *sometime:* former
liege: lord to whom allegiance is due

117 *Peace:* be silent

118 *Come ... wrath:* do not put yourself between me and the object of my anger [Cordelia]

119–20 *thought ... nursery:* hoped to set up my permanent home under her loving care

120 *Hence:* go away

121 *be ... peace:* may I rest in peace

121–2 *here ... her!* I hereby deprive ('give') her of her father's love ('heart')

122 *Who stirs?* get moving – Lear has to prompt his attendants to carry out his orders, which suggests they were so shocked by what had taken place that they failed to react to his command

124 *digest the third:* absorb Cordelia's share of the kingdom between you

125 *plainness:* honest speech, directness
marry her: be her dowry and get her a husband

126 *invest you jointly:* empower you equally

127 *Pre-eminence:* superiority

127–8 *large ... majesty:* magnificent trappings that accompany the position of monarch

128–31 *Ourself ... due turn:* I shall stay with each of you in turn for a month; I reserve to myself the privilege of having a personal retinue of one hundred knights who are to be maintained by you

131–2 *Only ... king:* the only privileges of royalty I shall retain are the name of king and all the marks of honour and distinction belonging to a king

133 *sway:* power, authority
revenue: income, yield
execution: performance, action

134 *which ... you:* to confirm this arrangement, divide this small crown [symbolising authority] between you

138 *patron:* protector, benefactor

139–41 *The bow ... heart:* Lear is telling Kent that his decision is not subject to change: what he has laid down is as inevitable as the flight of an arrow from a tightened bow. Lear is also warning Kent to avoid danger ('make from the shaft'): to oppose the decision, as Kent is about to do, is to risk one's life. The courageous Kent, however, is prepared to defy Lear: he challenges him to let the arrow of his power and displeasure fly, even if its forked head will pierce his heart

141–2 *be ... mad:* Kent is entitled to behave badly in response to Lear's insane decision to break up his kingdom and reject Cordelia

142 *What ... man?* this is a strong insult and breach of decorum; 'thou' was normally used to address inferiors and intimates, never to address kings

143–5 *Think'st ... folly:* do you think that I ('duty') shall be afraid to speak out when you ('power') submit to Goneril and Regan ('flattery')? I ('honour') am bound to speak plainly when you ('majesty') grow foolish

145 *Reserve thy state:* retain your royal power

146–7 *in ... rashness:* when you come to consider the matter properly, halt your sudden decision to abdicate

147 *Answer ... judgement:* I am prepared to stake my life on my opinion

149–50 *Nor ... hollowness:* the full-hearted sincerity of Cordelia cannot find expression in loud words (the emptiness of her sisters can). Kent is drawing on the proverb about empty vessels making most noise

150 *Reverb:* reverberate, echo
hollowness: insincerity

151–3 *My ... motive:* I have always been prepared to stake my life on your behalf in any conflict, and I would be prepared to lose my life to ensure your welfare

151 *pawn:* pledge
152 *wage:* stake, risk
153 *motive:* motivation

155 *blank:* white centre of a target, bullseye

156–7 *Now ... vain:* Kent accuses Lear of taking Apollo's name in vain (using it inappropriately) because Apollo (Greek and Roman god of light, the sun and truth) is associated with clear vision whereas Lear has been blinded by vanity, pride and anger. This exchange highlights one of the play's main themes: sight and blindness

157 *vassal:* slave
Miscreant: villain, unbeliever

158 *forbear:* be patient, control yourself
159–60 *Kill ... disease:* Kent sees himself as Lear's doctor, offering him health-giving advice, which Lear ignores and instead listens to the very people who will prove deadly to him. The reward ('fee') that Lear should bestow on the honest adviser, Kent, is given to Goneril and Regan ('foul disease')

160 *Revoke thy gift:* cancel your transfer of Cordelia's share of the kingdom to Goneril and Regan

LEAR   *don't mess with me*

The bow is bent and drawn, make from the shaft.

KENT   *rather say the truth then lie.*

140   Let it fall rather, though the fork invade   *impolite*

The region of my heart: be Kent unmannerly,   *will tell him*

When Lear is mad. What wouldst thou do, old man?   *when he is wrong.*

Think'st thou that duty shall have dread to speak,

When power to flattery bows? To plainness honour's bound,

145   When majesty falls to folly. Reserve thy state,

And in thy best consideration check

This hideous rashness. Answer my life my judgement,

Thy youngest daughter does not love thee least;

Nor are those empty-hearted, whose low sounds

Reverb no hollowness.

LEAR

150   Kent, on thy life, no more.

KENT   *I have always been by your side, I*

My life I never held but as a pawn   *will not stop now*

To wage against thine enemies, ne'er fear to lose it,

Thy safety being motive.

LEAR

                         Out of my sight!

KENT

See better, Lear, and let me still remain

155   The true blank of thine eye.

LEAR

Now by Apollo—

KENT

                         Now by Apollo, King,

Thou swear'st thy gods in vain.

LEAR   *get out of my sight!*

                         O vassal! Miscreant!

ALBANY, CORNWALL

Dear sir, forbear.

KENT *← he is a doctor (metaphorically)*

[*to LEAR*] Kill thy physician, and thy fee bestow

160   Upon the foul disease. Revoke thy gift,

Or, whilst I can vent clamour from my throat,

I'll tell thee thou dost evil.

LEAR

Hear me, recreant!

On thine allegiance, hear me!

That thou hast sought to make us break our vows,

Which we durst never yet; and with strained pride   165

To come betwixt our sentence and our power,

Which nor our nature nor our place can bear,

Our potency made good, take thy reward.

Five days we do allot thee for provision

To shield thee from diseases of the world;   170

And on the sixth to turn thy hated back

Upon our kingdom. If on the tenth day following,

Thy banished trunk be found in our dominions,

The moment is thy death. Away! By Jupiter,

This shall not be revoked.   175

KENT

Fare thee well, King; sith thus thou wilt appear,

Freedom lives hence and banishment is here.

[*to CORDELIA*] The gods to their dear shelter take thee, maid,

That justly think'st and hast most rightly said!

[*to GONERIL and REGAN*] And your large speeches may

your deeds approve,   180

That good effects may spring from words of love.

Thus Kent, O princes, bids you all adieu;

He'll shape his old course in a country new.

Exit.

Flourish. Enter GLOUCESTER, FRANCE, BURGUNDY, and ATTENDANTS.

GLOUCESTER

Here's France and Burgundy, my noble lord.

LEAR

My lord of Burgundy.   185

We first address toward you, who with this king

Hath rivalled for our daughter. What, in the least,

Will you require in present dower with her,   *sarcastic*

Or cease your quest of love?

161 *vent clamour:* utter cries (of protest)

162 *recreant:* one who breaks an oath of loyalty, a traitor

163 *thine allegiance:* your duty to me as your king

164 *That:* seeing that

165 *Which ... yet:* which I have never yet dared to do
     strained: excessive

166 *betwixt ... power:* between my words and my deeds

167 *Which ... bear:* which neither my temperament nor my royal status can put up with

168 *Our ... reward:* as an acknowledgment of my royal authority, take the reward that your misbehaviour has earned you. Lear forgets that he has handed over royal authority to Albany and Cornwall

169 *allot:* assign, give
     provision: dealing with necessities

170 *diseases:* troubles, discomforts

173 *trunk:* body
     dominions: lands, territories

174 *Jupiter:* the supreme Roman god

175 *This ... revoked:* earlier Kent asked Lear to 'revoke' (withdraw) his decision (line 160); now Lear is telling Kent that his decision (to banish him) will not be withdrawn

176–83 Kent uses rhyme for his parting speech, adding to the sense of resignation and finality. See also lines 250–61

176–7 *sith ... hence:* since ('sith') you are determined to be so self-willed and tyrannical, freedom must be sought elsewhere

178 *maid:* woman, virgin

180–1 *And ... love:* may your grandiose protestations of love for your father be matched by loving acts

182 *adieu:* farewell

183 *he'll ... new:* in his new country, Kent will continue to be the honest and plain-spoken man he has always been

Flourish: fanfare of trumpets

186 *We ... you:* I first address myself to you

187 *rivalled:* competed

187–9 *What ... love?* What is the least amount you will accept as an immediately available ('present') dowry with Cordelia, which, if you do not get, you will stop competing for her hand in marriage?

191 *tender:* offer

192 *When . . . so:* when I loved her, I considered her worth the large dowry I was prepared to offer earlier

194–7 *If . . . yours:* there she is. If anything about her pleases you, insignificant as she is, without a dowry, and labouring under the additional handicap of my disapproval, you can have her

194 *little-seeming substance:* Lear may be commenting ironically on Cordelia's sincerity as someone who values 'substance' (reality) a lot, and 'seeming' (appearance, pretence) comparatively little; in other words: this sincere creature who cannot bring herself to flatter. Or Lear may be simply expressing contempt for Cordelia, as someone who seems to have little to recommend her

195 *pieced:* added to it (the 'it' being 'that little-seeming substance' above)

196 *may . . . grace:* may please ('like') you by its suitability or fitness

198 *infirmities she owes:* defects she has

200 *strangered:* disowned, alienated

202 *Election . . . conditions:* nobody can be expected to make a choice under those terms

205–6 *I . . . hate:* I would not like to distance myself so much from your love as to ask you to marry someone I hate

206 *beseech:* may I ask

207 *T'avert . . . way:* to direct your love to somebody who deserves it more

208–9 *nature . . . hers:* Cordelia's 'unnatural' behaviour towards him causes Lear to feel that she scarcely deserves membership of the human race

209–14 *This . . . favour:* it is very strange indeed that Cordelia, who until now was the object of your most loving looks, the subject ('argument') of your praise, the comfort of your old age, your best and dearest daughter, should, within the space of a moment (a 'trice'), be guilty of so monstrous a crime as to be stripped ('dismantle') of your protective favour. France's comment underlines Lear's extreme fickleness, which is also noted by Goneril (lines 282–5)

215–16 *of . . . monsters it:* so unnatural as to be monstrous

BURGUNDY

                    Most royal majesty,

190 I crave no more than hath your highness offered,

     Nor will you tender less.   *don't expect little*

LEAR

                    Right noble Burgundy,

     When she was dear to us we did hold her so,

     But now her price is fallen. Sir, there she stands.

     If aught within that little-seeming substance,

195 Or all of it, with our displeasure pieced,

     And nothing more, may fitly like your grace,

     She's there, and she is yours.

BURGUNDY

                  I know no answer.

LEAR

     Will you, with those infirmities she owes,

     Unfriended, new-adopted to our hate,

200 Dowered with our curse, and strangered with our oath,

     Take her or leave her?

BURGUNDY

             Pardon me, royal sir;

     Election makes not up on such conditions.

LEAR

     Then leave her, sir; for by the power that made me,

     I tell you all her wealth. [*to FRANCE*] For you, great king,

205 I would not from your love make such a stray

     To match you where I hate, therefore beseech you

     T'avert your liking a more worthier way

     Than on a wretch whom nature is ashamed

     Almost t'acknowledge hers.

FRANCE

                  This is most strange,

210 That she, who even but now was your best object,

     The argument of your praise, balm of your age,

     The best, the dearest, should in this trice of time

     Commit a thing so monstrous, to dismantle

     So many folds of favour. Sure her offence

215 Must be of such unnatural degree

This is most strange

FRANCE, Act 1, Scene 1, 209

That monsters it, or your fore-vouched affection

Fall into taint, which to believe of her

Must be a faith that reason without miracle

Should never plant in me.

CORDELIA

               I yet beseech your majesty —

If for I want that glib and oily art   220

To speak and purpose not, since what I well intend

I'll do't before I speak — that you make known

It is no vicious blot, murder or foulness,

No unchaste action or dishonoured step,

That hath deprived me of your grace and favour: 225

But even for want of that for which I am richer:

A still-soliciting eye, and such a tongue

That I am glad I have not, though not to have it

Hath lost me in your liking.

216–17 *or ... taint:* or the sincerity of your previously declared ('fore-vouched') love for her must be doubted

217–19 *which ... me:* I cannot believe, on rational grounds, that she could be guilty of so monstrous an offence; it would take a miracle to convince me

220 *want:* lack
glib: eloquent, slick
oily: smooth, flattering
art: skill

221 *purpose not:* not to do what I promise

221–2 *since ... speak:* since I believe in doing something rather than talking about it

223 *vicious blot:* stain of vice

226 *But ... richer:* but because I lack a quality the very absence of which makes me a better person

227 *still-soliciting:* always looking out for favours

229 *Hath ... liking:* has deprived me of your love

LEAR

Better thou

230 Hadst not been born than not to have pleased me better.

FRANCE

Is it but this? A tardiness in nature

Which often leaves the history unspoken

That it intends to do? My lord of Burgundy,

What say you to the lady? Love's not love

235 When it is mingled with regards that stand

Aloof from th' entire point. Will you have her?

She is herself a dowry.

BURGUNDY

Royal King,

Give but that portion which yourself proposed

And here I take Cordelia by the hand,

240 Duchess of Burgundy.

LEAR

Nothing: I have sworn; I am firm.

BURGUNDY

[*to CORDELIA*] I am sorry then you have so lost a father

That you must lose a husband.

CORDELIA

Peace be with Burgundy!

Since that respect and fortunes are his love,

245 I shall not be his wife.

FRANCE

Fairest Cordelia, that art most rich being poor,

Most choice forsaken, and most loved despised;

Thee and thy virtues here I seize upon,

Be it lawful I take up what's cast away.

250 Gods, gods! 'Tis strange that from their cold'st neglect

My love should kindle to inflamed respect.

Thy dowerless daughter, King, thrown to my chance,

Is queen of us, of ours and our fair France.

Not all the dukes of waterish Burgundy

255 Can buy this unprized precious maid of me.

Bid them farewell, Cordelia, though unkind;

Thou losest here, a better where to find.

231–3 *Is … do?* Are you rejecting Cordelia only because her natural reserve prevents her from communicating her real feelings or intentions, which she proposes to act on?

232 *history:* story, inner narrative of a person

234–6 *Love's … point:* love is not genuine when it is joined to considerations ('regards') that have nothing to do with the essential matter ('th' entire point')

238 *portion:* dowry

244 *Since … love:* as considerations of status and fortune are the main focus of his interest

247 *Most choice forsaken:* specially chosen having been rejected

249 *Be … away:* let it be lawful for me to take what Burgundy has rejected

250–1 *Gods … respect:* it is strange that my love [for Cordelia] should grow so ardent, now that the gods have coldly neglected her

252 *my chance:* my lot

254 *waterish:* a descriptive term meaning 'abounding in rivers and streams', but also an insulting term meaning weak or underdeveloped and directed at Burgundy the man and/or the wine

255 *unprized precious:* not valued by others, but priceless to me

256 *unkind:* unnatural

257 *here:* in this place
where: place

LEAR

Thou hast her, France. Let her be thine, for we

Have no such daughter, nor shall ever see

That face of hers again. Therefore, be gone   260

Without our grace, our love, our benison.

Come, noble Burgundy.

Flourish. Exeunt LEAR, BURGUNDY, CORNWALL, ALBANY,
GLOUCESTER, EDMUND, and ATTENDANTS.

FRANCE

Bid farewell to your sisters.

CORDELIA

The jewels of our father, with washed eyes

Cordelia leaves you. I know you what you are   265

And, like a sister, am most loath to call

Your faults as they are named. Love well our father.

To your professed bosoms I commit him.

But yet, alas, stood I within his grace,

I would prefer him to a better place.   270

So farewell to you both.

REGAN

Prescribe not us our duty.

GONERIL

                    Let your study

Be to content your lord, who hath received you

At fortune's alms. You have obedience scanted,

And well are worth the want that you have wanted.   275

CORDELIA

Time shall unfold what plighted cunning hides,

Who covers faults, at last with shame derides.

Well may you prosper.

FRANCE

                    Come, my fair Cordelia.

Exeunt FRANCE and CORDELIA.

GONERIL

Sister, it is not little I have to say of what most nearly

appertains to us both. I think our father will hence tonight. 280

REGAN

That's most certain, and with you; next month with us.

261	*grace:* favour
	benison: blessing
	Exeunt: exit of more than one character
264	*jewels:* darlings, treasures
	washed eyes: eyes wet with tears
265	*what:* for what
266–7	*like ... named:* as a sister, I am most unwilling to give your faults their proper names
268	*To ... him:* I entrust our father to the love you have claimed to feel for him
270	*prefer:* promote, recommend
272	*Prescribe ... duty:* do not take it upon yourself to tell us what we must do
272	*study:* effort, aim
273	*content:* please
273–4	*hath ... alms:* took you when fortune was handing out charitable gifts; the implication is that France has got a poor bargain in Cordelia
274	*obedience scanted:* fallen short of the degree of obedience you owed to your father
275	*well ... wanted:* you well deserve to get the same lack of affection [from your husband] that you have shown to your father; or you well deserve to lose the dowry you have forfeited
276–7	*Time ... derides:* the hypocrisy of Goneril and Regan will be brought to light in time, which initially conceals sins but eventually ('at last') shames the sinners by exposing their offence
276	*plighted:* folded under, concealed
277	*derides:* mocks
278	*Well ... prosper:* this is ironical as Cordelia really believes that her sisters will not prosper
279–300	Note the return to prose for this private conversation between Goneril and Regan
279–80	*most ... both:* concerns both of us most intimately
280	*will hence:* will leave his palace

GONERIL

You see how full of changes his age is; the observation we have made of it hath not been little. He always loved our sister most, and with what poor judgement he hath now cast her off appears too grossly.

REGAN

'Tis the infirmity of his age; yet he hath ever but slenderly known himself.

GONERIL

The best and soundest of his time hath been but rash. Then must we look from his age to receive, not alone the imperfections of long-engrafted condition, but therewithal the unruly waywardness that infirm and choleric years bring with them.

REGAN

Such unconstant starts are we like to have from him as this of Kent's banishment.

GONERIL

There is further compliment of leave-taking between France and him. Pray you, let us sit together. If our father carry authority with such disposition as he bears, this last surrender of his will but offend us.

REGAN

We shall further think of it.

GONERIL

We must do something, and i' the heat.

Exeunt.

285 *grossly:* obviously, blatantly

286–7 *'Tis . . . himself:* it is a weakness of old age, although he has always had poor self-knowledge

288–92 *The . . . them:* even in the prime of life he was hot-headed ('rash'). Now that he is old we can expect to have to endure from him not only those faults that are deep-rooted ('long-engrafted') in his disposition ('condition'), but also the undisciplined contrariness ('waywardness') that feeble and angry old people exhibit
291 *therewithal:* in addition to that
292 *choleric:* prone to anger

293 *Such . . . have:* we are likely to see more such unpredictable whims

295 *compliment of leave-taking:* formal expression of farewells
296 *sit together:* discuss this matter together
296–8 *If . . . us:* if our father continues to exert royal authority in his usual rash, impulsive way, his abdication ('surrender') will only harm ('offend') us. Goneril fears that Lear will forget that he has given away his power

300 *We . . . heat:* we must strike while the iron is hot

285

290

295

300

Key points

This scene introduces all the main characters with the exception of Edgar and Lear's Fool. It shows the key event that acts as the catalyst for Lear's downfall.

- Lear's decision to break up a kingdom that has been united under his rule may seem unwise, but he gives valid reasons for it. He believes that 'younger strengths' (line 36) will govern the kingdom better than he now can. He also wants to ensure that there will be no rival claims to the throne after his death – in the absence of a settled arrangement, Albany and Cornwall might wage war against each other for the kingship.

- Lear's fatal error is to base this division on his daughters' public declarations of love for him.

- Goneril and Regan are well practised in the 'glib and oily art' (line 220) of telling people exactly what they wish to hear. Cordelia, on the other hand, is unable and unwilling to match her older sisters in their self-serving flattery.

- Lear is certain that Cordelia will outdo Goneril and Regan in expressing affection for him and is dismayed when she fails to meet his expectations.

- It is easy to understand why Lear's absurd love-test should offend Cordelia's sense of what is proper or reasonable. Nevertheless, her response is blunt and dismissive and she chooses not to make any allowance for Lear's old age or vanity.

- Cordelia's failure to acknowledge Lear as the exclusive object of her affections shatters his hopes for a blissful retirement in the loving care of his favourite daughter. He is outraged by her cold and formal statements of duty.

- Lear's response (disowning Cordelia and banishing Kent for trying to make him see reason) is violent and extreme. Perhaps, during his long reign as king, nobody ever questioned his orders, defied his wishes or dared to argue with him.

- Lear's ceremonial handing-over of royal power to Albany and Cornwall ('This coronet part between you'; line 135) is a symbolic moment in the scene, and in the play as a whole. He does not realise that he is giving up his power

and authority along with the crown. He will become a subject, at the mercy of whatever laws Goneril, Regan and their husbands decide should apply to him.

- Lear's poor judgement is further illustrated in the conditions he attaches to his abdication. He insists on retaining the title of king; the tokens of honour, respect and distinction due to a king; and a personal troupe of one hundred knights to be maintained at the expense of Albany and Cornwall at whose palaces he and his knights will stay on alternate months. He does not anticipate the problems this is likely to cause.

- Another parent–child relationship, shown briefly, is that between Gloucester and his younger son, Edmund. In Edmund's presence, Gloucester insensitively tells Kent that he has often been embarrassed to acknowledge Edmund and speaks of his illegitimacy in crude terms. He also seems happy to remark that Edmund has spent nine years in exile 'and away he shall again' (line 28).

- Edmund says little, but he cannot but feel slighted by his father's remarks, which are bound to leave him with a sense of grievance.

- Unlike Burgundy, France is ready to marry Cordelia for her own sake, even though Lear has deprived her of a share of the kingdom. Cordelia is fortunate in marrying a man who loves her and in being rejected by one who was only interested in her dowry.

- The closing conversation between Goneril and Regan indicates the true nature of these two women. They are cold, calculating and totally rational in their analysis of Lear's character and conduct.

- Goneril and Regan conclude that Lear is rash and has always lacked self-knowledge. As they are likely to be victims of these long-standing flaws, as well as the unpredictable changes of mind they associate with old age, they agree to stand together against him.

Useful quotes

aramatic effect → dramatic irony

> *I have so often blushed to acknowledge him that now I am brazed to't.*
> (Gloucester, lines 8–9)

soliloquy → exposition [explains how he [really feels]

> *be Kent unmannerly, When Lear is mad. What wouldst thou do, old man?*
> (Kent, 141–2)

> *Unhappy that I am, I cannot heave My heart into my mouth. I love your majesty According to my bond; no more nor less.*
> (Cordelia, lines 87–9)

→ Key quote

> *Thou hast her, France. Let her be thine, for we Have no such daughter, nor shall ever see That face of hers again.*
> (Lear, lines 258–60)

> *I loved her most, and thought to set my rest On her kind nursery.*
> (Lear, lines 119–20)

> *You see how full of changes his age is; the observation we have made of it hath not been little. He always loved our sister most, and with what poor judgement he hath now cast her off appears too grossly.*
> (Goneril, lines 282–5)

? Questions

1 Gloucester tells Kent that he has a son 'by order of law, some year elder' (line 16) than Edmund. What does this admission suggest about the kind of man Gloucester is or has been?

2 What indications are there in this scene that the 'love-test' is not really designed by Lear to determine which share of the kingdom each daughter will receive?

3 How would you characterise Cordelia's behaviour throughout this scene? Is she free from blame for what happens? How do her asides influence your view of her?

4 Suggest possible reasons for Lear's behaviour towards Cordelia and Kent.

5 What is Kent's function in this scene?

6 Why are France and Burgundy present at Lear's court? How are they contrasted?

7 Describe Goneril and Regan on the evidence of this scene.

8 'This coronet part between you' (line 135). Imagine you have been asked to direct this scene. What instructions would you give to the actors on how to handle this moment?

9 How might costumes and sound effects be used in this scene to help the audience understand what is taking place?

10 What indications are there in this scene that Goneril and Regan can expect to find Lear a very troublesome subject when they have to show him hospitality?

11 Look carefully at Kent's final speech in the scene (lines 176–83). What does this speech tell you about Kent?

12 Would you agree that Lear's main characteristic in this scene is selfishness? Give evidence for your answer.

ACT 1 † Scene 2

The action moves to Gloucester's castle. In a soliloquy, Edmund emerges as a lively, witty cynic, who despises conventional moral standards, laws and social customs. He intends to deprive his brother, Edgar, of his lawful inheritance by fraud and guile. He begins by using a forged letter, allegedly composed by Edgar, to destroy Gloucester's faith in his elder son. The letter outlines a plan to murder Gloucester. Edmund has little difficulty in convincing his gullible and superstitious father that Edgar is a treacherous plotter against his life. Soon after, he cunningly manipulates Edgar into hiding from their father. Edmund observes that both Gloucester and Edgar have innocent and trusting natures, which makes them easy victims of deception.

Now, gods, stand up for bastards!
EDMUND, Act 1, Scene 2, 22

Earl of Gloucester's castle.

Enter EDMUND (with a letter).

EDMUND

[handwritten: soliloquy → exposition explains how he actually feels]

Thou, nature, art my goddess; to thy law

My services are bound. Wherefore should I

Stand in the plague of custom, and permit

The curiosity of nations to deprive me,

5   For that I am some twelve or fourteen moonshines

Lag of a brother? Why 'bastard'? Wherefore 'base'?

When my dimensions are as well compact,

My mind as generous, and my shape as true,

As honest madam's issue? Why brand they us

10   With 'base'? With 'baseness bastardy'? 'Base, base'?

Who in the lusty stealth of nature take

More composition and fierce quality

Than doth, within a dull, stale, tired bed,

Go to th' creating a whole tribe of fops,

15   Got 'tween asleep and wake? Well, then,

Legitimate Edgar, I must have your land.

Our father's love is to the bastard Edmund

As to th' legitimate. Fine word, 'legitimate'.

Well, my legitimate, if this letter speed,

20   And my invention thrive, Edmund the base

Shall to th' legitimate. I grow, I prosper;

Now, gods, stand up for bastards!

Enter GLOUCESTER.

GLOUCESTER

Kent banished thus! And France in choler parted!

And the King gone tonight! Prescribed his power!

25   Confined to exhibition! All this done

Upon the gad! Edmund, how now! What news?

EDMUND

[*hiding the letter*] So please your lordship, none.

GLOUCESTER

Why so earnestly seek you to put up that letter?

EDMUND

I know no news, my lord.

[handwritten margin: dramatic effect → dramatic irony]

1   *nature:* Edmund's 'nature' is a selfish force concerned with fulfilling one's own desires, regardless of who else gets hurt in the process

2–6 *Wherefore . . . brother?* Why should I be blighted by a law that discriminates against younger and illegitimate sons? Edmund does not think that laws should deprive him of the right to inherit

3   *plague:* scourge, affliction
    custom: habit, usual practice

4   *curiosity:* scrupulousness

5   *moonshines:* months *[handwritten: → key quote]*

6   *lag of:* lagging behind (i.e. younger than)
    base: vile, despicable. Edmund's argument is that being born outside marriage does not mean that he is a bad person *[handwritten: haven't had affairs]*

7   *my dimensions . . . compact:* I am as well made and as well proportioned

8   *generous:* gallant, gentleman-like *[handwritten: marriage → procreation]*

9   *honest madam's issue:* a child of a chaste woman (he is using 'madam' ironically); a legitimate child

10 *With base . . . base?* Edmund is showing his contempt for the terms he is using

11–15 *Who . . . wake?* Edmund is suggesting that the lustful, secret, energetic ('fierce') passion involved in the conception of illegitimate children makes such children superior to the fools ('fops') brought into the world as a result of conventional married love

12 *composition:* putting together (i.e. are more complete, have a better make-up)

15 *Got 'tween:* created between

18 *As to:* as much as to

19 *speed:* succeeds

20 *And . . . thrive:* and if my plan goes well

20–1 *Edmund . . . legitimate:* the illegitimate Edmund will advance to, or take, the place of the legitimate Edgar

22 *Now . . . bastards!* Edmund's irreverence reaches its climax in the bawdy suggestiveness of this line, in which the gods are imagined as creating bastards as well as lending them moral support

23 *choler:* anger

24 *Prescribed:* limited. This is an understatement, as Lear has in fact surrendered his power

25 *exhibition:* the maintenance allowance (that Lear is to receive from Goneril and Regan)

26 *Upon the gad:* on the spur of the moment

28 *Why . . . letter?* Why are you so eager to pocket that letter? In fact, Edmund is eager to ensure that Gloucester sees the letter rather than to hide it from him

GLOUCESTER

What paper were you reading?   30

EDMUND

Nothing, my lord.

GLOUCESTER

No? What needed then that terrible dispatch of it into
your pocket? The quality of nothing hath not such need
to hide itself. Let's see: come, if it be nothing, I shall not
need spectacles.   35

EDMUND

I beseech you, sir, pardon me; it is a letter from my brother
that I have not all o'er-read, and for so much as I have
perused, I find it not fit for your o'er-looking.

GLOUCESTER

Give me the letter, sir.

EDMUND

I shall offend either to detain or give it. The contents, as in   40
part I understand them, are to blame.

GLOUCESTER

Let's see, let's see.

EDMUND

I hope, for my brother's justification, he wrote this but as
an essay or taste of my virtue.

Gives the letter to GLOUCESTER.

GLOUCESTER

[*reads*] 'This policy and reverence of age makes the world   45
bitter to the best of our times; keeps our fortunes from
us till our oldness cannot relish them. I begin to find an
idle and fond bondage in the oppression of aged tyranny
who sways, not as it hath power, but as it is suffered. Come
to me, that of this I may speak more. If our father would   50
sleep till I waked him, you should enjoy half his revenue
for ever, and live the beloved of your brother, Edgar.'
Hum! Conspiracy! 'Sleep till I waked him, you should
enjoy half his revenue.' My son Edgar! Had he a hand to
write this? A heart and brain to breed it in? When came   55
this to you? Who brought it?

32 *terrible dispatch:* he suggests that Edmund hid the letter in haste and terror

33–4 *The quality … itself:* if there were nothing in it, you would not need to hide it

34–5 *not need spectacles:* this is one of many references in the play to eyes and blindness

36 *beseech:* beg, implore

37 *not all o'er-read:* not entirely read through

38 *not fit … o'er-looking:* unsuitable for you to read

41 *to blame:* worthy of blame, objectionable. Edmund's 'protestations' are intended to make Gloucester even more curious about the letter

44 *essay … virtue:* means of testing my integrity. The assay (or 'essay') was the act of tasting food and drink before they were given to an eminent person

45–7 *This … them:* this custom of honouring old age (thought up by crafty old men) gives the world a bitter taste during the best years of our lives ('times') and means we do not receive our inheritance until we are too old to enjoy it

45 *policy:* crafty device, trick

47–8 *an idle … bondage:* a weak and foolish form of slavery

49 *sways:* holds power, oppresses
it is suffered: its victims are prepared to put up with it

50–1 *If … waked him:* if I had the power of life and death over our father

EDMUND

It was not brought me, my lord; there's the cunning of it. I found it thrown in at the casement of my closet.

GLOUCESTER

You know the character to be your brother's?

EDMUND

60   If the matter were good, my lord, I durst swear it were his; but in respect of that, I would fain think it were not.

GLOUCESTER

It is his.

EDMUND

It is his hand, my lord, but I hope his heart is not in the contents.

GLOUCESTER

65   Has he never before sounded you in this business?

EDMUND *ties into main plot (King Lear)*

Never, my lord; but I have heard him oft maintain it to be fit that, sons at perfect age and fathers declined, the father should be as ward to the son, and the son manage his revenue.

GLOUCESTER

70   O villain, villain! His very opinion in the letter! Abhorred villain! Unnatural, detested, brutish villain! Worse than brutish! Go, sirrah, seek him. I'll apprehend him. Abominable villain! Where is he?

EDMUND

I do not well know, my lord. If it shall please you to
75   suspend your indignation against my brother till you can derive from him better testimony of his intent, you should run a certain course; where, if you violently proceed against him, mistaking his purpose, it would make a great gap in your own honour, and shake in pieces the
80   heart of his obedience. I dare pawn down my life for him, that he hath writ this to feel my affection to your honour, and to no other pretence of danger.

GLOUCESTER

Think you so?

---

57   *cunning of it:* cleverness of the person who planned the scheme
58   *casement:* window
     closet: study

59   *character:* handwriting

60–1   *If ... not:* if the contents of the letter were good, I would swear it was his, but in view of what it really is, I would like to think it was not his

65   *sounded you:* tried to discover your thoughts or feelings

66   *oft:* often
67   *declined:* past their prime
68   *as ward:* like a ward (i.e. a person incapable of managing his or her own affairs, instead having them managed by a guardian)

70   *Abhorred:* hateful

72   *sirrah:* sir; here, the term expresses familiarity
     I'll apprehend him: it is unlikely that Gloucester intends to arrest Edgar himself; he presumably means that he will make sure that Edgar is arrested

75   *suspend your indignation:* hold back your anger
76   *testimony:* assurance, evidence
77   *run ... course:* follow a safe and reliable plan of action
     where: whereas
78   *mistaking his purpose:* misinterpreting his intentions
80   *pawn ... him:* stake my life on him
81   *feel:* test
82   *to no ... danger:* has no more dangerous intention ('pretence') in mind

EDMUND

If your honour judge it meet, I will place you where you shall hear us confer of this, and by an auricular assurance, have your satisfaction, and that without any further delay than this very evening.

GLOUCESTER

He cannot be such a monster—

EDMUND

Nor is not, sure.

GLOUCESTER

To his father, that so tenderly and entirely loves him. Heaven and earth! Edmund, seek him out, wind me into him, I pray you. Frame the business after your own wisdom. I would unstate myself to be in a due resolution.

EDMUND

I will seek him, sir, presently, convey the business as I shall find means, and acquaint you withal.

GLOUCESTER

These late eclipses in the sun and moon portend no good to us. Though the wisdom of nature can reason it thus and thus, yet nature finds itself scourged by the sequent effects. Love cools, friendship falls off, brothers divide. In cities, mutinies; in countries, discord; in palaces, treason; and the bond cracked 'twixt son and father. This villain of mine comes under the prediction; there's son against father. The King falls from bias of nature: there's father against child. We have seen the best of our time: machinations, hollowness, treachery and all ruinous disorders follow us disquietly to our graves. Find out this villain, Edmund; it shall lose thee nothing. Do it carefully. And the noble and true-hearted Kent banished! His offence, honesty! 'Tis strange!

Exit.

EDMUND

This is the excellent foppery of the world, that when we are sick in fortune, often the surfeits of our own behaviour, we make guilty of our disasters the sun,

85

90

95

100

105

110

84 *meet:* appropriate, proper

85–6 *auricular ... satisfaction:* satisfy yourself as to the facts of the situation by means of what you hear with your own ears

91–2 *wind ... him:* worm your way into his confidence for my sake

92 *Frame:* manage

93–4 *unstate ... resolution:* give up my title and revenues if I could dispel my uncertainty

94 *resolution:* conviction, assurance

95 *presently:* immediately

95–6 *convey ... withal:* manage the affair as well as I can, and inform you of my progress

96 *withal:* therewith, with this

97–107 Gloucester attributes the evils of the world around him to the influence of the heavenly bodies. An almost total eclipse of the sun occurred on 2 October 1605, around the time Shakespeare was writing the play, and had been preceded by a partial eclipse of the moon on 27 September 1605

97 *portend:* give warning of, foreshadow

98–100 *Though ... effects:* although natural science suggests various rational explanations (of eclipses), nevertheless, human nature is afflicted by the disastrous results that follow

103 *villain:* peasant. Edgar's supposed treachery causes Gloucester to see him as unworthy of his noble birth
under the prediction: Edgar's alleged wrongdoing is the kind of thing predicted by the eclipses and is evidence of the reliability of eclipses as guides to future events

104 *bias of nature:* behaviour that is contrary to one's natural instincts

105 *of our time:* years of our lives

106 *machinations:* plots, intrigues
hollowness: falseness, hypocrisy

107 *follow ... graves:* disturb our final years
Find out: discover, expose

111–25 Edmund ridicules Gloucester's failure to give human will its due

111 *foppery:* folly, stupidity

112 *sick in fortune:* down on our luck
surfeits: excesses

113 *we make ... disasters:* we blame our misfortunes on

114 *villains on necessity:* unable to do anything about our own bad behaviour

116 *treachers . . . predominance:* traitors just because particular planets, in their spheres, were most influential at the time of our birth

118–19 *divine thrusting on:* supernatural compulsion; as if heavenly influences impelled us to such activity

119–20 *An admirable . . . star!* it is a remarkable characteristic of lustful man that he should attribute his lecherous ('goatish') tendencies to the influence of a star

120–2 *My father . . . Ursa Major:* I was conceived under the constellation Draco (the Dragon) and born under that of the Great Bear

123 *I should . . . am:* I would still be the lecherous person that I am

124 *maidenliest:* most chaste
firmament: heavens

125 *bastardising:* being conceived outside marriage

126 *Pat:* just at the right time
catastrophe: in pre-Shakespearean comedy, the catastrophe was the final part of the play, in which the complications of the plot were unravelled

126–7 *My . . . melancholy:* I must play the part of a dark and gloomy ('melancholy') villain; the cue is a sign for actors, showing them when to enter and speak

127–8 *with . . . Bedlam:* making the characteristic sound of one of the beggars from the Bethlehem hospital in London (an asylum for the insane)

128 *eclipses . . . divisions!* Edmund is sarcastically summarising his father's superstitious beliefs

129 *Fa, sol, la, mi:* Edmund sings to imply that he does not notice Edgar's approach

132 *this other:* the other

134 Edgar did not expect Edmund to take that kind of thing seriously

135 *effects . . . unhappily:* the unfortunate consequences follow

137 *dearth:* shortages, famine
dissolutions . . . amities: the ending of old friendships

138 *menaces:* threats
maledictions: curses

139 *diffidences:* loss of trust

139–40 *dissipation of cohorts:* dispersal of bands of soldiers (the commonest causes being desertion and disease). A cohort was the tenth part of a Roman legion. The fact that Lear supposedly reigned long before the Roman occupation of Britain would not have troubled Shakespeare

140 *nuptial breaches:* marriage breakdowns

141 *sectary astronomical:* believer in the stars

144 *Spake you:* did you speak

---

the moon and stars, as if we were villains on necessity,
115 fools by heavenly compulsion, knaves, thieves and treachers by spherical predominance, drunkards, liars and adulterers by an enforced obedience of planetary influence; and all that we are evil in by a divine thrusting
120 on. An admirable evasion of whoremaster man, to lay his goatish disposition to the charge of a star! My father compounded with my mother under the Dragon's tail, and my nativity was under Ursa Major, so it follows that I am rough and lecherous. I should have been that I am had the maidenliest star in the firmament twinkled on
125 my bastardising. *don't blame anything/*
Enter EDGAR. anyone. It's your own fault

Pat he comes, like the catastrophe of the old comedy. My cue is villainous melancholy, with a sigh like Tom o' Bedlam. — Oh, these eclipses do portend these divisions! Fa, sol, la, mi. *dramatic irony.*

EDGAR

130 How now, brother Edmund! What serious contemplation are you in?

EDMUND

I am thinking, brother, of a prediction I read this other day, what should follow these eclipses.

EDGAR

Do you busy yourself with that?

EDMUND

135 I promise you, the effects he writes of succeed unhappily, as of unnaturalness between the child and the parent; death, dearth, dissolutions of ancient amities; divisions in state, menaces and maledictions against king and nobles; needless diffidences, banishment of friends, dissipation
140 of cohorts, nuptial breaches, and I know not what.

EDGAR

How long have you been a sectary astronomical?

EDMUND

When saw you my father last?

EDGAR

The night gone by.

EDMUND

Spake you with him?

EDGAR

Ay, two hours together. 145

EDMUND

Parted you in good terms? Found you no displeasure in him by word or countenance?

EDGAR

None at all.

EDMUND

Bethink yourself wherein you may have offended him, and at my entreaty forbear his presence till some little 150 time hath qualified the heat of his displeasure, which at this instant so rageth in him that with the mischief of your person it would scarcely allay.

EDGAR

Some villain hath done me wrong.

EDMUND

That's my fear. I pray you, have a continent forbearance 155 till the speed of his rage goes slower, and, as I say, retire with me to my lodging, from whence I will fitly bring you to hear my lord speak. Pray ye, go: there's my key. If you do stir abroad, go armed.

EDGAR

Armed, brother? 160

EDMUND

Brother, I advise you to the best. I am no honest man if there be any good meaning toward you. I have told you what I have seen and heard but faintly, nothing like the image and horror of it. Pray you, away.

EDGAR

Shall I hear from you anon? 165

EDMUND

I do serve you in this business. *irony*

Exit EDGAR. *gulable* *doesn't think anyone is doing any wrong*
A credulous father, and a brother noble,
Whose nature is so far from doing harms
That he suspects none; on whose foolish honesty
My practices ride easy. I see the business, 170
Let me, if not by birth, have lands by wit:
All with me's meet that I can fashion fit.

Exit.

---

147 *countenance:* demeanour, attitude towards you

149 *Bethink:* think about, consider
wherein: in what way

150 *entreaty:* earnest request
forbear his presence: avoid meeting him

151 *hath ... displeasure:* has reduced the intensity of his disapproval

152–3 *with ... allay:* even if he did you a physical injury, his anger would hardly subside ('allay')

155 *have ... forbearance:* exercise restraint

156 *retire:* retreat, withdraw

157 *lodging:* room, living quarters
whence: where
fitly: at an appropriate time

159 *stir abroad:* go outside

161–4 Edmund must derive immense satisfaction from the impudent irony of his remarks

163 *but faintly:* only slightly

165 *anon:* soon

167 *credulous:* one who is easily persuaded to believe
170 *practices:* intrigues, treacheries
171 *Let ... wit:* since I cannot inherit property because of my illegitimate birth, I must use my intelligence ('wit') to acquire it

172 *All ... fit:* I will regard as right and proper ('meet') whatever I can do to advance my own cause. Edmund believes that the end justifies the means
fashion fit: shape to suit my purpose or needs

Key points

This scene is devoted to outlining and developing the sub-plot, which involves Gloucester and his two sons, the legitimate Edgar and the illegitimate Edmund.

- Edmund's opening soliloquy immediately establishes his liveliness of mind, his cynical wit and his forceful personality. He has no time for social convention. He despises legitimacy of birth as a mere matter of law and custom; he associates illegitimacy with energy and imagination.

- Edmund has no respect for the rights of others ('Legitimate Edgar, I must have your land'; line 16).

- Parallels between the Lear plot (the main plot) and the sub-plot emerge in this scene. The self-centred, calculating and scheming Edmund shares these qualities with both Goneril and Regan. Their fathers, Lear and Gloucester, place too much trust in outward appearances and are shown to be easily manipulated by their deceptive children.

- Edgar's alleged views on the transfer of power from the old to the young (lines 66–9) ironically reflect Lear's practice in the opening scene.

- Gloucester draws an analogy between Lear's recent rejection of Cordelia and Edgar's supposed disloyalty to himself. His superstitious nature attributes such discord to astrological influences ('These late eclipses in the sun and moon'; line 97).

- If the opening scene raised questions of probability (no monarch in the real world would even pretend to base a division of the kingdom on the sort of love-test Lear contrives for his daughters), Scene 2 raises more acute problems of credibility. We are, for example, given no reason why Edgar, who, at the time, is living in the same house as Edmund, should write a self-incriminating letter to his brother when he might much more safely have whispered his plans in his ear.

- Gloucester should know Edgar much better than he knows Edmund, since the latter had been away for the previous nine years. Yet he seems ignorant of the true nature of both his sons. It appears as if Gloucester wants to be deceived. For example, he unhesitatingly accepts Edmund's lying account of Edgar's opinions as a confirmation of those contained in the forged letter, without looking for evidence of any kind (lines 70–3).

- Edgar is presented as a gullible character, like his father, but it is not easy to believe that he would simply accept Edmund's advice to avoid Gloucester instead of facing his father and finding out the cause of his anger.

- All of this suggests that *King Lear* is nonsensical and unconvincing if taken at a purely realistic level. Shakespearean drama, however, combines realism with symbolism, and the divisions between the two are blurred. Gloucester's failure to see, or even to seek, the truth about his sons may be taken as a sign of his weak spiritual state at this stage.

- Edgar is a pathetic figure in this scene. Just as Goneril and Regan provided testimony as to Cordelia's goodness, so Edmund conveys Edgar's noble nature, which 'is so far from doing harms that he suspects none' (lines 168–9). In Edgar, however, freedom from evil intent goes along with an almost incredible innocence. The equation of goodness with stupidity and of evil with intelligence is a disturbing feature of this scene.

- The whole scene is rich in irony. Note, for example, Edgar's remark 'Some villain hath done me wrong' (line 154).

Useful quotes

> Legitimate Edgar, I must have your land.
>
> (Edmund, line 16)

> Some villain hath done me wrong.
>
> (Edgar, line 154)

> I have heard him oft maintain it to be fit that, sons at perfect age and fathers declined, the father should be as ward to the son, and the son manage his revenue.
>
> (Edmund, lines 66–9)

> A credulous father, and a brother noble,
> Whose nature is so far from doing harms
> That he suspects none; on whose foolish honesty
> My practices ride easy. I see the business,
> Let me, if not by birth, have lands by wit:
> All with me's meet that I can fashion fit.
>
> (Edmund, lines 167–72)

> Find out this villain, Edmund; it shall lose thee nothing.
>
> (Gloucester, lines 107–8)

Questions ?

1 Give an assessment of Edmund's character on the basis of what he has to say in his first soliloquy.

2 Describe Edmund's motivation for what he is about to do.

3 What is your assessment of Gloucester on the evidence of his reaction to Edmund's forged letter?

4 Is there a family resemblance between Gloucester and Edgar?

5 What are the main points of contrast between Edmund on the one hand and Gloucester and Edgar on the other?

6 Edmund is in full control of what happens in this scene. What strategies does he use to achieve this control?

7 How does Edmund succeed so easily in deceiving his father and brother?

8 Comment on Shakespeare's use of soliloquies in this scene.

9 What parallels are already emerging between the main plot (involving Lear's family) and the sub-plot (involving Gloucester's family)?

10 Imagine you are either Edgar or Gloucester. Compose a diary entry giving your thoughts on your conversation with Edmund in this scene.

11 If you were choosing an actor to play Edmund in a stage or film version of King Lear, what characteristics or features would you look for?

Plot summary

Lear is staying with Goneril and Albany, obliging them to fulfil the conditions he imposed when he conferred half the kingdom on them. Goneril finds fault with her father and his followers. She initiates the process of humiliating Lear by encouraging her steward, Oswald, to be disrespectful and to make her palace a less hospitable place of residence for Lear.

By day and night he wrongs me

GONERIL, Act 1, Scene 3, 3

Duke of Albany's palace.

Enter GONERIL and OSWALD (her steward).

GONERIL

Did my father strike my gentleman for chiding of his fool?

OSWALD

Ay, madam.

GONERIL

By day and night he wrongs me; every hour

He flashes into one gross crime or other,

That sets us all at odds: I'll not endure it.   5

His knights grow riotous, and himself upbraids us

On every trifle. When he returns from hunting,

I will not speak with him; say I am sick.

If you come slack of former services,

You shall do well; the fault of it I'll answer.   10

OSWALD

He's coming, madam; I hear him.

GONERIL

Put on what weary negligence you please,

You and your fellows; I'd have it come to question.

If he distaste it, let him to my sister,

Whose mind and mine, I know, in that are one,   15

Not to be over-ruled. Idle old man,

That still would manage those authorities

That he hath given away! Now, by my life,

Old fools are babes again; and must be used

With checks as flatteries, when they are seen abused.   20

Remember what I have said.

OSWALD

                              Well, madam.

GONERIL

And let his knights have colder looks among you;

What grows of it, no matter; advise your fellows so.

I would breed from hence occasions, and I shall

That I may speak. I'll write straight to my sister   25

To hold my very course. Prepare for dinner.

Exeunt.   * if he doesn't like it, he can
                      leave.

steward: controller of the household's domestic affairs (see p. 249)

1 chiding of: rebuking
fool: jester; clever and funny entertainer in the royal court

4 flashes: breaks out without warning

6 upbraids us: finds fault with me. Goneril's use of the royal plural ('us' for 'me') shows that she now regards herself as exercising her father's kingly powers

7 trifle: petty issue

9 come ... services: are not as attentive to his needs as you used to be

10 the fault ... answer: I will take responsibility for any adverse consequences of your actions

12 Put ... negligence: show him whatever bored indifference

13 I'd ... question: I would like it (your neglectful treatment of him) to become an issue

14 distaste it: does not like it (finds it distasteful)
to: go to

15 Whose ... one: who thinks the same as me

16 Idle: foolish, lacking in seriousness and gravity

17–18 That still ... away! Goneril's accusation is that Lear wants to continue to exercise the kingly powers he has surrendered to Regan and herself

19–20 Old ... abused: foolish old men like Lear, in their second childhood, must be punished, instead of praised, when praise only makes them more foolish

20 checks: restraints, rebukes

21 Well: I shall remember well

23 grows of it: results from it

24–5 I would ... speak: I would like to use Lear's hostile response to our treatment of him as an excuse for speaking plainly to him

25 straight: immediately

26 To ... course: advising her to adopt the same course of action as the one I am embarking on

Key points

This short scene indicates that the arrangement between Lear, Goneril and Regan is unlikely to endure for long and suggests that life is about to become difficult for Lear.

- Oswald, Goneril's steward, is not merely a servant. He is an official of the palace and someone in whom Goneril can confide. She trusts him with her innermost thoughts, even telling him how she feels about her father and how she would like to have him treated.

- Whether there is any basis in reality for Goneril's complaints about her father and his followers, or whether she is merely fabricating excuses for hostile action against Lear, is an open question. In his 1962 Stratford production of the play, Peter Brook introduced riotous knights onto the stage, thereby suggesting that Goneril had cause to be offended. The text of the play, however, gives no explicit evidence for staging such behaviour.

- An argument can be made in support of the view that, in spite of their dishonesty, his daughters' reluctance to entertain Lear and his knights in the long term is not entirely unreasonable. Few people would relish the prospect of providing hospitality for an old, moody, demanding royal parent and his hundred knights, riotous or not, for six months of the year, every year.

- Goneril's unfeeling comments on the supposed senility and childishness of Lear, who has given her so much, justify all that he will later have to say on the subject of his daughters' ingratitude.

- Goneril is hoping that the hostile treatment she plans for Lear will cause him to become more troublesome. This will give her an excuse to rebuke him, making life even more unpleasant for him.

- If Lear finds her treatment intolerable, Goneril foresees that he will turn to Regan for comfort. She decides to write immediately to Regan, advising her to adopt similar tactics to those she is planning with Oswald. Together, they will be able to isolate Lear quickly.

Useful quotes

When he returns from hunting,
I will not speak with him; say I am sick.

(Goneril, lines 7–8)

Put on what weary negligence you please

(Goneril, line 12)

If he distaste it, let him to my sister,
Whose mind and mine, I know, in that are one,
Not to be over-ruled.

(Goneril, lines 14–16)

? Questions

1. Is Goneril telling Oswald about genuine grievances when she claims that Lear wrongs her 'by day and night' (line 3) or is she looking for excuses to take action against her father? Is there anything in this scene to suggest that any of these grievances are genuine?

2. What new information about Goneril's character does the scene convey?

3. Has anything in the two previous scenes prepared us for what happens in this one?

4. Describe Goneril's strategy for dealing with Lear. From her point of view, is this strategy a good one?

5. What impression do you get of Oswald from this scene?

ACT 1 † Scene 4

The banished Kent returns in disguise to help Lear, who accepts him into his service. Lear, not yet used to the idea that he has surrendered his royal power, is impatiently giving orders. He is infuriated by Oswald's lack of respect for him and succeeds in humiliating him, with Kent's help. Lear's Fool provides a touch of reality after this temporary triumph, mocking Lear's foolishness in abdicating the throne. Lear has played into Goneril's hands and she rebukes him violently, shattering his composure. She decides to reduce his retinue to fifty knights. Lear curses Goneril and determines to go to Regan. Goneril sends Oswald to inform Regan of what has happened. The scene closes with a glimpse of the Goneril–Albany relationship, during which she dismisses his advice.

Nothing can be made out of nothing.

LEAR, Act 1, Scene 4, 123

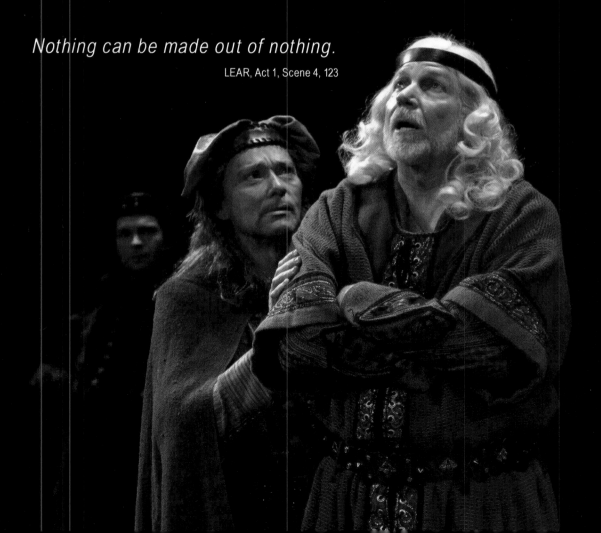

A hall in the Duke of Albany's palace.

Enter KENT (disguised).

KENT

If but as well I other accents borrow

That can my speech defuse, my good intent

May carry through itself to that full issue

For which I razed my likeness. Now, banished Kent,

5   If thou canst serve where thou dost stand condemned,

So may it come, thy master, whom thou lov'st,

Shall find thee full of labours.

Horns within. Enter LEAR, KNIGHTS, and ATTENDANTS.

LEAR

Let me not stay a jot for dinner; go get it ready.

Exit an ATTENDANT.

[*to KENT*] How now! What art thou?

KENT

10   A man, sir.

LEAR

What dost thou profess? What wouldst thou with us?

KENT

I do profess to be no less than I seem: to serve him truly that will put me in trust; to love him that is honest; to converse with him that is wise, and says little; to fear

15   judgement; to fight when I cannot choose; and to eat no fish.

LEAR

What art thou?

KENT

A very honest-hearted fellow, and as poor as the King.

LEAR

If thou be'st as poor for a subject as he's for a King, thou

20   art poor enough. What wouldst thou?

KENT

Service.

LEAR

Who wouldst thou serve?

1–4 *If ... likeness:* if, in addition to the disguise I am wearing, I can further conceal my identity by altering my speech so as to make it confused or indistinct, I shall be in a position to achieve the good purpose for which I disguised myself. The purpose of Kent's disguise (as the servant Caius) is to enable him to enter Lear's service

2 *defuse:* disguise, make obscure

4 *razed my likeness:* obliterated my previous appearance. Kent has shaved off his beard and may be punning on 'razed' and 'razor'

5 *If ... condemned:* if you can serve the man who condemned you to banishment

6 *So may it come:* may it come to pass

7 *full of labours:* ready to perform any number of difficult tasks

8 *stay:* wait
   jot: tiny bit, moment

11 *profess:* trade, profession
    What wouldst thou: what do you want

12 *profess:* claim. Kent deliberately misunderstands Lear's question. He says he can claim to be just what he appears to be; we know, of course, that he is much more

12–13 *to serve ... trust:* to be a loyal servant to the man who will trust me with responsibility

14 *converse:* associate or keep company with somebody – not to engage in conversation

15 *judgement:* divine judgement

KENT

You.

LEAR

Dost thou know me, fellow?

KENT

No, sir, but you have that in your countenance which I   25
would fain call master.

LEAR

What's that?

KENT

Authority.

LEAR

What services canst thou do?

KENT

I can keep honest counsel, ride, run, mar a curious tale in   30
telling it, and deliver a plain message bluntly. That which
ordinary men are fit for, I am qualified in, and the best of
me is diligence.

LEAR

How old art thou?

KENT

Not so young, sir, to love a woman for singing, nor so   35
old to dote on her for anything. I have years on my back
forty-eight.

LEAR

Follow me; thou shalt serve me. If I like thee no worse after
dinner, I will not part from thee yet. Dinner, ho, dinner!
Where's my knave, my fool? Go you, and call my fool hither.   40

Exit an ATTENDANT.

Enter OSWALD.

You, you, sirrah, where's my daughter?

OSWALD

So please you—

Exit.

LEAR

What says the fellow there? Call the clotpoll back.

25–6 *you ... master:* there is something about your bearing and demeanour that makes me want to call you master

30 *honest counsel:* an honourable secret
30–1 *mar ... telling it:* spoil an elegant story by telling it in a plain, inelegant fashion. This is Kent's oblique tribute to his own bluntness and plainness of speech. It provides an ironic reminder of his blunt speeches to Lear before he assumed his disguise
33 *diligence:* zeal in carrying out orders

35–6 *Not ... anything:* if he loved a woman merely for her singing, he would be immature, and therefore very young. On the other hand, he is not so old (with fewer choices) as to be prepared to love a woman who has few, if any, redeeming features

40 *hither:* here, to this place

41 *sirrah:* sir; here, the term expresses contempt and Lear's assumed authority

43 *clotpoll:* one who has a clod for a head ('poll'); blockhead, fool

45 *mongrel:* Oswald is characterised throughout this episode in terms of animal imagery that implies contempt for his behaviour and status; animal imagery is also used in the play to refer to Goneril and Regan, particularly their ferocity and menace

48 *roundest manner:* plainest, most straightforward way

52 *entertained:* treated
53 *wont:* accustomed
54 *abatement:* falling off
55 *dependants:* body of servants
duke: Albany. There is no direct evidence for this suggestion; indeed, Albany appears surprised at the growing hostility between Goneril and Lear later in this scene

61 *Thou ... conception:* you are merely reminding me of what I myself have been suspecting
62 *faint:* cold, indifferent
62–4 *which I ... unkindness:* Lear has been unwilling to attribute the discourtesy he has experienced to any deliberate unkindness on the part of Goneril and Albany; instead, he has explained it away as the result of his own tendency to feel that even the most trivial signs of neglect are major offences against his dignity
63 *jealous:* suspiciously watchful
curiosity: inquisitiveness, concern for one's rights
64 *very pretence:* actual intention
67 *young lady:* Cordelia

Exit a KNIGHT.

Where's my fool? Ho, I think the world's asleep.

Re-enter KNIGHT.

45 How now! Where's that mongrel?

KNIGHT

He says, my lord, your daughter is not well.

LEAR

Why came not the slave back to me when I called him?

KNIGHT

Sir, he answered me in the roundest manner: he would not.

LEAR

50 He would not?

KNIGHT

My lord, I know not what the matter is; but, to my judgement, your highness is not entertained with that ceremonious affection as you were wont; there's a great abatement of kindness appears as well in the
55 general dependants as in the duke himself also and your daughter.

LEAR

Ha! Say'st thou so?

KNIGHT

I beseech you pardon me, my lord, if I be mistaken; for my duty cannot be silent when I think your highness
60 wronged.

LEAR

Thou but rememberest me of mine own conception. I have perceived a most faint neglect of late, which I have rather blamed as mine own jealous curiosity than as a very pretence and purpose of unkindness. I will look
65 further into't. But where's my fool? I have not seen him this two days.

KNIGHT

Since my young lady's going into France, sir, the fool hath much pined away.

LEAR

No more of that; I have noted it well. Go you, and tell my
daughter I would speak with her.   70

Exit an ATTENDANT.

Go you, call hither my fool.

Exit an ATTENDANT.

Enter OSWALD.

O you sir, you, come you hither, sir. Who am I, sir?

OSWALD

My lady's father.

LEAR

'My lady's father'! My lord's knave, you whoreson dog!
You slave! You cur!   75

OSWALD

I am none of these, my lord, I beseech your pardon.

LEAR

Do you bandy looks with me, you rascal? [*striking him*]

OSWALD

I'll not be strucken, my lord.

KENT

[*tripping his heels*] Nor tripped neither, you base football
player.   80

LEAR

I thank thee, fellow; thou serv'st me, and I'll love thee.

KENT

[*to OSWALD*] Come, sir, arise, away! I'll teach you
differences, away, away! If you will measure your lubber's
length again, tarry; but away! Go to! Have you wisdom?
[*pushes OSWALD out*] So.   85

LEAR

Now, my friendly knave, I thank thee. There's earnest of
thy service.

Enter FOOL.

FOOL

Let me hire him too. [*to KENT*] Here's my coxcomb.

---

75 *cur:* dog

77 *bandy:* exchange. In tennis, to 'bandy' means to hit
to and fro; Lear is furious that Oswald should dare
to exchange looks with him

78–80 *I'll not ... player:* these lines extend the sporting
metaphor: Lear strikes Oswald as if he were a
tennis ball; when Oswald objects to this, Kent
treats him as a football by tripping him. To cast
Oswald in the role of a footballer is to insult
him. Unlike tennis, which was an aristocratic
pastime, football was regarded by Shakespeare's
contemporaries as a game for the lower ('base')
classes

83 *differences:* social positions (since you do not
appear to appreciate the differences between
yourself and a king)

83–4 *If ... tarry:* if you want to have your clumsy body
('lubber's length') stretched on the ground again,
stay ('tarry')

84 *wisdom:* sense (to leave while you are still safe)

86 *earnest:* money paid in advance to secure his
services, and as a pledge of further payments

88 *coxcomb:* cap worn by a professional fool

89 *pretty knave:* dainty fellow

90 *were best:* had better. The Fool is suggesting that Kent will make a good fool if he serves a master like Lear, who has come down in the world; the offer of the coxcomb is the Fool's parody of Lear's payment to Kent

93 *thou . . . sits:* if you cannot side with the party in power

93–4 *thou'lt . . . shortly:* you will soon suffer at their hands; or you will soon be out in the cold

95 *banished:* alienated, turned them against him by giving them power and independence
on's: of his

95–6 *blessing . . . will:* the Fool believes that by disowning and banishing Cordelia, Lear did her a favour, since she is blessed to be away from her father and she found a worthy husband

97 *How now, nuncle?* Hello, how are you, uncle? At this point the Fool condescends to speak to Lear, having ignored him so far. 'Nuncle' is a contraction of 'mine uncle' and was the standard form in which a fool would address his master
Would I had: I wish I had

100 *If . . . myself:* if the Fool did as Lear has done, and gave away all his property, he would retain his coxcomb, or fool's cap, as a reminder of his folly

101 *There's . . . daughters:* here is my coxcomb (as a first token of your folly); if you want a second one, ask your daughters (whose response will confirm what a fool you were when you gave them everything)

102 *the whip:* this was a common punishment for fools

103–4 *Truth's . . . stink:* truth is so little respected that it is whipped out of doors like an unwelcome dog, while flattery and deceit (represented by the fawning female hunting-hound or brach) are allowed to share the hospitable warmth of the fireside. The 'stink' represents the undesirable consequences of flattery

105 *A pestilent gall to me!* this means either: how intensely bitter my situation makes me feel; or: your remarks are deeply wounding in their exposure of my folly

106 *Sirrah:* the Fool's use of this term of authority impudently reverses the relationship between servant and master

108 *Mark:* pay attention to

109–18 *Have . . . score:* the essential point of this jingle is that the prudent, cautious man is bound to accumulate wealth. A paraphrase would run as follows: do not show all your wealth, do not tell all you know, do not lend unless you can well afford to, save shoe leather by riding rather than walking, listen a lot and believe little of what you hear, do not gamble everything on a single throw; avoid wine and loose women, and stay indoors; and if you follow this advice, your wealth will grow

111 *owest:* own

LEAR

How now, my pretty knave! How dost thou?

FOOL

90 Sirrah, you were best take my coxcomb.

KENT

Why, fool?

FOOL

Why? For taking one's part that's out of favour. Nay, and thou canst not smile as the wind sits, thou'lt catch cold shortly. There, take my coxcomb. Why, this fellow has

95 banished two on's daughters, and did the third a blessing against his will. If thou follow him, thou must needs wear my coxcomb. How now, nuncle? Would I had two coxcombs and two daughters.

LEAR

Why, my boy?

FOOL

100 If I gave them all my living, I'd keep my coxcombs myself. There's mine; beg another of thy daughters.

LEAR

Take heed, sirrah, the whip!

FOOL *flattery.* *Cordelia, Kent*

Truth's a dog must to kennel; he must be whipped out, when the Lady Brach may stand by the fire and stink.

two daughters.

LEAR

105 A pestilent gall to me!

FOOL

Sirrah, I'll teach thee a speech.

LEAR

Do.

FOOL

Mark it, nuncle:

Have more than thou showest,

110 Speak less than thou knowest,

Lend less than thou owest,

Ride more than thou goest,

Learn more than thou trowest,

Set less than thou throwest;

Leave thy drink and thy whore,   115

And keep in-a-door;   → be sensible
                                    and you will be ok.
And thou shalt have more

Than two tens to a score.

KENT

This is nothing, fool.

FOOL

Then 'tis like the breath of an unfee'd lawyer: you gave   120
me nothing for't. Can you make no use of nothing,
nuncle?

LEAR   repatition

Why, no, boy. Nothing can be made out of nothing.

FOOL

[*to KENT*] Prithee tell him, so much the rent of his land
comes to. He will not believe a fool.   125

LEAR

A bitter fool!

FOOL

Dost thou know the difference, my boy, between a bitter
fool and a sweet one?

LEAR

No, lad. Teach me.

FOOL

That lord that counselled thee   130

To give away thy land,

Come place him here by me;

Do thou for him stand:

The sweet and bitter fool

Will presently appear;   135

The one in motley here, [*points to himself*]

The other found out there. [*points to LEAR*]

LEAR

Dost thou call me fool, boy?

---

113   *trowest:* believe

114   *Set:* wager
      throwest: throw for

116   *in-a-door:* indoors

118   *two ... score:* your score (twenty units) of money
      will be worth more than two tens – presumably
      by earning interest

120   *breath ... lawyer:* speech of a lawyer who has not
      been paid (i.e. nothing, since, as the proverb has it,
      a lawyer will not plead but for a fee)

123   *Nothing ... nothing:* Lear is saying that the
      multiplication table shows that nothing as
      principal will yield nothing as interest. It reminds
      us of his previous assertion that 'Nothing will come
      of nothing' (Act 1, Scene 1, line 86)

124   *Prithee:* please
      so much: how much. The Fool's point is that the
      rent from Lear's land comes to nothing now that
      he has given it away

127–9 Lear and the Fool appear to have exchanged roles
       here (just as Lear and Goneril have)
127   *bitter:* shrewd, satirical
128   *sweet:* naïve, half-witted

130–7 *That ... there:* this may be paraphrased as: stand
       beside me, and represent the one who advised you
       to give away your land (i.e. yourself). You will then
       immediately discover that I am the gullible fool
       and that you are the shrewd one

136   *in motley:* dressed as a fool

137   *The other ... there:* the 'other' is Lear, who is
      discovered ('found out') to be a fool despite
      appearances; 'there' indicates that the Fool is
      pointing to where Lear is

139–40 *that ... with:* Lear was born with his share of foolishness ('that')

141 *This ... fool:* this man is not a total fool

142–5 *No ... snatching:* the Fool interprets Kent's 'altogether fool' to mean a person who embodies in himself the sum total of human folly. He then suggests that if he had been granted a monopoly of folly, courtiers, male and female, would be anxious to snatch part of it for themselves, just as they try to get a share of everything else

146 *two crowns:* two royal crowns; it also means ten shillings: an egg would have been worth less than a halfpenny in early Jacobean times, which makes him look like a silly fool for offering to pay so much. However, when he turns a pun on the crowns into a bitter jibe at Lear's expense (lines 148–53), we realise that the Fool is the sarcastic 'bitter' one, while his master is the naïve 'sweet' fool. The Fool merely offers to give away ten shillings for an egg; whereas Lear has given away his kingdom, and got ingratitude and persecution in return

149 *clovest:* split

151 *borest ... dirt:* Lear has acted as foolishly as the man in Aesop's fable who carried his ass over the dirt instead of letting it carry him

152 *wit:* intelligence
crown: further punning on the word 'crown'; this time it means 'head'

153–4 *If ... so:* the person who thinks that what I have just said is foolish deserves to be whipped as a fool

153 *like myself:* like a fool (foolishly honest in my speech)

155–8 *Fools ... apish:* fools have never been so little in demand as at present because wise men are taking their places. These 'wise' men show their lack of wisdom in their attempts to imitate current fashion

155 *grace:* favour
in a year: in any year to date

156 *foppish:* foolish

158 *apish:* imitative, copying like apes

160 *used it:* been in the habit of it

160–1 *e'er ... mothers:* ever since you gave your daughters the right to discipline and chastise you (and thus violated the natural law of parent–child relationships)

162 *put'st ... breeches:* forced down your own trousers

165–6 *play ... among:* behave like a child ('play bo-peep') and join the world's fools

168 *fain:* gladly

FOOL

All thy other titles thou hast given away; that thou wast
140 born with.

KENT

This is not altogether fool, my lord.

FOOL

No, faith, lords and great men will not let me. If I had a
monopoly out, they would have part on't, and ladies
too — they will not let me have all fool to myself: they'll
145 be snatching. Nuncle, give me an egg, and I'll give thee
two crowns.

LEAR

What two crowns shall they be?

FOOL

Why, after I have cut the egg i' the middle and eat up
the meat, the two crowns of the egg. When thou clovest
150 thy crown i' the middle and gavest away both parts, thou
borest thy ass on thy back o'er the dirt. Thou hadst little
wit in thy bald crown, when thou gavest thy golden one
away. If I speak like myself in this, let him be whipped that
first finds it so.

[handwritten: metaphor→ kept crown (two pieces but gave away of shell) everything else (power) ✱inside of egg]

155 Fools had ne'er less grace in a year;
For wise men are grown foppish,
And know not how their wits to wear,
Their manners are so apish.

LEAR

When were you wont to be so full of songs, sirrah?

FOOL

160 I have used it, nuncle, e'er since thou madest thy
daughters thy mothers; for when thou gavest them the
rod and put'st down thine own breeches,

Then they for sudden joy did weep,
And I for sorrow sung,
165 That such a king should play bo-peep,
And go the fools among.

Prithee, nuncle, keep a schoolmaster that can teach thy
fool to lie. I would fain learn to lie.

[handwritten: problem: fool cannot lie → the daughters have become mothers • image: they can spank you (power)]

LEAR

And you lie, sirrah, we'll have you whipped.

FOOL *rather be a fool then a king.*

I marvel what kin thou and thy daughters are: they'll have   170

me whipped for speaking true, thou'lt have me whipped

for lying; and sometimes I am whipped for holding my

peace. I had rather be any kind o' thing than a fool. And

yet I would not be thee, nuncle. Thou hast pared thy wit

o' both sides and left nothing i' the middle. Here comes   175

one o' the parings.

Enter GONERIL.

LEAR

How now, daughter? What makes that frontlet on? You

are too much of late i' the frown.

FOOL *mathemathemical image → zero without a figure (nothing)*

Thou wast a pretty fellow when thou hadst no need

to care for her frowning. Now thou art an O without a   180   *at least he has a job*

figure: I am better than thou art now: I am a fool, thou art

nothing. [*to GONERIL*] Yes, forsooth, I will hold my tongue;

so your face bids me, though you say nothing.

    Mum, mum!

    He that keeps nor crust nor crumb,   185

    Weary of all, shall want some.

That's a sheal'd peascod. [*points to LEAR*]

GONERIL

Not only, sir, this your all-licensed fool,

But other of your insolent retinue

Do hourly carp and quarrel, breaking forth   190

In rank and not-to-be-endured riots. Sir,

I had thought, by making this well known unto you,

To have found a safe redress; but now grow fearful,

By what yourself too late have spoke and done,

That you protect this course and put it on   195

By your allowance; which, if you should, the fault

Would not 'scape censure, nor the redresses sleep,

Which, in the tender of a wholesome weal,

Might in their working do you that offence,

Which else were shame, that then necessity   200

Will call discreet proceeding.

---

170 *I marvel ... are:* I wonder how you and your daughters can be related (because they behave towards him in such contradictory ways)

174–6 *Thou ... parings:* Lear, in sharing out his kingdom between Goneril and Regan, has also parted with whatever intelligence he had

175 *o' both sides:* on both sides of your brain
    i' the middle: for yourself

176 *one o' the parings:* one who has benefited from Lear's distribution of his wit and his kingdom

177 *What ... on?* Why are you frowning so much? Lear thinks of Goneril's frowns as forming a headboard ('frontlet')

178 *too ... frown:* frowning too much lately

179 *pretty:* fortunate

180–1 *thou art ... figure:* you are like a zero without another figure before it (i.e. worthless)

182 *forsooth:* indeed, in truth

184 *Mum:* silence. The Fool is telling himself that he must remain silent for fear of Goneril's displeasure; in spite of this, he continues to speak

186 *all:* cares and responsibilities (of kingship)
    want some: lack both crust (the outer trappings of power) and crumb (real power). Having given away his power and authority, Lear will not be able to keep the privileges he asked for

187 *sheal'd peascod:* emptied peapod

188 *all-licensed fool:* traditionally, fools were permitted ('licensed') to express themselves freely and frankly to those in authority

190 *carp:* find fault

191 *rank:* gross

193 *safe redress:* definite remedy

194 *too late:* only too recently

195 *course:* kind of behaviour

195–6 *put ... allowance:* encourage it

196–7 *which ... sleep:* if you are giving your approval to the misbehaviour of your followers, I will correct ('censure') you for it, and my remedial measures ('redresses') will follow swiftly

197 *'scape:* escape

198–201 *Which ... proceeding:* these penalties I am talking about, inspired by my concern for the health of the country ('weal'), may harm or offend you in a way that might reflect shame on me if conditions were normal. But since the welfare of the country is at stake, people will describe my punitive action as wise, indeed necessary

201 *discreet proceeding:* wise, a prudent course of action

FOOL

For, you know, nuncle,

    The hedge-sparrow fed the cuckoo so long,

    That it had it head bit off by it young.

205   So out went the candle, and we were left darkling.

LEAR

Are you our daughter?

GONERIL

I would you would make use of that good wisdom,

Whereof I know you are fraught, and put away

These dispositions which of late transport you

210   From what you rightly are.

FOOL

May not an ass know when the cart draws the horse?

    'Whoop, jug! I love thee!'

LEAR

Does any here know me? This is not Lear,

Does Lear walk thus? Speak thus? Where are his eyes?

215   Either his notion weakens, his discernings

Are lethargied — Ha! Walking? 'Tis not so.

Who is it that can tell me who I am?

203–4 *The hedge-sparrow ... young:* this is the Fool's image for the present relationship between Lear and Goneril. The well-nourished cuckoo [Goneril], hatched in the hedge-sparrow's [Lear's] nest, grows so big that it bites off the hedge-sparrow's head to make room for itself

205 *So ... darkling:* Lear has allowed his power to be extinguished like a candle, leaving his followers in the darkness of fear and misgovernment *darkling:* in the dark

207 *I would:* I wish

208 *fraught:* supplied

209 *dispositions:* attitudes

210 *you rightly are:* is your true nature

211 *May ... horse?* even a fool like me sees that there is something wrong when a daughter gives orders to her royal father

212 *Whoop ... thee!* this was probably the refrain of an old song. 'Jug' was a nickname for Joan, and a term of endearment. The Fool is ironically recalling Goneril's ardent protestations of love for Lear in the opening scene

213–17 *Does any ... am?* Lear has never before been confronted by such a challenge to his absolute authority and wonders whether his present experiences are real or imagined

215–16 *Either ... lethargied:* either his intellect is becoming enfeebled, or his understanding is impaired

216 *Ha ... so:* I must be dreaming

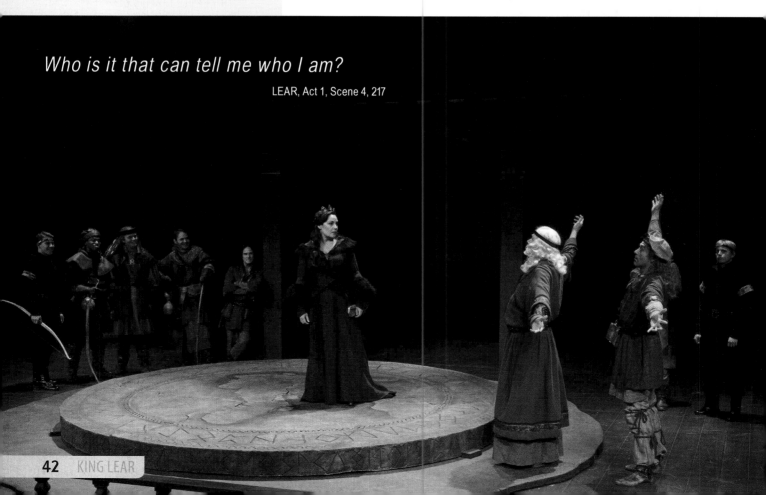

Who is it that can tell me who I am?

LEAR, Act 1, Scene 4, 217

FOOL

Lear's shadow.

LEAR

I would learn that; for by the marks of sovereignty, knowledge, and reason, I should be false persuaded I had   220
daughters.

FOOL

Which they will make an obedient father.

LEAR

Your name, fair gentlewoman?

GONERIL

This admiration, sir, is much o' the savour

Of other your new pranks. I do beseech you   225

To understand my purposes aright:

As you are old and reverend, should be wise.

Here do you keep a hundred knights and squires,

Men so disordered, so debosh'd and bold,

That this our court, infected with their manners,   230

Shows like a riotous inn; epicurism and lust

Makes it more like a tavern or a brothel

Than a graced palace. The shame itself doth speak

For instant remedy. Be then desired

By her, that else will take the thing she begs,   235

A little to disquantity your train,

And the remainders, that shall still depend,

To be such men as may besort your age,

And know themselves and you.

LEAR

                          Darkness and devils!

Saddle my horses! Call my train together!   240

Exeunt ATTENDANTS.

Degenerate bastard! I'll not trouble thee.

Yet have I left a daughter.

GONERIL

You strike my people, and your disordered rabble

Make servants of their betters.

Enter ALBANY.

218 *Lear's shadow:* the Fool is telling Lear that having given away his substance to his daughters, he is now a mere shadow of his old self

219 *I would learn that:* ignoring the Fool's last remark, Lear would like an answer to the question he asked about his real identity

219–21 *for ... daughters:* pursuing the subject of his identity, which, he claims, continues to puzzle him, Lear says: 'my royal insignia, my knowledge and my reason all suggest that I am King Lear, the father of the daughters who owe me respect. But since I can see no such daughters, I cannot claim to be King Lear'

224–5 *This ... pranks:* this false show of astonishment ('admiration') has the same undesirable features as other recent games of yours
224 *savour:* taste
226 *aright:* properly, correctly
227 *should:* you should

229 *debosh'd:* vicious (debauched)

231 *epicurism:* gluttony and drunken behaviour

233 *graced:* stately
233–4 *The ... remedy:* immediate measures are required to rid us of the shame arising from this situation
235 *that ... begs:* who will otherwise ('else') take by force what she asks you to yield voluntarily
236 *disquantity:* reduce the size of
train: retinue, band of followers and servants
237 *the remainders ... depend:* those members of your train who remain on as your dependants
238 *besort:* be suitable for

241 *Degenerate bastard!* Goneril has so abandoned the qualities (kindness, loyalty, respect) proper to a daughter of his that she is no longer fit to be regarded as his daughter (hence 'bastard')
242 *Yet:* still

245 *Woe . . . repents!* pity the person who, like myself, repents too late

246 *Is it your will?* Lear is asking Albany if he supports Goneril in her treatment of him

247 *marble-hearted fiend:* hard-hearted devil

248-9 *More . . . sea-monster!* Lear's suggestion is that filial ingratitude is monstrously ugly

250 *Detested kite:* hateful bird of prey. The reference associates Goneril with death, meanness and cruelty

251 *men . . . parts:* men who display qualities of rare excellence

252 *particulars:* details

253-4 *in the . . . name:* they take the utmost care to live up to their honourable reputations

254-8 *O . . . gall:* Cordelia's minor mistake, acting like a destructive instrument ('an engine'), ripped my natural affection away from her, around whom my world had previously revolved, drew the love from my heart, and increased my store of anger and bitterness ('gall')

259 *gate:* entrance; here, Lear's head

262 *moved:* provoked, aroused (your anger)

263 *nature:* the creative force in the universe

264-5 *Suspend . . . fruitful:* nature, if you intended to make Goneril ('this creature') capable of bearing children, withhold that capacity from her

267 *increase:* reproduction

268 *derogate:* degraded, deviating from the course of nature

269 *teem:* prove fruitful, have a child

270 *Create . . . spleen:* give her a child composed of nothing but malice and ill humour

271 *And . . . her:* and torment her by showing her the same perverse lack of natural feeling as she has shown to her father

273 *cadent:* flowing
fret: wear

274-5 *Turn . . . contempt:* Lear is asking nature to mock at the pains and troubles Goneril may have to suffer as a mother and to show contempt for whatever maternal happiness she may feel

---

LEAR

245 Woe, that too late repents! — O sir, are you come?

Is it your will? Speak, sir. — Prepare my horses.

Exeunt ATTENDANTS.

Ingratitude, thou marble-hearted fiend,   *reference to nature*

More hideous when thou show'st thee in a child

Than the sea-monster!

ALBANY

Pray, sir, be patient.

LEAR

250 [*to GONERIL*] Detested kite, thou liest!

My train are men of choice and rarest parts,

That all particulars of duty know,

And in the most exact regard support

The worships of their name. O most small fault,

255 How ugly didst thou in Cordelia show!

Which, like an engine, wrenched my frame of nature

From the fixed place, drew from my heart all love,

And added to the gall. O Lear, Lear, Lear!

Beat at this gate that let thy folly in [*strikes his head*]

260 And thy dear judgement out! — Go, go my people!

ALBANY

My lord, I am guiltless, as I am ignorant

Of what hath moved you.

LEAR

It may be so, my lord.

[*kneeling*] Hear, nature, hear; dear goddess, hear!

Suspend thy purpose, if thou didst intend

265 To make this creature fruitful.

Into her womb convey sterility;

Dry up in her the organs of increase,

And from her derogate body never spring

A babe to honour her! If she must teem,

270 Create her child of spleen, that it may live

And be a thwart disnatured torment to her.

Let it stamp wrinkles in her brow of youth;

With cadent tears fret channels in her cheeks;

Turn all her mother's pains and benefits

275 To laughter and contempt, that she may feel

How sharper than a serpent's tooth it is
To have a thankless child! Away, away!

Exeunt LEAR, KENT, and ATTENDANTS.

ALBANY
Now, gods that we adore, whereof comes this?

GONERIL
Never afflict yourself to know more of it,
But let his disposition have that scope   280
As dotage gives it.

Re-enter LEAR.

LEAR
What, fifty of my followers at a clap?
Within a fortnight?

ALBANY
                    What's the matter, sir?

LEAR
I'll tell thee. [*to GONERIL*] Life and death! I am ashamed
That thou hast power to shake my manhood thus;   285
That these hot tears, which break from me perforce,
Should make thee worth them. Blasts and fogs upon thee!
Th' untented woundings of a father's curse
Pierce every sense about thee! Old fond eyes,
Beweep this cause again, I'll pluck ye out,   290
And cast you, with the waters that you loose,
To temper clay. Yea, is't come to this?
Ha! Let it be so. I have another daughter
Who, I am sure, is kind and comfortable.
When she shall hear this of thee, with her nails   295
She'll flay thy wolfish visage. Thou shalt find
That I'll resume the shape which thou dost think
I have cast off for ever. Thou shalt, I warrant thee.

Exit.

GONERIL
Do you mark that?

ALBANY
I cannot be so partial, Goneril,   300
To the great love I bear you—

Notes:

278 *whereof comes this:* what is the reason for this outburst

279 *Never ... it:* do not trouble yourself with further enquiries into this matter

280–1 *let ... gives it:* allow his senile moods to take their course

282 *at a clap:* at a stroke, in one go

286 *perforce:* involuntarily

287 *Should ... them:* should make you sufficiently valuable to be worth the shedding of royal tears
Blasts and fogs: blighting and plague-bearing influences

288 *Th' untented woundings:* wounds so deep as to be untentable (impossible to probe or cleanse, and therefore incurable). A tent was an instrument for examining or cleansing a wound

289 *fond:* foolish

290–2 *Beweep ... clay:* Lear is saying that if his eyes shed tears again over his differences with Goneril, he will pluck them out and use them, along with the water they discharge ('loose') when plucked out, to soften ('temper') clay

294 *comfortable:* comforting, prepared to give comfort

295–6 *with ... visage:* Lear fondly imagines his 'kind' daughter Regan attacking Goneril as one wolf might attack another

297–8 *resume ... for ever:* again take on the office of kingship, which you thought I had permanently renounced

298 *warrant:* promise, assure

299 *mark:* note. Goneril is referring to Lear's threat to resume the kingship, which would be an act of treason

300–1 *I cannot ... you:* even though my love for you means I should take your side, I cannot allow this to influence me in your favour on this occasion

KING LEAR   45

GONERIL

Pray you, content. — What, Oswald, ho! —

[*to FOOL*] You, sir, more knave than fool, after your master.

FOOL

Nuncle Lear, nuncle Lear, tarry; take the fool with thee.

305   A fox, when one has caught her,

    And such a daughter,

    Should sure to the slaughter,

    If my cap would buy a halter.

    So the fool follows after.

Exit.

GONERIL

310 This man hath had good counsel! A hundred knights!

'Tis politic and safe to let him keep

At point a hundred knights! Yes, that on every dream,

Each buzz, each fancy, each complaint, dislike,

He may enguard his dotage with their powers

315 And hold our lives in mercy. — Oswald, I say!

ALBANY

Well, you may fear too far.

GONERIL

                 Safer than trust too far.

Let me still take away the harms I fear,

Not fear still to be taken. I know his heart.

What he hath uttered I have writ my sister;

320 If she sustain him and his hundred knights,

When I have showed the unfitness—

Enter OSWALD.

                 How now, Oswald!

What, have you writ that letter to my sister?

OSWALD

Ay, madam.

GONERIL

Take you some company, and away to horse.

325 Inform her full of my particular fear,

And thereto add such reasons of your own

As may compact it more. Get you gone,

And hasten your return.

Exit OSWALD.

---

302 *Pray you, content:* do not interfere – be content with my handling of the affair

304 *tarry:* wait for me

305–9 *A fox … after:* if he could afford a halter, he would use it to hang her, as he would a fox. The Fool can afford this show of defiance because he is about to leave with Lear. 'Halter' and 'after' were pronounced hauter and auter, and so rhymed with 'daughter' and 'slaughter'

310 *This … counsel!* he would not insult me in this way had he not been encouraged by Lear
counsel: advice. Goneril is being sarcastic
311 *politic:* good policy
312 *At point:* in full preparation for any emergency
313 *buzz:* whispered rumour
fancy: imagined grievance
314 *enguard … powers:* use the power of his knights to surround and protect his senile waywardness
dotage: the childishness of old age
315 *in mercy:* at his mercy

316 *you … far:* your fears may be exaggerated

317–18 *Let … taken:* allow me always ('still') to move to eliminate potentially harmful influences rather than remain in fear of being overcome by them

320 *sustain:* endures, provides for

321 *unfitness:* inappropriateness, unsuitability

322 *have you writ:* Oswald has written the letter at Goneril's dictation

325 *full:* fully, completely
particular: personal
326 *thereto:* to that
327 *compact:* strengthen, make more credible

No, no, my lord,
This milky gentleness and course of yours
Though I condemn not, yet, under pardon,   330
You are much more at task for want of wisdom
Than praised for harmful mildness.

ALBANY
How far your eyes may pierce I cannot tell:
Striving to better, oft we mar what's well.

GONERIL
Nay, then—   335

ALBANY
Well, well; th' event.

Exeunt.

329 *This ... yours:* your mild and gentle way of doing things
330 *under pardon:* if you will pardon my saying so
331 *at task:* taken to task; open to censure or blame

333 *may pierce:* see into the future
334 *Striving ... well:* Albany's advice is 'leave well enough alone in case you make things worse'

336 *th' event:* we'll see what happens. The 'event' is the outcome

Striving to better, oft we mar what's well.
ALBANY, Act 1, Scene 4, 334

Key points

The conflict between Lear and his remaining daughters, dimly anticipated in Scene 1, and prepared for in Scene 3, now breaks out in earnest as Goneril advances the plan to alienate Lear.

- Kent has concealed his identity by changing his outward appearance and his way of speaking. It may still seem odd that Lear does not recognise Kent, but in Shakespeare's plays, convention dictates that once a character assumes a disguise, that disguise is impenetrable.

- Oswald, in carrying out Goneril's orders to make life less pleasant for Lear and his knights, is humiliated by Kent, to Lear's delight. This apparent victory over her agent, however, only serves to further Goneril's scheme to get rid of him.

- The Fool's main function is to make Lear recognise his true position, to make him realise that he is out of favour with the two daughters to whom he has foolishly handed over his power. He also reminds him of Cordelia, whose truthfulness he represents in her absence.

- The role of the Fool in Shakespeare's plays was a unique one (see p. 244). Convention dictated that a Fool was, as Goneril puts it, 'all-licensed' (line 188) to speak his mind freely to those in authority, even kings, without having to expect to endure punishment for doing so. This kind of immunity gives him the confidence to point out Lear's folly in placing himself at the mercy of his daughters.

- There is a paradoxical element in the Fool's treatment of Lear. There can be no doubt that everything the Fool says is intended for Lear's good. Frequently, however, his remarks have the effect of torturing Lear.

- The Fool's persistent nagging sometimes has a more stimulating effect, encouraging Lear to challenge Goneril's hostile attitude to him.

- A central theme of this scene is the disastrous effect on Lear's personality of his abdication. The possession and exercise of his royal power, which was absolute, meant he could strike terror into all who crossed him. In the opening scene, when Cordelia and Kent challenged him, they were banished from his sight. The benefits associated with the exercise of absolute power are essential to Lear's well-being. Their loss means a loss of his identity. Before he gave away his kingdom, his children were defined in relation to him. Now he is defined in relation to them: he is merely, as Oswald points out, 'my lady's father' (line 73). This is an unwelcome truth that he cannot easily face.

- When Goneril attacks Lear bitterly, he wonders what has happened to the old Lear who was never spoken to in this fashion: 'This is not Lear … Who is it that can tell me who I am?' (lines 213–17). He cannot accept that Goneril can treat him as she does in this scene; hence his question to her: 'Your name, fair gentlewoman?' (line 223).

- The theme of the 'thankless child', powerfully expressed in this scene, will become an obsession with Lear, as he comes to believe that all evils that befall parents inevitably stem from filial ingratitude. This is the main impulse behind his terrible, but logical, curse on Goneril: he hopes that Goneril will not have a child, but if she does, he hopes the child will torment her as she is tormenting him, so that she may feel the pain that only 'a thankless child' (line 277) like herself can inflict.

- The scene exposes the nature of the relationship between Goneril and Albany. Albany's half-hearted attempt to intercede for Lear is contemptuously brushed aside by his domineering wife. In Shakespeare's time the aggressive, tough, ruthless and dominant qualities shown by Goneril were strongly associated with men, whereas Albany's 'milky gentleness' (line 329), which Goneril dismisses, was considered a feminine trait.

Useful quotes

Let me not stay a jot for dinner; go get it ready.

(Lear, line 8)

Why came not the slave back to me when I called him?

(Lear, line 47)

Not only, sir, this your all-licensed fool,
But other of your insolent retinue
Do hourly carp and quarrel, breaking forth
In rank and not-to-be-endured riots.

(Goneril, lines 188–91)

Does any here know me? This is not Lear,
Does Lear walk thus? Speak thus? Where are his eyes?

(Lear, lines 213–14)

Ingratitude, thou marble-hearted fiend,
More hideous when thou show'st thee in
    a child
Than the sea-monster!

(Lear, lines 247–9)

If she must teem,
Create her child of spleen, that it may live
And be a thwart disnatured torment to her.

(Lear, lines 269–71)

Inform her full of my particular fear,
And thereto add such reasons of your own
As may compact it more.

(Goneril, lines 325–7)

Questions ?

1 What characteristics does Kent exhibit in this scene?

2 What evidence is there in this scene that Lear has not yet accepted the fact that he is no longer king?

3 Why is Lear so angry when Oswald calls him 'my lady's father' (line 73)?

4 Imagine you are Goneril. Make a case for your treatment of Lear in this scene. Your case should be based on evidence from the play so far.

5 In this scene Lear appears to see himself as the centre of his universe. He also appears to see loyalty to himself as the sole measure of goodness, and disloyalty as the sole measure of wickedness, in those around him. Develop these ideas.

6 What is the point of the Fool's remarks to Kent and Lear in this scene?

7 Are Lear and Kent justified in their treatment of Oswald? Explain your answer.

8 On the evidence provided by this scene, do you think Lear and Goneril have qualities in common? What are the main differences between their characters?

9 Would you agree that in this scene Lear learns some painful truths about the consequences of abdication for him? Give evidence from the play in support of your answer.

10 Is there any evidence in the text of the play that Lear is beginning to acknowledge his folly and perhaps recognise that he punished Cordelia for a relatively small fault?

ACT 1 ✝ Scene 5

Plot summary

Lear sends Kent with a written message to Regan, giving his version of what happened with Goneril. The Fool warns Lear that he cannot expect any better treatment at Regan's hands. Another ominous note is sounded by Lear himself when he prays that he will not go mad.

O let me not be mad, not mad, sweet heaven!

Courtyard in front of the Duke of Albany's palace.

Enter LEAR, KENT and FOOL.

LEAR

[*to KENT*] Go you before to Gloucester with these letters. Acquaint my daughter no further with any thing you know than comes from her demand out of the letter. If your diligence be not speedy, I shall be there afore you.

KENT

I will not sleep, my lord, till I have delivered your letter.   5

Exit.

FOOL

If a man's brains were in's heels, were't not in danger of kibes?

LEAR

Ay, boy.

FOOL

Then, I prithee, be merry; thy wit shall not go slip-shod.

LEAR

Ha, ha, ha!   10

FOOL

Shalt see, thy other daughter will use thee kindly; for though she's as like this as a crab's like an apple, yet I can tell what I can tell.

LEAR

What canst tell, boy?

FOOL

She will taste as like this as a crab does to a crab. Thou   15
canst tell why one's nose stands i' the middle on's face?

LEAR

No.

FOOL

Why, to keep one's eyes of either side's nose, that what a man cannot smell out he may spy into.

LEAR

I did her wrong—   20

FOOL

Canst tell how an oyster makes his shell?

LEAR

No.

1 *before:* ahead of me
to Gloucester: this refers not to the Earl of Gloucester but to the town near which Cornwall and Regan have their residence; it is a night's journey from this residence to the Earl of Gloucester's castle
2–3 *Acquaint . . . letter:* Kent should not comment on the events recorded in Act 1, Scene 4, and confine himself to answering questions arising from the contents of the letter
3 *demand:* query, question
3–4 *If . . . speedy:* if you do not get there with all possible speed
4 *afore:* before, sooner than
6 *in's:* in his

7 *kibes:* chilblains

9 *be merry:* cheer up
go slip-shod: need to wear slippers (instead of shoes to protect your brains from irritation, since you do not have brains, even in your heels). The Fool's main point is that Lear shows his lack of intelligence ('wit') in undertaking a visit to Regan

11 *Shalt see:* you will see
use: treat
kindly: according to her nature (kind), which in Regan's case is cruel
12 *she's . . . apple:* she resembles Goneril as a sour apple resembles an eatable one: both are of the same kind
12–13 *I can tell . . . tell:* I know what I know

15 *She . . . to a crab:* Lear's experience of Regan will be as distasteful as his experience of Goneril has been
16 *on's:* of his

18 *of . . . nose:* on either side of one's nose
18–19 *that . . . into:* so that what his sense of smell cannot tell him, his eyes may investigate. The Fool is suggesting that a man's senses are there to preserve him from the kind of folly that Lear has been guilty of
20 *her:* Cordelia

FOOL

Nor I neither, but I can tell why a snail has a house.

LEAR

Why?

FOOL

25   Why, to put's head in; not to give't away to his daughters, and leave his horns without a case.

LEAR

I will forget my nature. So kind a father! Be my horses ready?

FOOL

Thy asses are gone about 'em. The reason why the seven
30   stars are no more than seven is a pretty reason.

LEAR

Because they are not eight?

FOOL

Yes, indeed: thou wouldst make a good fool.

LEAR

To take't again perforce! Monster ingratitude!

FOOL

If thou wert my fool, nuncle, I'd have thee beaten for
35   being old before thy time.

LEAR

How's that?

FOOL

Thou shouldst not have been old till thou hadst been wise.

LEAR

O let me not be mad, not mad, sweet heaven!

Keep me in temper; I would not be mad!

Enter a GENTLEMAN.

40   How now! Are the horses ready?

GENTLEMAN

Ready, my lord.

LEAR

Come, boy.

Exeunt all except FOOL.

FOOL

She that's a maid now, and laughs at my departure

Shall not be a maid long, unless things be cut shorter.

Exit.

---

25   *put's:* put his

26   *leave ... case:* leave himself without the protection of a home

27   *forget my nature:* forget that I was once Goneril's father

29   *Thy ... 'em:* your servants are attending to the matter

33   *To ... perforce!* Lear is thinking either: of Goneril's action in taking away the privileges she had agreed to grant him; or: of restoring himself to royal authority by force
perforce: of necessity

39   *in temper:* in a proper frame of mind, sane

43–4   *She ... shorter:* the Fool's indecent couplet is addressed to the audience. He is suggesting that the virgin ('maid') who can see only the comic side of his witticisms, and who does not understand the tragic implications of Lear's journey, will not have enough intelligence to preserve her chastity

Key points

Lear is regretting his rash decision to divide his kingdom between Goneril and Regan, and realising that he will have to fight to keep his sanity.

- Lear's instructions to Kent when sending him with his letter to Regan suggest that he does not entirely trust her. This is why he tells Kent not to discuss with her what has happened during his terrible confrontation with Goneril in the previous scene. Instead, Kent must deal only with matters arising from Lear's letter.

- Lear appears too distracted by his own problems to pay full attention to the wise and troubling remarks of the Fool. Lear's own remarks are taken up with Goneril's ingratitude ('I will forget my nature. So kind a father!' and 'To take't again perforce! Monster ingratitude!';

lines 27, 33). When he says that he will forget his nature he means that he will try to forget that he was ever Goneril's father, because so kind and generous a father as he has been should not be cursed with so monstrously ungrateful a daughter as Goneril has shown herself to be.

- Lear's despairing cry: 'O let me not be mad' (line 38) indicates that, at this point, his greatest fear is that Goneril's behaviour may drive him to insanity.

- Lear's obsessive focus on the cruelty of Goneril (and later of Regan) will soon become a central feature of the madness theme.

Useful quotes

> Shalt see, thy other daughter will use thee kindly; for though she's as like this as a crab's like an apple, yet I can tell what I can tell.
>
> (Fool, lines 11–13)

> Thou shouldst not have been old till thou hadst been wise.
>
> (Fool, line 37)

> O let me not be mad, not mad, sweet heaven!
> Keep me in temper; I would not be mad!
>
> (Lear, lines 38–9)

? Questions

1 What characteristics does the Fool exhibit in this scene?

2 'So kind a father!' (line 27). Is Lear's assessment of himself accurate given what has happened in the first five scenes of the play? Explain your thinking.

3 Imagine you are either Lear or Goneril and compose your letter to Regan, informing her of recent events.

4 What do you think is Lear's state of mind in this scene? Is he regretting his actions in the opening scene? Support your answers with reference to the text of the play.

Scene 1

- Lear, King of Britain, decides to abdicate and divide his kingdom between his three daughters.
- Cordelia, Lear's youngest and best-loved daughter, refuses to match her sisters, Goneril and Regan, in their hypocritical declarations of love for their father.
- An angry Lear disinherits Cordelia, who is then married to the King of France without a dowry.
- Lear banishes the Earl of Kent for defending Cordelia.
- Goneril and Regan and their husbands, Albany and Cornwall, inherit the kingdom between them.

Scene 2

- The sub-plot involving the Earl of Gloucester and his two sons, Edgar (his heir) and Edmund (his illegitimate son), is introduced in this scene.
- Edmund intends to deprive Edgar of his inheritance and have himself made heir.
- Edmund deceives Gloucester into believing that Edgar is planning to murder him.
- Edmund persuades Edgar that he has upset their father and must keep out of his way.

Scene 3

- Lear is staying with Goneril under the conditions he imposed when he gave up the throne.
- Goneril has become impatient with Lear and his followers for their unruly behaviour.
- Goneril instructs her steward, Oswald, to make Lear and his followers feel unwelcome.
- Goneril will advise Regan of her plans, so that she can adopt the same strategy.

Scene 4

- Kent, heavily disguised, offers his services to Lear, and is accepted.
- When Oswald is negligent, Lear strikes him and Kent trips him up.
- The Fool reminds Lear of his folly in putting himself at the mercy of his daughters.
- Goneril tells Lear to reduce the number of his followers from one hundred to fifty.
- Lear calls down curses on Goneril, before leaving to seek the hospitality of Regan.

Scene 5

- The Fool warns Lear that Regan will treat him just as badly as Goneril has treated him.
- Lear worries that he may lose his sanity.

ACT 1 Speaking and listening

1 Your class has recently attended a performance of the play. In Act 1, Scene 4 of that production, Lear's knights destroy Goneril's dining hall, throwing plates and drinking vessels at each other, upending the dining table and engaging in drunken quarrels. In pairs, discuss whether this interpretation is true to the text of the play and how it might affect the audience.

2 In small groups, discuss the role of Cordelia in Act 1, Scene 1. What sort of person is she? Is her behaviour justified? Should she have handled the situation differently? Decide whether or not you support her stance. Each group should then contribute to a class discussion on Cordelia's role, followed by a vote on whether you condone or condemn her position.

Plot summary

The main plot and sub-plot come together in this scene. Hearing that Regan and Cornwall are coming to visit Gloucester's castle, Edmund manipulates Edgar into believing that he has offended them. Edgar flees the castle. The quick-witted Edmund wounds himself and then claims that Edgar tried to kill him when he refused to murder their father. Gloucester believes Edmund's story and intends to disinherit Edgar. Regan and Cornwall arrive and Regan manages to link Edgar with Lear's riotous knights and with Lear himself (whose godson Edgar is). Edgar is deemed a criminal and Lear's name is blackened by association. Meanwhile, Edmund wins praise from Gloucester and Cornwall.

This weaves itself perforce into my business.

EDMUND, Act 2, Scene 1, 15

severally: separately (i.e. they arrive on stage from different directions)

1 *Save thee:* God save thee

6 *abroad:* everywhere, at large
7 *the whispered ones:* the news discussed in whispers
7–8 *ear-kissing arguments:* topics of conversation, details of which are whispered into the ear

10 *toward:* impending, at hand
'twixt: between

14 *The better!* so much the better
15 *This ... business:* the arrival of Cornwall will inevitably ('perforce') involve him in my schemes ('business')
17–18 *one ... act:* a piece of business to dispose of that requires delicate handling
18 *Briefness ... work!* may speedy action and good fortune help me to achieve my goal
19 *descend:* Edgar is to come down from his hiding place in Edmund's lodging

20 *watches:* is looking for you
fly: leave, flee
21 *Intelligence:* information
22 *advantage:* help, benefit

A courtyard within the Earl of Gloucester's castle.

Enter EDMUND and CURAN, severally.

EDMUND
Save thee, Curan.

CURAN
And you, sir. I have been with your father, and given him notice that the Duke of Cornwall and Regan, his duchess, will be here with him this night.

EDMUND
5 How comes that?

CURAN
Nay, I know not. You have heard of the news abroad? — I mean the whispered ones, for they are yet but ear-kissing arguments.

EDMUND
Not I. Pray you, what are they?

CURAN
10 Have you heard of no likely wars toward, 'twixt the Dukes of Cornwall and Albany?

EDMUND
Not a word.

CURAN
You may do then in time. Fare you well, sir.

Exit.

EDMUND
The duke be here tonight? The better! Best!
15 This weaves itself perforce into my business.
My father hath set guard to take my brother;
And I have one thing, of a queasy question,
Which I must act. Briefness and fortune, work!
Brother, a word; descend! Brother, I say!

Enter EDGAR.

20 My father watches! O sir, fly this place!
Intelligence is given where you are hid!
You have now the good advantage of the night.

Have you not spoken 'gainst the Duke of Cornwall?

He's coming hither, now, i'th' night, i'th' haste,

And Regan with him. Have you nothing said   25

Upon his party 'gainst the Duke of Albany?

Advise yourself.

EDGAR
                    I am sure on't, not a word.

EDMUND

I hear my father coming! Pardon me;

In cunning I must draw my sword upon you.

Draw. Seem to defend yourself. Now quit you well.   30

[*calling*] Yield! Come before my father! Light, ho, here!

[*to Edgar*] Fly, brother! [*calling*] Torches, torches!

[*to Edgar*] So, farewell.

Exit EDGAR.

Some blood drawn on me would beget opinion

Of my more fierce endeavour. I have seen drunkards   35

Do more than this in sport. [*wounds himself*] Father,
        father!

Stop, stop! No help?

Enter GLOUCESTER and SERVANTS (with torches).

GLOUCESTER

Now, Edmund, where's the villain?

EDMUND

Here stood he in the dark, his sharp sword out,

Mumbling of wicked charms, conjuring the moon   40

To stand auspicious mistress.

GLOUCESTER
                    But where is he?

EDMUND

Look, sir, I bleed!

GLOUCESTER
                    Where is the villain, Edmund?

EDMUND

Fled this way, sir, when by no means he could—

23–6 *Have ... Albany?* it is only a few moments since Edmund learned about a possible conflict between Cornwall and Albany, and his quick use of this information to alarm Edgar shows his capacity for turning circumstances to his advantage. He first asks Edgar whether he has not spoken against Cornwall, and then, reversing the question, asks whether Edgar has said something on the side of Cornwall against Albany. His motive is to confuse Edgar, to suggest to him that he is beset by dangers and to encourage him to run away

26 *Upon his party:* in support of his faction

27 *Advise yourself:* recollect, think carefully
    on't: of it
    not a word: I have not spoken a word against either Albany or Cornwall

29 *In cunning:* as a trick (to avoid giving the impression that we are conspiring together)

30 *quit you well:* give a good account of yourself

31 *Yield ... here:* Edmund shouts out so that Gloucester will hear

34–5 *beget ... endeavour:* give the impression that I have been engaged in a violent encounter

35–6 *I ... sport:* a reference to the custom, common in Shakespeare's time among gallants (men of fashion), of stabbing their arms and mixing the blood with wine as they drank to the health of their mistresses

37 *No help?* Is there nobody to help me?

40 *Mumbling ... charms:* muttering devilish spells. Edmund is deftly playing on his father's superstitious nature. He is also showing his imaginative skill in devising a scene that makes Edgar appear in a sinister light to Gloucester

40–1 *conjuring ... mistress:* solemnly calling on the moon to exert a favourable ('auspicious') influence on his activities

41 *stand:* assume the role of

42 *Look ... bleed!* this is a delaying tactic; Edmund does not want Edgar captured until Gloucester is fully convinced of his guilt

43 *Fled this way:* presumably Edmund points in the wrong direction

GLOUCESTER

Pursue him, ho! Go after.

Exeunt SERVANTS.

'By no means' what?

EDMUND

45   Persuade me to the murder of your lordship;

But that I told him, the revenging gods

'Gainst parricides did all the thunder bend;

Spoke with how manifold and strong a bond

The child was bound to the father — sir, in fine,

50   Seeing how loathly opposite I stood

To his unnatural purpose, in fell motion,

With his prepared sword he charges home

My unprovided body, latched mine arm;

But whe'r he saw my best alarum'd spirits

55   Bold in the quarrel's right, roused to th' encounter,

Or whether gasted by the noise I made,

Full suddenly he fled.

GLOUCESTER

Let him fly far,

Not in this land shall he remain uncaught;

And found — Dispatch! The noble duke my master,

60   My worthy arch and patron, comes tonight.

By his authority I will proclaim it,

That he which finds him shall deserve our thanks,

Bringing the murderous coward to the stake;

He that conceals him, death.

EDMUND

65   When I dissuaded him from his intent,

And found him pight to do it, with curst speech

I threatened to discover him. He replied:

'Thou unpossessing bastard! Dost thou think

If I would stand against thee, would the reposal

70   Of any trust, virtue or worth in thee

Make thy words faithed? No, what I should deny —

As this I would; ay, though thou didst produce

My very character — I'd turn it all

To thy suggestion, plot and damned practice;

75   And thou must make a dullard of the world,

---

46 *But that:* but when

47 *'Gainst ... bend:* directed all their thunderbolts against those who murdered their fathers

48 *manifold:* numerous

49 *in fine:* in short, finally

51 *in fell motion:* with a deadly thrust

52 *prepared:* unsheathed, ready for use
    charges home: makes a sharp thrust

53 *unprovided:* unprotected
    latched mine arm: caught, nicked my arm

54 *whe'r:* whether
    best alarum'd spirits: energies, fully alert

55 *Bold ... right:* confidently asserting themselves in the rightness of my cause

56 *gasted:* frightened, scared (as if by a ghost)

57 *Full:* very

57 *Let him fly far:* however far he flies

59 *And found – Dispatch!* one interpretation is: and when he is found – kill him; other commentators suggest that 'dispatch' may mean 'hurry' (to find him) or 'get on with your [Edmund's] story'

60 *worthy:* honourable
    arch and patron: chief patron, arch-patron

61 *proclaim it:* officially declare Edgar an outlaw

63 *the stake:* the place of execution

64 *He ... death:* death is to be the punishment for anybody hiding Edgar

65 *dissuaded ... intent:* advised him against carrying out his intention

66 *pight:* fixed in his determination
    curst: angry, vehement, harsh

67 *discover him:* reveal the truth about him

68 *unpossessing bastard:* illegitimate child incapable of inheriting property

69 *If I ... thee:* if it came to a question of my word against yours
    reposal: the act of placing; here, the word refers to the trust and confidence placed in Edmund by Gloucester

71 *faithed:* believed

71–4 *No ... practice:* no, you would not be believed; in denying the truth of your accusations, which is what I would do, even if you were to produce my handwriting ('character'), I would explain everything you accused me of as being due to your instigation, your plotting and your wicked intrigue ('damned practice')

75 *thou ... world:* you would suppose all men ('the world') stupid (a 'dullard' is a slow-witted person)

If they not thought the profits of my death
Were very pregnant and potential spirits
To make thee seek it.'

GLOUCESTER
                    O strange and fastened villain!
Would he deny his letter, said he? I never got him.

Tucket within.

Hark! The duke's trumpets. I know not why he comes.   80
All ports I'll bar; the villain shall not 'scape;
The duke must grant me that. Besides, his picture
I will send far and near, that all the kingdom
May have due note of him; — and of my land,
Loyal and natural boy, I'll work the means   85
To make thee capable.

Enter CORNWALL, REGAN, and ATTENDANTS.

CORNWALL
How now, my noble friend! Since I came hither,
Which I can call but now, I have heard strange news.

REGAN
If it be true, all vengeance comes too short
Which can pursue th' offender. How dost, my lord?   90

GLOUCESTER
Oh, madam, my old heart is cracked, it's cracked!

REGAN
What, did my father's godson seek your life?
He whom my father named, your Edgar?

GLOUCESTER
O lady, lady, shame would have it hid!

REGAN
Was he not companion with the riotous knights   95
That tended upon my father?

GLOUCESTER
I know not, madam; 'tis too bad, too bad.

EDMUND
Yes, madam, he was of that consort.

REGAN
No marvel, then, though he were ill affected.
'Tis they have put him on the old man's death,   100

76–8 *If . . . it:* if they did not think that what you stand to gain from my death would provide you with very obvious ('pregnant') and powerful incentives ('potential spirits') to make you try to get rid of me. This is a wonderfully subtle way of suggesting to Gloucester that Edmund should replace Edgar as his heir

78 *strange:* unnatural, unheard of
    fastened: determined

79 *I . . . him:* he is not my son

Tucket within: a personal trumpet call is heard from off stage

80 *Hark!* listen

81 *ports:* means of escape (sea ports, town gates)
    bar: block

82 *his picture:* Edgar's picture. The circulation of pictures of wanted people was common in Shakespeare's time

84 *due note:* proper knowledge

84–6 *of my . . . capable:* I will go about the business of legitimising you, so that you will be legally entitled to inherit my land

85 *natural:* illegitimate. Gloucester is also implicitly contrasting Edmund's supposedly natural feeling for him with Edgar's seemingly unnatural conduct

89 *all . . . short:* no punishment can match (Edgar's offence)

91 *cracked:* broken

92–105 *What . . . be there:* Regan is pleased to find new evidence, however tenuous, against her father and his associates. She is far less concerned with Gloucester's sufferings than with using his predicament to strengthen her own case against Lear. She traces Edgar's allegedly evil behaviour to his association with Lear's knights, and, using the classic technique of guilt by association, manages to suggest that Lear's role as Edgar's godson may have had something to do with the latter's 'crime'

96 *tended:* waited upon

98 *consort:* company, group, fraternity

99 *No . . . affected:* it is no wonder, then, that he proved disloyal

100 *put him on:* encouraged him to bring about

101 *th' expense and waste:* the extravagant spending and squandering

103 *cautions:* warnings

104 *sojourn:* make a temporary stay

105 *assure thee:* you may be assured

107 *A child-like office:* true filial devotion. The moral values of Cornwall and Regan are confused. They express outrage at Edgar's 'disloyalty' to his father, and admire Edmund's show of loyalty, while at the same time refusing to accept any obligation of loyalty to Lear, to whom they owe so much

108 *He . . . practice:* Edmund disclosed Edgar's treacherous scheme (his 'practice')

109 *apprehend:* arrest

111–12 *If . . . harm:* if he is captured, there need be no further fear that he will do harmful deeds

112–13 *Make . . . please:* make your own plans for his capture, knowing that you may rely on my backing ('strength')

114–15 *Whose . . . itself:* whose virtuous obedience is so praiseworthy at this time

115 *ours:* part of my following. Cornwall is using the royal plural

116 *we . . . need:* Cornwall will be in real need of trustworthy followers in the civil strife ahead

117 *seize on:* take legal possession of (as my subject)

117–18 *I . . . else:* even if my personal defects prevent me from serving you to your total satisfaction, I shall, at any rate, be totally loyal to you

118 *For him:* on his behalf

120 *out of season:* at an inappropriate time
threading dark-eyed night: travelling through the darkness with the same painful effort as might be expended on threading a needle in the dark

121 *Occasions . . . prize:* there are matters of some importance

To have th' expense and waste of his revenues.
I have this present evening from my sister
Been well informed of them, and with such cautions
That if they come to sojourn at my house,
I'll not be there.

CORNWALL

105   Nor I, assure thee, Regan.
Edmund, I hear that you have shown your father
A child-like office.

EDMUND

             It was my duty, sir.

GLOUCESTER

He did bewray his practice, and received
The hurt you see, striving to apprehend him.

CORNWALL

Is he pursued?

GLOUCESTER

110   Ay, my good lord.

CORNWALL

If he be taken, he shall never more
Be feared of doing harm. Make your own purpose,
How in my strength you please. For you, Edmund,
Whose virtue and obedience doth this instant

115 So much commend itself, you shall be ours.
Natures of such deep trust we shall much need;
You we first seize on.

EDMUND

              I shall serve you, sir,
Truly, however else.

GLOUCESTER

            For him I thank your grace.

CORNWALL

You know not why we came to visit you—

REGAN

120 Thus out of season, threading dark-eyed night:
Occasions, noble Gloucester, of some prize;
Wherein we must have use of your advice.
Our father he hath writ, so hath our sister,

Of differences, which I best thought it fit

To answer from our home; the several messengers 125

From hence attend dispatch. Our good old friend,

Lay comforts to your bosom and bestow

Your needful counsel to our businesses,

Which craves the instant use.

GLOUCESTER

                            I serve you, madam,

Your graces are right welcome. 130

Flourish. Exeunt.

124	*differences:* quarrels (between Lear and Goneril)
124–5	*which … home:* Regan wants to answer the letters while she is away from home
125–6	*several … dispatch:* messengers carrying letters from Lear and Goneril respectively are waiting to be sent away
127	*Lay … bosom:* console yourself (about Edgar)
127–8	*bestow … businesses:* give us your much-needed advice on our affairs and activities
129	*Which … use:* which require to be dealt with immediately

Key points

This scene marks a decisive step in the separation of the good characters from the evil ones. Cornwall and Regan offer support to Edmund. Meanwhile, Edgar is forced into exile, sharing a common fate with Cordelia and Kent.

- Edmund manages events to his own advantage with notable skill. He easily conscripts his two victims, Edgar and Gloucester, into his service. It is a tribute to his ingenuity and his ability to appear to be what he is not (and play the part of the honest man) that everyone seems convinced by what he says. He is a man with a grievance, and as such is highly motivated.

- Edmund has no trouble in persuading Edgar to take part in what the latter must think is a pointless swordfight. Honest Edgar, incapable of suspecting wrong in others, obeys Edmund instinctively. The contrast between the cunning of Edmund and the simplicity of Edgar makes the triumph of evil over good a mere matter of course.

- Edmund's main purpose – to establish himself as Gloucester's heir by undoing his noble, trusting brother – is progressing with relative ease. As a clever manipulator and an imaginative creator of 'evidence', Edmund confronts Gloucester with plausible 'proof' of Edgar's guilt. Gloucester, as Edmund knows, is easily deceived.

- Regan is another opportunist. She seeks to convict her father of wrongdoing, using the technique of guilt by association (see lines 92–105). She makes an assertion (linking Edgar and Lear's knights) for which there is no evidence in the text of the play. We may be intended to find a parallel between Regan's attempt to associate Lear and Edgar with riotous behaviour, and Edmund's successful attempt to convince Gloucester that Edgar wants him killed. Edmund ensures that Gloucester never sees Edgar and therefore cannot test the truth or falsehood of his accusations. Similarly, we only have Goneril's word for it that Lear's knights behaved riotously. We know that Edmund's accusations are false, and also that Goneril and Regan have a strong motive for spreading falsehoods about their father.

- Shakespeare provides a subtle indication that the relationship between Regan and Cornwall is not notably different from that between Goneril and Albany. Cornwall is about to explain why they have unexpectedly come to visit Gloucester, when Regan brushes him aside and finishes his speech for him (lines 119–20). The stated aim of the visit is that Regan wants to answer the communications from Lear and Goneril while she is away from home, but the real purpose is that she does not want to receive or entertain Lear without first consulting Goneril.

Useful quotes

> *I hear my father coming! Pardon me;*
> *In cunning I must draw my sword upon you.*
>
> (Edmund, lines 28–9)

> *Loyal and natural boy, I'll work the means*
> *To make thee capable.*
>
> (Gloucester, lines 85–6)

> *Some blood drawn on me would beget opinion*
> *Of my more fierce endeavour.*
>
> (Edmund, lines 34–5)

> *What, did my father's godson seek your life?*
> *He whom my father named, your Edgar?*
>
> (Regan, lines 92–3)

> *when by no means he could …*
> *Persuade me to the murder of your lordship;*
> *But that I told him, the revenging gods*
> *'Gainst parricides did all the thunder bend;*
> *Spoke with how manifold and strong a bond*
> *The child was bound to the father*
>
> (Edmund, lines 43–9)

> *Was he not companion with the riotous knights*
> *That tended upon my father?*
>
> (Regan, lines 95–6)

> *For you, Edmund,*
> *Whose virtue and obedience doth this instant*
> *So much commend itself, you shall be ours.*
>
> (Cornwall, lines 113–15)

? Questions

1 Curan provides Edmund with news of rumours that Cornwall and Albany are likely to go to war. What use does Edmund make of this news? Has there been any previous indication of trouble between the dukes?

2 Why, do you think, does Edmund describe his brother as 'Mumbling of wicked charms, conjuring the moon' (line 40)?

3 Examine the irony of Edmund's speech beginning 'when by no means he could' (lines 43–57).

4 Regan talks of Edgar as Lear's godson and as a 'companion with the riotous knights' (line 95) who attended on Lear. What is the significance of these attempts to associate Edgar with Lear?

5 Who is the dominant partner in the Cornwall–Regan marriage? Explain your answer.

6 Why have Cornwall and Regan arrived in such haste at Gloucester's castle?

7 Can you find any parallels between Gloucester's behaviour in this scene and Lear's behaviour in Act 1, Scene 1?

8 Why, do you think, does Cornwall choose to make himself Edmund's patron?

9 In your opinion, is Regan being honest in her comments during this scene? Explain your answer.

10 Imagine you are Edmund. Write a brief account of your thoughts and feelings at this point in the play.

ACT 2 † Scene 2

Plot summary

Oswald and Kent have reached Gloucester's castle and delivered their letters to Regan. Oswald greets Kent politely, thinking he is a servant in Gloucester's household. Kent's response is extremely rude, and his language becomes abusive and threatening. Oswald cannot understand why a person he does not know should be treating him in this fashion. Kent draws his sword, and challenges Oswald to a duel, having reminded him that only two days previously he had tripped him up and beat him in the presence of Lear. Oswald calls for help. When Edmund answers the call, Kent threatens to fight him. Cornwall intervenes, but Kent shows little respect for him as well. Cornwall sentences Kent to a period in the stocks, a punishment reserved for low-born petty criminals. Gloucester pleads with Cornwall not to proceed with this punishment, which will offend Lear, but his plea is dismissed out of hand. The scene ends with a philosophical meditation from Kent.

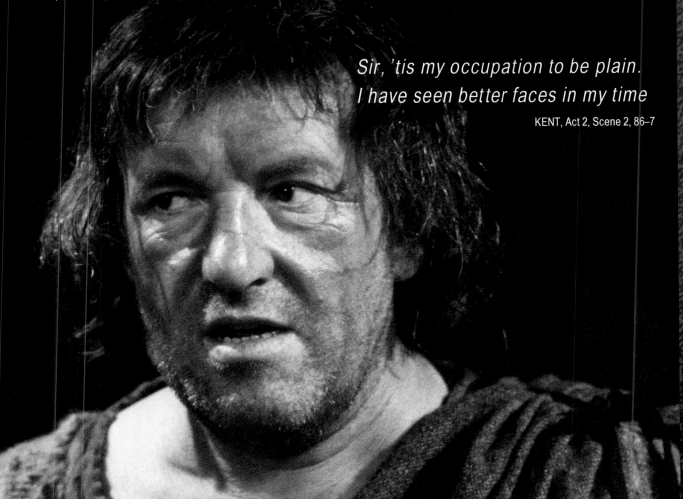

Sir, 'tis my occupation to be plain.
I have seen better faces in my time

KENT, Act 2, Scene 2, 86–7

severally: separately. Both men have delivered their letters to Regan, who has since travelled, in haste, to Gloucester's castle

1 *Good dawning:* Oswald wishes Kent, whom he does not recognise in the dark, good morning
Art . . . house? Are you a servant here?

2 *Ay:* Kent does not belong to Gloucester's household, but pretends he does, thus giving his insulting behaviour to Oswald a false warrant

4 *mire:* mud

5 *Prithee . . . lov'st me:* this was a conventional phrase used before a question or request, but Kent takes it literally

8 *in Lipsbury pinfold:* between my teeth, in my clutches; a 'pinfold' is a pound or pen in which animals are kept

10 *use:* treat
13–18 *an eater . . . service:* Kent is tracing Oswald's rise from kitchen servant to Goneril's confidant
13 *broken meats:* scraps left over after meals
base, proud: the lowly bred Oswald is proud of his new status as a steward
14–15 *three-suited . . . knave:* Oswald is a servant masquerading as a gentleman. He is 'three-suited' because servants were entitled to three suits a year; he is a 'hundred-pound' knave because this was the minimum property qualification for the title of gentleman; and his worsted ('woosted') stockings make him a mock-gentleman – real gentlemen wore silk stockings
15 *lily-livered:* cowardly
action-taking: one who takes legal action instead of settling disputes by combat
16 *glass-gazing:* admiring himself in mirrors
super-serviceable: overanxious to be of service
finical: affected, overly fastidious
17 *one-trunk-inheriting:* having so few possessions that they all fit in a single trunk
17–18 *a bawd . . . service:* prepared to do any service for his mistress
18 *composition:* mixture
19 *pander:* a go-between in illicit love affairs
20 *clamorous:* noisy
21 *thy addition:* the 'noble' titles I have conferred on you

Before the Earl of Gloucester's castle.

Enter KENT and OSWALD, severally.

OSWALD
Good dawning to thee, friend. Art of this house?

KENT
Ay.

OSWALD
Where may we set our horses?

KENT
In the mire.

OSWALD
5   Prithee, if thou lov'st me, tell me.

KENT
I love thee not.

OSWALD
Why then, I care not for thee.

KENT
If I had thee in Lipsbury pinfold, I would make thee care for me.

OSWALD
10   Why dost thou use me thus? I know thee not.

KENT
Fellow, I know thee.

OSWALD
What dost thou know me for?

KENT
A knave, a rascal, an eater of broken meats, a base, proud, shallow, beggarly, three-suited, hundred-pound, filthy, 15 woosted-stocking knave; a lily-livered, action-taking whoreson, glass-gazing, super-serviceable, finical rogue, one-trunk-inheriting slave; one that would be a bawd in way of good service, and art nothing but the composition of a knave, beggar, coward, pander, and the son and heir 20 of a mongrel bitch; one whom I will beat into clamorous whining if thou deniest the least syllable of thy addition.

OSWALD

Why, what a monstrous fellow art thou, thus to rail on one that is neither known of thee nor knows thee!

KENT

What a brazen-faced varlet art thou, to deny thou knowest me! Is it two days ago since I tripped up thy heels, and beat thee before the King? Draw, you rogue, for though it be night, yet the moon shines. I'll make a sop o' the moonshine of you. [*drawing his sword*] You whoreson cullionly barber-monger, draw!

25

OSWALD

Away! I have nothing to do with thee.

30

KENT

Draw, you rascal! You come with letters against the King, and take Vanity the puppet's part against the royalty of her father. Draw, you rogue, or I'll so carbonado your shanks. Draw, you rascal! Come your ways!

OSWALD

Help, ho! Murder! Help!

35

KENT

Strike, you slave! Stand, rogue, stand! You neat slave, strike! [*beats him*]

OSWALD

Help, ho! Murder! Murder!

Enter EDMUND.

EDMUND

How now! What's the matter? Part!

KENT

With you, goodman boy, if you please! Come, I'll flesh ye; come on, young master.

40

Enter CORNWALL, REGAN, GLOUCESTER, and SERVANTS.

GLOUCESTER

Weapons! Arms! What's the matter here?

CORNWALL

Keep peace, upon your lives! He dies that strikes again.

What is the matter?

22 *rail on:* utter abusive language at

24 *varlet:* low, mean person

28 *sop o' the moonshine:* a 'sop' is a piece of bread or cake soaked in liquid, so it has been suggested that Kent's intention may be either: to steep Oswald in his own blood, under the light of the moon; or: to perforate Oswald so that his body may soak up the moonlight through his wounds

29 *cullionly barber-monger:* base, foolish frequenter of barbers' shops

32 *Vanity the puppet:* Goneril. Kent sees her as a figure from a puppet show, representing self-conceit. Kent is speaking as though Lear still out-ranks Goneril

33–4 *carbonado your shanks:* cut your legs crosswise as if they were meat for grilling

34 *Come your ways!* come on

36 *neat slave:* pure rogue

39 *Part:* it has been suggested that this should be a stage direction, rather than part of the dialogue. Excluding 'Part' from the text would make more sense of Kent's reply

40 *With . . . please!* Kent is answering Edmund's question about the subject of the quarrel by saying: my quarrel is with you, my fine young fellow; if you want a fight, I'm your man
goodman boy: master, boy, or my fine young man; the title is used contemptuously or mockingly
flesh ye: introduce you to bloodshed

45 *messengers:* Oswald is Goneril's messenger; Kent is Lear's

46 *difference:* quarrel

48 *No marvel ... valour:* no wonder (you are out of breath), your brave exertions have made you so

49 *disclaims in thee:* renounces any share in making you a tailor: as Oswald's clothes are the best part of him, and in Kent's eyes the only worthwhile part, he suggests that a tailor made him

53 *ill:* badly
53–4 *o' the trade:* at his trade

56 *at suit of:* out of sympathy for (his age)
58 *Thou whoreson ... letter!* Kent is suggesting that Oswald is an unwanted member of the human race. The letter z ('zed') was regarded as superfluous ('unnecessary') because s could serve most of its purposes
59–60 *I ... him:* Kent thinks of Oswald as being composed of lumpy, unsifted ('unbolted') lime, which must be trodden on before it can be made into mortar. Kent would be glad to perform this task, and to smear ('daub') the wall of a lavatory ('jakes') with the product of his labour
61 *wagtail:* this is a reference to Oswald's nervous jerky movements
63 *You beastly ... reverence?* Cornwall finds Kent's behaviour more appropriate to the animal kingdom than to human society, since he shows no respect or good manners
64 *anger ... privilege:* an angry man has the right to ignore the conventions of good behaviour
66–7 *That ... honesty:* I am angry that a man like Oswald should wear a sword, the mark of a gentleman, and at the same time be totally lacking in decency and integrity ('honesty')
67–9 *Such ... t'unloose:* evil-minded servants such as Oswald are often prepared to untie the most sacred family bonds (between husband and wife, between father and child). Such bonds are too tightly knotted to be easily loosened, and so violent or sinister means (hence the reference to 'rats') must be used to sever them

REGAN
45 The messengers from our sister and the King.

CORNWALL
What is your difference? Speak.

OSWALD
I am scarce in breath, my lord.

KENT
No marvel, you have so bestirred your valour. You cowardly rascal, nature disclaims in thee; a tailor made 50 thee.

CORNWALL
Thou art a strange fellow. A tailor make a man?

KENT
Ay, a tailor, sir. A stone-cutter or painter could not have made him so ill, though he had been but two years o' the trade.

CORNWALL
55 [*to OSWALD*] Speak yet, how grew your quarrel?

OSWALD
This ancient ruffian, sir, whose life I have spared at suit of his grey beard—

KENT
Thou whoreson zed! Thou unnecessary letter! — My lord, if you will give me leave, I will tread this unbolted villain 60 into mortar, and daub the wall of a jakes with him. — Spare my grey beard, you wagtail?

CORNWALL
Peace, sirrah!
You beastly knave, know you no reverence?

KENT
Yes, sir; but anger hath a privilege.

CORNWALL
65 Why art thou angry?

KENT
That such a slave as this should wear a sword,
Who wears no honesty. Such smiling rogues as these,

Like rats, oft bite the holy cords a-twain

Which are too intrince t'unloose; smooth every passion

That in the natures of their lords rebel;   70

Bring oil to fire, snow to their colder moods;

Renege, affirm, and turn their halcyon beaks

With every gall and vary of their masters,

Knowing nought, like dogs, but following.

[*to OSWALD*] A plague upon your epileptic visage!   75

Smile you my speeches, as I were a fool?

Goose, if I had you upon Sarum plain,

I'd drive ye cackling home to Camelot.

CORNWALL

What! Art thou mad, old fellow?

GLOUCESTER

How fell you out? Say that.   80

KENT

No contraries hold more antipathy

Than I and such a knave.

CORNWALL

Why dost thou call him a knave? What is his fault?

KENT

His countenance likes me not.

CORNWALL

No more, perchance, does mine, nor his, nor hers.   85

KENT

Sir, 'tis my occupation to be plain.

I have seen better faces in my time

Than stands on any shoulder that I see

Before me at this instant.

CORNWALL

              This is some fellow,

Who, having been praised for bluntness, doth affect   90

A saucy roughness, and constrains the garb

Quite from his nature. He cannot flatter, he!

An honest mind and plain, he must speak truth!

And they will take it, so; if not, he's plain.

---

68 *holy cords:* bonds of marriage and the family
a-twain: in two

69 *intrince:* tightly knotted, hence hard to unravel ('t'unloose')

69–70 *smooth ... rebel:* flattering servants, such as Oswald, encourage and promote the wayward passions of their masters

72–3 *Renege ... masters:* these flattering servants are prepared to deny and renounce ('renege') or, on the other hand, to affirm anything – depending on what they think will please their masters. Kent uses the halcyon or kingfisher as an emblem of Oswald and his kind; the kingfisher, when hung up, was thought to turn with the wind, like a weathercock

73 *gall and vary:* varying gale, changing breeze

75 *epileptic visage:* Oswald, shaking with fear, gives Kent the impression that he has epilepsy

76 *Smile ... fool?* Are you smiling at my speeches as if I were a professional jester?

77 *Goose:* proverbial name for a fool
Sarum plain: Salisbury plain

78 *I'd ... Camelot:* the precise location of Camelot, the legendary capital of King Arthur's kingdom, is unknown. It may be Camelford in Cornwall, a possible residence of Regan and her husband. Kent may thus be saying: I would like to chase you all the way from Salisbury to Cornwall

81 *No ... antipathy:* no two people could be less compatible, more opposed to each other

84 *His ... not:* his face does not please me

85 *perchance:* perhaps

90–2 *doth ... nature:* puts on an air of insolent rudeness and distorts ('constrains') the style ('garb') of plain speech from its true nature, which is the sincere expression of feeling, making it instead a cloak for cunning

94 *And ... plain:* if ('And') people are prepared to accept his rudeness ('it'), then Kent is satisfied; if they take exception to his rudeness, he can always say that he is a simple, plain-spoken man

95–8 *These . . . nicely:* I am familiar with scoundrels like this fellow, who, beneath a blunt exterior, conceal more cunning ('craft') and more corrupt purposes than twenty fawning, cringing attendants ('observants'), bowing and scraping in ludicrous fashion as they try to perform their duties with the utmost refinement and exactness ('nicely')

99–102 Kent adopts a courtly style and flatters his critic, in absurdly exaggerated language
99 *verity:* truth
100–2 *th' allowance . . . front:* the approval ('allowance') of your magnificent looks, whose astrological power (acting upon the characters and destinies of human beings and affecting events on earth), like the bright coronet of fire on the flaming forehead of the sun ('Phoebus')

103 *To . . . dialect:* to change my style of speech
discommend: disapprove of
104 *beguiled:* deceived

106–7 *though . . . to' t:* even if I were able to persuade your disapproving self to beg me to be a plain knave by flattering you

110 *late:* recently
111 *upon his misconstruction:* as a result of his misinterpretation of what I said and did. Oswald is lying; he was struck by Lear for the offensively negligent attitude Goneril ordered him to adopt
112–18 *When . . . again:* following the King's assault on me, he [Kent], being in league with the King, and in an effort to encourage by his support the King's angry mood, tripped me from behind. When I was on the ground, he enjoyed a scornful and abusive triumph over me, and acted the part of hero so well that he won honour for himself. He won the praise of the King for attacking an opponent who offered no resistance, and in the bloodthirsty mood induced by his first success as a warrior, drew his sword on me again, this time here
118–19 *None . . . fool:* any rogue or coward (such as Oswald) can make a fool of someone like Ajax (or Cornwall), by deceiving him or by imposing on him. Ajax fought at the siege of Troy and was a man with more strength than intelligence. Users of the name 'Ajax' (pronounced 'age aches') frequently intended to pun on 'jakes' (a lavatory) – this would account for Cornwall's angry reaction
119 *stocks:* a timber frame with holes for the feet, where offenders were confined for public punishment

95 These kind of knaves I know, which in this plainness

Harbour more craft and more corrupter ends

Than twenty silly-ducking observants,

That stretch their duties nicely.

KENT

Sir, in good faith, in sincere verity,

100 Under th' allowance of your great aspect

Whose influence, like the wreath of radiant fire

On flickering Phoebus' front—

CORNWALL

What mean'st by this?

KENT

To go out of my dialect, which you discommend so much.

I know, sir, I am no flatterer. He that beguiled you in a

105 plain accent was a plain knave; which, for my part, I will

not be, though I should win your displeasure to entreat

me to't.

CORNWALL

[*to OSWALD*] What was th' offence you gave him?

OSWALD

I never gave him any.

110 It pleased the King his master very late

To strike at me, upon his misconstruction,

When he, compact, and flattering his displeasure,

Tripped me behind; being down, insulted, railed,

And put upon him such a deal of man,

115 That worthied him, got praises of the King

For him attempting who was self-subdued;

And in the fleshment of this dread exploit,

Drew on me here again.

KENT

None of these rogues and cowards

But Ajax is their fool.

CORNWALL

Fetch forth the stocks!

Exit some SERVANTS.

You stubborn, ancient knave, you reverend braggart,   120
We'll teach you.

KENT
                    Sir, I am too old to learn:
Call not your stocks for me. I serve the King,
On whose employment I was sent to you.
You shall do small respect, show too bold malice
Against the grace and person of my master   125
Stocking his messenger.

CORNWALL
                    Fetch forth the stocks!
As I have life and honour, there shall he sit till noon.

REGAN
Till noon? Till night, my lord, and all night too.

KENT
Why, madam, if I were your father's dog,
You should not use me so.

REGAN
                    Sir, being his knave, I will.   130

CORNWALL
This is a fellow of the self-same colour
Our sister speaks of. Come, bring away the stocks!
Stocks brought out.

GLOUCESTER
Let me beseech your grace not to do so.
His fault is much, and the good King his master
Will check him for't. Your purposed low correction   135
Is such as basest and contemn'd wretches
For pilferings and most common trespasses
Are punished with. The King must take it ill,
That he, so slightly valued in his messenger,
Should have him thus restrained.

CORNWALL
                    I'll answer that.   140

REGAN
My sister may receive it much more worse
To have her gentleman abused, assaulted,
For following her affairs. Put in his legs.

---

120 *You ... braggart:* being old ('ancient'), Kent should be respected/respectful ('reverend'); instead, he is rude and rough ('stubborn') and a boaster ('braggart')

125 *Against ... master:* against the office of kingship, and against the person of the King
126 *Stocking:* placing in the stocks

130 *use me so:* treat me thus

130 *being:* since you are

131 *self-same colour:* identical character
132 *Our sister speaks of:* the reference is to Goneril's letter; Cornwall is accusing Kent of behaving like Lear's (supposedly) riotous knights

135 *check:* rebuke, reprimand

136 *basest and contemn'd:* lowest and most despised

140 *answer:* be accountable for

142 *her gentleman:* Oswald

143 *following her affairs:* attending to her business

146 *disposition:* tendency of mind and character, mood

147 *be rubbed:* put up with being hindered
entreat for thee: speak on your behalf

148 *watched:* gone without sleep

150 *A . . . heels:* even a good man may suffer a decline in fortune. Kent's image for this is of a man down at heel; a man in the stocks was said to be 'punished by the heels'
151 *Give you:* God give you

152 *'twill be ill taken:* Lear will take it badly

153–5 *Good King . . . sun!* the example of Lear is about to confirm ('approve') the truth of the common proverb ('saw') describing the fate of someone destined to go from better to worse, from the comfort of the shade to the discomfort of the hot sun and open air
156 *beacon:* sun
under globe: lower world, the earth
157 *comfortable:* comforting
158–9 *Nothing . . . misery:* the meaning of this is not certain, but may be: only the most miserable person believes in/gets a miracle; or: to those in despair, almost any relief seems like a miracle
161 *obscured course:* hidden, disguised way of life
161–3 *and shall . . . remedies:* a possible meaning is that Cordelia, away from this monstrous situation, will try to restore what has been lost; however, most commentators believe the text to be corrupt here. Another explanation for the fragmented style is that Kent is reading extracts from the letter
163 *o'er-watched:* too long without sleep
164–5 *Take vantage . . . lodging:* let me take advantage of the opportunity offered by sleep not to have to look on the degrading stocks
165–6 *Fortune . . . wheel:* Kent is at the bottom of fortune's wheel; he is hoping that it will turn and he and Lear may climb upward again

KENT is put in the stocks.

Come, my good lord, away.

Exeunt all but GLOUCESTER and KENT.

GLOUCESTER

145   I am sorry for thee, friend. 'Tis the duke's pleasure,

Whose disposition, all the world well knows,

Will not be rubbed nor stopped. I'll entreat for thee.

KENT

Pray do not, sir. I have watched and travelled hard.

Some time I shall sleep out, the rest I'll whistle.

150   A good man's fortune may grow out at heels.

Give you good morrow!

GLOUCESTER

The duke's to blame in this: 'twill be ill taken.

Exit.

KENT

Good King, that must approve the common saw,

That out of heaven's benediction com'st

155   To the warm sun!

Approach, thou beacon to this under globe,

That by thy comfortable beams I may

Peruse this letter. Nothing almost sees miracles,

But misery. I know 'tis from Cordelia,

160   Who hath most fortunately been informed

Of my obscured course, and shall find time

From this enormous state, seeking to give

Losses their remedies. All weary and o'er-watched,

Take vantage, heavy eyes, not to behold

165   This shameful lodging. Fortune, good night.

Smile once more; turn thy wheel.

He sleeps.

Key points

The events depicted in this scene amount to a comic parody of the more serious conflicts between Lear and his daughters and between Gloucester and Edgar.

- It should be remembered that none of the other characters in the scene know that the puzzling and bad-tempered man acting as Lear's servant and messenger is the Earl of Kent in disguise.

- Kent's lengthy list of insults and his vigorous actions against Oswald are inspired by the fact that Oswald has come from Goneril with a communication that is hostile to Lear. Kent is devoted to Lear and will always do what he can to protect Lear's interests.

- Kent's loss of self-control is a faint reflection of Lear's outbursts against Cordelia, Kent and Goneril. Like his master, Kent is no respecter of persons or their feelings. He insults Oswald, then the company in general ('I have seen better faces in my time'; line 87) and then Cornwall in particular ('None of these rogues and cowards but Ajax is their fool'; lines 118–19). However, his refusal to be taken in by surface appearances is in marked contrast to Lear's folly.

- Kent's plainness of speech resembles Cordelia's refusal to flatter Lear in the opening scene. Similarly, Cornwall's sarcastic treatment of Kent's truthfulness and angry response to his offence is reminiscent of Lear's hasty banishment of Kent and Cordelia. This time Kent's punishment is to be a night in the stocks.

- Regan's vindictive nature is also on display in this scene when she increases the time Kent must spend in the stocks. Having experienced at first hand the rigours of Regan's 'hospitality', Kent knows that Lear can expect no better when he arrives.

- Kent's identification with Lear is stressed just before and after he is put in the stocks. Gloucester points out that Lear will regard any humiliation inflicted on Kent as a personal insult. And Kent's soliloquy (lines 153–66) suggests that his own confinement in the stocks is an emblem of Lear's fall from high estate.

- We see the first signs that Gloucester's attitude to Regan and Cornwall is beginning to change. He is sorry to see Kent in the stocks and fearful of how Lear will react to the contempt that has been shown to his representative. At this stage, however, Gloucester is unable to influence events.

- The image of the wheel of fortune at the end of Kent's soliloquy is particularly appropriate ('Fortune, good night. Smile once more; turn thy wheel'; lines 165–6). Kent feels that he is now at the bottom of fortune's wheel, from which point things must improve. His hopes have been raised by a letter from Cordelia, who will seek 'to give losses their remedies' (lines 162–3). Although Cordelia does not appear on stage for much of the play, her presence is always felt in the background.

Useful quotes

> Sir, 'tis my occupation to be plain.
>
> (Kent, line 86)

> You shall do small respect, show too bold malice
> Against the grace and person of my master
> Stocking his messenger.
>
> (Kent, lines 124–6)

> Why, madam, if I were your father's dog,
> You should not use me so.
>
> (Kent, lines 129–30)

> The King must take it ill,
> That he, so slightly valued in his messenger,
> Should have him thus restrained.
>
> (Gloucester, lines 138–40)

> My sister may receive it much more worse
> To have her gentleman abused, assaulted,
> For following her affairs. Put in his legs.
>
> (Regan, lines 141–3)

? Questions

1 Describe Kent's attitude to Oswald in this scene. Is it justified? Is he being deliberately provocative?

2 Imagine you are Oswald. Write your impressions of Lear's messenger, Caius (i.e. Kent).

3 What qualities does Cornwall display in this scene? Do you think he is a suitable husband for Regan?

4 Kent changes his manner of speech in lines 99–102. Explain why he does this.

5 Oswald provides his version of events in lines 109–18 ('I never gave him any …'). On the evidence of the play so far, is his version accurate and reasonable? Explain your answer.

6 Does Kent deserve to be put in the stocks? Does he deserve to be punished at all? Give reasons for your answers.

7 At the end of Act 2, Scene 1, Gloucester appeared to be sympathetic to Regan and Cornwall. How do you explain his changing position in this scene?

8 What does this scene tell you about the way Regan is thinking? Explain your answer with reference to the play.

9 This scene has some grim and terrible moments, some humorous ones and some hopeful ones. Comment on one example of each kind.

10 Imagine that you are Kent and write a short note to Cordelia to inform her of the recent behaviour of Regan and Cornwall.

Plot summary

The main dramatic function of this soliloquy is to explain the transformation of Edgar into Poor Tom, thus ensuring that audiences will recognise the true identity and significance of the character when he next appears. The disguise enabled Shakespeare to keep Edgar in Britain (and on the stage), even though he has a price on his head.

My face I'll grime with filth,
Blanket my loins, elf all my hair in knots,
And with presented nakedness outface
The winds and persecutions of the sky.

EDGAR, Act 2, Scene 3, 9–12

edgar disguise,
reality of the kingdom.

1 *proclaimed:* declared an outlaw

2 *happy:* opportune, lucky

4–5 *That ... taking:* that is not strictly guarded with a view to capturing me

6 *am bethought:* have decided, have the idea

7–20 *To take ... Tom:* Edgar plans to disguise himself as a Bedlam beggar. He describes the plight and behaviour of these seventeenth-century social outcasts. They were pauper lunatics, who had been released from the mental hospital of St Mary of Bethlehem in London with a licence to beg. They wandered up and down the country and were thought to be possessed by demons. As Edgar speaks, he may be removing his clothing, smearing himself with dirt and knotting his hair

7 *basest:* most debased, lowest

8–9 *That ... beast:* Edgar is about to assume the appearance of extreme destitution ('penury'); almost to the level of a beast

10 *Blanket my loins:* wear a blanket as a loincloth
elf: twist

11–12 *with presented ... sky:* with a show of nakedness, defiantly confront ('outface') the ferocity of the elements

13 *proof and precedent:* examples to imitate

15 *Strike:* stick
mortified: insensible to pain (because of exposure to the cold)

17 *this horrible object:* the frightful spectacle of wounded bodies
low: humble

18 *pelting:* mean, insignificant

19 *bans:* curses

20 *Enforce their charity:* compel country people to be charitable to them
Turlygod: the meaning is no longer known; perhaps it was a made-up word to indicate his 'madness'
Poor Tom: Edgar is practising the distinctive whine of the Bedlam beggar

21 *That's ... am:* as Poor Tom, I have some hope; as Edgar, I am doomed

contrast between
King Lear going mad,
and Edgar pretending
to be mad.

Simular to Cordelia.

Near the Earl of Gloucester's castle.

Enter EDGAR.

EDGAR
I heard myself proclaimed,
And by the happy hollow of a tree
Escaped the hunt. No port is free, no place
That guard and most unusual vigilance
5   Does not attend my taking. Whiles I may 'scape
I will preserve myself, and am bethought
To take the basest and most poorest shape
That ever penury, in contempt of man,
Brought near to beast. My face I'll grime with filth,
10 Blanket my loins, elf all my hair in knots,
And with presented nakedness outface
The winds and persecutions of the sky.
The country gives me proof and precedent
Of Bedlam beggars, who, with roaring voices
15 Strike in their numbed and mortified arms
Pins, wooden pricks, nails, sprigs of rosemary;
And with this horrible object from low farms,
Poor pelting villages, sheep-cotes and mills,
Sometimes with lunatic bans, sometimes with prayers,
20 Enforce their charity. Poor Turlygod, Poor Tom!
That's something yet. Edgar I nothing am.

Exit.

Key points

Edgar's soliloquy introduces a few new themes.

- It provides the first indication that Britain consists of more than the 'shadowy forests', 'champains rich'd', 'plenteous rivers and wide-skirted meads' mentioned in Act 1, Scene 1, lines 60–1. Edgar gives us a picture of 'poor pelting villages, sheep-cotes and mills' (line 18). Lear has yet to become familiar with this side of his former kingdom.

- The Bedlam beggar, whom Edgar is about to impersonate, was an English institution in Shakespeare's time. Inmates of Bethlehem (hence 'Bedlam') hospital in London, an asylum for the insane, were released after a period of time with a licence to beg throughout the kingdom. Edgar's soliloquy gives a graphic picture of their frightening appearance and conduct as they enforced charity with the aid of wild curses ('lunatic bans'; line 19) and prayers.

- Another significant new theme is expressed in Edgar's determination 'to take the basest and most poorest shape that ever penury, in contempt of man, brought near to beast' (lines 7–9). As with Kent's humiliating predicament (in the stocks) in the previous scene, Edgar's proposal anticipates Lear's condition later in the play. However, Edgar chooses this state as a disguise, whereas Lear is forced into it by cruel circumstances.

- In spite of his fear of capture, Edgar has a positive outlook and is determined to preserve his life as long as he can.

- There is no scene division in the First Folio version of the play between Act 2, Scenes 2 and 3, which means that Kent would remain on the stage, presumably asleep, during Edgar's soliloquy. This indicates the non-realistic nature of the play. It also hints at Shakespeare's dramatic style, as the bringing together on stage of two loyal men who have both been forced by circumstances to adopt a disguise would be a poignant symbol of Lear's world.

Useful quotes

> No port is free, no place
> That guard and most unusual vigilance
> Does not attend my taking.
>
> (Edgar, lines 3–5)

> My face I'll grime with filth,
> Blanket my loins, elf all my hair in knots,
> And with presented nakedness outface
> The winds and persecutions of the sky.
>
> (Edgar, lines 9–12)

? Questions

1 Do you think Edgar has chosen a good method of evading capture? Give reasons for your answer.

2 In deciding to pretend to be somebody he is not, Edgar has something in common with some other characters in the play, although his motives for pretending differ from theirs. Comment on this statement, referring to the text of the play.

3 What do we learn about the life of a Bedlam beggar from this scene?

4 Imagine that you are directing a production of King Lear. Write out a brief for the costume, hair and make-up department about the look you want them to achieve for 'Poor Tom'. You may find it helpful to include sketches or other visual material.

ACT 2 † Scene 4

Plot summary

Confronted by the spectacle of Kent in the stocks, Lear refuses to face the fact that Regan and Cornwall have thus humiliated his messenger, and by implication himself. When Kent finally convinces him of the truth, he must fight with all his strength to control his mounting hysteria. He resolves to confront Regan at whatever cost. However, she refuses to speak with him. His fearful anticipation of the interview with her leads to another attack of hysteria. When Cornwall and Regan finally appear, Lear's worst fears are realised. Lear wants to believe, for the sake of his sanity, that Regan is comforting, tender-hearted and welcoming. The evidence to the contrary is not long in coming.

Regan symbolically takes the newly arrived Goneril by the hand, and Lear must endure a cleverly orchestrated bullying session at the hands of his two daughters. They play a cruel game as they suggest reductions in the number of his followers. The final humiliation comes when Goneril decides to deprive him of all his followers. Lear has no choice but to rush out. The increasing disorder of Lear's mind is reflected in the approaching storm and tempest. Goneril and Regan tell Gloucester not to offer shelter to their father, but to let him face the fury of the storm. Gloucester's protests are ignored.

*O how this mother swells
up toward my heart!*
Hysterica passio, *down,
thou climbing sorrow!*

LEAR Act 2 Scene 4, 54–5

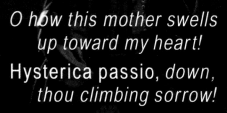

Before the Earl of Gloucester's castle.

Enter LEAR, FOOL and GENTLEMAN.

LEAR

'Tis strange that they should so depart from home
And not send back my messenger.

GENTLEMAN

As I learned,
The night before there was no purpose in them
Of this remove.

KENT

[*in the stocks*] Hail to thee, noble master.   5

LEAR

Ha! Mak'st thou this shame thy pastime?

KENT

No, my lord.

FOOL

Ha, ha! He wears cruel garters. Horses are tied by the
heads, dogs and bears by the neck, monkeys by the loins,
and men by the legs. When a man's over-lusty at legs
then he wears wooden nether-stocks.   10

LEAR

[*to KENT*] What's he that hath so much thy place mistook
To set thee here?

KENT

It is both he and she,
Your son and daughter.

LEAR

No.

KENT

Yes.   15

LEAR

No, I say.

KENT

I say, yea.

LEAR

No, no, they would not.

1 *they:* Regan and Cornwall, who have hastily left their home in response to Goneril's letter warning them about Lear and his knights

2 *And ... messenger:* Lear expected Regan and Cornwall to send back Kent with a message about their departure

3–4 *there ... remove:* they had no intention to leave home

6 *Mak'st ... pastime?* Are you sitting there in these degrading stocks to amuse yourself?

7 *cruel:* there is a double meaning here based on the similarity of sound between 'cruel' (painful) and 'crewel' (a worsted yarn used in the making of cross-garters)

9–10 *When ... nether-stocks:* when a man is too much of a wanderer (i.e. when his legs are too strong or 'lusty') he wears wooden stocks (to restrain him), instead of stockings ('nether-stocks')

11–12 *What's ... here?* Lear angrily wonders who can have shown such scant regard for Kent's position as his messenger to humiliate him like this. On top of Goneril's treatment of him, this is a further shock to Lear's mental and emotional balance

KENT

Yes, they have.

LEAR

20   By Jupiter, I swear, no.

KENT

By Juno, I swear, ay.

LEAR

They durst not do't,

They could not, would not do't. 'Tis worse than murder,

To do upon respect such violent outrage.

Resolve me, with all modest haste, which way

25   Thou mightst deserve, or they impose, this usage,

Coming from us.

KENT

My lord, when at their home

I did commend your highness's letters to them,

Ere I was risen from the place that showed

My duty kneeling, came there a reeking post,

30   Stewed in his haste, half breathless, panting forth

From Goneril his mistress salutations;

Delivered letters, spite of intermission,

Which presently they read; on whose contents

They summoned up their meiny, straight took horse,

35   Commanded me to follow and attend

The leisure of their answer, gave me cold looks;

And meeting here the other messenger,

Whose welcome, I perceived, had poisoned mine —

Being the very fellow that of late

40   Displayed so saucily against your highness —

Having more man than wit about me, drew.

He raised the house with loud and coward cries.

Your son and daughter found this trespass worth

The shame which here it suffers.

FOOL

45   Winter's not gone yet, if the wild-geese fly that way.

Fathers that wear rags

Do make their children blind,

But fathers that bear bags

Shall see their children kind.

50   Fortune, that arrant whore,

Ne'er turns the key to the poor.

Notes (left column):

20   *Jupiter:* the supreme Roman god

21   *Juno:* wife of Jupiter, and goddess of marriage and childbirth

durst: dare

23   *To ... outrage:* to perform ('do') so violently outrageous an act as the stocking of Kent deliberately and after mature consideration. Another explanation is: to offend so violently and outrageously against a man whose status as the King's messenger demanded respect

24–6   *Resolve ... us:* explain to me ('resolve me') quickly and reasonably how you could deserve this treatment ('usage'), or how they could give it out to you, my messenger

27   *commend:* deliver

28–9   *Ere ... kneeling:* before I had risen from the kneeling position that showed my respect for Regan and Cornwall

29–30   *came ... haste:* a messenger ('post') rushed in, soaked in the sweat his hurrying had caused

31   *salutations:* greetings

32   *spite of intermission:* in spite of the fact that he was interrupting my business, and delaying the answer I was about to receive

33   *presently:* immediately

34   *meiny:* retinue, household company, servants
      straight: immediately

39   *the very fellow:* the same fellow (Oswald)

40   *Displayed ... against:* acted with such insolence towards

41   *more ... drew:* more courage than common sense, I drew my sword

42   *raised the house:* aroused the household

43   *trespass:* offence

45   *Winter's ... way:* the wild geese that desert the country as they fly south with the approach of winter are images of Goneril and Regan in the process of forsaking Lear and revolting against him

46–51   *Fathers ... poor:* fathers who wear ragged clothing make their children indifferent to their miseries, whereas fathers who keep their money will experience kindness from their children. Fortune, that notorious whore, never admits the poor to her favours

But for all this thou shalt have as many dolours for thy daughters as thou canst tell in a year.

LEAR
O how this mother swells up toward my heart! *[panic attack]*
Hysterica passio, down, thou climbing sorrow! 55
Thy element's below. — Where is this daughter?

KENT
With the earl, sir, here within.

LEAR
Follow me not; stay here.

Exit.

GENTLEMAN
Made you no more offence but what you speak of?

KENT
None. How chance the King comes with so small a 60 number?

FOOL
And thou hadst been set i' the stocks for that question, thou'dst well deserved it.

KENT
Why, fool?

FOOL *duty, definiton of friendship*
We'll set thee to school to an ant, to teach thee there's 65 no labouring i' the winter. All that follow their noses are led by their eyes but blind men; and there's not a nose among twenty but can smell him that's stinking. Let go thy hold when a great wheel runs down a hill, lest it break thy neck with following. But the great one that goes 70 upward, let him draw thee after. When a wise man gives thee better counsel, give me mine again; I would have none but knaves follow it, since a fool gives it.

That sir which serves and seeks for gain
And follows but for form, 75
Will pack when it begins to rain,
And leave thee in the storm.
But I will tarry; the fool will stay,
And let the wise man fly:
The knave turns fool that runs away, 80
The fool no knave, perdie.

Margin glosses:

52–3 *But ... year:* because of all this, you will have as many sorrows on account of your daughters as you can count ('tell') in a year
52 *dolours:* griefs, sorrow; with a pun on 'dollars'
54–6 *O ... below:* Lear, his heart ready to break with grief and indignation, is now feeling the first symptoms of hysteria. He attributes these feelings to an illness known as *hysterica passio*, the more distressing symptoms of which are raised blood pressure, a racing heart and a sense of suffocation. Lear, recognising that his extreme distress ('climbing sorrow') originates in the pit of his stomach ('below'), asks it to return to its proper place ('element')
60 *How chance:* how does it happen that
62 *And thou hadst:* if you had
[sinical] stupidness – moral cleverness – evil
65–6 *We'll ... winter:* Kent can learn from the ant in Aesop's fable, which, unlike Lear, provided for the winter when labour was no longer possible. Lear has left himself without resources in the winter of his life; many of his followers have deserted him now that he is no longer able to provide for them
66–8 *All ... stinking:* those who can see straight know that Lear's fortunes have declined; even the blind can smell that his fortunes are decayed
68–71 *Let ... after:* when a great man's fortunes are fast declining, desert him; when a man is rising in the world, attach yourself to his cause. The Fool's cynical comments indicate the general desertion of Lear's followers in his time of adversity
71–3 *When ... gives it:* the Fool dismisses his own advice as foolish and suitable only for knaves, to be returned to the giver as soon as better advice becomes available
74–81 *That sir ... perdie:* the man who serves his master, not out of loyalty but for what he can gain from him, and whose service is merely a formal thing, will desert that master when times are hard. But I, the Fool, will remain loyal, and let the worldly servant flee. The 'prudent' servant who deserts his master is eventually shown up as a fool, since wisdom implies loyalty to one's master. A fool, who, like myself, remains loyal is, at any rate, no knave
81 *perdie:* in God's name

you'd have to be stupid to follow someone who has no power.

KENT

Where learned you this, fool?

FOOL

Not i' the stocks, fool.

Enter LEAR and GLOUCESTER.

Fool says its because he has no money.

LEAR *has been disrespected as a father + as a king.*

Deny to speak with me! They are sick! They are weary!

85 They have travelled all the night! Mere fetches,

The images of revolt and flying off.

Fetch me a better answer.

GLOUCESTER

                    My dear lord,

You know the fiery quality of the duke;

How unremovable and fixed he is

90 In his own course.

LEAR

Vengeance! Plague! Death! Confusion!

Fiery? What 'quality'? Why, Gloucester, Gloucester,

I'd speak with the Duke of Cornwall and his wife.

GLOUCESTER   *→ wrong language.*

Well, my good lord, I have informed them so.

LEAR *colapse in status.*

95 Informed them! Dost thou understand me, man?

GLOUCESTER   *1st time*
                   → has to find a reason/excuses
Ay, my good lord.   *for being disrespected.*

LEAR *mental health.*

The King would speak with Cornwall; the dear father

Would with his daughter speak, commands, tends, service.

Are they 'informed' of this? My breath and blood!

100 Fiery? The fiery duke? Tell the hot duke that Lear— *disjointed speech.*

No, but not yet. Maybe he is not well.   *'language changing'*

Infirmity doth still neglect all office

Whereto our health is bound. We are not ourselves

When nature, being oppressed, commands the mind

105 To suffer with the body. I'll forbear,

And am fall'n out with my more headier will,

To take the indisposed and sickly fit

For the sound man. — Death on my state! Wherefore

Should he sit here? This act persuades me

beginning to realise loss of status

not himself

Handwritten note (left margin): lear still thinks/believes he is the most important person in the country + in his daughter's life.

---

83 *Not ... fool:* this is the Fool's tribute to Kent's loyalty to Lear, which is as genuine as his own. He is suggesting: if you had been selfishly wise instead of foolishly loyal, you would not have ended up in the stocks

84 *Deny:* refuse

85 *fetches:* tricks, tactics

86 *images ... off:* signs or tokens of disobedience and desertion

88 *quality:* nature, character

89–90 *How ... course:* how determined he is in pursuit of any course of action he undertakes

92 *What 'quality'?* from Lear's point of view, questions of character are irrelevant when kings give commands

93 *I'd:* I wish to

98 *commands, tends, service:* orders Regan and Cornwall to show him respect, and awaits ('tends') their show of duty; 'tends' is a conciliatory modification of 'commands'

100 *hot:* hot-tempered

102–5 *Infirmity ... body:* when we are ill, we always ('still') neglect those duties that we are bound to fulfil when we are well. Bodily illness so preoccupies the mind that we are unable to behave normally

105 *forbear:* restrain myself, have patience

106–8 *And ... man:* I have abandoned my earlier, more impetuous inclination to blame Cornwall for conduct that, I now feel, is out of character and promoted by a bout of illness

108 *Death on my state!* may my royal power perish – Lear's exclamation is ironic, since his royal power has already perished. His mercurial temperament is indicated by another sudden change of mood

108–9 *Wherefore ... here?* Why should he [Caius/Kent] sit here in the stocks?

That this remotion of the duke and her   *[angry / calm / angry]*   110

Is practice only. Give me my servant forth.

Go tell the duke and 's wife I'ld speak with them

Now, presently! Bid them come forth and hear me,

Or at their chamber door I'll beat the drum

Till it cry sleep to death.   115

GLOUCESTER

I would have all well betwixt you.

Exit.

LEAR   *maddness.*

O me, my heart, my rising heart! But down!

FOOL

Cry to it, nuncle, as the cockney did to the eels, when
she put 'em i' the paste alive; she knapped 'em o' the
coxcombs with a stick, and cried 'Down, wantons, down!'   120
'Twas her brother that, in pure kindness to his horse,
buttered his hay.

Enter GLOUCESTER, CORNWALL, REGAN, and SERVANTS.

LEAR

Good morrow to you both.

CORNWALL

               Hail to your grace!

KENT is set at liberty.

REGAN

I am glad to see your highness.

LEAR   *mother cursing.*

Regan, I think you are. I know what reason   125

I have to think so. If thou shouldst not be glad,

I would divorce me from thy mother's tomb,

Sepulchring an adult'ress. [*to KENT*] O, are you free?

Some other time for that.

Exit KENT.

               Beloved Regan,   *change in tone*

Thy sister's naught. O Regan, she hath tied   130

Sharp-toothed unkindness, like a vulture here

I can scarce speak to thee — thou'lt not believe

With how depraved a quality — O Regan!
               begging.

---

110 *remotion:* two distinct meanings have been proposed: (a) moving from one house (their own) to another's (Gloucester's), (b) holding themselves at a distance, keeping aloof

111 *practice:* trickery, fraud
    Give . . . forth: release my servant from the stocks

112 *and 's:* and his
    I'ld: I would, I wish to

113 *presently:* immediately

114–15 *Or . . . death:* or I shall beat the drum at their bedroom door until the noise kills off their sleep

116 *I . . . you:* I would like to see peace and harmony prevail between you

117 *my rising heart:* see note on lines 54–6

118–22 *cockney . . . hay:* a Cockney woman who, out of tenderness of heart, put live eels into her pastry ('paste') because she had not the heart to kill them. All she could do when they emerged wriggling was to rap ('knapped') them on the head ('coxcombs') and tell them to stay down. Her brother, equally soft-hearted, buttered his horse's hay. The suggestion is that Lear has been foolishly kind towards his daughters and it is too late to start playing the strict father now

120 *wantons:* carefree, playful things

123 *Good morrow:* good morning – the greeting is sarcastic and indicates that Lear has been waiting too long

125–6 *I know . . . so:* I have every reason to think that you should be glad to see me

127–8 *I . . . adult'ress:* if Regan refused to show gladness at the sight of her father, this would suggest to him that she was not really his daughter and that his late wife was an adulteress. Accordingly, he would divorce her posthumously, and refuse to be buried in the same tomb

130 *naught:* wicked

130–1 *she . . . here:* the cruelty he has experienced from Goneril reminds Lear of the fate of Prometheus, whose liver was daily torn by a vulture sent by Zeus. The actor playing Lear may point to his heart as he says the word 'here'

132–3 *thou'lt . . . quality:* you would scarcely credit the vileness of her manner towards me. The distraught Lear is unable to complete his statement

134–6 *I have ... duty:* I trust that you are less aware of her good qualities than she is of her duty. Regan is telling Lear that he is in the wrong

REGAN *defending Goneril.*

I pray you, sir, take patience. I have hope.

135 You less know how to value her desert

Than she to scant her duty.

LEAR

Say, how is that?

REGAN

I cannot think my sister in the least

Would fail her obligation. If, sir, perchance

She have restrained the riots of your followers

140–1 *'Tis ... blame:* her treatment of your riotous followers is so soundly based and so properly motivated as to make her wholly blameless

140 'Tis on such ground, and to such wholesome end,

As clears her from all blame.

LEAR

My curses on her!

REGAN

O sir, you are old. *your quite old, let people take care/control you.*

143–4 *Nature ... confine:* your natural life is nearing its end

Nature in you stands on the very verge *(who know better)*

Of her confine. You should be ruled and led

145–6 *some ... yourself:* someone discreet who understands your situation and your physical and mental condition better than you yourself do

145 By some discretion that discerns your state

Better than you yourself. Therefore, I pray you,

That to our sister you do make return.

Say you have wronged her. *apoligise to her.*

LEAR

Ask her forgiveness?

149 *Do ... house:* observe how the following prayer, which I make at your suggestion, is appropriate to my position as father of a royal household

Do you but mark how this becomes the house:

150 *Dear ... old:* dear Goneril, I ask your forgiveness for the sin of being an old man

150 [*he kneels*] 'Dear daughter, I confess that I am old;

151 *Age is unnecessary:* this may mean either: an old man like me has few needs; or: since I am old, and therefore useless, my continued existence cannot be defended on rational grounds

Age is unnecessary: on my knees I beg

That you'll vouchsafe me raiment, bed and food.'
    sarcastic [rear of truth]

152 *vouchsafe ... food:* condescend to grant me clothing, lodging and food

REGAN

Good sir, no more! These are unsightly tricks.

Return you to my sister.

LEAR [*rising*]

Never, Regan:

155 *abated:* deprived

155 She hath abated me of half my train;

156–7 *struck ... heart:* launched a venomous verbal attack on me that pierced my heart with sorrow

Looked black upon me; struck me with her tongue,

Most serpent-like, upon the very heart.

159 *ingrateful top:* ungrateful head

159–60 *Strike ... lameness!* may infectious vapours ('airs') blast her unborn child so that it may be born deformed

All the stored vengeances of heaven fall *cursing Goneril*

160 *taking:* bewitching, infecting with disease

On her ingrateful top! Strike her young bones,

You taking airs, with lameness!

CORNWALL

Fie, sir, fie!   160

LEAR

You nimble lightnings, dart your blinding flames

Into her scornful eyes! Infect her beauty,

You fen-sucked fogs, drawn by the pow'rful sun,

To fall and blister. *alliteration.*

REGAN

O the blest gods!

So will you wish on me when the rash mood is on.   165

LEAR

No, Regan, thou shalt never have my curse.   • *pleading tone* ✓

Thy tender-hefted nature shall not give

Thee o'er to harshness. Her eyes are fierce, but thine

Do comfort and not burn. 'Tis not in thee

To grudge my pleasures, to cut off my train,   170

To bandy hasty words, to scant my sizes,

And, in conclusion, to oppose the bolt

Against my coming in. Thou better know'st

The offices of nature, bond of childhood,

Effects of courtesy, dues of gratitude.   175

Thy half o' the kingdom hast thou not forgot,

Wherein I thee endowed. *reminds Regan of bond.*

• *flattering Regan*

REGAN

Good sir, to the purpose.

LEAR

Who put my man i' the stocks?

Tucket within.

CORNWALL

What trumpet's that?

REGAN

I know't, my sister's. This approves her letter,

That she would soon be here.

Enter OSWALD.

Is your lady come?   180

LEAR

This is a slave, whose easy-borrowed pride

Dwells in the sickly grace of her he follows.

[left margin, vertical] realises bond (cordelia)

160   *Fie:* an expression of disgust or disapproval

161   *nimble:* swift

162–4   *Infect . . . blister:* may her beauty be marred by those poisonous vapours that rise from the marshes (fens) in the sunshine, and blister the faces of those on whom they fall

167   *tender-hefted:* Lear imagines that Regan is softer than Goneril and that her body heaves with gentler feelings

170   *grudge:* resent, complain about

171   *bandy:* hit to and fro, like a tennis ball
       scant my sizes: reduce my allowances

172–3   *And . . . coming in:* and, as a final insult, shut the door in my face. There is irony in the fact that this is just what Regan is about to do to Lear

173–5   *Thou . . . gratitude:* you know better than Goneril the duties that nature imposes on children, duties such as kindness towards their parents, displays ('effects') of courteous behaviour and gratefulness for benefits conferred

177   *thee endowed:* provided for you

179   *approves:* confirms the contents of

181–2   *whose . . . follows:* Oswald's pride is a borrowed thing that originates in the corrupt ('sickly') favour extended to him by his mistress, Goneril

183 *varlet:* base fellow

185 *on't:* of it

186 *sway:* rule, government, authority

187 *Allow:* approve, sanction, be well pleased with

188 *Make . . . cause!* make my cause yours

189 *this beard:* Lear considers his beard to be a sign of age and authority and entitled to respect

192–3 *All's . . . so:* the fact that a person lacking in judgement, and who is also senile (in his 'dotage'), finds offence in a particular action (Regan's taking Goneril by the hand), does not necessarily make this action offensive

193–4 *O . . . hold?* Lear marvels that his chest ('sides') does not burst as a result of the violent agitation of his heart

195–6 *his . . . advancement:* degrading as the stocks may be as a form of punishment, they are better than what Kent deserved for his misbehaviour ('disorders')

199 *sojourn:* lodge, stay

201 *from home:* far from home

202 *entertainment:* proper reception and maintenance

204–7 *No . . . pinch:* no, I would prefer to renounce ('abjure') all dwellings, to have the wolf and the owl as my companions, to wager ('wage') my own painful poverty against the cruelty of the hostile elements

205–6 The order of lines 205 and 206 has been reversed here to ensure clarity

208 *hot-blooded France:* ardent King of France

210 *knee . . . beg:* kneel in submission before him, and, like the body servant to some nobleman, plead for an allowance

---

[*to OSWALD*] Out, varlet, from my sight!

CORNWALL
What means your grace?

LEAR
Who stocked my servant? Regan, I have good hope
Thou didst not know on't.

Enter GONERIL.

185 Who comes here? O heavens,
If you do love old men, if your sweet sway
Allow obedience, if yourselves are old,
Make it your cause! Send down and take my part!
[*to GONERIL*] Art not ashamed to look upon this beard?
190 O Regan, wilt thou take her by the hand?

GONERIL
Why not by the hand, sir? How have I offended?
All's not offence that indiscretion finds
And dotage terms so. *cursing.*

LEAR
O sides, you are too tough!
Will you yet hold? How came my man i' the stocks?
asked this question a lot before, never answered

CORNWALL
195 I set him there, sir; but his own disorders
Deserved much less advancement.

LEAR
You? Did you?

REGAN
I pray you, father, being weak, seem so.
If, till the expiration of your month,
You will return and sojourn with my sister,
200 Dismissing half your train, come then to me.
I am now from home, and out of that provision
Which shall be needful for your entertainment.

LEAR
Return to her, and fifty men dismissed?
No, rather I abjure all roofs, and choose
205 To be a comrade with the wolf and owl,
To wage against the enmity of the air
Necessity's sharp pinch. Return with her!
Why, the hot-blooded France, that dowerless took
Our youngest born, I could as well be brought
210 To knee his throne, and, squire-like, pension beg

I pray you, father, being weak, seem so.

REGAN, Act 2, Scene 4, 197

To keep base life afoot. Return with her!

Persuade me rather to be slave and sumpter

To this detested groom. [*pointing at OSWALD*]

GONERIL

               At your choice, sir. *ok if you want to*

LEAR

I prithee, daughter, do not make me mad, *ref to maddness*

I will not trouble thee, my child. Farewell.   215

We'll no more meet, no more see one another.

But yet thou art my flesh, my blood, my daughter —

Or rather a disease that's in my flesh

Which I must needs call mine. Thou art a boil,

A plague-sore, or embossed carbuncle,   220

In my corrupted blood. But I'll not chide thee.

Let shame come when it will, I do not call it.

I do not bid the thunder-bearer shoot,

Nor tell tales of thee to high-judging Jove.

Mend when thou canst, be better at thy leisure;   225

I can be patient, I can stay with Regan,

I and my hundred knights.

211 *To ... afoot:* to sustain me in a miserable condition

212 *sumpter:* drudge; literally, a horse that carries necessities for a journey

213 *detested groom:* detestable servant

220 *embossed carbuncle:* swollen tumour

221 *my corrupted blood:* the cause of the corruption is Goneril, the 'disease' in his flesh
chide: scold, rebuke

222 *Let ... call it:* I know that disgrace will eventually come upon you, without any need on my part to summon ('call') it

223–4 *I ... Jove:* I am not asking Jupiter to launch his thunderbolts in your direction, nor am I reporting your misbehaviour to the supreme god who judges human affairs from the heavenly heights

225 *Mend ... canst:* reform yourself whenever you are able

228 *I . . . you:* I did not expect you

230–1 *For . . . so:* because those who consider your passionate, irrational outbursts with a rational eye must come to the conclusion that you are senile, I do not need to say any more

232 *well spoken:* a proper way for a daughter to speak to her father

233 *avouch:* confirm, guarantee

234 *Is it not well?* Is that not adequate?

235 *sith:* since
charge: expense

238 *Hold amity:* maintain friendship

241 *chanced . . . ye:* happened to neglect you

242 *control them:* call them to account

245 *place or notice:* residence or recognition

247 *Made . . . depositaries:* appointed you stewardesses and trustees of the kingdom in my place
248 *reservation:* this is a reference to Lear's earlier 'reservation of an hundred knights' (Act 1, Scene 1, line 129) – a condition he attached to the granting of the kingdom to Goneril and Regan

251 *No . . . me:* you cannot have more than twenty-five knights if you want to stay with me
252–4 *Those . . . praise:* some people are more wicked than others and that can make the less wicked appear relatively attractive ('well favoured'). It now seems that Goneril is not as bad as Regan – an offer of fifty knights being better than one of twenty-five – and that is at least something in her favour

REGAN
                                    Not altogether so.
I looked not for you yet, nor am provided
For your fit welcome. Give ear, sir, to my sister,
230 For those that mingle reason with your passion
Must be content to think you old, and so —
But she knows what she does.

LEAR
                                    Is this well spoken?

REGAN
I dare avouch it, sir. What, fifty followers?
Is it not well? What should you need of more?
235 Yea, or so many, sith that both charge and danger
Speak 'gainst so great a number? How in one house
Should many people under two commands
Hold amity? 'Tis hard, almost impossible.

GONERIL
Why might not you, my lord, receive attendance
240 From those that she calls servants, or from mine?

REGAN
Why not, my lord? If then they chanced to slack ye,
We could control them. If you will come to me,
For now I spy a danger, I entreat you
To bring but five-and-twenty. To no more
245 Will I give place or notice.

LEAR
I gave you all—

REGAN
                    And in good time you gave it. *and in good time (old)*

LEAR
Made you my guardians, my depositaries,
But kept a reservation to be followed
With such a number. What, must I come to you
250 With five-and-twenty? Regan, said you so?

REGAN
And speak't again, my lord. No more with me.

LEAR *he hasn't learnt that love is not materialistic*
Those wicked creatures yet do look well favoured
When others are more wicked. Not being the worst
Stands in some rank of praise. [*to GONERIL*] I'll go with thee.

Thy fifty yet doth double five-and-twenty,   255

And thou art twice her love.

GONERIL

                       Hear me, my lord.

What need you five-and-twenty, ten, or five,

To follow in a house where twice so many

Have a command to tend you?

REGAN

                    What need one?

the need is not there

LEAR

O, reason not the need! Our basest beggars   260

Are in the poorest thing superfluous.

Allow not nature more than nature needs,

Man's life is as cheap as beast's. Thou art a lady;

If only to go warm were gorgeous,

Why, nature needs not what thou gorgeous wear'st,   265

Which scarcely keeps thee warm. But, for true need —

You heavens, give me that patience, patience I need!

You see me here, you gods, a poor old man,

As full of grief as age; wretched in both!

If it be you that stir these daughters' hearts   270

Against their father, fool me not so much

To bear it tamely. Touch me with noble anger,

And let not women's weapons, water-drops,

Stain my man's cheeks! No, you unnatural hags,

I will have such revenges on you both   275

That all the world shall — I will do such things —

What they are yet I know not, but they shall be

The terrors of the earth! You think I'll weep —

No, I'll not weep. I have full cause of weeping,

Storm and tempest.

But this heart shall break into a hundred thousand flaws   280

Or ere I'll weep. — O fool, I shall go mad!

Exeunt LEAR, GLOUCESTER, GENTLEMAN and FOOL.

CORNWALL

Let us withdraw, 'twill be a storm.

REGAN

This house is little; the old man and 's people

Cannot be well bestowed.

Marginal handwritten notes:
if he only has what he needs, he is no better! nothing more than an animal.

Printed marginal glosses:

255–6 *Thy ... love:* since Goneril can offer fifty knights to Regan's twenty-five, she must love him twice as much. This is a comic illustration of Lear's tendency to calculate degrees of affection mathematically

257 *need you:* need have you of

258 *follow:* be your servants or attendants

260–3 *O ... beast's:* do not go on arguing in coldly rational terms about my needs; even the poorest beggars possess a few miserable items over and above what is absolutely essential for their survival. If we do not allow human beings to possess more than they need merely to sustain life, then we are condemning them to live at the level of animals

263–6 *Thou ... warm:* Lear is looking at the splendid, if rather flimsy, garments worn by Regan as he says: if your only purpose in wearing these gorgeous clothes is your need for warmth, then your body does not need them, since they do very little to keep you warm anyway. Goneril and Regan have been trying to define his needs in terms of standards they do not accept for themselves. Mere need, as Lear points out, cannot be the criterion for possessing things; by wearing fine, largely useless clothes, his daughters accept that human need goes beyond what is necessary for survival

266–7 *for ... I need!* as far as true need is concerned — Lear is about to explain what true need is (respect and affection from his daughters), but he is overcome by mounting sorrow and anger and can think only of his immediate need, which is patience

270–4 *If ... cheeks!* if you [the gods] have inspired the unnatural conduct of these daughters towards me, do not cause me to be such a fool as to endure it passively. Let manly anger, rather than womanly tears, be my response

280–1 *this ... weep:* instead of melting in grief and tears, Lear's heart, stimulated by 'noble anger', will break into small fragments. 'Flaws' are also outbursts of feeling or passion

281 *O ... mad!* Lear instinctively realises that his overwrought condition will lead to madness

283 *This house:* Gloucester's castle

284 *bestowed:* accommodated

285 *'Tis . . . rest:* it is his own fault that he has nowhere to stay; he is the author of his own disturbed condition

287–8 *For . . . follower:* I am readily prepared to receive him for his own sake, but I shall not consider taking any of his followers. It is noteworthy that Regan offers this concession only after Lear has gone, when she will not have to go through with it

288 *So . . . purposed:* I am of the same mind

290 *forth:* out

292 *will . . . whither:* I do not know where he intends to go

293 *'Tis . . . himself:* it is best to let him go; he will not accept direction from anybody else

294 *entreat . . . stay:* under no circumstances are you to ask him to stay

295 *Alack:* alas (a common expression of regret, grief, sorrow)
296 *sorely ruffle:* blow with fierce intensity

297–9 *to wilful . . . schoolmasters:* obstinate people are chastised by the consequences of their own actions, just as obstinate children are chastised by their teachers

300 *a desperate train:* a band of reckless followers

301–2 *And . . . fear:* Regan is saying that as Lear is too willing to listen to those who would mislead him, it is prudent to fear what his knights may provoke him into doing and to take precautions accordingly by locking him out

GONERIL

285 'Tis his own blame; hath put himself from rest,

And must needs taste his folly.

REGAN

For his particular, I'll receive him gladly,

But not one follower.

GONERIL

              So am I purposed.

Where is my lord of Gloucester?

CORNWALL

Followed the old man forth.

Enter GLOUCESTER.

290   He is returned.

GLOUCESTER

The King is in high rage.

CORNWALL

              Whither is he going?

GLOUCESTER

He calls to horse, but will I know not whither.

CORNWALL

'Tis best to give him way; he leads himself.

GONERIL

My lord, entreat him by no means to stay.

GLOUCESTER

295 Alack, the night comes on, and the high winds

Do sorely ruffle. For many miles about

There's scarce a bush.

REGAN

            O sir, to wilful men

The injuries that they themselves procure

Must be their schoolmasters. Shut up your doors.

300 He is attended with a desperate train,

And what they may incense him to, being apt

To have his ear abused, wisdom bids fear.

CORNWALL

Shut up your doors, my lord; 'tis a wild night.

My Regan counsels well. Come out o' the storm.

Exeunt.

Key points

This is one of the great scenes of the play and represents a significant turning point for Lear as his relationship with Goneril and Regan totally breaks down. Remarkable strains are placed on Lear's self-control and on the balance of his mind throughout this scene.

- What Goneril and Regan have been planning since the end of Act 1, Scene 1 comes to pass, as they cynically toss Lear back and forth between them, forcing him to realise how utterly powerless he is, depriving him of his dignity and his sustenance.

- The attitude of Goneril and Regan is simple and crude. They are determined not to treat Lear as a retired monarch, unloved but still feared. Instead, they force him to see himself as a silly, raving old fool, an inconvenient domestic nuisance costing too much to maintain, a useless burden whom neither they nor anybody else would want to bear.

- Lear suffers two major shocks in the scene. The first comes when he discovers Kent in the stocks. This insult to his status and dignity causes him to suffer the first symptoms of hysteria: a racing heart and a feeling of suffocation. The true explanation of Kent's imprisonment in the stocks is a reality too cruel to bear, and threatens Lear's mental composure.

- The second shock is his rejection by Regan. In the aftermath of this his reason is extinguished and a terrible anger takes over. He behaves like a helpless, bullied child, breathlessly threatening the bullies with frightful but unspecified punishments (lines 275–8). These threats sound all the more pathetic because Lear is totally powerless to carry them out.

- The debate about the size of Lear's entourage is a grotesque parody of what happened in Act 1, Scene 1, when Lear encouraged his three daughters to quantify their love for him: the more words, the more love. He sees the cruel joke of which he is now the victim. Love is to be weighed and measured. The sister who is willing to allow Lear to keep the greater number of knights must love him more than the one who allows him fewer knights (lines 255–6).

- The first rumblings of the storm are significant in a symbolic sense: the tempest in Lear's mind is reflected in the tempest in the heavens. Lear knows from the thunder that what he has been fearing is about to come to pass ('O fool, I shall go mad'; line 281). His exposure to the storm will complete the torture that the cruelty and ingratitude of his daughters has inflicted on him. Further evidence of Lear's mental confusion can be found in his fragmented speech patterns (lines 275–81).

- Regan decides that Gloucester's home is too small to accommodate 'the old man and 's people' (line 283). This detached comment tells us a lot about the kind of woman she is. The father she flattered in Act 1, Scene 1 is now dismissed as 'the old man'. Furthermore, the house she has shut against Lear's people is not her own, it is Gloucester's, whose feelings on the subject she does not consider.

- Notice that the inhuman behaviour of Goneril, Regan and Cornwall is having an effect on Gloucester, who follows Lear into the storm but returns to impress on them the perils Lear is now exposed to (lines 295–7). Unmoved, they order him to leave Lear to the mercy of the storm.

- Goneril callously blames Lear for causing his own disturbed condition, and claims that he must be punished for this (lines 285–6). Regan also dissociates herself from the horrors facing her father, saying that he needs to learn the error of his ways (lines 297–9).

- There is no certainty that Regan is telling the truth when she claims that Lear 'is attended with a desperate train' (line 300). During the scenes that follow, there is no sign of this 'desperate train', which either deserted Lear immediately or was merely a fabrication designed to justify Regan's exclusion of Lear.

Useful quotes

Hysterica passio, *down, thou climbing sorrow!*

(Lear, line 55)

Let go
thy hold when a great wheel runs down a hill, lest it break
thy neck with following. But the great one that goes
upward, let him draw thee after.

(Fool, lines 68–71)

Nature in you stands on the very verge
Of her confine. You should be ruled and led
By some discretion that discerns your state
Better than you yourself.

(Regan, lines 143–6)

Return to her, and fifty men dismissed?
No, rather I abjure all roofs, and choose
To be a comrade with the wolf and owl

(Lear, lines 203–5)

Thy fifty yet doth double five-and-twenty,
And thou art twice her love

(Lear, lines 255–6)

Allow not nature more than nature needs,
Man's life is as cheap as beast's.

(Lear, lines 262–3)

? Questions

1 Why does Lear not want to accept Kent's statement that Cornwall and Regan have put him in the stocks?

2 What do we learn from this scene about the character and outlook of the Fool?

3 What is the Fool trying to teach Lear?

4 Summarise Regan's case against Lear.

5 Lear says sarcastically, 'age is unnecessary' (line 151). Consider this as a statement of a major theme of the play so far.

6 Lear calls on the heavens to make his cause their cause, to 'send down and take my part' (line 188). How is his prayer answered?

7 Lear tells Goneril that he will go with her, soon after he has called down curses on her head. How can this change of attitude be accounted for?

8 Comment on the symbolism of the storm that begins (around line 280) in this scene.

9 Regan thinks that Lear is 'apt to have his ear abused' (lines 301–2). Comment on the irony of this remark, particularly given what happened in Act 1, Scene 1.

10 Goneril says of her father, ''Tis his own blame; hath put himself from rest, and must needs taste his folly' (lines 285–6). Is her comment in any way justified? Explain your answer.

Scene 1

- Edmund warns Edgar to flee as his life is in danger, stages a mock-duel with him, and wounds himself in a successful attempt to convince Gloucester that Edgar had tried and failed to persuade him to murder their father, attacked him, and then fled.
- Gloucester persuades his overlord, Cornwall, to allow him to proclaim Edgar a criminal.
- Regan has already been warned by Goneril about Lear's alleged misbehaviour, and has travelled to Gloucester's castle so as not to be at home when Lear calls.
- Cornwall takes Edmund on as part of his following.

Scene 2

- Kent expresses hatred for Oswald in his role as Goneril's agent, and beats him.
- Kent insults Cornwall, who has him put in the stocks as if he were a common criminal.
- Gloucester pleads in vain with Cornwall not to treat Kent in this way, as Lear, his master, will be displeased.

Scene 3

- Edgar, now a fugitive, will preserve his life by disguising himself as a Bedlam beggar, a former inmate of a mental hospital, with a licence to roam the countryside, seeking charity.

Scene 4

- Lear is shocked to find Kent in the stocks and seeks an explanation.
- When Regan eventually appears, she gives Lear no comfort, and coldly rejects his criticisms of Goneril, suggesting that he return to her and apologise for having wronged her.
- Goneril arrives. She and Regan further humiliate Lear by telling him he does not need any followers.
- Lear threatens vengeance on Goneril and Regan, and then goes out into the raging storm. Cornwall and Regan shut the doors on him.

ACT 2 ✝ Speaking and listening

1 In groups of four, assign the parts of Regan, Goneril, Kent and the Fool. Each person should select and recite a short speech (from either Act 1 or Act 2) that indicates their character's true nature. As a group, identify and discuss the characteristics revealed.

2 Assign the part of Edmund. He will then be interviewed by members of the entire class chosen at random. He may be questioned closely on, for example, how he feels about his successful deception of both Gloucester and Edgar, his opinion of Cornwall and Regan, his ambitions for the future and whether his conscience ever troubles him.

ACT 3 ✝ Scene 1

Plot summary

A Gentleman updates Kent on Lear's suffering. Kent informs him that the King of France is getting reports of events in England through his spies, and that divisions are emerging between Albany and Cornwall. Cordelia is on her way to help her father, and Kent sends the Gentleman to Dover with a message about the persecution Lear is undergoing. The two men part to search for Lear.

*I am a gentleman of blood
and breeding*

KENT, Act 3, Scene 1, 40

A heath.

A storm. Enter KENT and a GENTLEMAN, severally.

KENT
Who's there, besides foul weather?

GENTLEMAN
One minded like the weather, most unquietly.

KENT
I know you. Where's the King?

GENTLEMAN
Contending with the fretful elements:
Bids the winds blow the earth into the sea,   5
Or swell the curled water 'bove the main,
That things might change or cease. Tears his white hair,
Which the impetuous blasts with eyeless rage
Catch in their fury and make nothing of;
Strives in his little world of man to out-storm   10
The to-and-fro-conflicting wind and rain.
This night, wherein the cub-drawn bear would couch,
The lion and the belly-pinched wolf
Keep their fur dry, unbonneted he runs,
And bids what will take all.

KENT
               But who is with him?   15

GENTLEMAN
None but the fool, who labours to out-jest
His heart-strook injuries.

KENT
            Sir, I do know you,
And dare, upon the warrant of my note,
Commend a dear thing to you. There is division,
Although as yet the face of it is covered   20
With mutual cunning, 'twixt Albany and Cornwall,
Who have — as who have not, that their great stars
Throned and set high? — servants, who seem no less,
Which are to France the spies and speculations
Intelligent of our state. What hath been seen,   25
Either in snuffs and packings of the dukes,

---

2   *One ... unquietly:* someone whose mind is as disturbed as the weather (see also lines 10–11)

4   *Contending ... elements:* Lear is struggling to survive the onslaught of the violent storm; he is also competing (in his own violent behaviour) with the anger of the weather ('elements', i.e. wind, rain, thunder, lightning)

5–7   *Bids ... cease:* commands the world to return to the state in which it was before land became separated from water, so that the natural order may either be transformed or cease to exist

6   *curled water:* the wind makes the waves of the ocean look like curls of human hair
     main: mainland

8   *impetuous blasts:* forceful, violent winds
     eyeless rage: blind fury, indiscriminate violence

9   *make nothing of:* the reference is to Lear's hair, for which the winds show no respect

10–11   *Strives ... rain:* Lear, in his tempestuous behaviour, struggles to outdo the angry, conflicting movements of the elements. Shakespeare is here expressing a commonplace of his time: the 'little world of man' (or microcosm) is a miniature version or model of the universe (or macrocosm), whose behaviour it mirrors

12   *cub-drawn ... couch:* the ravenous bear is forced (by the weather) to keep to her lair; the bear is ravenous because her cubs have drained her milk

13   *belly-pinched:* starved

14   *unbonneted:* hatless. In Shakespeare's time, to go outdoors without a hat was frowned upon

15   *And ... all:* Lear is seen as a reckless gambler, staking all he has left on one final throw. 'Take all' is the cry of a gambler; it is also a cry of despair

16–17   *who ... injuries:* who works hard to drive out Lear's sorrows by the force of his witticisms

18–19   *And ... you:* my observation ('note') of you gives me the confidence to entrust an important ('dear') piece of business to you

20–1   *the face ... cunning:* both Albany and Cornwall are taking shrewd steps to prevent their differences from becoming public knowledge

22–3   *that ... high:* those who were born under planetary influences that assured their rise to power

24   *speculations:* speculators, observers

25   *Intelligent:* giving information

25–9   *What ... furnishings:* according to Kent, the French invasion may be due to: (a) what has been seen and reported to the King of France about the quarrels ('snuffs') and plots against each other ('packings') of Albany and Cornwall; (b) the rigid and harsh control the dukes have exercised over Lear; or (c) some deeper, more obscure, causes that make reasons (a) and (b) mere pretexts or excuses

27 *rein:* the metaphor is from riding; Lear is pictured as a horse on a tight rein. There is also a pun on 'reign'

29 *furnishings:* trimmings, excuses, pretexts

30–2 *from France ... feet:* the French army ('power'), taking advantage of their knowledge of ('wise in') our neglect of Britain's security, have secretly set foot

31 *scattered:* disunited, unsettled

33 *at point:* ready

34 *show ... banner:* proceed openly against us
to you: as for my business with you

35–6 *If ... Dover:* if you have sufficient faith in me to follow my instructions and hurry to Dover

37 *making just report:* for giving an accurate account

39 *plain:* complain of

41 *assurance:* reliable information

42 *office:* duty, assignment (to report to Dover)

44–5 *For ... out-wall:* if you wish to satisfy yourself that I am a person of greater importance than my outward appearance suggests (Kent is disguised as the servant Caius)

48 *fellow:* companion

49 *Fie:* an expression of disgust or reproach

52 *to ... yet:* of greater importance than any I have spoken so far

53–4 *in which ... this:* in which task (that of finding Lear) you go that way and I'll go this

54 *lights on him:* comes upon him

55 *Holla:* halloo, call out to

Exeunt severally: they go their separate ways (leave the stage in different directions)

Or the hard rein which both of them have borne
Against the old kind King, or something deeper,
Whereof perchance these are but furnishings—
30 But true it is, from France there comes a power
Into this scattered kingdom, who already,
Wise in our negligence, have secret feet
In some of our best ports, and are at point
To show their open banner. Now to you:
35 If on my credit you dare build so far
To make your speed to Dover, you shall find
Some that will thank you, making just report
Of how unnatural and bemadding sorrow
The King hath cause to plain.
40 I am a gentleman of blood and breeding,
And from some knowledge and assurance offer
This office to you.

GENTLEMAN
I will talk further with you.

KENT
                              No, do not,
For confirmation that I am much more
45 Than my out-wall, open this purse, and take
What it contains. If you shall see Cordelia —
As fear not but you shall — show her this ring,
And she will tell you who your fellow is
That yet you do not know. — Fie on this storm!
50 I will go seek the King.

GENTLEMAN
Give me your hand. Have you no more to say?

KENT
Few words, but, to effect, more than all yet:
That, when we have found the King — in which your pain
That way, I'll this — he that first lights on him
55 Holla the other.

Exeunt severally.

Key points

The hopeful notes in this scene are fragile tokens of a possible restoration of order, sounded as they are against the backdrop of a raging storm.

- Up to this point, Lear's enemies have had the initiative and his friends have been passive. In this scene there are the first signs of a counter-movement.

- The backdrop to this scene is a raging storm, from which the strongest and fiercest of animals (bears, lions and wolves) have been forced to seek shelter; yet Lear confronts the elements, trying to outdo them in fury.

- Instead of showing Lear on the stage in angry contention with the storm, Shakespeare relies on descriptive language to create the effects of a storm on man and beast. He uses the Gentleman as his vehicle for doing so. Shakespeare's stage lacked the realistic sound and lighting effects available to modern theatres, and so his words had to suggest what could not otherwise be convincingly presented.

- Kent changes the emphasis from description to revelation and plotting. His first revelation is of differences between Albany and Cornwall; the second is that French spies are active, and French forces are already secretly present, in Britain.

- Kent's description of Britain as 'this scattered kingdom' (line 31) embraces a wide range of meaning. He has three kingdoms in mind. The first is Britain, which is no longer united under a single ruler. The second is the natural world, which is disrupted by a terrible storm. The third is Lear's inner world, which is in chaos as he begins to lose his mind.

Useful quotes

> *Bids the winds blow the earth into the sea,*
> *Or swell the curled water 'bove the main,*
> *That things might change or cease.*
>
> (Gentleman, lines 5–7)

> *Strives in his little world of man to out-storm*
> *The to-and-fro-conflicting wind and rain.*
>
> (Gentleman, lines 10–11)

> *I am a gentleman of blood and breeding*
>
> (Kent, line 40)

? Questions

1 Is there any indication that the Gentleman mistrusts Kent? Give reasons for your answer.

2 Kent speaks of a division between Cornwall and Albany. Is there anything in the play so far to alert us to this possibility? Suggest reasons why Cornwall and Albany might not be seeing eye to eye.

3 On the evidence provided by the Gentleman in this scene, describe Lear's state of mind. For example, can Lear, at this point, accept the reality of what he has been exposed to? Is he now totally out of control? Give reasons for your answers.

4 How does Shakespeare inform the audience about the severity of the storm? Give examples to support your answer.

ACT 3 ✝ Scene 2

Plot summary

The storm is exceptional in its severity. Lear is overpowered by his sense of human ingratitude and wants to see an end to humanity. He identifies the punishing fury of the storm with the cruelty of his two daughters, believing that they and nature are conspiring to destroy him. The elements are slaves to his daughters, joining with them against a pitiful old victim. The elements also inspire in Lear a vision of a corrupt world of secret criminals who deserve such punishments as those the storm is capable of unleashing on them. The Fool wants Lear to ask his daughters for refuge. Kent also encourages Lear to find shelter. These pleas distract Lear from his self-pity and make him consider others. Eventually, he agrees to go to a hovel.

Things that love night
Love not such nights as these.

KENT, Act 3, Scene 2, 41–2

weather – human behaviour
↑
connected

Another part of the heath.

language
* no special effects

Storm still. Enter LEAR and FOOL.

imagery → thunder lightening.

LEAR [*Destroy the world storm*]

link → storm – mind

Blow, winds, and crack your cheeks! Rage! Blow!

You cataracts and hurricanoes, spout

Till you have drenched our steeples, drowned the cocks!

You sulph'rous and thought-executing fires,

Vaunt-couriers to oak-cleaving thunderbolts,   5

Singe my white head! And thou, all-shaking thunder,

Strike flat the thick rotundity o' the world!

feels hard done by

Crack nature's moulds, all germens spill at once

That make (ingrateful) man!

FOOL

O nuncle, court holy-water in a dry house is better than   10
rain-water out o' door. Good nuncle, in and ask thy
daughters' blessing. Here's a night pities neither wise
men nor fools.

LEAR

Rumble thy bellyful! Spit, fire! Spout, rain!

Nor rain, wind, thunder, fire, are my daughters.   15

I tax not you, you elements, with unkindness;

I never gave you kingdom, called you children;

You owe me no subscription; then let fall

Your horrible pleasure. Here I stand, your slave,   *realisation of his new*

A poor, infirm, weak and despised old man.   *position in*   20
the world.

But yet I call you servile ministers,

That will with two pernicious daughters join

Your high-engendered battles 'gainst a head

*dragon?
(contrast)* So old and white as this. O, ho! 'Tis foul!   *behaviour of daughters ~ storm*
link

FOOL

He that has a house to put 's head in has a good headpiece.   25

    The codpiece that will house

    Before the head has any,

    The head and he shall louse;

    So beggars marry many.

    The man that makes his toe   30

    What he his heart should make

    Shall of a corn cry woe,

    And turn his sleep to wake.

1–9 *Blow . . . man!* the storm is identified with Lear, who acts it out in speeches such as this one

1 *crack:* puff

2 *cataracts and hurricanoes:* water from the heavens and from the seas

3 *cocks:* weathercocks. Lear is calling for a flood that will submerge the church steeples and weathercocks

4 *thought-executing fires:* lightning ('fires') moving as fast as thoughts

5 *Vaunt-couriers:* heralds or harbingers. The lightning heralds the arrival of the thunderbolts, which split ('cleave') the oak trees

6–9 *Singe . . . man!* Lear asks the elements to destroy him. Such is his conception of his own central importance that he sees no point in the survival of mankind or nature after his death: both must follow him to destruction

7 *Strike . . . world!* make the round earth flat, destroy life in the earth's womb

8–9 *Crack . . . man!* Lear calls for an end to the process of human birth, and so for the extinction of the race of ungrateful ('ingrateful') human beings

8 *nature's moulds:* the forms in which all things, including human beings, are made
  germens: germs or seeds out of which matter is formed
  spill: destroy

10 *court holy-water:* flattery, which is dispersed as freely at court as holy water is sprinkled in a church

14 *thy bellyful:* to your heart's content

16 *I tax . . . unkindness:* I am not accusing the weather of ingratitude

18 *subscription:* obedience, allegiance

19 *pleasure:* things that please you

21–4 *I call . . . this:* I call you slavish agents in that you are willing to ally your armies ('battles'), formed in the high heavens, with my two wicked daughters against an old white-haired man like myself

25 *He . . . headpiece:* this is a bitter reminder to Lear of his folly in leaving himself homeless; 'headpiece' means both 'helmet' and 'brain'

26–33 *The . . . wake:* the man who satisfies his sexual desires (who finds a home for his 'codpiece' or genitalia) before he has a roof over his head, will marry and share his wife's lice and her beggary; many beggars marry in this way. The man who showers his affection on base creatures [Goneril and Regan] and rebuffs those who love him [Cordelia], will suffer such heartache at the hands of those he has cherished that he will not enjoy a night's sleep

32 *Shall . . . woe:* shall cry in pain because of a corn

34–5 *For ... glass:* the reference is to pretty women practising facial expressions before a mirror; there may be an allusion to the vanity and hypocrisy of Goneril and Regan

36 *pattern:* model, perfect example

For there was never yet fair woman but she made mouths

35 in a glass.

LEAR
No, I will be the pattern of all patience.
I will say nothing.

Enter KENT.

KENT
Who's there?

39 *Marry:* by the Virgin Mary (an oath)
39–40 *here's ... fool:* 'grace' is Lear ('the King's grace' was the name commonly given to the monarch in Jacobean times) and 'codpiece' is the Fool; they represent the spiritual and the physical respectively. The Fool appears to be suggesting that he himself is the wise man and Lear the fool for having had children before he acquired wisdom

FOOL
Marry, here's grace and a codpiece: that's a wise man and
40 a fool.

KENT
Alas, sir, are you here? Things that love night
Love not such nights as these. The wrathful skies

43 *Gallow ... dark:* terrify even the wild beasts who wander by night
44 *keep:* remain within

Gallow the very wanderers of the dark,
And make them keep their caves. Since I was man,
45 Such sheets of fire, such bursts of horrid thunder,
Such groans of roaring wind and rain, I never
Remember to have heard. Man's nature cannot carry

47–8 *Man's ... fear:* human nature can bear ('carry') neither the suffering inflicted by the storm, nor the fear of that suffering

Th' affliction nor the fear.

deal with reveal all mans sins.

LEAR
�001   Let the great gods,
That keep this dreadful pudder o'er our heads,

49 *pudder:* turmoil
50 *Find out:* uncover

50 Find out their enemies now. Tremble, thou wretch,
That hast within thee undivulged crimes

justice [theme]

52 *Unwhipped of:* unpunished by
bloody hand: murderer
53 *perjured:* perjurer
53–4 *simular ... incestuous:* hypocritical pretender to chastity ('virtue') who is secretly guilty of incest
54 *Caitiff:* wretch
55–6 *That ... life:* who plotted murder while putting on a show of innocence
56 *practised on:* plotted against
Close pent-up guilts: guilty secrets or impulses carefully concealed by those who harbour them
57 *Rive ... continents:* burst through the protective covering that conceals you from view
continents: containers, enclosures
57–8 *cry ... grace:* beg mercy ('grace') from the angry elements
58 *summoners:* officers who brought offenders before ecclesiastical courts
58–9 *I ... sinning:* in contrast to the hypocritical wrongdoers he has been describing, he is the victim, rather than the agent, of sinful deeds
60 *hard:* close, near
hovel: poor-quality shelter
63 *raised:* built up

Unwhipped of justice. Hide thee, thou bloody hand,
Thou perjured, and thou simular of virtue
That art incestuous. Caitiff, to pieces shake,
55 That under covert and convenient seeming
Hast practised on man's life. Close pent-up guilts,
Rive your concealing continents and cry
These dreadful summoners grace. I am a man   NB
More sinned against than sinning.

KENT
                               Alack, bare-headed?
60 Gracious my lord, hard by here is a hovel;
Some friendship will it lend you 'gainst the tempest;
Repose you there while I to this hard house —
More harder than the stones whereof 'tis raised;

Which even but now, demanding after you,

Denied me to come in — return and force   65

Their scanted courtesy.

LEAR 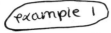 *example 1*

             My wits begin to turn.

Come on, my boy. How dost, my boy? Art cold?

I am cold myself. Where is this straw, my fellow?

<u>The art of our necessities is strange</u>

That can make <u>vilde things precious</u>. Come, your hovel.   70

Poor fool and knave, I have one part in my heart

That's sorry yet for thee.

— example of kindness
— thinking about some one else (caring)
— humility.

FOOL

    He that has and a tiny little wit

    With heigh-ho, the wind and the rain,

    Must make content with his fortunes fit,   75

    Though the rain it raineth every day.

LEAR

True, boy. [*to KENT*] Come, bring us to this hovel.

Exeunt LEAR and KENT.

FOOL

This is a brave night to cool a courtesan. I'll speak a

prophecy ere I go: *Justice*

    When priests are more in word than matter;   80

    When brewers mar their malt with water;

    When nobles are their tailors' tutors;

    No heretics burned but wenches' suitors;

    Then shall the realm of Albion → *Britian*

    Come to great confusion.   85

    When every case in law is right;

    No squire in debt, nor no poor knight;

    When slanders do not live in tongues;

    Nor cut-purses come not to throngs;

    When usurers tell their gold i' the field;   90

    And bawds and whores do churches build;

    Then comes the time, who lives to see't

    That going shall be used with feet.

unfair

justice

This prophecy Merlin shall make; for I live before his time. *normal*   95

Exit.

64–6 *Which ... courtesy:* the occupants of which, only now, when I made enquiries as to your whereabouts, refused me admittance. Kent will return in order to force some kind of hospitality from those who earlier withheld ('scanted') it

69–70 *The ... precious:* need ('poverty') can make us value things, such as straw, that we despised when we were prosperous

69 *art:* magic, skill

70 *vilde:* vile

73 *He ... wit:* the man who has little intelligence, and that 'little' is a very little indeed

75–6 *Must ... day:* must make his happiness match his fortune in an endlessly hostile world, or must be satisfied with a fortune to match his small intelligence. The Fool is reminding Lear that both of them have only a small share of wit, with which they must manage as best they can

78 *brave:* splendid
courtesan: a female who satisfies the lusts of kings and courtiers. The Fool is saying that the stormy night would cool the ardour of such a woman

80–5 *When priests ... confusion:* when priests are better at preaching about good behaviour than at practising it; when brewers water down their beer; when noblemen care for nothing but fashion; when people are no longer burned at the stake for preaching heresy, and the only ones who suffer (are 'burned') are those with sexually transmitted diseases; then shall the kingdom of Britain come to ruin. These lines are a satirical account of abuses that were rife in Shakespeare's England

84–5 In the First Folio, these lines are placed after the present line 91 'And bawds ... build'

86–93 *When every ... feet:* these lines convey a Utopian vision of society and are meant ironically. The Fool is imagining a time when, paradoxically, justice is the main feature of the legal system; when neither knights nor squires are impoverished; when slanderous comment is no longer heard; when people who congregate are not pestered by purse-stealing thieves; when moneylenders openly count their money; when those who have lived on the profits of sexual immorality build churches as an act of repentance. When all these things happen, whenever that may be, people will use their feet for walking (i.e. the true and natural order of things will be restored)

94–5 *This ... time:* Merlin, King Arthur's magician, is said to have flourished during the sixth century AD. Lear is thought to have become King of Britain in the ninth century BC – around 1,500 years before Merlin's time

Key points

This is the first of Lear's three storm scenes. The greatness, violence and power of the storm are a measure of these qualities in Lear himself: this is a storm fit for a king to confront. The storm also symbolises the turmoil in his mind and in the kingdom.

- Having experienced the cruelty of Goneril and Regan, Lear is now struck by another kind of force: the cruelty of nature, exemplified in the storm. Of course, Lear would not be experiencing the cruelty of nature if his daughters had not forced him to confront the storm, making them the instruments of this second kind of cruelty.

- The early part of this scene suggests two things about Lear: that he is obsessed with himself, and that he is unable to come to terms with no longer being a king. Where the royal crown used to rest is now his 'white head' (line 6). This head, as Lear imagines it, is still a royal one. His reference to 'oak-cleaving thunderbolts' (line 5) is significant as the royal oak, monarch among trees, is a prime target for lightning strikes. Thunderbolts strike the highest and greatest figures on the landscape. On the heath, Lear, the only royal figure, is the appropriate target.

- Lear's self-regard reaches an extreme pitch when he decides that if he is to die, the world must die with him, ending the human race.

- Lear's apocalyptic vision is interrupted by the Fool's down-to-earth remark that since Lear's daughters are in a dry house and protected from the storm, it might be best for him to return to them and ask for their blessing. The Fool's common sense is a deflating contrast to Lear's magnificent self-dramatising rhetoric. It is all very well for Lear to look to the heavens to destroy creation, but realities must be faced. That the Fool feels able to make this suggestion is another way of indicating the extreme severity of the storm.

- The speech beginning 'Rumble thy bellyful!' (line 14) shows that Lear is haunted by the thought of his daughters' ingratitude. The suffering inflicted by the storm is not the worst form of suffering. He cannot charge the elements with the depth of unkindness shown to him by his daughters. After all, he never gave his kingdom over to the elements, so, unlike his daughters, they owe him nothing. Then, in a sudden change of mood, he sees the storm as taking his daughters' side against him, joining their forces against an infirm old man.

- Lear imagines a role for the storm in uncovering for 'the great gods' (line 48) the secret crimes committed by their enemies, such as perjurers, those who commit incest and those who plot against the lives of others. The storm will, in Lear's imagination, force them through fear to confess their crimes and cry out for mercy. The implication here is that where human justice has failed to detect and punish major crimes, the elements, as agents of 'the great gods', must intervene.

- Notice that Lear distinguishes between himself and the major sinners he condemns. He himself, he claims, is 'a man more sinned against than sinning' (lines 58–9). However, in this pronouncement he is at least acknowledging that he has sinned.

- So far, Lear's tone has been mainly one of self-regard and self-pity. As his 'wits begin to turn' (line 66), he looks beyond himself and wonders if the Fool is cold. This concern is followed by an expression of pity: 'I have one part in my heart that's sorry yet for thee' (lines 71–2). This small episode is part of a larger theme: when hitherto fortunate people are exposed to extreme misery it makes them sympathetic to the plight of others.

- By the end of this scene we feel that Lear's exclusive concern for himself is giving way to compassion for others.

- Kent emphasises the storm's unprecedented fury (lines 42–7). Shakespeare's theatres had little or no provision for special effects, which meant that he had to keep relying on the power of language to suggest and create the storm in the minds and imaginations of his audience.

- Kent concludes that human nature is not capable of withstanding the storm's terrible force or the fear it engenders. He wants to return to Gloucester's castle to ask Goneril and Regan to allow Lear to seek refuge there. Instead, Lear prefers the modest comfort offered by a hovel on the heath.

Useful quotes

> I tax not you, you elements, with unkindness;
> I never gave you kingdom, called you children
>
> (Lear, lines 16–17)

> I am a man
> More sinned against than sinning.
>
> (Lear, lines 58–9)

> Since I was man,
> Such sheets of fire, such bursts of horrid thunder,
> Such groans of roaring wind and rain, I never
> Remember to have heard.
>
> (Kent, lines 44–7)

> My wits begin to turn.
> Come on, my boy. How dost, my boy? Art cold?
> I am cold myself.
>
> (Lear, lines 66–8)

Questions ?

1 Why, do you think, does Lear reach the conclusion that the world should be destroyed?

2 It has been suggested by some commentators that Lear sees the battering he is getting from the storm as a relief. Is there any evidence for this suggestion in the text of the play?

3 Lear declares: 'No, I will be the pattern of all patience. I will say nothing' (lines 36–7). Comment on these lines as a reflection of Cordelia's attitude in Act 1, Scene 1. Do the lines imply that Lear has arrived at an understanding of her response?

4 'Lear enacts the storm in heightened language.' Identify examples of this type of language in this scene.

5 Comment on how Lear is beginning to acquire some understanding of injustice in human society. What do you think has helped him to acquire this understanding?

6 The Fool wants to teach Lear the lesson that they must be satisfied with a small share of happiness to match their small share of intelligence (lines 73–6). On the evidence of this scene, is Lear beginning to learn this lesson? Explain your answer.

ACT 3 † Scene 3

Plot summary

Gloucester confides in Edmund that he is disturbed about the unnatural behaviour of Goneril and Regan towards their father. He talks about the growing hostility between Albany and Cornwall. He also gives Edmund important information about the counter-movement in Lear's favour. He has a letter stating that the first division of an army from France has established itself in Britain. He asks Edmund to cover for him while he searches for Lear. Edmund is now in a position to betray his father to Cornwall, and to reveal to Lear's enemies all he knows about the French invasion. The motive for this betrayal is self-interest: Edmund will inherit what his father will lose.

These injuries the King now bears will be revenged home.

GLOUCESTER, Act 3, Scene 3, 10–11

A room in the Earl of Gloucester's castle.
Enter GLOUCESTER and EDMUND (with lights).

[handwritten: daughters have done to lear]

GLOUCESTER

[circled handwritten: irony]

Alack, alack, Edmund, I like not this unnatural dealing.
When I desired their leave that I might pity him, they took
from me the use of mine own house, charged me on pain
of perpetual displeasure, neither to speak of him, entreat
for him, or any way sustain him.   5

EDMUND

Most savage and unnatural!   *[handwritten: irony]*

GLOUCESTER

Go to. Say you nothing. There is a division between the
dukes, and a worse matter than that. I have received a
letter this night; 'tis dangerous to be spoken; I have
locked the letter in my closet. These injuries the King now   10
bears will be revenged home. There is part of a power
already footed. We must incline to the King. I will look him
and privily relieve him. Go you and maintain talk with
the duke, that my charity be not of him perceived. If he
ask for me, I am ill and gone to bed. If I die for it (as no   15
less is threatened me), the King my old master must be
relieved. There is strange things toward, Edmund; pray
you, be careful.

[handwritten: plans to revenge king against daughters.]

Exit.

EDMUND

This courtesy forbid thee, shall the duke
Instantly know, and of that letter too.   20
This seems a fair deserving, and must draw me
That which my father loses — no less than all.
The younger rises when the old doth fall.

Exit.

---

2 *desired their leave:* requested permission from Goneril, Regan and Cornwall
pity him: take pity on Lear
3 *charged:* ordered
4 *perpetual displeasure:* being always out of favour
5 *sustain:* support or care for

6 *Most ... unnatural!* this is another of Edmund's ironies

7 *Go to:* this is an expression of disapproval, meaning 'come, come'. Gloucester thinks he needs to restrain Edmund from openly expressing criticism of Goneril, Regan and their husbands
8 *a worse matter:* i.e. the French invasion
10 *closet:* cabinet in which confidential material is kept
11 *home:* fully
12 *footed:* landed
incline to: take the side of
look him: search for him
13 *privily:* secretly

15–17 *If I ... relieved:* this marks the emergence of Gloucester as a character of moral stature and fundamental decency. His support for Lear is now unconditional and humanitarian, offered at the risk of his own life
17 *There ... toward:* strange events are at hand

19 *This ... thee:* your decision to extend the kindness to Lear that you were forbidden to

21 *This ... deserving:* it seems to me that I will merit a decent reward for this (the information he is about to give Cornwall)
21–2 *draw ... all:* bring into my hands what my father is about to lose (all his possessions)

Key points

This scene marks a significant development in the sub-plot, particularly in Gloucester's character. Gloucester knows he must help Lear, even if it may cost him his life.

- Gloucester confirms earlier reports of an invasion of Britain by forces from France sent to relieve Lear, and of a falling out between Albany and Cornwall.

- Gloucester is facing a difficult choice: driven by force of circumstances he must choose between ancient loyalties and human decency on the one hand and self-interest and self-preservation on the other.

- We are invited to see Gloucester in a more favourable light than previously when he determines to relieve Lear, even if this means that he himself is to die for doing so (in earlier scenes he appeared to accept the cruel treatment of Lear by Goneril and Regan as something he could not do anything about).

- Gloucester is not quite a heroic martyr and would prefer to relieve Lear without the knowledge of Cornwall: 'Go you and maintain talk with the duke, that my charity be not of him perceived. If he ask for me, I am ill and gone to bed' (lines 13–15).

- Just as Gloucester gains new esteem, Edmund's character degenerates sharply. His condemnation of Goneril and Regan as 'most savage and unnatural' (line 6) exposes new depths of hypocrisy, as he is now ready to betray his father in order to take possession of his title and his lands.

- Gloucester has made the fatal mistake of confiding in Edmund, just as Lear did earlier when he entrusted his kingdom and his welfare to Goneril and Regan. This error has sealed Gloucester's fate.

- In Edmund's closing soliloquy we once again see him seizing an opportunity and taking decisive action to further his interests. He is prepared to betray his father without a second thought.

- Gloucester's compassion for Lear, and trust in his son Edmund, mean that he is now in grave danger.

- On a practical level, this scene gives the actor playing Lear a necessary rest.

Useful quotes

If I die for it (as no less is threatened me), the King my old master must be relieved.

(Gloucester, lines 15–17)

The younger rises when the old doth fall.

(Edmund, line 23)

? Questions

1 Both Gloucester and Edmund use the word 'unnatural' in this scene, but with differing meaning. Explain.

2 Imagine you are Gloucester. Write to a trusted friend setting out the problems facing you at this point.

3 Compose a diary entry for Edmund, recording his impressions of what has transpired between his father and himself in this scene.

4 'While we admire Gloucester's determination to help Lear, we cannot yet regard him as a moral hero.' Comment on this view.

Plot summary

Now that they have reached the hovel, Lear resists Kent's repeated attempts to persuade him to enter it. The violent storm paradoxically provides Lear with relief and distraction from a more injurious storm: the one that is now racking his mind and threatening his sanity. If he enters the hovel, his mind will again be free to torture itself with the contemplation of filial ingratitude, with which he is now obsessed. Lear urges the others to enter the hovel first. He talks feelingly and at length about the sufferings of those who are even more miserable than he is. He raises fundamental questions about human and divine justice. His remarkable awareness of social and economic inequality shows a new feeling for the common humanity of beggar and king.

The Fool discovers Edgar (disguised as Poor Tom) in the hovel and runs out in fear; Edgar follows. Lear assumes that Poor Tom's daughters mistreated him and are responsible for his wretched condition. Kent points out in vain that Tom/Edgar has no daughters. Lear's mind has given way: he has left reality behind and is technically insane. The exchanges between Lear (now at the height of his madness), the Fool and Edgar penetrate to the essential condition of humanity. Lear finds the half-naked Edgar a true image of the basic humanity he wants to share.

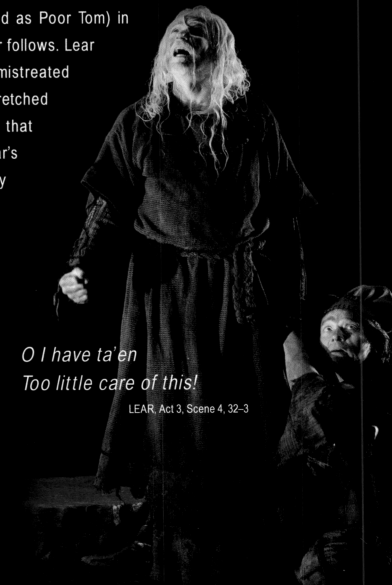

O I have ta'en
Too little care of this!

LEAR, Act 3, Scene 4, 32–3

Gloucester tells the disguised Kent that he is losing his own mind and regrets his treatment of Edgar. Gloucester leads them to better shelter.

2–3 *The . . . endure:* the merciless violence of such a night as this spent in the open is beyond human endurance

4 *Wilt:* do you want to

6–7 *Thou . . . skin:* you are appalled that this violent storm drenches me to the skin

8–9 *But . . . felt:* if a man is burdened with two sources of grief, the greater, more obsessive ('fixed') one makes the lesser one seem trivial. Lear's greater grief is the heartbreaking ingratitude of his daughters; the storm is less of a threat

9–11 *Thou'dst shun . . . mouth:* you would run from a bear, but if it meant running into a violent sea (a greater danger), you would turn to face the bear

11–12 *When . . . delicate:* a mind free from care tends to focus on relatively minor bodily ailments

12–14 *the tempest . . . ingratitude:* my tormented mind is insensitive to anything except the thought of my daughters' ingratitude

15–16 *Is . . . to't?* Lear imagines his daughters and himself as parts of a single body. By turning against him, they have violated the integrity of that body

16 *home:* thoroughly

21–2 *O . . . of that:* Lear senses that his preoccupation with his daughters' ingratitude is threatening his sanity

let storm distract him of his thoughts

24–5 *This . . . more:* fierce as it is, Lear welcomes the storm as the lesser of two evils, the greater one being his sense of 'filial ingratitude' (line 14). While he confronts the storm, he has less time to dwell on his obsession, which would be more damaging

→ Obsessive

→ repatition

example of kindess → Kent

The heath. Before a hovel.

Enter LEAR, KENT and FOOL.

KENT
Here is the place, my lord. Good my lord, enter.
The tyranny of the open night's too rough
For nature to endure.

Storm still.

LEAR
                              Let me alone.

KENT
Good my lord, enter here.

LEAR
                                        Wilt break my heart?

KENT
5   I had rather break mine own. Good my lord, enter.

LEAR
Thou think'st 'tis much that this contentious storm
Invades us to the skin; so 'tis to thee,
But where the greater malady is fixed,
The lesser is scarce felt. Thou'dst shun a bear;
10   But if thy flight lay toward the roaring sea
Thou'dst meet the bear i' the mouth. When the mind's free
The body's delicate; the tempest in my mind
Doth from my senses take all feeling else
Save what beats there — filial ingratitude!
15   Is it not as this mouth should tear this hand
For lifting food to't? But I will punish home:
No, I will weep no more. — In such a night
To shut me out? Pour on; I will endure.
In such a night as this! O Regan, Goneril!
20   Your old kind father, whose frank heart gave all —
O that way madness lies; let me shun that;
No more of that.

KENT
                              Good my lord, enter here.

LEAR
Prithee, go in thyself; seek thine own ease.
This tempest will not give me leave to ponder
25   On things would hurt me more. But I'll go in.

kindness | *example 3*

[*to FOOL*] In boy, go first. You houseless poverty —
Nay, get thee in. I'll pray, and then I'll sleep. [*FOOL goes in*]
Poor naked wretches, wheresoe'er you are
That bide the pelting of this pitiless storm,
How shall your houseless heads and unfed sides,   30
Your looped and windowed raggedness, defend you
From seasons such as these? O I have ta'en
Too little care of this! Take physic, pomp;
Expose thyself to feel what wretches feel,
That thou mayst shake the superflux to them   35
And show the heavens more just.

social injustice

× redistribution of wealth
× experience what they do → more empathy → help

EDGAR [*within*]
Fathom and half, fathom and half! Poor Tom!

FOOL [*within*]
Come not in here, nuncle; here's a spirit.
Help me, help me! [*runs out from the hovel*]

KENT
Give me thy hand. Who's there?   40

FOOL
A spirit, a spirit! He says his name's Poor Tom.

KENT
What art thou that dost grumble there i' the straw?
Come forth.

Enter EDGAR (disguised as Poor Tom).

EDGAR
Away! The foul fiend follows me! Through the sharp
hawthorn blow the cold winds. Humh! Go to thy cold bed   45
and warm thee.

LEAR
Didst thou give all to thy daughters? And art thou come
to this?

EDGAR *fake mad*   *× feels the cold → Lear doesn't*

Who gives anything to Poor Tom? Whom the foul fiend
hath led through fire and through flame, through   50
ford and whirlpool, o'er bog and quagmire, that hath
laid knives under his pillow and halters in his pew, set
ratsbane by his porridge; made him proud of heart to
ride on a bay trotting-horse over four-inched bridges, to

maddness

---

26 *You houseless poverty:* Lear is beginning his prayer, which he momentarily interrupts in the next line. Lear prays, not to the gods, but to poverty and its wretched victims, who are most vulnerable to the ferocity of the elements
29 *bide:* abide, endure
social awareness.
31 *looped ... raggedness:* ragged clothes full of holes and openings
32 *seasons:* weather conditions
ta'en: taken
33–4 *Take ... wretches feel:* let the great and powerful (such as Lear himself) learn by sharing in the wretchedness of common men
33 *physic:* medicine
pomp: powerful, ostentatious people
35 *shake:* distribute, cast off
superflux: superfluity, your surplus possessions

37 *Fathom and half:* overwhelmed by the downpour, he pretends to be a sailor sounding the depths of the ocean. Edgar's entrance – pretending to be the insane Poor Tom, a Bedlam beggar – adds another dimension to the madness and disorder depicted on stage
38–9 Edgar's whine and appearance are sufficiently terrifying to send the Fool running

44 *Away!* keep away from me
foul fiend: mad people were thought to be possessed by devils
45 *Humh!* he is cold and shivering

51 *quagmire:* soft, wet ground
51–3 *that ... porridge:* the devil, knowing that the possessed man is in despair and will consider suicide, provides him with knives, halters and rat poison ('ratsbane')
52 *pew:* his seat in church, or a gallery in his house
53 *porridge:* broth
53–4 *to ride ... bridges:* to perform difficult and dangerous feats. He imagines being led by the devil to ride a high-stepping horse over ridiculously narrow bridges

55 *course:* chase
for: as though it is
five wits: these were: common wit, imagination, fantasy, estimation and memory

56 *Tom's a-cold:* this was the peculiar cry of Bedlam beggars in all seasons. Note that Lear's real madness makes him unaware of the cold, whereas Edgar's false madness seems to focus on the cold
do de: his teeth are chattering

57 *starblasting:* coming under the hostile influence of a star, and hence contracting an illness
taking: being bewitched, which often implied being infected with disease

58-9 *There . . . there:* Edgar is searching his body for lice and devils

60-1 *Has . . . all?* Lear, now convinced that all the world's evils spring from filial ingratitude, wonders if Tom's daughters have reduced him to his present condition and if he has acted with the same thoughtless generosity as Lear

62 *Nay . . . shamed:* no, he has kept a blanket, which he is wearing as a loincloth; otherwise we would all have been affronted by his nakedness

63 *plagues:* calamities
pendulous: suspended

64 *light:* descend, fall

66 *subdued nature:* reduced his human qualities or natural powers to this state

68-9 *Is . . . flesh?* Do fathers whose children have rejected them normally punish their bodies by sticking things in their flesh (as Edgar has done)?

70-1 *Judicious . . . daughters:* we should be punished in the flesh, since it created daughters who demand the ultimate sacrifice from us. According to legend, the pelican sustained its young on blood drawn from its breast

72 *Pillicock . . . Hill:* 'Pillicock' is suggested by 'pelican' in the previous line. It is a term of endearment, meaning 'darling'. There may also be a crude allusion to Lear's 'this flesh begot', since 'pillicock' was another word for 'penis'

75-7 *Obey . . . array:* Edgar is providing a version of the Ten Commandments. The suggestion is that if these rules are not broken, 'the foul fiend' may be kept in check

76-7 *commit . . . spouse:* do not commit adultery with the lawful wife of another

77 *set . . . array:* do not desire fine clothes

81 *gloves . . . cap:* gifts from a mistress, tokens of her favour

82 *did . . . darkness:* had sexual intercourse

---

55 course his own shadow for a traitor. Bless thy five wits! Tom's a-cold. O do de, do de, do de. Bless thee from whirlwinds, starblasting and taking! Do Poor Tom some charity, whom the foul fiend vexes. There could I have him now, and there, and there again, and there.

Storm still.

LEAR

60 Has his daughters brought him to this pass?
Couldst thou save nothing? Wouldst thou give 'em all?

FOOL

Nay, he reserved a blanket, else we had been all shamed.

LEAR

Now all the plagues that in the pendulous air
Hang fated o'er men's faults light on thy daughters!

justice

KENT

65 He hath no daughters, sir.

LEAR

Death, traitor! Nothing could have subdued nature
To such a lowness but his unkind daughters.
Is it the fashion that discarded fathers
Should have thus little mercy on their flesh?

70 Judicious punishment! 'Twas this flesh begot
Those pelican daughters.

EDGAR

Pillicock sat on Pillicock Hill
Alow, alow, loo, loo!

FOOL

This cold night will turn us all to fools and madmen.

EDGAR

75 Take heed o' the foul fiend. Obey thy parents; keep thy words justice; swear not; commit not with man's sworn spouse; set not thy sweet heart on proud array. Tom's a-cold.

LEAR

What hast thou been?

EDGAR

80 A serving man, proud in heart and mind, that curled my hair, wore gloves in my cap, served the lust of my mistress's heart, and did the act of darkness with her, swore as many

oaths as I spake words, and broke them in the sweet face of heaven; one that slept in the contriving of lust, and waked to do it. Wine loved I deeply, dice dearly, and in women out- 85
paramoured the Turk. *racism* False of heart, light of ear, bloody of hand; hog in sloth, fox in stealth, wolf in greediness, dog in madness, lion in prey. Let not the creaking of shoes nor the rustling of silks betray thy poor heart to woman. Keep thy foot out of brothels, thy hand out of plackets, thy pen from 90
lenders' books, and defy the foul fiend. Still through the hawthorn blows the cold wind, says suum, mun, nonny. Dolphin my boy, boy, sessey! Let him trot by.

Storm still.

LEAR

everyone is the same

Thou wert better in a grave than to answer with thy uncovered body this extremity of the skies. Is man no 95
more than (this?) Consider him well. Thou ow'st the worm no silk, the beast no hide, the sheep no wool, the cat no *clothes give status* perfume. Ha! Here's three on's are sophisticated. Thou art the thing itself! Unaccommodated man is no more but such a poor, bare, *fancy* forked animal as thou art. Off, off, you 100
lendings! Come, unbutton here. [*tears off his clothes*]

FOOL

Prithee, nuncle, be contented; 'tis a naughty night to swim in.

Enter GLOUCESTER (with a torch)

Now a little fire in a wild field were like an old lecher's heart; a small spark, all the rest on's body cold. Look! Here 105
comes a walking fire.

EDGAR

This is the foul fiend Flibbertigibbet. He begins at curfew and walks at first cock. He gives the web and the pin, squints the eye, and makes the harelip, mildews the white wheat, and hurts the poor creature of earth. 110

Swithold footed thrice the old;

He met the night-mare, and her nine-fold;

Bid her alight,

And her troth plight,

And aroint thee, witch, aroint thee! 115

---

84 *contriving:* plotting, thinking about

85–6 *in women ... Turk:* had more lovers than the Sultan of Turkey

86 *light of ear:* believing malicious reports
bloody: murderous

87–8 *hog ... prey:* the seven deadly sins (pride, covetousness, lust, anger, gluttony, envy and sloth) were conventionally represented by animals

90 *plackets:* slits in the fronts of petticoats

91 *defy ... fiend:* by following the instructions given above, you will be keeping the devil at bay

92 *says ... nonny:* Edgar may be imitating the sound of the wind

93 *Dolphin:* appears to mean 'dauphin', and consequently 'devil'; English hatred of the French led to the identification of the French crown prince (the dauphin) with the prince of hell
sessey: cease, be quiet; from the French *cessez*

94 *Thou wert better:* you would be better off
answer: confront

96–7 *Thou ... silk:* you are not indebted to the silkworm for silken garments

97 *cat:* civet cat, a source of perfume

98 *three on's:* three of us (Lear, Kent, the Fool)

98–9 *Thou ... itself!* you, Poor Tom, represent mankind in its pure, naked, natural state

99 *Unaccommodated man:* human beings without the trappings of civilisation (here, principally clothing)

100 *forked:* two-legged

101 *lendings:* clothes 'borrowed' from the animals (i.e. hides, wool)
Come, unbutton here: Lear removes his clothes in an effort to be at one with Poor Tom (i.e. a man reduced to his simplest terms)

104 *fire:* torch carried by Gloucester

107 *begins:* first appears
curfew: in feudal times, the curfew bell was the signal to put out fires and lights

108 *walks ... cock:* goes away at first cock-crow (i.e. at midnight)
web ... pin: cataract

111–15 *Swithold ... thee!* Edgar is reciting a charm against the nightmare, a demon who troubles people in their sleep. St Withold walked the rolling upland ('the old' or wold). When he met the nightmare and her nine offspring or imps, he ordered her to alight from the chest of her victim sleeper and promise ('her troth plight') not to do further harm

115 *aroint:* be gone

121 *wall-newt:* wall lizard
water: water-newt

122–3 *for sallets:* as a substitute for salads or tasty morsels

123 *ditch-dog:* a dog thrown dead into a ditch

124 *green . . . pool:* scum on a stagnant pond

124–5 *whipped . . . to tithing:* a statute of 1572 governing the punishment of vagabonds stipulated that such people were to be whipped publicly from one parish ('tithing') to another

125 *stocked:* put in the stocks

126 *three . . . body:* this was the allowance for a gentleman's servant

128 *deer:* animals, game

130 *Beware . . . fiend!* Edgar is warning the others of the dangers posed by his familiar demon ('follower'), whose name is Smulkin

131 *your grace:* your majesty

132–3 *The . . . Mahu:* with a nice sense of grotesque comedy, Edgar pretends that Gloucester's anxious question is addressed to him, rather than to Lear, so he answers: the devil I have as my attendant is a nobleman; his names are Modo and Mahu (captain or commander of the other devils)

134–5 *Our . . . gets it:* such is the present vileness of human nature that our children hate their parents

135 *gets:* begets, generates, creates

136 *suffer:* allow me

138 *injunction:* order

KENT
How fares your grace?

LEAR
What's he?

KENT
[*to GLOUCESTER*] Who's there? What is't you seek?

GLOUCESTER
What are you there? Your names?

EDGAR
120 Poor Tom, that eats the swimming frog, the toad, the tadpole, the wall-newt and the water; that in the fury of his heart, when the foul fiend rages, eats cow-dung for sallets, swallows the old rat and the ditch-dog, drinks the green mantle of the standing pool; who is whipped from
125 tithing to tithing and stocked, punished and imprisoned, who hath had three suits to his back, six shirts to his body,

    Horse to ride and weapon to wear

    But mice and rats and such small deer,

    Have been Tom's food for seven long year.

130 Beware, my follower! Peace, Smulkin! Peace, thou fiend!

GLOUCESTER
[*to LEAR*] What, hath your grace no better company?

EDGAR
The Prince of Darkness is a gentleman; Modo he's called, and Mahu.

GLOUCESTER
Our flesh and blood, my lord, is grown so vilde,
That it doth hate what gets it.

EDGAR
135   Poor Tom's a-cold.

GLOUCESTER
Go in with me. My duty cannot suffer
T'obey in all your daughters' hard commands;
Though their injunction be to bar my doors
And let this tyrannous night take hold upon you,
140 Yet have I ventured to come seek you out
And bring you where both fire and food is ready.

LEAR

First let me talk with this philosopher.

[*to EDGAR*] What is the cause of thunder?

KENT

Good my lord, take his offer; go into the house.

LEAR

I'll talk a word with this same learned Theban.   145

[*to EDGAR*] What is your study?

EDGAR

How to prevent the fiend, and to kill vermin.

LEAR

Let me ask you one word in private.

LEAR and EDGAR talk apart.

KENT

Importune him once more to go, my lord.

His wits begin t' unsettle.

GLOUCESTER

                Canst thou blame him?   150

Storm still.

His daughters seek his death. Aha, that good Kent,

He said it would be thus, poor banished man!

Thou say'st the King grows mad. I'll tell thee, friend,

I am almost mad myself. I had a son,

Now outlawed from my blood; he sought my life   155

But lately, very late, I loved him, friend,

No father his son dearer. Truth to tell thee,

The grief hath crazed my wits. What a night's this!

[*to LEAR*] I do beseech your grace—

LEAR

                    O cry your mercy, sir.

[*to EDGAR*] Noble philosopher, your company.   160

EDGAR

Tom's a-cold.

GLOUCESTER

In fellow, there, into the hovel; keep thee warm.

---

142 *this philosopher:* Edgar, wearing only his blanket, looks like a traditional philosopher. Lear is referring to the belief that philosophers (who would now be called scientists) were expected to live in reduced circumstances, and to content themselves with the basic items of food and dress

145 *learned Theban:* Lear is not paying the highest possible compliment to the learning of Poor Tom, since Thebans were regarded as less skilled in learned pursuits than were Athenians. But see note to line 168 below

146 *study:* research area, speciality

147 *prevent the fiend:* avoid or hinder the devil
vermin: pests

148 *Let . . . private:* it has been suggested that Lear is thinking of his daughters as vermin, and wants to ask about getting rid of them
apart: to one side, away from the other characters on stage

149 *Importune:* urge

151 *Kent:* of course, Gloucester is unaware that he is in fact talking to Kent in disguise

154–8 *I am . . . wits:* Edgar does not hear Gloucester's comments on these matters that vitally concern him; instead, he is talking separately with Lear

155 *Now . . . blood:* disowned as my son and deprived of the right to inherit my estate

159 *cry your mercy:* pardon me – I did not notice you

163 *let's in all:* Lear wants to go into the hovel if Edgar is going in

163 *This way:* Kent is directing Lear away from the hovel and towards the house mentioned at line 144

163 *With him:* I want to go with him (i.e. Edgar)

164 *still:* all the time, always. Lear is saying: I insist on being continuously in the company of my philosopher

165 *soothe him:* humour him (i.e. Lear)

166 *Take ... on:* Gloucester is asking Kent to bring Edgar ahead with him to the house adjoining Gloucester's castle so that Lear will follow

168 *Athenian:* Lear is now placing a higher value on Poor Tom's expertise as a philosopher; he previously called him a Theban, a less cultivated and less learned person than an Athenian

170–2 *Child ... man:* in these lines, a reference to Roland (Charlemagne's heroic nephew) is amalgamated with a famous quotation from the story of Jack the giant-killer. Edgar probably sees himself as a British Roland, about to encounter the dangers lurking in his father's castle, where his blood (his kinship with Gloucester) may be smelled by the ogre Cornwall

171 *His ... still:* his motto or password was always

LEAR
Come, let's in all.

KENT
                              This way, my lord.

LEAR
                                        With him.
I will keep still with my philosopher.

KENT
165 Good my lord, soothe him: let him take the fellow.

GLOUCESTER
Take him you on.

KENT
Sirrah, come on. Go along with us.

LEAR
Come, good Athenian.

GLOUCESTER
No words, no words! Hush!

EDGAR
170   Child Roland to the dark tower came,
          His word was still 'Fie, foh, and fum,
          I smell the blood of a British man.'

Exeunt.

Fie, foh, and fum,
I smell the blood of a British man.

EDGAR, Act 3, Scene 4, 171–2

Key points

This tremendous scene is one of the highlights of the play. It confronts us with an extraordinary vision of the breakdown of normal human nature.

- Lear is fearful of sheltering from the storm – because while he has to contend with the violence of the wind and rain, he is not free to think of his greater mental suffering ('This tempest will not give me leave to ponder on things would hurt me more'; lines 24–5).

- Lear's prayer (lines 28–36) is unusual in that it is addressed, not to heavenly powers, but to poverty and its wretched victims who are most exposed to the ferocity of the elements. Lear's mind turns to the miseries of those who are worse off than he is. The insightful prayer signifies that suffering has little value unless it is shared with the great mass of humanity, and also is something for which the individual sufferer takes some responsibility.

- Lear confesses that during his reign he did not pay proper attention to the needs of others ('O I have ta'en too little care of this!'; lines 32–3). He recommends that people in power should rid themselves of unnecessary luxury and distribute their surplus wealth among the needy. In other words, resources should be shared more evenly.

- Lear has come to these conclusions, not by reflecting on poverty in the abstract, but by gaining personal experience of what poverty is really like.

- Lear's encounter with Edgar as Poor Tom shows him crossing the line between sanity and madness. His great controlling obsession – 'filial ingratitude' (line 14) and how it reduces human beings to misery – comes to the fore. Notice that in his curse on Tom's imaginary daughters, Lear is remembering his similar curses on Goneril and Regan.

- The imaginative high point of the scene is the dialogue between Lear (at this stage a real madman), the Fool (a professional madman) and Edgar (pretending to be a madman). They communicate by means of a new visionary language that explores depths of experience far beyond the reach of normal discourse. They reach a level of truth and insight that makes the mundane, practical concerns of Gloucester and Kent appear shallow and superficial.

- Gloucester's arrival adds to the parent–child theme. He reinforces Lear's obsession with filial ingratitude by remarking that human nature has now become so debased that children hate their parents ('Our flesh and blood, my lord, is grown so vilde, that it doth hate what gets it'; lines 134–5). This echoes Lear's reference to Poor Tom's 'pelican daughters' (line 71).

- Gloucester offers to rescue Lear from 'this tyrannous night' (line 139). Lear, unaware of the reality around him, does not understand that Gloucester is risking his life to help him. Instead, he wants to talk with Poor Tom, whom he imagines to be an ancient Greek philosopher. The remainder of the scene takes on the character of grotesque comedy as Lear insists on ignoring Gloucester and speaking only to Tom/Edgar.

- Lear's response to Poor Tom has its own logic. He is remembering that ancient philosophers were supposed to live in modest circumstances, eating and wearing little. Thus, the disguised Edgar, dressed only in a blanket, would appear like a philosopher. When Lear asks him, 'What is the cause of thunder?' (line 143), he is seeking an answer both to an urgent problem he is facing (a thunderstorm) and to a question that ancient philosophers were frequently asked.

- Gloucester exposes the extent and cause of his own intense mental anguish and gives a harrowing statement of his present feelings for Edgar. The irony here is that Edgar, talking apart with Lear, does not hear Gloucester's words, which concern him more deeply than they do anyone else present.

- This scene is the climax of both the main plot and the sub-plot. This point is borne out by the fact that Gloucester and Edgar (disguised as a beggar) join Lear and Kent (disguised as Lear's servant) to go to better lodgings.

Useful quotes

> When the mind's free
> The body's delicate; the tempest in my mind
> Doth from my senses take all feeling else
> Save what beats there — filial ingratitude!
>
> (Lear, lines 11–14)

> Your old kind father, whose frank heart gave all —
> O that way madness lies; let me shun that;
> No more of that.
>
> (Lear, lines 20–2)

> O I have ta'en
> Too little care of this! Take physic, pomp;
> Expose thyself to feel what wretches feel,
> That thou mayst shake the superflux to them
> And show the heavens more just.
>
> (Lear, lines 32–6)

> Has his daughters brought him to this pass?
> Couldst thou save nothing? Wouldst thou give 'em all?
>
> (Lear, lines 60–1)

> Unaccommodated man is no more but
> such a poor, bare, forked animal as thou art.
>
> (Lear, lines 99–100)

> My duty cannot suffer
> T'obey in all your daughters' hard commands
>
> (Gloucester, lines 136–7)

> Thou say'st the King grows mad. I'll tell thee, friend,
> I am almost mad myself.
>
> (Gloucester, lines 153–4)

? Questions

1 Why does Lear prefer to endure the storm rather than accept the shelter of the hovel? Refer to the text of the play in support of your answer.

2 Comment on the significance of Lear's prayer beginning 'Poor naked wretches' (line 28). What is unusual about this speech?

3 Edgar's presence as Poor Tom has a decisive effect on Lear. Describe this effect.

4 Discuss the grotesque comedy of this scene.

5 What is Lear's main concern in this scene?

6 Why does Lear tear off his clothes?

7 Why does Lear think of Poor Tom/Edgar as a philosopher? Why is he so determined to seek his company? Is Edgar a source of wisdom in this scene? Explain your answers.

8 Describe your feelings about Gloucester in this scene.

9 Comment on the various versions of madness depicted in this scene.

10 Imagine you are the set designer for a theatrical production of *King Lear*. How would you create the setting for this scene? Consider issues such as scenery, props and lighting.

ACT 3 ✝ Scene 5

Cornwall is out for revenge – clearly Edmund has given him details of Gloucester's sympathy for Lear. The letter Gloucester spoke of in confidence to Edmund is now in Cornwall's hands. Edmund's reward for betraying his father, with cynical opportunism, is a rich one: the Earldom of Gloucester. Cornwall and Edmund plan the capture of Gloucester. Edmund is symbolically 'adopted' by Cornwall as his son.

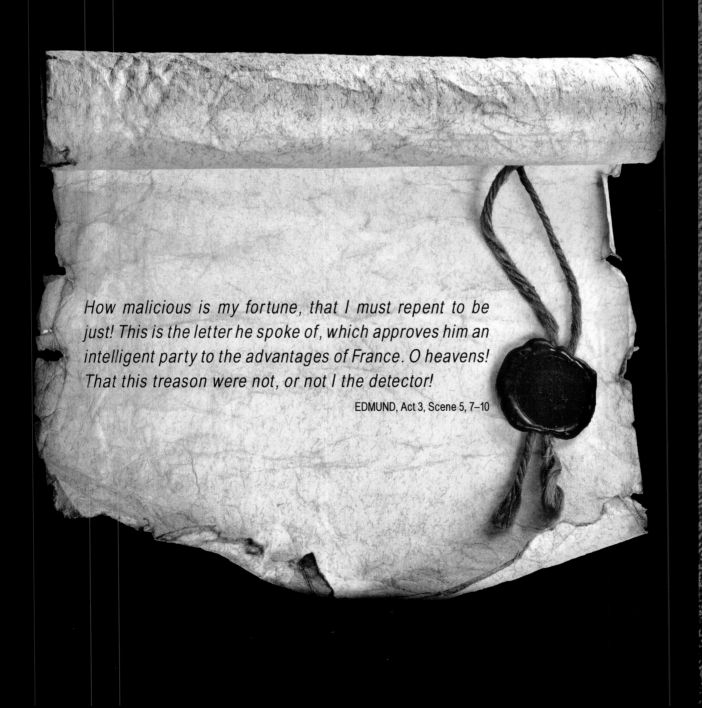

How malicious is my fortune, that I must repent to be just! This is the letter he spoke of, which approves him an intelligent party to the advantages of France. O heavens! That this treason were not, or not I the detector!

EDMUND, Act 3, Scene 5, 7–10

A room in the Earl of Gloucester's castle.

Enter CORNWALL and EDMUND.

CORNWALL

I will have my revenge ere I depart his house.

EDMUND

How, my lord, I may be censured, that nature thus gives way to loyalty, something fears me to think of.

CORNWALL

I now perceive it was not altogether your brother's evil disposition made him seek his death, but a provoking merit, set a-work by a reprovable badness in himself.

EDMUND

How malicious is my fortune, that I must repent to be just! This is the letter he spoke of, which approves him an intelligent party to the advantages of France. O heavens! That this treason were not, or not I the detector!

CORNWALL

Go with me to the duchess.

EDMUND

If the matter of this paper be certain, you have mighty business in hand.

CORNWALL

True or false, it hath made thee Earl of Gloucester. Seek out where thy father is, that he may be ready for our apprehension.

EDMUND [*aside*]

If I find him comforting the King, it will stuff his suspicion more fully. [*to CORNWALL*] I will persever in my course of loyalty, though the conflict be sore between that and my blood.

CORNWALL

I will lay trust upon thee, and thou shalt find a dearer father in my love.

Exeunt.

5

10

15

20

---

my revenge: Cornwall will take revenge on Gloucester
ere: before

How ... of: it scares me a little to think of how I will be judged ('censured') for allowing my duty to the state ('loyalty') to take precedence over my natural feelings as a son ('nature')

I ... himself: I now observe that it was not merely Edgar's wicked nature that caused him to plot to kill Gloucester; another influence was the blameworthy depravity ('reprovable badness') of Gloucester, which provoked Edgar to mete out to him the punishment he deserved

repent to be just: regret doing the right thing

approves ... France: proves that he is a French spy, or a collaborator with the French cause

That ... detector! I wish my father had not committed treason, and that I had not been the one to uncover it

matter: subject matter, contents
certain: accurate, reliable

that ... apprehension: that we will be able to arrest him without difficulty

comforting: giving help or support to
stuff ... fully: give Cornwall further reason for suspecting that Gloucester is an enemy of Britain
persever: continue, persist
my blood: my natural affection for my father

I ... love: I will give you duties to perform that will show my confidence in you; you shall find in me a loving substitute for your father

Key points

- Edmund's consummate hypocrisy is evident in his pretence that he is troubled by a conflict between his loyalty to his father and his duty to his country. This concern is just a front for Cornwall's benefit. His aside to the audience reveals Edmund's true feelings: he hopes that when he tracks down Gloucester he will find him with Lear, as that will further convince Cornwall of Gloucester's treachery.

- With such ruthless men as Edmund and Cornwall conspiring against him, it is clear that Gloucester is in deep trouble.

- Cornwall's opening words, 'I will have my revenge' (line 1), set the tone for this short scene. His main emphasis is on Gloucester's wickedness, which, to his mind, is so extreme as to provide an excuse for Edgar's alleged scheme of parricide. From his point of view, Gloucester has been disloyal and must be punished. He will then reward Edmund for his loyalty: 'it hath made thee Earl of Gloucester' (line 14).

- The main plot (Lear, Goneril, Regan, Cornwall, Albany, Cordelia) and the sub-plot (Gloucester, Edgar, Edmund) again come together in this scene when Cornwall and Edmund plan the capture of Gloucester. Family bonds mean nothing to Edmund and he is only too happy to replace his natural father with a more powerful and useful patron in Cornwall.

Useful quotes

> How malicious is my fortune, that I must repent to be just!
>
> (Edmund, lines 7–8)

> I will lay trust upon thee, and thou shalt find a dearer father in my love.
>
> (Cornwall, lines 21–2)

Questions ?

1. 'O heavens! That this treason were not, or not I the detector!' (lines 9–10). Comment on the ironies implicit in this statement.

2. When Edmund tells Cornwall of the difficulty he has in betraying his father, what impression is he trying to create?

3. Discuss the origin and significance of the letter Edmund is discussing with Cornwall.

4. Why does Edmund think that Cornwall has 'mighty business in hand' (lines 12–13)? What kind of business is he talking about?

5. What do we learn about Cornwall in this scene?

6. 'Go with me to the duchess' (line 11). Write a short sketch (twenty to thirty lines) in which Edmund and Cornwall tell Regan about Gloucester's loyalty to Lear.

ACT 3 † Scene 6

Plot summary

In a basic farmhouse on Gloucester's estate, Lear conducts a mock-trial of Goneril and Regan (in their absence). It is presided over by Lear, Edgar (as Poor Tom) and the Fool. The fact that Lear appoints an apparent lunatic and a court jester as his daughters' judges suggests that sanity and reason are not necessary parts of the judicial process. Eventually Lear gives in to the need for rest. Gloucester returns with transport to take Lear to Dover. His well-meant intervention is presented as a mixed blessing: Kent needs to get Lear to safety but Lear's greatest need at that moment is rest, which might calm his broken nerves.

Come, come away.
GLOUCESTER, Act 3, Scene 6, 98

A chamber in a farmhouse adjoining the Earl of Gloucester's castle.

Enter KENT and GLOUCESTER.

GLOUCESTER

Here is better than the open air. Take it thankfully. I will piece out the comfort with what addition I can. I will not be long from you.

KENT

All the power of his wits have given way to his impatience. The gods reward your kindness!   5

Exit GLOUCESTER.

Enter LEAR, EDGAR and FOOL.

EDGAR

Frateretto calls me, and tells me Nero is an angler in the lake of darkness. Pray, innocent, and beware the foul fiend.

FOOL

Prithee, nuncle, tell me whether a madman be a gentleman or a yeoman?   10

LEAR

A king, a king!

FOOL

No, he's a yeoman that has a gentleman to his son, for he's a mad yeoman that sees his son a gentleman before him.

LEAR

To have a thousand with red burning spits

Come hizzing in upon 'em—   15

EDGAR

The foul fiend bites my back.

FOOL

He's mad that trusts in the tameness of a wolf, a horse's health, a boy's love, or a whore's oath.

LEAR

It shall be done; I will arraign them straight.

[*to EDGAR*] Come, sit here, most learned justice.   20

[*to FOOL*] Thou, sapient sir, sit here. Now, you she-foxes!

mad (justices)

1–2 *I will . . . can:* I will do what I can to add to the amenities of the place

3 *from you:* away from you

4 *All . . . impatience:* passion has overwhelmed his reason

5 *The . . . kindness!* Gloucester's 'reward' will in fact be a cruel punishment, delivered by guests in his own house. The ironic disappointment of morally justified hopes is a feature of *King Lear*

6 *Frateretto:* the devil
Nero: Roman emperor from 54 to 68 AD, who arranged the murder of his mother (and is therefore linked with Edgar, who has been accused of plotting to kill his father) and is (incorrectly) said to have fiddled while Rome burned in a great fire
angler: can mean a fiddler or a fisherman

7 *Pray, innocent:* Edgar is addressing the Fool. Fools were called innocents

10 *yeoman:* land-owning farmer but not of high birth like a gentleman

12–13 *for he's . . . him:* only a mad yeoman would allow his son to become a gentleman before he did. The reference to Lear's own situation is clear: in a mad gesture he has allowed his daughters to become his superiors in status and power

14–15 *To . . . 'em:* this is Lear's idea of an appropriate punishment for his daughters. He imagines, with relish, a thousand tormentors, armed with burning spits, attacking them. In Lear's fantasy, his daughters are suffering the torments of hell. A spit is a slender, sharp-pointed end of metal or wood, which is thrust through meat that is to be roasted over a fire

16 *The . . . back:* Edgar imagines being bitten by a devil in the form of a louse

17 *tameness of a wolf:* the Fool is suggesting that a wolf cannot be tamed

17–18 *horse's health:* a horse is notoriously subject to disease

19 *arraign them straight:* bring them to trial immediately

20 *justice:* judge

21 *sapient:* wise
she-foxes: Goneril and Regan (in his imagination)

22 *Look ... glares:* presumably he is referring to one of the fiends that possess him
eyes: a spectator

24 *Come ... me:* this is the first line of a 'Songe between the Queen's majesty and England'

25–7 *Her ... thee!* the Fool supplies his own vulgar version of the song

28–9 *The ... nightingale:* Edgar pretends to mistake the Fool's singing for the voice of a fiend disguised as a nightingale

29–30 *Hoppedance ... thee:* Edgar pretends that an evil spirit lodged in his stomach (called Hoppedance), is calling for unsmoked herring

30 *Croak not, black angel:* the devil in his stomach ('black angel') is likened to a toad; the croaking is the rumbling of an empty stomach

32 *Stand ... amazed:* do not stand there dumbfounded

34 *the evidence:* those who are to give evidence against them

35 *robed ... justice:* Lear imagines that Edgar is the Lord Chief Justice, presiding over a court of law. Edgar's blanket suggests a judge's robe

36 *yoke-fellow of equity:* Lear thinks of the Fool as the Lord Chancellor, presiding over one of the courts of equity. 'Yoke-fellow' means 'partner' – the Fool is Edgar's judicial colleague

37 *Bench:* take your seat on the judge's bench

38 *You ... commission:* Kent is a King's Justice of the Peace under the Great Seal

41 *corn:* cornfield; if the sheep eat too much corn too quickly, they may die

42 *And ... mouth:* and for the time it takes you to play one strain on your shepherd's pipe
minikin: can mean either 'dainty' or 'shrill'

43 *take:* come to

44 *Pur ... grey:* devils were believed to assume the form of a grey cat

45 *Arraign her:* call her to answer on a criminal charge

EDGAR

Look where he stands and glares! Want'st thou eyes at trial, madam?

Come o'er the bourn, Bessy, to me—

FOOL [*sings*]

25 Her boat hath a leak,

And she must not speak

Why she dares not come over to thee!

EDGAR

The foul fiend haunts Poor Tom in the voice of a nightingale. Hoppedance cries in Tom's belly for two 30 white herring. Croak not, black angel. I have no food for thee.

KENT

[to LEAR] How do you, sir? Stand you not so amazed.
Will you lie down and rest upon the cushions?

LEAR

I'll see their trial first. Bring in the evidence.

35 [*to EDGAR*] Thou robed man of justice, take thy place.

[*to FOOL*] And thou, his yoke-fellow of equity,

Bench by his side.

[*to KENT*] You are o' the commission, sit you too.

EDGAR

Let us deal justly,

40 Sleepest or wakest thou, jolly shepherd?

Thy sheep be in the corn;

And for one blast of thy minikin mouth,

Thy sheep shall take no harm.

Pur! The cat is grey.

LEAR

45 Arraign her first. 'Tis Goneril. I here take my oath before this honourable assembly she kicked the poor King her father.

FOOL

Come hither, mistress. Is your name Goneril?

LEAR

She cannot deny it.

FOOL

Cry you mercy. I took you for a joint-stool. 50

LEAR

And here's another, whose warped looks proclaim

What store her heart is made on. Stop her there!

Arms, arms, sword, fire! Corruption in the place!

False justicer, why hast thou let her 'scape?

EDGAR

Bless thy five wits! 55

KENT

[to LEAR] O pity! Sir, where is the patience now

That thou so oft have boasted to retain?

EDGAR [aside]

My tears begin to take his part so much

They mar my counterfeiting.

LEAR

The little dogs and all — Tray, Blanch and Sweetheart — 60

see, they bark at me.

EDGAR

Tom will throw his head at them. Avaunt, you curs.

Be thy mouth of black or white,

Tooth that poisons if it bite,

Mastiff, greyhound, mongrel grim, 65

Hound or spaniel, brach or lym;

Or bobtail tike or trundle-tail;

Tom will make them weep and wail:

For, with throwing thus my head,

Dogs leapt the hatch, and all are fled. 70

Do de, de, de. Sese! Come, march to wakes and fairs and

market towns. Poor Tom, thy horn is dry.

LEAR

Then let them anatomise Regan, see what breeds about her heart. Is there any cause in nature that make these hard-hearts? [to EDGAR] You, sir, I entertain for one 75 of my hundred, only I do not like the fashion of your garments. You will say they are Persian, but let them be changed.

---

50 *Cry you mercy:* I beg your pardon
took ... joint-stool: deliberately offensive 'apology' for overlooking or ignoring somebody

51 *another:* Regan
warped looks: unnatural, twisted features

52 *store:* material
Stop her there: Lear imagines that Regan is trying to escape

53–4 *Corruption ... 'scape:* Lear is accusing a corrupt judge ('false justicer') of allowing Regan to escape

55 *five wits:* these were: common wit, imagination, fantasy, estimation and memory

58–9 *My ... counterfeiting:* I am so overcome with grief at Lear's plight that my tears are ruining my performance as a madman (or judge)

60–1 *The ... me:* this is Lear's pathetic image of his much-reduced state: he is now so despised that his own small dogs feel free to bark at him with impunity – or so he imagines. The names of the three dogs in Lear's hallucination carry subtle allusions to his experience of his daughters. 'Tray' suggests 'betray'; 'Blanch' suggests 'turn pale, with horror'; while 'Sweetheart' evokes Cordelia, the first syllable of whose name is the same as the Latin word for 'heart'

62 *Tom ... curs:* I will frighten them off with a jerk of my head. Be off ('avaunt'), you watchdogs

63–70 *Be ... fled:* Edgar addresses an imaginary collection of dogs, telling them that no matter what kind they are, he will banish them

64 *Tooth ... bite:* the reference is to a rabid dog

66 *brach:* bitch-hound
lym: bloodhound

67 *bobtail tike:* a watchdog with its tail cut short
trundle-tail: a dog whose drooping tail drags heavily behind it

69 *with ... head:* he jerks his head menacingly

70 *leapt the hatch:* jumped over the lower half of a dividing door (i.e. retreated hastily)

71 *Do de, de, de:* Edgar's teeth are again chattering
Sese! cease, be quiet
wakes: annual parish festival with sports and merrymaking, where a beggar might do well

72 *horn is dry:* Bedlam beggars wore an ox-horn around their necks into which they put whatever they got to drink. Edgar may also be suggesting that he is unable to play the part of Poor Tom any longer

73–4 *Then ... heart:* Lear is saying: if the beggar's horn is dry (and hard) let an anatomical dissection of Regan reveal the nature of her heart. Is it as dry as the horn? As hard? As inhuman? As bloodless?

75–8 *You ... changed:* Lear offers to engage ('entertain') Poor Tom as one of his hundred knights. But Tom must find more suitable garments, since he is wearing only a blanket, which now suggests Persian attire to Lear

80 *draw the curtains:* Lear thinks that he is in a richly appointed bed, with a servant to draw the bed-curtains

81 *We'll ... morning:* there is no food (as Gloucester has not yet returned), so Lear must sleep first and have his supper when he wakes

82 *And ... noon:* bed at noon follows supper in the morning because sleep is natural after an evening meal. Since these are the last words spoken by the Fool, some commentators have suggested that the line foretells the Fool's premature death ('bed' can mean 'grave')

87 *litter:* a vehicle containing a couch shut in by curtains, and here drawn by animals to judge from 'drive toward Dover' (line 88)

92 *Stand ... loss:* are certain to be lost
Take up, take up: this is Gloucester's urgent order to Kent to take Lear in his arms and carry him

93–4 *that ... conduct:* who will lead you quickly to where supplies may be found

94 *Oppressed nature sleeps:* Lear, his physical and mental functions having been overcome ('oppressed') by intolerable strain, has taken refuge in sleep

95–7 *This ... cure:* this sleep might have soothed your shattered nerves; such a cure will hardly be possible if favourable circumstances do not arise to bring it about

99–112 *When ... lurk!* when we see people of higher standing than ourselves suffering the same calamities as we do, we hardly think of our sufferings as ours at all, but associate them with our superiors. The severest burden carried by those who suffer on their own is a mental one; such people leave behind them carefree ('free') experiences and happy sights ('shows'). →

KENT
Now, good my lord, lie here and rest awhile.

LEAR
80 Make no noise, make no noise; draw the curtains, so, so.
We'll go to supper i' the morning.

FOOL
And I'll go to bed at noon.

Enter GLOUCESTER.

GLOUCESTER
Come hither, friend: where is the King my master?

KENT
Here, sir; but trouble him not; his wits are gone.

GLOUCESTER
85 Good friend, I prithee take him in thy arms;
I have o'er-heard a plot of death upon him.
There is a litter ready; lay him in't,
And drive toward Dover, friend, where thou shalt meet
Both welcome and protection. Take up thy master,
90 If thou shouldst dally half an hour, his life,
With thine and all that offer to defend him,
Stand in assured loss. Take up, take up,
And follow me, that will to some provision
Give thee quick conduct.

KENT
Oppressed nature sleeps.
95 This rest might yet have balmed thy broken sinews
Which, if convenience will not allow
Stand in hard cure. [*to FOOL*] Come, help to bear thy master;
Thou must not stay behind.

GLOUCESTER
Come, come away.

Exeunt all but EDGAR.

EDGAR
When we our betters see bearing our woes,
100 We scarcely think our miseries our foes,
Who alone suffers, suffers most i' the mind,
Leaving free things and happy shows behind;
But then the mind much sufferance doth o'er-skip,

When grief hath mates, and bearing fellowship.

How light and portable my pain seems now,   105

When that which makes me bend, makes the King bow.

He childed as I fathered. Tom, away!

Mark the high noises, and thyself bewray

When false opinion, whose wrong thoughts defile thee,

In thy just proof repeals and reconciles thee.   110

What will hap more tonight, safe 'scape the King!

Lurk, lurk!

Exit.

But much of this suffering ('sufferance', 'bearing') is avoided by those who experience companionship. My burden of grief now seems light and endurable ('portable') when I see the King bowed to the ground by heavier woes than mine. His children seek to destroy him, just as my father seeks to destroy me. Go on your way, Tom. Take note of the rumours of conflict among those in power ('high noises'). Reveal ('bewray') yourself as Edgar when the false rumours that make you appear morally tainted are dispelled, and when your innocence is established, thus recalling you from your predicament as an outlaw and restoring you to friendship with your father. Whatever else happens tonight, may Lear come safely through! Hide!

Key points

This scene centres on a fantasy court trial. Chaos prevails; a chaos that undermines the social, moral, psychological and judicial worlds. This episode is farcical, but its point is to expose the entire system of justice as a farce.

- The Fool continues to offer words of wisdom, even though Lear's 'wits have given way to his impatience' (line 4). Lear is still obsessed with his own situation and does not listen to what the Fool is trying to tell him.

- Lear has decided that he will avenge himself on his wicked daughters by making them defendants in a fantasy trial. Although this trial is a ludicrous parody of normal court proceedings, it sets out to demonstrate that the administration of justice is a mere mockery, lacking any moral basis, a charade. For example, the sentence passed upon Goneril and Regan, and devised by Lear, their accuser ('To have a thousand with red burning spits come hizzing in upon 'em'; lines 14–15) precedes, rather than concludes, their trial.

- The mock-trial consists of a few charges brought by Lear: that Goneril 'kicked the poor King her father' (lines 46–7) and that Regan has 'warped looks' (line 51) and a hard heart.

- Although Lear uses proper judicial language in choosing the members of his court, he appoints a lunatic and a jester to judge his daughters.

- Edgar, wearing his blanket, is the Lord Chief Justice; the Fool is the Lord Chancellor; they are joined on the bench by Kent as the King's Justice of the Peace. As it happens, these three characters are among the most honest in the play. The distinction between sanity and insanity has clearly been abolished.

- There are blatant moments of farce in this scene. For example, the Fool calls on Goneril to come forward. Looking at a stage-property (prop) representing Goneril, he then exclaims, 'Cry you mercy. I took you for a joint-stool' (line 50). He is saying to Lear: where you see Goneril, I can see only a stool. However, he may also be suggesting, ironically, that Goneril is more like a judge (on a joint-stool or bench) than a prisoner, since she, not Lear, exercises power.

- Similarly, the fantasy Regan 'escapes', or attempts to, causing Lear to accuse a corrupt judge of facilitating her escape.

- The mock-trial, for all its apparent insane defiance of logic and reason, nevertheless has an important thematic function. It suggests that human systems of justice are an absurd pretence. Lear's comment on 'Corruption in the place' (line 53) refers to a judicial system in which judges are inherently corrupt and which does not produce fair outcomes.

- Lear's mock-trial of his wicked daughters is not part of the revised version of the play found in the First Folio.

- Lear soon lapses into a different kind of fantasy: Edgar's blanket, which had reminded Lear of a judge's robe, now looks to him like a Persian costume, which he does not like. He offers to make Edgar one of his hundred knights if he changes into a more suitable garment. Lear falls asleep, and the fantasy ends.

- In Act 3, Scene 4 Edgar, posing as a Bedlam beggar, unhinged Lear's mind; in this scene it is Edgar's father who unwittingly interrupts Lear's recovery from madness. The sudden, but urgent, journey to Dover that Gloucester has arranged may disturb Lear's rest and so prevent his recovery.

Useful quotes

Arraign her first. 'Tis Goneril. I here take my oath before this honourable assembly she kicked the poor King her father.

(Lear, lines 45–7)

My tears begin to take his part so much They mar my counterfeiting.

(Edgar, lines 58–9)

And here's another, whose warped looks proclaim What store her heart is made on.

(Lear, lines 51–2)

How light and portable my pain seems now, When that which makes me bend makes the King bow. He childed as I fathered.

(Edgar, lines 105–7)

? Questions

1 Discuss the comic elements in this scene.

2 Examine the attitude of each of the other characters in this scene to Lear.

3 This scene depicts a world in chaos. What are the factors contributing to this?

4 Why, do you think, is Lear so concerned with justice?

5 Does Lear's behaviour in this scene suggest to you that he is seeking justice or simply looking for revenge? Give reasons for your answer.

6 Has Lear totally lost touch with reality in this scene? Support your answer with evidence from the text of the play.

7 Is there any significance in the fact that in the mock-trial episode Lear appoints the three most honest men in the play to be his judges? Explain your answer.

8 Imagine you are either Edgar or Kent. Compose a diary entry giving your thoughts on Lear's health and on the mock-trial he conducts in this scene.

Plot summary

Cornwall instructs Goneril to return home to inform Albany of the threat from France. Edmund is sent with her so that he will not be a party to Gloucester's punishment. The captured Gloucester is bound and questioned. He faces his ordeal with courage and dignity. Cornwall plucks out one of Gloucester's eyes. When he goes to remove the second eye, one of his servants intervenes and a swordfight ensues. The servant inflicts a mortal wound on Cornwall before Regan intervenes to kill him. Cornwall plucks out Gloucester's remaining eye. Regan adds to Gloucester's agony by revealing that Edmund betrayed him. She then instructs the servants to throw him out of the castle. The servants agree that Gloucester should not be left to fend for himself and decide to make sure he is looked after.

Lest it see more, prevent it. Out, vile jelly!

CORNWALL, Act 3, Scene 7, 82

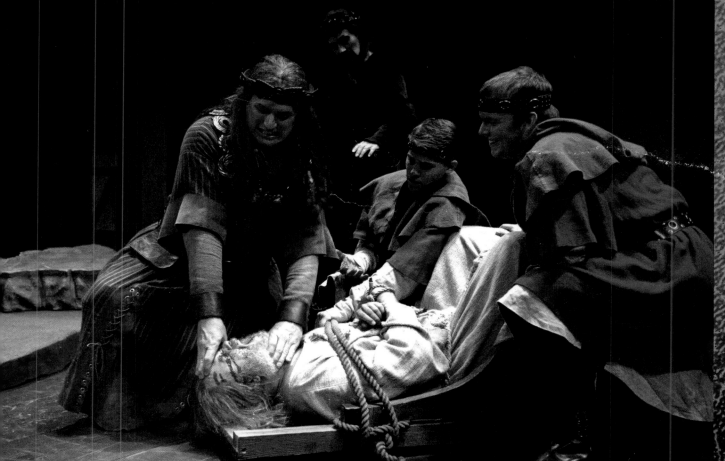

A room in the Earl of Gloucester's castle.

Enter CORNWALL, REGAN, GONERIL, EDMUND, and SERVANTS.

CORNWALL

[*to GONERIL*] Post speedily to my lord your husband; show him this letter. The army of France is landed. [*to SERVANTS*] Seek out the traitor Gloucester.

Exeunt some SERVANTS.

REGAN

Hang him instantly.

GONERIL

5   Pluck out his eyes.

CORNWALL

Leave him to my displeasure. Edmund, keep you our sister company. The revenges we are bound to take upon your traitorous father are not fit for your beholding. Advise the duke, where you are going, to a most festinate

10   preparation; we are bound to the like. Our posts shall be swift and intelligent betwixt us. Farewell, dear sister; farewell, my lord of Gloucester.

Enter OSWALD.

How now! Where's the King?

OSWALD

My lord of Gloucester hath conveyed him hence.

15   Some five — or six — and thirty of his knights,

Hot questrists after him, met him at gate,

Who, with some other of the lord's dependants,

Are gone with him toward Dover; where they boast

To have well-armed friends.

CORNWALL

                        Get horses for your mistress.

GONERIL

20   Farewell, sweet lord, and sister.

CORNWALL

Edmund, farewell.

Exeunt GONERIL, EDMUND and OSWALD.

                   Go seek the traitor Gloucester;

Pinion him like a thief; bring him before us.

Exeunt remaining SERVANTS.

---

1 *Post:* ride

7–8 *The . . . beholding:* this is a fine ironic touch as Edmund is quite capable of witnessing the horrors Cornwall is contemplating

9 *duke . . . going:* the duke [Albany], to whom you are going
most festinate: quick and urgent

10 *bound . . . like:* ready to do the same (prepare for war)
posts: messengers on horseback

11 *intelligent betwixt:* give information between
sister: sister-in-law (Goneril)

12 *lord of Gloucester:* Edmund has now been given his father's title, even though the latter is alive and active (and is still referred to as Gloucester for the rest of the play; see, for example, line 14)

14 *conveyed him hence:* taken him away from here

16 *Hot . . . gate:* enthusiastic in their quest for him, met Lear at the entrance to Gloucester's castle

17 *the lord's:* Gloucester's

19 *your mistress:* Goneril

22 *Pinion:* bind

Though well we may not pass upon his life
Without some form of justice, yet our power
Shall do a court'sy to our wrath, which men 25
May blame but not control. Who's there? The traitor?

Enter GLOUCESTER, brought in by two or three SERVANTS.

REGAN
Ingrateful fox, 'tis he!

CORNWALL
Bind fast his corky arms.

GLOUCESTER
What means your grace? Good my friends, consider
You are my guests. Do me no foul play, friends. 30

CORNWALL
Bind him, I say.

SERVANTS bind him.

REGAN
                    Hard, hard. O filthy traitor!

GLOUCESTER
Unmerciful lady as you are, I'm none.

CORNWALL
To this chair bind him. Villain, thou shalt find—

REGAN plucks GLOUCESTER's beard.

GLOUCESTER
By the kind gods, 'tis most ignobly done
To pluck me by the beard. 35

REGAN
So white, and such a traitor!

GLOUCESTER
                    Naughty lady,
These hairs, which thou dost ravish from my chin,
Will quicken, and accuse thee. I am your host:
With robbers' hands my hospitable favours
You should not ruffle thus. What will you do? 40

CORNWALL
Come, sir, what letters had you late from France?

REGAN
Be simple-answered, for we know the truth.

23–6 *Though . . . control:* although we cannot pass a judicial sentence of death on him without a formal trial, we will not allow our legal authority ('power') to interfere with the punishment our anger will make us inflict on him. Although we may be censured for what we do in anger, nobody can restrain us

25 *do a court'sy:* obey, give way to, gratify

27 *Ingrateful fox:* Gloucester has proved ungrateful by being disloyal to his patron, Cornwall; and fox-like in his secret assistance to Lear

28 *corky:* withered, dry (because Gloucester is old)

31 *Hard, hard:* bind him tightly

32 *none:* no traitor

34 *ignobly:* shamefully, dishonourably

[handwritten: unjust / unnatural.]

36 *Naughty:* wicked

37 *ravish:* snatch, tear

38 *quicken:* come to life

39–40 *my hospitable . . . thus:* you should not treat the facial features ('favours') of your host in such a violent fashion. The gesture of yanking at a beard was grossly offensive in Shakespeare's day

39 *hospitable:* belonging to the host

41 *late:* lately

42 *Be simple-answered:* give a straight answer

43–4 *And ... kingdom?* And what conspiracy ('confederacy') are you engaged in with the traitors who have recently landed in Britain?

46 *guessingly set down:* written without certain knowledge

48 *opposed:* opposed to Cornwall

50 *at peril:* on peril of your life

52 *I am ... course:* I am like a bear being attacked by dogs at a bear-baiting, and I must endure my suffering until the cruel attack is ended
course: one of a succession of attacks by dogs on a bear, in bear-baiting

55 *anointed:* holy. The English monarch is anointed with holy oil during the coronation ceremony. Shakespeare is here thinking of Lear as a Christian king, and ignoring the pagan setting of the play
58 *Would ... fires:* would have risen, like a buoy, high enough to quench the light of the stars
59 *holp:* helped
60 *stern:* grim, dismal
61–2 *Thou ... subscribe:* you would have told the porter to turn the key and let the wolves in. All other cruel creatures ('cruels') give way ('subscribe') to pity in cases of extreme distress such as Lear's; you alone remain pitiless

---

CORNWALL
And what confederacy have you with the traitors
Late footed in the kingdom?

REGAN
            To whose hands
45 You have sent the lunatic King; speak!

GLOUCESTER
I have a letter guessingly set down,
Which came from one that's of a neutral heart,
And not from one opposed.

CORNWALL
            Cunning.

REGAN
               And false.

CORNWALL
Where hast thou sent the King?

GLOUCESTER
          To Dover.

REGAN
50 Wherefore to Dover? Wast thou not charged at peril—

CORNWALL
Wherefore to Dover? Let him answer that.

GLOUCESTER
I am tied to the stake, and I must stand the course.

REGAN
Wherefore to Dover?

bravery
GLOUCESTER
          Because I would not see
Thy cruel nails pluck out his poor old eyes;
55 Nor thy fierce sister in his anointed flesh
Stick boarish fangs. The sea, with such a storm
As his bare head in hell-black night endured,
Would have buoyed up, and quenched the stelled fires;
Yet, poor old heart, he holp the heavens to rain.
60 If wolves had at thy gate howled that stern time,
Thou shouldst have said, 'Good porter, turn the key',
All cruels else subscribe; but I shall see
The winged vengeance overtake such children.

CORNWALL

See't shalt thou never — fellows, hold the chair —

Upon these eyes of thine I'll set my foot. 65

GLOUCESTER

He that will think to live till he be old,

Give me some help! — O cruel! O you gods!

CORNWALL removes one of GLOUCESTER's eyes.

REGAN

One side will mock another. Th' other too!

CORNWALL

If you see vengeance—

FIRST SERVANT

　　　　　　　　Hold your hand, my lord!

I have served you ever since I was a child, 70

But better service have I never done you

Than now to bid you hold.

REGAN

　　　　　　　How now, you dog!

FIRST SERVANT

If you did wear a beard upon your chin

I'd shake it on this quarrel.

CORNWALL draws his sword.

What do you mean? 75

CORNWALL

My villain!

FIRST SERVANT *brave*

[*drawing his weapon*] Nay then, come on, and take the

chance of anger.

He wounds CORNWALL.

REGAN

Give me thy sword. A peasant stand up thus!

She takes a sword and strikes him.

FIRST SERVANT

Oh, I am slain. My lord, you have one eye left 80

To see some mischief on him. Oh! [*he dies*]

CORNWALL *cruelty. (enjoys)*

Lest it see more, prevent it. Out, vile jelly!

CORNWALL removes GLOUCESTER's other eye.

lack of justice

Where is thy lustre now?

68　*One . . . another:* the side of Gloucester's face with an eye will make the other side, which lacks one, appear ridiculous

69　*vengeance:* before his servant interrupts him, Cornwall is about to comment on the hope expressed by Gloucester at lines 62–3

69　*Hold:* stop

73–4　*If . . . quarrel:* if Regan had a beard, the servant would pull it, just as Regan earlier pulled Gloucester's beard. This could also mean that the servant does not want to fight with Regan because she is a woman

75　*mean:* intend to do

76　*My villain!* Cornwall is astonished that his own servant, a menial employee, should thus challenge him

77–8　*take . . . anger:* this means either: take the risk of fighting with an angry opponent; or: take the risk of a combat in which the outcome will be decided by anger, rather than swordsmanship (in which case, the servant's chances might be as good as Cornwall's)

79　*Give . . . sword:* Regan may be addressing the wounded Cornwall, or a loyal servant
A . . . thus! Regan is echoing Cornwall's astonishment that a servant should stand up to his master

81　*mischief on him:* harm done to him

82　*Lest . . . prevent it:* in case the remaining eye should see 'some mischief' done to me, I shall knock that eye out

83　*lustre:* brightness

85 *nature:* filial love

86 *quit:* avenge

88 *overture:* disclosure, discovery

93 *How look you?* How do you feel?

94 *hurt:* wound, injury

95 *Turn ... villain:* Cornwall's wound is giving him such trouble that he does not notice that Gloucester has already gone
this slave: the First Servant

96 *apace:* profusely

97 *Untimely:* at a bad time

99 *If ... good:* if Cornwall thrives and escapes divine vengeance

99 *she:* Regan

100 *And ... death:* and dies a natural death
old: customary

102–6 *Let's ... him!* there is a contradiction between these Quarto lines and the opening lines of the next act, where Gloucester is led by an old man, and apparently meets Edgar by accident

103–4 *His ... anything:* being a mad beggar, he can be persuaded to do anything he is asked

---

GLOUCESTER

All dark and comfortless. Where's my son Edmund?

85 Edmund, enkindle all the sparks of nature

To quit this horrid act.

REGAN

Out, treacherous villain!

Thou call'st on him that hates thee. It was he

That made the overture of thy treasons to us,

Who is too good to pity thee.

GLOUCESTER *dramatic metaphor — now he sees the truth.*

90 O my follies! Then Edgar was abused.

Kind gods, forgive me that, and prosper him!

REGAN *cruel.*

Go thrust him out at gates, and let him smell

His way to Dover.

GLOUCESTER is led out.

How is't, my lord? How look you?

CORNWALL

I have received a hurt. Follow me, lady.

95 Turn out that eyeless villain. Throw this slave

Upon the dunghill. Regan, I bleed apace.

Untimely comes this hurt. Give me your arm.

Exit CORNWALL, supported by REGAN.

SECOND SERVANT

I'll never care what wickedness I do,

If this man come to good.

THIRD SERVANT

If she live long,

100 And in the end meet the old course of death,

Women will all turn monsters.

SECOND SERVANT

Let's follow the old earl, and get the bedlam

To lead him where he would. His roguish madness

Allows itself to anything.

THIRD SERVANT

105 Go thou. I'll fetch some flax and whites of eggs

To apply to his bleeding face. Now, heaven help him!

Exeunt severally.

Key points

An important function of this scene is to show the depth of cruelty and inhumanity of which human beings are capable.

- Lear has suffered severely in mind and his dignity and self-esteem have been savagely undermined. It is now Gloucester's turn to undergo parallel suffering, the nature of which is physical. This difference may be because Lear's initial fault was an error of moral judgement, for which the appropriate punishment is psychological, whereas Gloucester's lapse was sensual (in fathering Edmund) and his punishment is directed at one of his senses: his sight.

- The theme of justice is again brought into focus in this scene. Cornwall debates the fate of Gloucester, deciding that he cannot pass a death sentence on him without a formal trial. This rules out Regan's advice to 'Hang him instantly' (line 4), but not Goneril's 'Pluck out his eyes' (line 5). However, Cornwall and Regan will not allow their legal authority to interfere with whatever punishment their anger wants to inflict. In any case, nobody can hold them to account. Cornwall's idea of justice, therefore, is that punishment is to be inflicted at the whim of those holding power.

- In Shakespeare's day the presence of women was expected to reduce the level of brutality. It is significant that here it is the female characters who are most dedicated to violence and cruelty. Even the intense physical suffering inflicted on Gloucester does not satisfy Regan's appetite for revenge. She also torments him with the revelation that it was Edmund who betrayed him.

- The 'trial' of Gloucester is a perversion of justice. But at the darkest moment of the play, Shakespeare introduces an episode that does something to redeem human nature. The intervention of Cornwall's servant on Gloucester's behalf is an instinctively humane act and parallels Gloucester's earlier decision to help Lear. A further token of decent humanity is provided by the other servants who come to Gloucester's assistance after he is blinded.

- At first, the contest between the good and evil characters appears heavily weighted in favour of the latter, who have all the power. However, the exercise of an extreme act of cruelty by Cornwall, Goneril and Regan has its price, provoking a servant into a fatal assault on Cornwall. The servant's self-sacrifice marks the first major defeat for the evil characters and plays a vital role in the evolution of the plot. Cornwall's death will open the way for a love triangle to develop between the widow Regan, Goneril and Edmund. The lust of the two sisters for Edmund will ultimately result in the deaths of all three.

- At the end of the previous scene Edgar made two observations of relevance to this scene. First, he said that mental torture is worse than physical torture: 'Who alone suffers, suffers most i' the mind' (line 101); however, the sheer physical horror of the blinding of Gloucester challenges that assertion. As far as the audience is concerned, watching this beastliness enacted on stage is bound to have a more profound effect than the mental suffering Edgar talks about. Second, Edgar's observation that he will reveal himself when the false rumours of his guilt have been dispelled (lines 108–10) finds its echo in this scene when Edmund's treachery is revealed by Regan, and Gloucester acknowledges Edgar's innocence.

Useful quotes

> *Edmund, keep you our sister company. The revenges we are bound to take upon your traitorous father are not fit for your beholding.*
>
> (Cornwall, lines 6–8)

> *I am tied to the stake, and I must stand the course.*
>
> (Gloucester, line 52)

> *Lest it see more, prevent it. Out, vile jelly! Where is thy lustre now?*
>
> (Cornwall, lines 82–3)

> *Thou call'st on him that hates thee. It was he That made the overture of thy treasons to us, Who is too good to pity thee.*
>
> (Regan, lines 87–9)

> *Go thrust him out at gates, and let him smell His way to Dover.*
>
> (Regan, lines 92–3)

> *If she live long, And in the end meet the old course of death, Women will all turn monsters.*
>
> (Third Servant, lines 99–101)

? Questions

1 Shakespeare excludes Edmund from being present at the murder of his father. Suggest possible reasons for this.

2 Why are Goneril, Regan and Cornwall so angry with Gloucester?

3 What attitudes to law and justice are displayed in this scene? Compare Lear's mock-trial in the previous scene with this scene's trial of Gloucester.

4 What impressions of human nature are conveyed in this scene? Refer to the text of the play in your answer.

5 Comment on the irony of Gloucester's 'Because I would not see thy cruel nails pluck out his poor old eyes' (lines 53–4). Identify two other examples of irony in this scene and explain where the irony resides in each case.

6 Trace the role that Regan plays in this scene. What more do we learn about her character?

7 How does Gloucester face his accusers and his punishment? Is he a different person from the man we met in the first Act of the play?

8 Is it significant that Cornwall is killed by his servant? Give reasons for your answer.

9 At the end of this scene, do you think a playgoer has reason to expect that things are about to get better for the 'good' characters, or that they are about to get worse? Give reasons for your answer. Assume that the playgoer in question is not familiar with the plot of *King Lear*.

10 Imagine you are the props manager for a production of *King Lear*. Make a list of the items needed for this scene.

ACT 3 🗡 Key moments

Scene 1

- We learn from Kent that French agents have established themselves in Britain as a prelude to an invasion in support of Lear.
- We also learn of a conflict between Albany and Cornwall, and that servants of both dukes are helping the French with information.
- The terrors of the storm to which Lear is exposed on the heath are graphically described.

Scene 2

- Lear acts out the storm in a number of powerfully descriptive passages, seeing its cruelties as an extension of those inflicted on him by his daughters.
- Kent and the Fool are not impressed by Lear's pleas for universal destruction: they urge him to go back to his daughters to seek shelter.

Scene 3

- Gloucester confirms Kent's news of a division between Albany and Cornwall.
- Gloucester tells Edmund of his intention to take Lear's side against his enemies, and to relieve him of his distress.
- Edmund decides to betray his father to Cornwall, with a view to acquiring Gloucester's title and assets.

Scene 4

- Lear reveals that what he suffers in the storm distracts him from the ingratitude of his daughters.
- Lear persists in thinking that all the troubles endured by men must be caused by their ungrateful daughters. He extends this belief to Edgar, who is disguised as Poor Tom.
- Lear has lost touch with external reality, thinking Edgar/Poor Tom is a philosopher who can tell him the cause of thunder.
- Gloucester says that the grief he is enduring as a result of Edgar's supposed crime has almost driven him mad.

Scene 5

- Edmund has betrayed Gloucester to Cornwall, but pretends to the latter that this betrayal is causing him distress.
- Cornwall makes Edmund the Earl of Gloucester in his father's place, and promises to treat him as a son.

ACT 3 ⚔ Key moments

Scene 6

- Lear, playing the part of King, conducts a mock-trial of Goneril and Regan in their absence. The trial is presided over by the Fool and Edgar/Poor Tom. Its purpose is to show the absurdity of real-life systems of justice.

- This scene marks the final appearance of the Fool.

- Gloucester intervenes on Lear's behalf, telling Kent to take him to Dover before his enemies can catch and kill him.

Scene 7

- Cornwall sends Edmund away to prevent him from witnessing the punishments Regan and he will inflict on Gloucester.

- Gloucester admits that he sent Lear to Dover to save him from further torture at the hands of Regan.

- Cornwall blinds Gloucester, but in the process is fatally wounded by one of his own servants.

- Regan derives a cruel pleasure from informing Gloucester that he has been betrayed by Edmund.

- Gloucester acknowledges the innocence of Edgar.

ACT 4 † Scene 1

Edgar's opening soliloquy is optimistic, almost buoyant, in tone. He suggests that once people reach the lowest depths of misery, matters can only improve. His moralising about the power of good to overcome evil is horribly shattered by the arrival of the blinded Gloucester. Edgar overhears his father tell the Old Man leading him that he was wrong about Edgar and longs for his presence. When they meet, the disguised Edgar does not reveal his true identity and must endure the painful ordeal of withholding comfort and recognition from a father who desperately needs both. Gloucester's initial response to his experiences is to desire a speedy death by suicide. He asks Edgar to lead him to the cliffs at Dover.

O gods! Who is't can say 'I am at the worst'?
I am worse than e'er I was.

EDGAR, Act 4, Scene 1, 25–6

→ *It is better to know people don't like you then for them to talk about you* behind your back

1–4 *Yet ... fear:* it is better to be a Bedlam beggar, and openly despised, than to be flattered as a lord and at the same time ('still') secretly despised. The man who is utterly cast down by fortune is able to enjoy a permanent state of hopefulness, and nothing worse can happen to him

4 *still in esperance:* always in hope

5–6 *The ... laughter:* those at the peak of good fortune are at risk of a painful change in their circumstances, whereas those who have reached the lowest depths can expect only an improvement in their fortunes

6–9 *Welcome ... blasts:* Edgar, wearing only a blanket, cheerfully accepts the company of the open air, which has nothing of value or substance to give him. It has done nothing for Edgar other than assist his journey into misery; he therefore owes nothing to it and can embrace it without fear of obligation

10 *poorly led:* led by a poor man

11 *mutations:* changes (from prosperity to misery)

12 *Life ... age:* we would resist the effects and consequences of age and go on living

14 *fourscore:* eighty

16 *comforts:* attempts to help me

18 *I have ... eyes:* Gloucester is contemplating suicide. His road through life (his 'way') is at an end, therefore he has no need of his eyesight

20–1 *Our means ... commodities:* our material resources ('means') give us blind and false confidence in our own security, whereas deprivation and adversity prove advantageous

20 *our mere defects:* our very lack of resources

22 *The ... wrath:* Gloucester used Edgar to nourish or feed his anger ('wrath') when he was deceived ('abused') by Edmund

23–4 *Might ... again!* Gloucester's only hope of 'seeing' Edgar again is to touch him; if only he could do that he would be as happy as if his sight were restored

The heath.

Enter EDGAR.

EDGAR
Yet better thus, and known to be contemn'd,
Than still contemn'd and flattered. To be worst,
The lowest and most dejected thing of fortune,
Stands still in esperance, lives not in fear.
5   The lamentable change is from the best:
The worst returns to laughter. Welcome, then,
Thou unsubstantial air that I embrace.
The wretch that thou hast blown unto the worst
Owes nothing to thy blasts.
Enter GLOUCESTER, led by an OLD MAN.
                          But who comes here?
10   My father, poorly led! World, world, O world!
But that thy strange mutations make us hate thee,
Life would not yield to age.

OLD MAN
                          O my good lord:
I have been your tenant, and your father's tenant,
These fourscore years.

GLOUCESTER
15   Away, get thee away! Good friend, be gone.
Thy comforts can do me no good at all;
Thee they may hurt.

OLD MAN
                          You cannot see your way.

GLOUCESTER
I have no way, and therefore want no eyes;
I stumbled when I saw. Full oft 'tis seen,
20   Our means secure us, and our mere defects
Prove our commodities. O dear son Edgar,
The food of thy abused father's wrath —
Might I but live to see thee in my touch,
I'd say I had eyes again!

OLD MAN
                          How now! Who's there?

EDGAR [*aside*]

O gods! Who is't can say 'I am at the worst'?　　　25

I am worse than e'er I was.

contradiction

OLD MAN

　　　　　　　'Tis poor mad Tom.

EDGAR [*aside*]

And worse I may be yet; the worst is not

So long as we can say 'This is the worst'.

OLD MAN

Fellow, where goest?

GLOUCESTER

　　　　　　　Is it a beggar-man?

OLD MAN

Madman and beggar too.　　　　　　　　　　30

GLOUCESTER

He has some reason, else he could not beg.

I' the last night's storm I such a fellow saw,

Which made me think a man a worm. My son

Came then into my mind, and yet my mind

Was then scarce friends with him. I have heard more since.　35

bold

As flies to wanton boys are we to the gods.

They kill us for their sport.

irony
(it was his son)

— *unlucky people*

EDGAR [*aside*] *— being messed with.*

　　　　　　　How should this be?

Bad is the trade that must play fool to sorrow,

Ang'ring itself and others. [*aloud*] Bless thee, master!

GLOUCESTER

Is that the naked fellow?

OLD MAN

　　　　　　　Ay, my lord.　　　　　　　　40

GLOUCESTER

Get thee away. If, for my sake,

Thou wilt o'er-take us, hence a mile or twain,

I' the way toward Dover, do it for ancient love;

And bring some covering for this naked soul,

Which I'll entreat to lead me.

25–6　*O ... was:* Edgar realises that the optimism of his opening speech in this scene was foolish: he has reached new depths of misery on hearing his father's heartbreaking words

27–8　*And ... worst:* bad as Edgar's situation now is, it may get even worse. We are not at the lowest point in our misery ('the worst') as long as we can console ourselves by saying that we are, because such false consolation tends to be followed, as Edgar has just learned, by a descent into deeper levels of misery

31　*reason:* intelligence
　　else: otherwise

35　*scarce:* hardly

36–7　*As ... sport:* this bleak view of divine justice and mercy, with its image of the gods recklessly amusing themselves as they inflict misery and death on mankind, must be considered in context: Gloucester is speaking out of the depths of his own despair and heartbreak
36　*wanton:* skittishly playful
37　*How ... be?* Edgar may be wondering how his father can have altered so much, or can forgive him, or can be so pessimistic
38–9　*Bad ... others:* it is a bad course of action to pretend to be merry ('play fool') in the presence of such sorrow as my father's; this can only cause grief and distress to myself, and to him. Edgar is now to Gloucester as the Fool is to Lear

42–3　*hence ... Dover:* a mile or two from here on the road to Dover
43　*for ancient love:* for the sake of the love you have long shown to my family and myself
44　*And ... soul:* Gloucester's consideration for Tom mirrors Lear's kindness towards the Fool in Act 3
45　*Which ... me:* whom I'll beg to guide me

walk around the world with senseless direction

46 *'Tis ... blind:* the 'mad' Edgar is to lead the blind Gloucester, who, based on his own predicament, suggests it is a suitable image of the state of things in the world in general

47 *Do as ... pleasure:* Gloucester modifies a command to a request, asking the Old Man to do what he thinks best

48 *Above the rest:* above all

49 *'parel:* apparel, clothing

50 *Come ... will:* no matter what happens as a result

51 *I ... further:* I cannot continue to put on a false show (i.e. pretend to be Poor Tom)
daub: pretend, fake

53 *And yet I must:* and still I must persist in trying. It is part of Edgar's elaborate plan to save Gloucester from despair
Bless ... bleed! on a closer inspection, Edgar now sees the full horror of Gloucester's condition

55 *horse-way:* bridle path

58 *as:* named

60 *mopping and mowing:* grinning and grimacing
60–1 *who ... waiting-women:* after the fiend left Poor Tom, it took possession of female servants

63–4 *thou ... strokes:* you whom the punishments of the gods have reduced to such an abject state that you humbly accept extreme misery

65 *happier:* he gets Gloucester's purse, and he has a fellow-sufferer to share his misery
Heavens ... still! may the heavenly powers always act in this way (i.e. to ensure a more just and equitable distribution of resources)

66–8 *Let ... quickly:* let the man who is living in luxury, who satisfies his lusts and desires, who shows contempt for divine law, who refuses to see the needs of others because he has no feeling for them, now feel humbled by heavenly justice

66 *superfluous:* having more than enough

67 *slaves your ordinance:* treats divine law as his slave by bending it to conform to his self-interest

OLD MAN

45   Alack, sir, he is mad.

GLOUCESTER

'Tis the times' plague, when madmen lead the blind.

Do as I bid thee, or rather do thy pleasure;

Above the rest, be gone.

OLD MAN

I'll bring him the best 'parel that I have,

Come on't what will.

Exit.

GLOUCESTER

50   Sirrah, naked fellow—

EDGAR

Poor Tom's a-cold. [*aside*] I cannot daub it further.

GLOUCESTER

Come hither, fellow.

EDGAR [*aside*]

And yet I must. [*to GLOUCESTER*] Bless thy sweet eyes,
          they bleed!

GLOUCESTER

Know'st thou the way to Dover?

EDGAR

55   Both stile and gate, horse-way and foot-path. Poor Tom
hath been scared out of his good wits. Bless thee, good
man's son, from the foul fiend! Five fiends have been in
Poor Tom at once; of lust, as Obidicut; Hobbididence,
prince of dumbness; Mahu, of stealing; Modo, of murder;
60   Flibbertigibbet, of mopping and mowing, who since
possesses chambermaids and waiting-women. So, bless
thee, master!

GLOUCESTER

Here, take this purse, thou whom the heavens' plagues

Have humbled to all strokes. That I am wretched

65   Makes thee the happier. Heavens deal so still!

Let the superfluous and lust-dieted man

That slaves your ordinance, that will not see   *ref to*

Because he doth not feel, feel your power quickly;   *Poor Tom*

come down to poor Toms level.

So distribution should undo excess

And each man have enough. Dost thou know Dover?　　70

[handwritten: repatition social justice]

EDGAR

Ay, master.

[handwritten: let that be my reason · learn from being with people like Poor Tom · expirience to understand.]

GLOUCESTER

There is a cliff, whose high and bending head

Looks fearfully in the confined deep;

Bring me but to the very brim of it

And I'll repair the misery thou dost bear　　75

With something rich about me. From that place

I shall no leading need.

[handwritten: Gloucester plans on killing himself.]

EDGAR

　　　　　　　Give me thy arm;

Poor Tom shall lead thee.

Exeunt.

69　*So ... excess:* Gloucester is asking the gods to induce those who have too much to distribute their surplus wealth among those in need

73　*fearfully:* causing fear
confined deep: sea hemmed in by land; here, the reference is to the Straits of Dover

74　*Bring ... it:* take me to the very edge of the cliff

77–8　*Give ... thee:* there is deliberate ambiguity in Edgar's words. He is promising to lead Gloucester to the place of his (Gloucester's) intended suicide; but his real intention is to lead Gloucester out of his despair

Key points

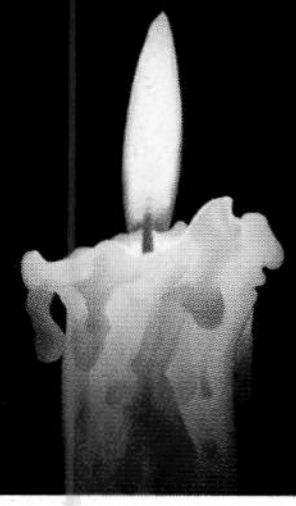

This scene marks the slow start of a process in which broken relationships will be repaired, and tension between Lear's enemies will increase.

- The encounter between Edgar (as Poor Tom) and the blinded Gloucester forms the substance of this scene. There is profound and cruel irony involved in their meeting. Edgar's opening remarks prove embarrassingly optimistic when his fortunes take a further turn for the worse. His hopeful moralising gives way to gloomy reflection at the sight of his blinded father.

- There is a further contrast between some of Edgar's banal statements and Gloucester's more insightful and moving revelations. Edgar's ponderous reflection ('O world! But that thy strange mutations make us hate thee, life would not yield to age'; lines 10–12) rings hollow when set against Gloucester's memorable comment on his own plight ('I have no way, and therefore want no eyes; I stumbled when I saw'; lines 18–19).

- It is Edgar's asides that maintain our sympathy for him. For example, his aside in response to Gloucester's wish to live long enough to 'see' Edgar by touching him is heartfelt ('O gods! Who is't can say "I am at the worst"? I am worse than e'er I was'; lines 25–6).

- There is great pathos in Gloucester's references to Edgar and some commentators have wondered why Edgar does not, at this stage, reveal his true identity to his father and thus gratify Gloucester's longing to 'see' him. Not to do so, after all, can only prolong Gloucester's pain. Edgar's own answer to this criticism will come later ('Why I do trifle thus with his despair is done to cure it'; Act 4, Scene 6, lines 33–4).

Useful quotes

> I have no way, and therefore want no eyes;
> I stumbled when I saw.
>
> (Gloucester, lines 18–19)

> As flies to wanton boys are we to the gods.
> They kill us for their sport.
>
> (Gloucester, lines 36–7)

> Let the superfluous and lust-dieted man
> That slaves your ordinance, that will not see
> Because he doth not feel, feel your power quickly;
> So distribution should undo excess
> And each man have enough.
>
> (Gloucester, lines 66–70)

? Questions

1 Imagine you are Edgar. Write an account of your meeting with Gloucester, and of its effect on you.

2 Comment on Edgar's views on life and fortune in this scene.

3 What makes this scene so sad and moving?

4 There are significant parallels between this scene and the previous scene. Mention some of these.

5 Gloucester sounds rather like Lear at times. Elaborate on this idea.

6 Why, do you think, does Gloucester voice his concern for deprived people (lines 63–70)? Show how this speech expresses one of the central themes of the play.

7 The scene ends with Edgar's 'Poor Tom shall lead thee' (line 78). Edgar's understanding of these words is quite different from Gloucester's. Explain the difference.

> O Goneril,
> You are not worth the dust which the rude wind
> Blows in your face.
>
> ALBANY, Act 4, Scene 2, 30–2

ACT 4 ✝ Scene 2

Plot summary

As Goneril and Edmund approach Albany's palace, Oswald informs them that Albany has changed and appears to be on the opposite side to Goneril. Goneril sends Edmund back to Cornwall with this news. She also makes it clear to Edmund that she wants him to take Albany's place by her side. Albany and Goneril argue bitterly. She accuses him of cowardice. He claims he would kill her if she was not a woman. A messenger brings news of Cornwall's death. Goneril is troubled by the thought that Regan, now widowed, may also have designs on Edmund, and so destroy the fantasy that is making her life tolerable. Albany's stand is reinforced when he hears of Gloucester's blinding. He finds in Cornwall's death a confirmation of the justice of the gods, and the scene closes with a determined resolve on his part to acknowledge Gloucester's kindness to Lear and to avenge his blinding.

Before the Duke of Albany's palace.

Enter GONERIL and EDMUND.

GONERIL
Welcome, my lord: I marvel our mild husband
Not met us on the way.

Enter OSWALD.

Now, where's your master?

OSWALD
Madam, within, but never man so changed.
I told him of the army that was landed:

5   He smiled at it. I told him you were coming:
His answer was 'The worse'. Of Gloucester's treachery,
And of the loyal service of his son,
When I informed him, then he called me sot,
And told me I had turned the wrong side out.

10   What most he should dislike seems pleasant to him;
What like, offensive.

GONERIL [*to EDMUND*]
Then shall you go no further.
It is the cowish terror of his spirit
That dares not undertake. He'll not feel wrongs
Which tie him to an answer. Our wishes on the way

15   May prove effects. Back, Edmund, to my brother;
Hasten his musters and conduct his powers.
I must change arms at home, and give the distaff
Into my husband's hands. This trusty servant
Shall pass between us; ere long you are like to hear,

20   If you dare venture in your own behalf,
A mistress's command. Wear this [*gives a favour*]; spare
speech.
Decline your head; this kiss, if it durst speak,
Would stretch thy spirits up into the air.
[*kisses him*] Conceive, and fare thee well.

EDMUND
Yours in the ranks of death.

GONERIL

25   My most dear Gloucester!

Exit EDMUND.

---

1 *Welcome:* Goneril welcomes Edmund to her palace, as he arrives there in her company

1–2 *I ... way:* I am amazed that my tame, domesticated husband has not come to meet us on our way here

8 *sot:* fool, blockhead

9 *I ... out:* I was giving a false account of Gloucester's 'treachery' and Edmund's 'loyal service' as it should be the other way around

11 *What like, offensive:* what one would expect him to like seems offensive to him

12 *cowish:* faint-hearted, cowardly

13 *undertake:* take the initiative

13–14 *He'll ... answer:* he will ignore any insult or threat that might oblige him to challenge an aggressor

14–15 *Our ... effects:* the desires we expressed on our journey may be fulfilled. This suggests that they have considered how they might further their relationship, presumably by disposing of Albany

15 *my brother:* my brother-in-law (Cornwall)

16 *Hasten ... powers:* speed up the assembly of his forces and lead his army

17–18 *I ... hands:* I will exchange the kind of work done (with our arms) at home, swopping my distaff (symbol of female domesticity) for Albany's sword

17 *distaff:* a staff on which wool or flax was wound; the word came to mean 'female, female authority, or the female branch of the family'

18 *trusty servant:* Oswald

19–21 *ere ... command:* if you have the courage to pursue your own interests ('venture in your own behalf'), you are likely, before ('ere') long, to hear me commanding you as your liege-lady and as your lady-love. Goneril is quibbling on 'mistress'

21 *favour:* token of love

22 *Decline your head:* bend your head forward

22–5 *this kiss ... death:* Goneril's speech and Edmund's reply involve bawdy double meanings, 'stretch thy spirits' and 'conceive' have sexual implications, as has Edmund's reference to 'the ranks of death', which signifies sexual enjoyment

22 *durst:* dared to

O the difference of man and man!

To thee a woman's services are due:

My fool usurps my body.

OSWALD

Madam, here comes my lord.

Exit.

Enter ALBANY.

GONERIL

I have been worth the whistling.

ALBANY

O Goneril,   30

You are not worth the dust which the rude wind

Blows in your face. I fear your disposition:

That nature, which contemns its origin,

Cannot be bordered certain in itself;

She that herself will sliver and disbranch   35

From her material sap, perforce must wither

And come to deadly use.

GONERIL

No more; the text is foolish.

ALBANY

Wisdom and goodness to the vilde seem vilde;

Filths savour but themselves. What have you done?   40

Tigers, not daughters, what have you performed?

A father, and a gracious, aged man

Whose reverence even the head-lugged bear would lick,

Most barbarous, most degenerate, have you madded.

Could my good brother suffer you to do it?   45

A man, a prince, by him so benefacted!

If that the heavens do not their visible spirits

Send quickly down to tame these vilde offences,

It will come,

Humanity must perforce prey on itself,   50

Like monsters of the deep.

GONERIL

Milk-livered man!

That bear'st a cheek for blows, a head for wrongs;

Who hast not in thy brows an eye discerning

Thine honour from thy suffering,

27–8 *To ... body:* Edmund deserves a woman's favours (by the law of nature), whereas my fool-husband has wrongful possession of my body (by the law of marriage)

30 *I ... whistling:* Goneril is thinking of the proverb: it is a poor dog that is not worth the whistling. She seems to be saying: so you decided at last to seek me out, since even a poor dog is worth whistling for

31–2 *You ... face:* not alone are you not worth whistling for, you are not even worth the dust the whistling wind throws in your face

32–7 *I ... use:* the tendency of your character frightens me because of what it may lead to. A human being who shows such contempt for her parentage cannot be depended upon to keep within the bounds of the moral law. A woman who severs herself from the nourishing stock from which she grew must inevitably meet the fate of a withered branch, and be destroyed ('and come to deadly use')

35 *sliver:* tear off, sever
   disbranch: cut off

36 *material sap:* what gives life and sustenance
   perforce: of necessity

38 *the text is foolish:* your sermon makes no sense to me

39 *vilde:* vile

40 *Filths ... themselves:* those who are filthy-minded relish only the taste of their own filth

43 *Whose ... lick:* Lear is so deserving of respect and homage that even an angry bear would lick him affectionately and reverently
   head-lugged: pulled by a chain tied around the neck, and therefore angry

44 *madded:* made (your father) mad

45–6 *Could ... benefacted:* Albany cannot understand how Cornwall allowed Goneril and Regan to treat Lear so badly. He believes Cornwall should have defended Lear as 'a man' (i.e. on basic humanitarian grounds); as 'a prince', who should uphold superior moral values; and because he is heavily indebted to Lear for the benefits that have been conferred upon him ('benefacted')

47–51 *If ... deep:* if the gods do not quickly send thunderbolts ('their visible spirits') to chastise these loathsome offenders ('vilde offences'), human beings will become cannibals and prey upon each other as sea creatures do, the strong devouring the weak

51 *Milk-livered:* cowardly

52 *That ... wrongs:* you are prepared to endure insults and wrongs without retaliating

53–4 *Who ... suffering:* you are unable to judge what you can and what you cannot endure without loss of honour

54–6 *that ... mischief:* you do not realise that only fools pity criminals (such as Lear), whose intended crimes are prevented by punishment

56 *Where's thy drum?* Why are you not preparing to muster your soldiers?

57 *France ... land:* the forces of the King of France are advancing without resistance; the noise of British war preparations is not to be heard

58 *With ... threats:* the French soldiers wearing plumed helmets threaten the flaxen-capped British troops

59 *moral:* moralising

60 *'Alack ... so?':* Goneril imagines Albany crying: 'Alas, why is the King of France threatening us?'

61–2 *Proper ... woman:* ugliness (physical and moral) seems more revolting in a woman than in the devil; in the devil's case at least ugliness is appropriate ('proper')

63 *self-covered thing:* a devil with its real self concealed in a woman's body

64 *Be-monster ... feature:* do not assume the monstrous shape of the devil you are
Were't my fitness: if it were the proper thing for me to do

65 *blood:* inclination, natural impulse

66 *apt:* ready

67 *Howe'er ... fiend:* but although you are a devil

68 *shield:* protect

69 *Marry ... mew:* Goneril is about to launch another verbal attack on her husband, questioning his manhood, when she is interrupted by the arrival of the messenger

74 *bred:* maintained in his household
thrilled with remorse: intensely moved with compassion

75–6 *bending ... master:* directing his sword against Cornwall

76–9 *who ... after:* Cornwall, enraged at his servant's attack on him, rushed at the offending servant and, with the aid of others, slew him, not, however, before he (Cornwall) had received the wound that has since caused him to follow his servant ('plucked him after') in death

77 *amongst ... dead:* between them they killed him. It was actually Regan who killed the First Servant by running at him with a sword

---

                      that not know'st

55   Fools do those villains pity who are punished

Ere they have done their mischief. Where's thy drum?

France spreads his banners in our noiseless land,

With plumed helm thy flaxen biggin threats;

Whilst thou, a moral fool, sits still and cries

'Alack, why does he so?'

ALBANY

60   See thyself, devil!

Proper deformity seems not in the fiend

So horrid as in woman.

GONERIL

              O vain fool!

ALBANY

Thou changed and self-covered thing, for shame,

Be-monster not thy feature. Were't my fitness

65   To let these hands obey my blood,

They are apt enough to dislocate and tear

Thy flesh and bones. Howe'er thou art a fiend,

A woman's shape doth shield thee.

GONERIL

Marry, your manhood, mew—

Enter a MESSENGER.

ALBANY

70   What news?

MESSENGER

O my good lord, the Duke of Cornwall's dead,

Slain by his servant, going to put out

The other eye of Gloucester.

ALBANY

                  Gloucester's eyes!

MESSENGER

A servant that he bred, thrilled with remorse,

75   Opposed against the act, bending his sword

To his great master, who, thereat enraged,

Flew on him, and amongst them felled him dead,

But not without that harmful stroke, which since

Hath plucked him after.

ALBANY

This shows you are above,
You justicers, that these our nether crimes   80
So speedily can venge! But, O poor Gloucester!
Lost he his other eye?

MESSENGER

Both, both, my lord.
This letter, madam, craves a speedy answer.
'Tis from your sister.

GONERIL [*aside*]

One way I like this well,
But being widow, and my Gloucester with her,   85
May all the building in my fancy pluck
Upon my hateful life. Another way
The news is not so tart. [*aloud*] I'll read, and answer.

Exit.

ALBANY

Where was his son when they did take his eyes?

MESSENGER

Come with my lady hither.

ALBANY

He is not here.   90

MESSENGER

No, my good lord; I met him back again.

ALBANY

Knows he the wickedness?

MESSENGER

Ay, my good lord. 'Twas he informed against him,
And quit the house on purpose that their punishment
Might have the freer course.

ALBANY

Gloucester, I live   95
To thank thee for the love thou showed'st the King,
And to revenge thine eyes. — Come hither, friend:
Tell me what more thou know'st.

Exeunt.

79–81 *This . . . venge!* the fact that crimes committed down here on earth ('nether crimes') are so quickly avenged shows that heavenly judges ('justicers') preside over the affairs of men

83 *craves:* demands

84–8 *One . . . tart:* an expanded paraphrase of Goneril's divided response to this news would run as follows: in one respect I welcome the news of Cornwall's death. But Regan is now a widow and has my Edmund with her; this may result in the collapse of my dream of marrying Edmund, and force me to live in the hateful contemplation of Regan and Edmund living together as husband and wife. Then again, the news is not so bitter ('tart') because Cornwall's death opens up the possibility of single rule over Britain

86 *building . . . fancy:* my castles in the air. Goneril is referring to the hope she has formed of possessing Edmund and the kingdom

90 *Come . . . hither:* Edmund came here with Goneril

91 *back again:* on his way back

92 *the wickedness:* about the plucking out of Gloucester's eyes

94–5 *quit . . . course:* deliberately left Gloucester's castle so that the punishment of Gloucester by Cornwall and Regan might proceed without trouble

Key points

This scene marks an important step in the restoration of good in the play. Albany has begun to reject his wife's influence and his new-found determination to support Lear's cause offers hope.

- The breakdown of moral, social and natural values, which is a feature of the play as a whole, is illustrated in this scene when Goneril, out of lust, reveals that Edmund should take her husband's place ('To thee a woman's services are due: my fool usurps my body'; lines 27–8).

- It is Goneril who initiates this relationship. Edmund is much more reticent about his feelings for her. His ambiguous reply to her enthusiastic proposal ('Yours in the ranks of death'; line 25) makes the affair appear rather one-sided. This remark is also an ironic anticipation of the common fate of Edmund and Goneril in the play's final scene.

- Goneril's behaviour is in marked contrast to her earlier stated concern for rules and standards, and her stern disapproval of lust (see Act 1, Scene 4, lines 228–39).

- Cornwall's death casts a shadow over Goneril's plans. Revealing a total lack of sympathy for her bereaved sister, her only concern is that Regan, as a widow, is now free to marry Edmund. This, as she frankly admits, would leave her in jealous torment. Her fears are later proved correct, as Regan does turn to Edmund, giving him a new sense of self-importance.

- Cornwall's death might also have its advantages for Goneril: the way is now open for single rule over Britain (for her and Edmund). The implication here is that Albany and Regan would have to be eliminated.

- We have already heard rumours of disagreements between Albany and Cornwall and now Oswald confirms that Albany has 'changed' (line 3) and is taking a different position to Goneril, Regan and Cornwall. This offers hope that the evil characters will be challenged and stopped.

- During a bitter row with Goneril, Albany describes her as a devil in a woman's shape, and warns her not to cast off that disguise as it is the only thing that protects her from his fury (lines 63–8). Albany was easily dismissed by his wife in Act 1, Scene 4, but now he is prepared to stand his ground and voice his concerns.

- Albany receives the news of Cornwall's death as an affirmation of divine justice ('This shows you are above, you justicers, that these our nether crimes so speedily can venge'; lines 79–81). Albany's gods exact swift punishment. He has already affirmed that if they do not intervene quickly to punish vile offenders against the moral law, 'Humanity must perforce prey on itself, like monsters of the deep' (lines 50–1). In other words, human beings with the power to do so will prey on weaker human beings to their own advantage, as Goneril and Regan have done in the case of Lear, as Edmund has done in the case of Gloucester and Edgar, and as Goneril is planning to do in the case of those who may be obstacles on her way to greater power. The trouble about Albany's deities is that their punishments fall equally on the good (Gloucester and the servant who tries to save his sight) and on the wicked (Cornwall).

- It is important to remember that in this scene Albany knows nothing of Goneril's passion for Edmund. His anger is motivated by Goneril's cold-hearted neglect of Lear, and increased by the brutal punishment inflicted on Gloucester.

- Mysteriously, Albany appears to do little to fulfil his impressive and resounding promises to avenge the cruel treatment of Lear and Gloucester.

this kiss, if it durst speak,
Would stretch thy spirits up into the air

GONERIL, Act 4, Scene 2, 22–3

Useful quotes

> ere long you are like to hear,
> If you dare venture in your own behalf,
> A mistress's command.
>
> (Goneril, lines 19–21)

> O Goneril,
> You are not worth the dust which the rude wind
> Blows in your face.
>
> (Albany, lines 30–2)

> Milk-livered man!
> That bear'st a cheek for blows, a head for wrongs
>
> (Goneril, lines 51–2)

> Howe'er thou art a fiend,
> A woman's shape doth shield thee.
>
> (Albany, lines 67–8)

Questions ?

1 In what ways does this scene indicate a change in Albany's role?

2 A new Goneril is also beginning to emerge. Explain.

3 Do you agree that the relationship between Goneril and Albany represents an inversion of traditional gender roles? Explain your answer with reference to the text of the play.

4 Goneril is faced with a new problem in this scene. What is it? How would she like to solve it?

5 Describe Goneril's attitude to her marriage to Albany and to marriage in general.

6 Albany and Goneril exchange insults. Summarise the content of these insults. Do you think any of their insults can be justified? Explain your answer.

7 Imagine you are Edmund. Compose a diary entry giving your thoughts on what you learned from Goneril and Oswald as you approached Albany's palace.

8 If you were choosing actors to play Goneril and Albany in a stage or film version of *King Lear*, what characteristics or features would you look for?

ACT 4 ⚲ Scene 3

Plot summary

The action moves to Dover, where we learn that the King of France has returned home and that Cordelia has been greatly distressed by Lear's treatment at the hands of her sisters. We also hear of Lear's presence in Dover, and of his guilty reluctance to meet Cordelia, conscious as he is that he has mistreated her.

> *There she shook*
> *The holy water from her heavenly eyes;*
> *And clamour-moistened, then away she started*
> *To deal with grief alone.*
>
> GENTLEMAN, Act 4, Scene 3, 29–32

The French camp near Dover.

Enter KENT and GENTLEMAN.

KENT

Why the King of France is so suddenly gone back, know
you no reason?

GENTLEMAN

Something he left imperfect in the state, which since his
coming forth is thought of, which imports to the kingdom
so much fear and danger that his personal return was   5
most required and necessary.

KENT

Who hath he left behind him general?

GENTLEMAN

The Marshal of France, Monsieur La Far.

KENT

Did your letters pierce the queen to any demonstration
of grief?   10

GENTLEMAN

Ay, sir; she took them, read them in my presence,
And now and then an ample tear trilled down
Her delicate cheek. It seemed she was a queen
Over her passion, who, most rebel-like,
Sought to be king o'er her.

KENT

                              O, then it moved her?   15

GENTLEMAN

Not to a rage; patience and sorrow strove
Who should express her goodliest. You have seen
Sunshine and rain at once; her smiles and tears
Were like a better way; those happy smilets,
That played on her ripe lip seemed not to know   20
What guests were in her eyes, which parted thence
As pearls from diamonds dropped. In brief,
Sorrow would be a rarity most beloved
If all could so become it.

This entire scene is omitted from the First Folio version
of the play. It is frequently left out in stage productions
because it is purely descriptive and because the idea that
Lear knows Cordelia is in England and is refusing (out of
shame) to see her is not supported by his behaviour in
the remainder of the play.

3–6 *Something . . . necessary:* the King of France left
some unfinished business in his own kingdom,
and this has come to mind since his arrival in
Britain. The implications of this business are so
fearful and dangerous for France that his presence
there was absolutely essential. Shakespeare has to
send the King of France home to avoid making a
foreign invasion of Britain a major issue in the play

7 *general:* as his commander-in-chief

9 *pierce:* provoke, impel

12 *ample:* big
    trilled: trickled
13 *delicate:* beautiful
13–14 *queen . . . who:* able to control her emotion, which

15 *it:* the letter, the news
    moved her: stirred her emotions

16–17 *patience . . . goodliest:* self-control and grief
struggled with her as if in an effort to discover
which would give her the lovelier facial expression
17–19 *You . . . way:* Cordelia's smiles and tears were like
simultaneous sunshine and rain, but even more
attractive ('a better way')
19 *smilets:* little smiles
20 *ripe:* full

21 *guests:* tears
    parted thence: left from there

23–4 *Sorrow . . . it:* sorrow would be a coveted jewel
if it could appear as lovely in others as it does in
Cordelia

24 *Made ... question?* the emphasis is on 'verbal';
Kent is asking whether she had anything to say,
apart from what her looks expressed
question: speech

25 *heaved:* spoke with difficulty

29 *Let ... believed!* Cordelia finds it impossible to
believe in the existence of pity in the light of what
her sisters have done to her father

29–32 *There ... alone:* at that point she wept, and her
tears sprinkled ('moistened') her outburst of grief;
then she went away to commune silently with her
sorrow. Cordelia's emotion is subdued by tears as a
shower calms a storm. These lines offer a striking
example of the Christian symbolism surrounding
Shakespeare's presentation of Cordelia

32–5 *It ... issues:* our natures ('conditions') must be
governed by planetary influences, otherwise one
and the same husband ('mate') and wife ('make')
could not have had children so different as Goneril
and Regan on the one hand, and Cordelia on the
other

37 *King:* King of France, Cordelia's husband

38 *Lear's i' the town:* this report as to Lear's
whereabouts contradicts what Cordelia says on
the subject in the next scene, where she orders a
search to be made for her father

39 *sometime ... tune:* sometimes during his intervals
of sanity

41 *yield:* agree, consent

42 *A ... him:* an overpowering sense of shame forces
him back, thus overmastering his desire to see
Cordelia

43 *benediction:* blessing

43–4 *turned ... casualties:* turned her out, thereby
forcing her to take her chances abroad

45 *dog-hearted:* cruel, pitiless

KENT

                                        Made she no verbal question?

GENTLEMAN

25   Faith, once or twice she heaved the name of father
      Pantingly forth, as if it pressed her heart,
      Cried 'Sisters! Sisters! Shame of ladies! Sisters!
      Kent! Father! Sisters! — What, i' the storm? I' the night?
      Let pity not be believed!' There she shook
30   The holy water from her heavenly eyes;
      And clamour-moistened, then away she started
      To deal with grief alone.

KENT

                                        It is the stars,
      The stars above us govern our conditions;
      Else one self mate and make could not beget
35   Such different issues. You spoke not with her since?

GENTLEMAN

      No.

KENT

      Was this before the King returned?

GENTLEMAN

                                        No, since.

KENT

      Well, sir, the poor distressed Lear's i' the town,
      Who sometime in his better tune remembers
40   What we are come about, and by no means
      Will yield to see his daughter.

GENTLEMAN

                                        Why, good sir?

KENT

      A sovereign shame so elbows him: his own unkindness
      That stripped her from his benediction, turned her
      To foreign casualties, gave her dear rights
45   To his dog-hearted daughters — these things sting
      His mind so venomously that burning shame
      Detains him from Cordelia.

GENTLEMAN

                                        Alack, poor gentleman!

KENT

Of Albany's and Cornwall's powers you heard not?

GENTLEMAN

'Tis so, they are afoot.

KENT

Well, sir, I'll bring you to our master Lear,   50

And leave you to attend him. Some dear cause

Will in concealment wrap me up awhile.

When I am known aright, you shall not grieve

Lending me this acquaintance. I pray you go

Along with me.   55

Exeunt.

48   *powers:* forces

49   *'Tis so:* I have indeed heard of them
     afoot: on the march

50–1   *I'll ... him:* why Kent should leave Lear in the
       care of the Gentleman is not made clear. Note
       the contradiction between these lines and
       the opening of the next scene, where Lear is
       wandering mad through the fields

51–2   *Some ... awhile:* an important reason will keep
       me in disguise for a while longer. We are not told
       what this reason is

53   *aright:* properly (i.e. as Kent)

53–4   *you ... acquaintance:* you will not be sorry for
       having been acquainted with me

Key points

The outstanding moment in this scene is the celebrated description of Cordelia reading accounts of her father's sufferings at the hands of Goneril and Regan. Some commentators consider her reported grief to be embarrassingly sentimental.

- The contrast between this scene and the previous one could scarcely be greater. The controlling impulse in Goneril's case is undiluted selfishness. The satisfaction of her lustful impulses and of her desire for supreme power is her sole focus. Her discourse is marked by violence of language. Cordelia does not appear in person in this scene, but the Gentleman's account of her responses to her father's sufferings conveys an impression of self-control, gentleness, patience and, above all, heartfelt concern for her father.

- The contrast between Cordelia and her sisters moves Kent to the conclusion that our natures are not the result of hereditary factors but of planetary influences.

Otherwise, Kent claims, the same parents could not have had children so utterly different as Cordelia is from Goneril and Regan.

- While Goneril and Regan are denatured, lacking any humane or natural impulses, this scene explicitly associates Cordelia with natural forces. Her smiles and tears, for example, are reminiscent of 'sunshine and rain at once' (line 18). They are a sequel to the storm, or a spring shower that follows a harsh winter.

- As for Lear, the scene provides some indication that his broken mind is slowly healing, but shame for what he has done to Cordelia detains him from seeing her.

Useful quotes

> And now and then an ample tear trilled down
> Her delicate cheek. It seemed she was a queen
> Over her passion, who, most rebel-like
> Sought to be king o'er her.
>
> (Gentleman, lines 12–15)

> the poor distressed Lear's i' the town,
> Who sometime in his better tune remembers
> What we are come about, and by no means
> Will yield to see his daughter.
>
> (Kent, lines 38–41)

> O dear father!
> It is thy business that I go about.
>
> CORDELIA, Act 4, Scene 4, 23–4

? Questions

1 Kent raises an important point about human nature (lines 32–5). Explore this in the context of the behaviour of the characters in the play up to now.

2 The explanation given for the King of France leaving Britain is unconvincing. Suggest reasons why Shakespeare had to make him return home at this vital stage.

3 Suggest reasons why Shakespeare chooses to delay Cordelia's return to the stage and opts for the Gentleman's description of her response instead.

4 How does the imagery associated with Cordelia in this scene compare with that applied to her sisters up to this point in the play? Refer to the text in support of your answer.

5 Consider Kent's role as a go-between or intermediary in the play.

ACT 4 ✝ Scene 4

Cordelia has returned to Britain to show her love for her father by restoring him to the throne. She has been told of Lear's insanity and wants to see him. It is hoped that nature in its benevolent aspects will restore his health. Meanwhile, the British forces are approaching Dover.

drum and colours: a drummer and standard-bearers

1   *Alack, 'tis he!* alas, the man you have been describing is my father

2   *As . . . sea:* at the mercy of his unpredictable passions

3   *rank:* luxuriant

3–5   *fumiter . . . darnel:* all the plants named are weeds with unpleasant properties; for example, hemlock is poisonous and nettles sting

5   *idle:* useless, unprofitable

6   *sustaining:* maintaining life, nurturing
     A century: one hundred soldiers. This is a Roman term and therefore an anachronism, since Lear's rule was before Roman times

8–9   *What . . . sense?* What can human science ('wisdom') do to restore his impaired ('bereaved') sanity?

10   *outward worth:* material possessions

11   *means:* a way (of treating Lear's illness)

12   *Our . . . repose:* sleep acts as a fostering and supporting influence

13–15 *that . . . anguish:* to induce sleep ('that') in him, there are many effective medicinal herbs ('simples') that have the power to ease pain

15–17 *All . . . tears!* may all those herbs with hidden healing powers spring from the earth as I weep. Cordelia thinks of her tears as having the same effect as a spring shower

17   *aidant and remediate:* helpfully healing

19   *ungoverned rage:* uncontrolled madness

20   *That . . . it:* that lacks reason ('the means') to control or guide ('lead') it

21   *hitherward:* towards this place

22–3   *'Tis . . . them:* we already know that and our troops are ready to do battle with them

24–8   *It . . . right:* I am making war in Britain, not out of a desire for personal conquest, but to restore my father to the throne

25–6   *Therefore . . . pitied:* because of that, my husband, the King of France, has taken pity on my sad, pleading tears

27   *No . . . incite:* our military activities are not inspired by an exaggerated desire for conquest
     blown: puffed up

The French camp near Dover.

Enter, with drum and colours, CORDELIA, GENTLEMAN and SOLDIERS.

CORDELIA
Alack, 'tis he. Why, he was met even now
As mad as the vexed sea, singing aloud,
Crowned with rank fumiter and furrow-weeds,
With hardokes, hemlock, nettles, cuckoo-flowers,

5   Darnel, and all the idle weeds that grow
In our sustaining corn. A century send forth;
Search every acre in the high-grown field,
And bring him to our eye.

Exit an OFFICER.
               What can man's wisdom
In the restoring his bereaved sense?

10   He that helps him take all my outward worth.

GENTLEMAN
There is means, madam.
Our foster-nurse of nature is repose,
The which he lacks; that to provoke in him
Are many simples operative, whose power
Will close the eye of anguish.

CORDELIA
15   All blest secrets,
All you unpublished virtues of the earth,
Spring with my tears! Be aidant and remediate
In the good man's distress! Seek, seek for him,
Lest his ungoverned rage dissolve the life
That wants the means to lead it.

Enter MESSENGER.

MESSENGER
20   News, madam:
The British powers are marching hitherward.

CORDELIA
'Tis known before. Our preparation stands
In expectation of them. — O dear father!
It is thy business that I go about.

25   Therefore great France
My mourning and importuned tears hath pitied.
No blown ambition doth our arms incite
But love, dear love, and our aged father's right.
Soon may I hear and see him.

Exeunt.

Key points

Cordelia, who has not been on the stage since Act 1, Scene 1, now re-appears with the French army.

- Shakespeare emphasises the fact that Cordelia has invaded Britain, not with any desire for conquest ('No blown ambition doth our arms incite'; line 27), but to relieve and assist her father. This emphasis meant that his early audiences did not reject Lear and Cordelia as anti-British.

- Despite all Cordelia has endured at Lear's hands, she has not only forgiven him, but she is prepared to give all her worldly possessions to anybody who can ease his acute mental distress.

- The nature imagery in the scene, which features the disorderly and luxuriant growth of 'idle weeds' (line 5), suggests Lear's uncontrolled state of mind.

- Lear's crown is made of plants that can cause hurt or discomfort. It is therefore representative of both the causes and the results of his suffering.

- Whereas Lear is linked with the harsher aspect of nature, Cordelia is characteristically associated with the natural remedies, the 'unpublished virtues of the earth' (line 16), which will help to restore her father's sanity.

- Cordelia has deep concern and compassion for her father, even though he harshly rejected her earlier in the play. Her behaviour in this respect is similar to Edgar's.

- Healing herbs and sleep – 'Our foster-nurse of nature' (line 12) – are considered the best remedies for Lear's illness, which has been caused by the unnatural behaviour of his daughters.

- In the Quarto version of the play, this scene featured a 'Doctor' rather than a 'Gentleman'.

Useful quotes

> What can man's wisdom
> In the restoring his bereaved sense?
> He that helps him take all my outward worth.
>
> (Cordelia, lines 8–10)

> No blown ambition doth our arms incite
> But love, dear love, and our aged father's right.
> Soon may I see and hear him.
>
> (Cordelia, lines 27–9)

? Questions

1 Discuss the function of the nature imagery in this scene.

2 In what way does Cordelia's concern for her father stand in marked contrast to the attitudes of her sisters? Comment on this contrast in the light of Lear's dealings with his three daughters in Act 1, Scene 1.

3 Has Cordelia's outlook changed since her last appearance (in Act 1, Scene 1)? Explain your answer.

4 If you were staging this scene, how would you portray the French camp on stage? What impression might your decisions give the audience?

ACT 4 † Scene 5

Plot summary

Oswald has brought Goneril's letter to Regan and also tells her that Albany's forces are on their way. Edmund has gone to search for Gloucester to put him out of his misery. Regan realises that they should have killed Gloucester as his blinding is bad publicity. Regan tries to persuade Oswald to let her read her sister's letter to Edmund. Oswald refuses and remains loyal to Goneril. Through Oswald, Regan delivers a warning to her married older sister that it is Regan who is Edmund's fitting mate. She also urges Oswald to kill Gloucester if he should come upon him.

Edmund and I have talked
And more convenient is he for my hand
Than for your lady's.

REGAN, Act 4, Scene 5, 30–2

Earl of Gloucester's castle.

Enter REGAN and OSWALD.

REGAN
But are my brother's powers set forth?

OSWALD
                            Ay, madam.

REGAN
Himself in person there?

OSWALD
                   Madam, with much ado:
Your sister is the better soldier.

REGAN
Lord Edmund spake not with your lord at home?

OSWALD
No, madam.   5

REGAN
What might import my sister's letter to him?

OSWALD
I know not, lady.

REGAN
Faith, he is posted hence on serious matter.
It was great ignorance, Gloucester's eyes being out,
To let him live. Where he arrives he moves   10
All hearts against us. Edmund, I think, is gone,
In pity of his misery, to dispatch
His nighted life — moreover to descry
The strength o' the enemy.

OSWALD
I must needs after him, madam, with my letter.   15

REGAN
Our troops set forth tomorrow: stay with us,
The ways are dangerous.

OSWALD
                    I may not, madam.
My lady charged my duty in this business.

---

1 *But … forth?* Have Albany's forces set out to do battle?

2 *with much ado:* after a great deal of fuss and persuasion. It seems that Albany, uncertain of his duty, had to be persuaded to take the field against Lear's supporters

4 *your lord:* Albany

6 *What … him?* Regan is asking Oswald what he thinks Goneril's letter to Edmund might contain or signify. He must have told Regan earlier that he is carrying a letter from Goneril to Edmund
import: have as its purpose

8 *he … matter:* he has gone away on important business ('serious matter')
9 *ignorance:* political misjudgement, stupidity
10–11 *Where … us:* everywhere he goes, the sight of him turns people against us

12 *In … misery:* there is heavy irony in this phrase
12–13 *to … life:* to put an end to a life darkened ('nighted') by blindness
13 *descry:* discover

17 *ways:* roads

18 *charged … business:* emphasised the importance of following her instructions in this matter

20 *Transport ... word:* bring him a verbal account of her intentions
Belike: probably

21 *Some ... much:* Regan's unaccustomed incoherence of speech reflects her confusion of mind and emotional turmoil. She is troubled by the thought that Goneril and Edmund are lovers

22 *Madam ... rather:* the embarrassed Oswald would rather not hand over Goneril's letter

24 *at ... here:* when she was here recently

25 *oeillades:* amorous winks and glances
speaking looks: looks expressing love

26 *of her bosom:* in her confidence

28 *I ... understanding:* I know what I am talking about

29 *take this note:* take note of this

31 *convenient:* suitable, fitting

32 *gather:* deduce, surmise (from the hints I have been giving you)

33 *give him this:* Regan is sending Edmund a love letter or token

34–5 *And ... to her:* Regan is giving Oswald the task of reporting her views ('thus much') to Goneril, and of attempting to restore Goneril to wiser modes of thinking by inducing her to give up all thoughts of Edmund

37 *chance:* happen
blind traitor: Gloucester

38 *Preferment:* promotion
cuts him off: puts Gloucester to death

REGAN

Why should she write to Edmund? Might not you

20 Transport her purposes by word? Belike —

Some things — I know not what. I'll love thee much —

Let me unseal the letter.

OSWALD

                Madam, I had rather—

REGAN

I know your lady does not love her husband —

I am sure of that — and at her late being here

25 She gave strange oeillades and most speaking looks

To noble Edmund. I know you are of her bosom.

OSWALD

I, madam?

REGAN

I speak in understanding. Y'are; I know't.

Therefore I do advise you, take this note.

30 My lord is dead; Edmund and I have talked

And more convenient is he for my hand

Than for your lady's. You may gather more.

If you do find him, pray you give him this

And when your mistress hears thus much from you,

35 I pray desire her call her wisdom to her.

So, fare you well.

If you do chance to hear of that blind traitor,

Preferment falls on him that cuts him off.

OSWALD

Would I could meet him, madam. I should show

What party I do follow.

REGAN

40   Fare thee well.

Exeunt.

Key points

The previous scene was dominated by the loving concern and kindness felt by one family member for another. This contrasting scene dramatises the destructive power of hatred.

- In Act 4, Scene 2 we saw that Goneril, disturbed by the idea that Regan would be her rival for Edmund's affections, began to regard Regan as an enemy. Now we see Regan identifying Goneril as a hostile rival. It is clear that family bonds mean nothing to either sister.

- Regan is apparently not a grieving widow. Her primary concern is to replace her late husband with Edmund. Consumed with jealousy, she seeks to convince Oswald that Edmund would make a much 'more convenient' (line 31) husband for a widow like her than for the married Goneril.

- Regan's confused emotions, insecurity and fears are reflected in her disordered, fragmentary speech ('Belike – Some things – I know not what. I'll love thee much – Let me unseal the letter'; lines 20–2).

- Oswald has an interesting role in this scene. His primary duty is to Goneril, since he is her steward. However, Regan, her mind confused and in a jealous turmoil, wants Oswald to let her open a letter that he is carrying from Goneril to Edmund. When Oswald refuses, she gives him a verbal message of her own for Edmund, and asks him to convince Goneril of her folly in pursuing Edmund. Her final instruction, with which Oswald agrees to comply, is to kill 'that blind traitor' (line 37) Gloucester if he meets him.

Useful quotes

> *It was great ignorance, Gloucester's eyes being out,*
> *To let him live.*
>
> (Regan, lines 9–10)

> *Why should she write to Edmund? Might not you*
> *Transport her purposes by word? Belike —*
> *Some things — I know not what. I'll love thee much —*
> *Let me unseal the letter.*
>
> (Regan, lines 19–22)

> *If you do chance to hear of that blind traitor,*
> *Preferment falls on him that cuts him off.*
>
> (Regan, lines 37–8)

> *Would I could meet him, madam. I should show*
> *What party I do follow.*
>
> (Oswald, lines 39–40)

? Questions

1 Oswald reports that Albany is leading his forces 'with much ado' (line 2). What does this suggest about Albany's outlook at this point in the play?

2 Regan's thoughts, feelings and concerns have changed by the time we meet her in this scene. In what way, and for what reasons, has this change happened?

3 Why does Regan not want Gloucester to live any longer?

4 This scene gives us an insight into the kind of man Oswald is. Develop this idea.

5 Imagine you are Oswald. Write a diary entry giving an account of your thoughts and feelings after your meeting with Regan.

6 It has been said that the cruellest sentiments in the play are expressed by Regan and Goneril. Do you agree, based on the action so far? Give reasons for your answer.

ACT 4 ✝ Scene 6

Plot summary

This scene has three distinct episodes. The first (lines 1–81) involves Edgar's rescue of Gloucester from despair and suicide. Gloucester wants to throw himself from the cliff and asks to be led to the edge. Edgar deceives him into thinking that he survives his imagined leap from the cliff. He persuades the despairing Gloucester to accept his cruel fate and endure until the gods call him. Edgar's kindly deception inspires in his father a new determination to bear his fate until it grows weary of tormenting him.

The second episode (lines 82–220) involves the meeting of the mad Lear and the blinded Gloucester. Lear's imagination, free from rational control, creates magnificently compelling fantasies, governed by an insane logic of their own. Lear offers a profoundly depressing vision of life. In contrast, Gloucester takes a positive view of his condition, as he comes to terms with his fate. He submerges his own grief and suffering in the larger ordeal that Lear must endure.

In the third episode (lines 220–79) Edgar must protect his father from Oswald. Edgar kills Oswald and reads Goneril's letter to Edmund. He will use it to provide Albany with evidence of Goneril's relationship with Edmund and the pair's murderous intentions.

You're much deceived. In nothing am I changed
But in my garments.

EDGAR, Act 4, Scene 6, 9–10

The countryside near Dover.

Enter GLOUCESTER, and EDGAR (dressed like a peasant).

GLOUCESTER

When shall I come to the top of that same hill?

EDGAR

You do climb up it now. Look how we labour.

GLOUCESTER

Methinks the ground is even.

EDGAR

                    Horrible steep.

Hark, do you hear the sea?

GLOUCESTER

                    No, truly.

EDGAR

Why, then your other senses grow imperfect   5

By your eyes' anguish.

GLOUCESTER

                    So may it be, indeed.

Methinks thy voice is altered, and thou speak'st

In better phrase and matter than thou didst.

EDGAR

You're much deceived. In nothing am I changed

But in my garments.

GLOUCESTER

                    Methinks you're better spoken.   10

EDGAR

Come on, sir; here's the place. Stand still. How fearful

And dizzy 'tis to cast one's eyes so low!

The crows and choughs that wing the midway air

Show scarce so gross as beetles. Half way down

Hangs one that gathers samphire, dreadful trade!   15

Methinks he seems no bigger than his head.

The fishermen that walk upon the beach

Appear like mice, and yon tall anchoring bark

Diminished to her cock, her cock a buoy

Almost too small for sight. The murmuring surge,   20

That on th' unnumbered idle pebble chafes

Cannot be heard so high. I'll look no more,

Lest my brain turn, and the deficient sight

Topple down headlong.

---

dressed like a peasant: the Old Man has fulfilled his promise (made in Act 4, Scene 1) to bring Edgar some clothes

1   *that same hill:* Dover cliff

2   *labour:* work hard (to climb)

3   *Methinks:* it seems to me
even: flat, level

Horrible: extremely, terribly

5–6   *your other ... anguish:* the pain ('anguish') in your eyes impairs your other senses

7–8   *Methinks ... didst:* Gloucester notices the change in the style and contents of Edgar's speech, a change that Shakespeare emphasises by having Edgar speak blank verse

9   *You're much deceived:* there are several layers of irony in this remark. Gloucester has been, and still is, the victim of deception. He has been deceived by Edmund, he is being deceived by Edgar for his own good, and he is deceived by his own despair

12   *to ... low:* to look down

13   *choughs:* crow-like birds with red beaks and legs (the word is pronounced 'chuffs')
wing ... air: fly halfway between us and the ground below
14   *Show ... beetles:* look hardly as big as beetles
15   *samphire:* an aromatic rock-plant used in pickling

18   *yon ... bark:* that sailing-vessel at anchor there
19   *Diminished ... cock:* looking as small as her dinghy
her cock a buoy: her dinghy looks as small as a buoy
20   *surge:* ocean
21   *That ... chafes:* that rubs against ('chafes') the innumerable pebbles, moving them to and fro without purpose (in an 'idle' fashion)
23   *Lest ... turn:* in case I should lose my mental and physical balance
23–4   *and ... headlong:* and in case my failing eyesight should cause me to fall head first

26–7 *For . . . upright:* for all the world I would not jump up into the air, never mind jumping forward

29 *Fairies:* these were traditional guardians of buried treasure, and were reputed to cause it to multiply when it was discovered

30 *Prosper . . . thee:* make it multiply when it is in your possession

32 *With . . . heart:* I heartily concur with your wish that I may fare well: I shall fare well in death

33–4 *Why . . . it:* I am playing with his despair in order to cure it

37 *Shake . . . off:* end my tormented life in patience rather than in angry despair

38–41 *If . . . out:* if I were to endure my life any longer, and not begin to rebel against your irresistible wills, my small residue of life would burn itself out like a reeking, guttering candle-end. Gloucester finds suicide preferable to a life of rebellious hostility to the gods, and to a miserable old age

40 *snuff:* the smouldering wick of a candle is used here as an image of senile decay
loathed: loathsome, hateful
nature: human life

change of character

43–5 *And . . . theft:* Edgar is wondering whether Gloucester's imagining that he is dying may actually kill him, all the more so since he is willing to end his life

43 *conceit:* imagination

45–6 *Had . . . past:* if he had been where he thought he was (at the edge of the cliff), thinking would have been over for him by now

48 *Thus . . . indeed:* he might die ('pass') in reality

GLOUCESTER
                            Set me where you stand.

EDGAR

25 Give me your hand. You are now within a foot
Of th' extreme verge. For all beneath the moon
Would I not leap upright.

GLOUCESTER
                    Let go my hand.
Here, friend, is another purse; in it a jewel
Well worth a poor man's taking. Fairies and gods
30 Prosper it with thee! Go thou further off.
Bid me farewell, and let me hear thee going.

EDGAR
Now fare you well, good sir.

GLOUCESTER
                        With all my heart.

EDGAR [*aside*] *to audience.*
Why I do trifle thus with his despair
Is done to cure it.

GLOUCESTER
35 [*kneeling*] O you mighty gods!
This world I do renounce, and in your sights
Shake patiently my great affliction off.
If I could bear it longer, and not fall
To quarrel with your great opposeless wills,
40 My snuff and loathed part of nature should
Burn itself out. If Edgar live, O bless him!
Now, fellow, fare thee well.

EDGAR
                        Gone, sir. Farewell.

GLOUCESTER throws himself forward.
[*aside*] And yet I know not how conceit may rob
The treasury of life, when life itself
45 Yields to the theft. Had he been where he thought,
By this had thought been past. Alive or dead?
[*to GLOUCESTER*] Ho, you sir, friend; hear you, sir, speak.
[*aside*] Thus might he pass indeed, yet he revives.
[*to GLOUCESTER*] What are you, sir?

GLOUCESTER
                        Away, and let me die.

EDGAR

Hadst thou been aught but gossamer, feathers, air,   50

So many fathom down precipitating,

Thou'dst shivered like an egg: but thou dost breathe,

Hast heavy substance, bleed'st not, speak'st, art sound.

Ten masts at each make not the altitude

Which thou hast perpendicularly fell: 55

Thy life's a miracle. Speak yet again.

GLOUCESTER

But have I fall'n or no?

EDGAR

From the dread summit of this chalky bourn.

Look up a-height: the shrill-gorged lark so far

Cannot be seen or heard. Do but look up.   60

GLOUCESTER

Alack, I have no eyes.

Is wretchedness deprived that benefit

To end itself by death? 'Twas yet some comfort

When misery could beguile the tyrant's rage

And frustrate his proud will.

EDGAR

                    Give me your arm.   65

Up, so. How is't? Feel you your legs? You stand.

GLOUCESTER

Too well, too well.

EDGAR

               This is above all strangeness.

Upon the crown o' the cliff what thing was that

Which parted from you?

GLOUCESTER

               A poor unfortunate beggar.

EDGAR

As I stood here below me thought his eyes   70

Were two full moons. He had a thousand noses,

Horns whelked and waved like the enraged sea:

It was some fiend. Therefore, thou happy father,

Think that the clearest gods, who make them honours

Of men's impossibilities, have preserved thee.   75

---

50 *aught but gossamer:* anything but floating cobweb threads

51 *precipitating:* falling headlong

52 *Thou'dst shivered:* you would have broken in pieces

53 *Hast heavy substance:* are a solid body
sound: unbroken, whole

54 *at each:* one on top of the other

55 *fell:* fallen

56 *Thy life's:* your survival is

58 *dread:* terrifying, frightening
chalky bourn: chalk boundary (Dover cliff, the boundary of England)

59 *a-height:* on high

59–60 *the shrill-gorged . . . heard:* even the shrill-throated lark cannot be seen or heard from these depths

63–5 *'Twas . . . will:* there was a time when the unhappy victim of tyranny could, through suicide, cheat ('beguile') the vindictive anger of the tyrant, and thus defy his power and his hostile intentions

66 *Feel you:* do you have any feeling or power in

67 *This . . . strangeness:* this is the strangest thing that has ever happened

72 *whelked:* twisted, contorted

73 *happy father:* fortunate old man

74–5 *Think . . . thee:* bear in mind that the most just and sinless gods, who achieve honour among us by doing things that we regard as impossible, have saved your life

76–8 *Henceforth ... die:* from now on I will endure whatever misery befalls me, until misery itself decides that I have endured enough and ceases to trouble me (or perhaps, allows me to die)

81 *Bear ... thoughts:* keep your thoughts free of worry, and calm ('patient')

82–3 *The ... thus:* no man in his right mind would dress ('accommodate') himself in this fashion. Lear has dressed himself in wild flowers

84–94 *No ... Pass:* there is an inspired association of ideas in Lear's apparently incoherent speech. He has lost touch with the real world, and is moving rapidly from one fantasy to another. The idea that he cannot be arrested for minting coins (a royal prerogative) leads him to imagine that he is paying out money for newly enlisted soldiers ('press-money'). He then imagines himself reviewing recruits, and criticises one of them for awkwardness ('handles his bow like a crow-keeper'). He looks for a standard arrow ('a clothier's yard' in length). He offers his imaginary gauntlet as a token that he will fight even a giant to assert the justice of his cause. He asks for pikes ('brown bills'). He imagines that one of his archers has hit the bullseye (the 'clout'). The 'bird' is the arrow in flight. 'Hewgh!' is his imitation of the flight of an arrow. He thinks an unauthorised person is trying to gain admission and, like a sentry, asks for the password ('Give the word'). Edgar obliges with an appropriate password ('Sweet marjoram') – this plant is a traditional remedy for mental illness; the pronouncer of this password is obviously a friend, and Lear allows him to pass on the strength of it. In the midst of his meanderings, Lear imagines himself catching a mouse with a piece of cheese

86 *Nature's ... respect:* his authority as king derives from nature, which no art (human law) can modify
87 *crow-keeper:* one who keeps off crows from a field
96 *Goneril ... beard!* the demented Lear mistakes Gloucester for Goneril in disguise, since Gloucester flatters him by kneeling before him, reminding him that his daughters and courtiers, too, flattered him 'like a dog'
96–7 *like a dog:* in Shakespeare, dogs are often associated with fawning and fulsome flattery
97–8 *I ... there:* I had achieved the ripe wisdom associated with maturity ('white hairs') before I was even old enough to grow a beard
98–9 *To say ... divinity:* they agreed with everything I said, right or wrong, in order to flatter me; by doing this, they violated the scriptures
102 *smelt 'em out:* detected their flattery

104 *ague-proof:* immune from the illnesses that afflict other men; the ague is a fever

GLOUCESTER
I do remember now. Henceforth I'll bear
Affliction till it do cry out itself
'Enough, enough' and die. That thing you speak of,
I took it for a man; often 'twould say
80 'The fiend, the fiend'; he led me to that place.

EDGAR
Bear free and patient thoughts.

Enter LEAR (fantastically dressed with wild flowers).
                    But who comes here?
The safer sense will ne'er accommodate
His master thus.

LEAR
No, they cannot touch me for coining. I am the King himself.

EDGAR
85 O thou side-piercing sight!

LEAR   *nothing can change that he is King.*
MAD   Nature's above art in that respect. There's your press-
money. That fellow handles his bow like a crow-keeper.
Draw me a clothier's yard. Look, look, a mouse! Peace,
peace! This piece of toasted cheese will do't. There's my   *Thoughts*
90 gauntlet; I'll prove it on a giant. Bring up the brown bills.
O well flown, bird! I' the clout, i' the clout! Hewgh! Give
the word.   *Sense in his madness*

EDGAR
Sweet marjoram.

LEAR
Pass.

GLOUCESTER
95 I know that voice. *[he kneels]*   *realises he is human.*

LEAR   *tragic hero → learn what they have done wrong,*
Ha! Goneril, with a white beard! They flattered me like a
dog, and told me I had white hairs in my beard ere the
black ones were there. To say 'ay' and 'no' to everything
that I said 'ay' and 'no' to was no good divinity. When
100 the rain came to wet me once and the wind to make
me chatter, when the thunder would not peace at my   *realisation of them lying.*
bidding, there I found 'em, there I smelt 'em out. Go
to, they are not men o' their words. They told me I was
everything. 'Tis a lie: I am not ague-proof.
                    invincable.

GLOUCESTER

The trick of that voice I do well remember.   105

Is't not the King?

LEAR

WOMEN   Ay, every inch a King.   *Justice*

When I do stare, see how the subject quakes.

I pardon that man's life. What was thy cause?
many relationships
Adultery? Thou shalt not die. Die for adultery? No:

The wren goes to't, and the small gilded fly   110

Does lecher in my sight.
                    sex outside marriage
⌐ Let copulation thrive; for Gloucester's bastard son

irony ⌐ Was kinder to his father than my daughters

Got 'tween the lawful sheets.

To't, luxury, pell-mell, for I lack soldiers.   115

Behold yond simpering dame

Whose face between her forks presages snow,

That minces virtue and does shake the head

To hear of pleasure's name —
                    prostitute
The fitchew nor the soiled horse goes to't   120

With a more riotous appetite.

Down from the waist they are Centaurs,
                                    extremely
Though women all above;   *misogynistic*

But to the girdle do the gods inherit,
                    devil
Beneath is all the fiend's;   125

There's hell, there's darkness, there's the sulphurous pit
cenial   *sexual diesese*   *they smell*
burning, scalding, stench, consumption! Fie, fie, fie!

Pah, pah! Give me an ounce of civet, good <u>apothecary</u>, to

sweeten my imagination. There's money for thee.

GLOUCESTER

O let me kiss that hand!   130

LEAR   * *respect towards*

Let me wipe it first; it smells of mortality.   *Gloucester*

GLOUCESTER   * *he is not a God*
                            only human
O ruined piece of nature! This great world

Shall so wear out to naught. Dost thou know me?

LEAR

I remember thine eyes well enough. Dost thou squiny at

me? No, do thy worst, blind Cupid; I'll not love. Read thou   135

this challenge; mark but the penning of it.

---

105   *trick:* distinctive quality or character

108   *thy cause:* the charge against you. Lear imagines himself sitting in judgement on the kneeling Gloucester

111   *lecher:* copulate, mate

⌐ No soldiers = need more
followers = have sex for
more.

115   *To't . . . soldiers:* let lust ('luxury') be unconfined; an increased birth rate will supply my depleted army with recruits
pell-mell: promiscuously, indiscriminately

116–21   *Behold . . . appetite:* look at that woman smiling self-consciously, a woman whose countenance suggests extreme chastity, who puts on a coy display of virtue, and who shakes her head in disapproval at the very mention of pleasure. Not even a polecat or a frisky, well-fed horse engages in such uncontrolled lust as she does

117   *Whose . . . snow:* whose face indicates ('presages') icy chastity ('snow') between her legs ('forks')

120   *fitchew:* polecat, also prostitute
soiled: fed with freshly cut fodder, and therefore lustfully energetic

122–5   *Down . . . fiend's:* the worst in woman makes her akin to the animal, the best to the angel. The centaur was a creature of myth, half-man half-horse, an image of lustful tendencies. The gods hold power over women only above the waist ('girdle'); all that is below belongs to the devil

126–8   *There's hell . . . pah!* 'There' means 'below the waist'. The images of burning suggest both lustful desire and the flames of hell

127   *consumption:* destruction, the act of consuming

128–9   *Give . . . imagination:* Lear, anxious to induce more wholesome thoughts, wants to buy perfume ('civet') from Gloucester, whom he mistakes for a druggist ('apothecary')

129   *money:* Lear perhaps offers flowers as payment

131   *mortality:* death; and also human existence

132–3   *O . . . naught:* Lear, old, mad and dishevelled, is a ruined masterpiece ('piece of nature'). Gloucester, in moralising mood, remarks that the universe is also destined to decay to nothingness

133   *so:* in the same way

134   *I . . . enough:* Lear is commenting cruelly and grotesquely on the blinded Gloucester
squiny: squint

136   *mark . . . it:* just observe the way it is written

GLOUCESTER

Were all the letters suns, I could not see.

EDGAR [*aside*]

I would not take this from report. It is;

And my heart breaks at it.

LEAR

140 Read.

GLOUCESTER

What, with the case of eyes?

LEAR

O, ho, are you there with me? No eyes in your head, nor no money in your purse? Your eyes are in a heavy case, your purse in a light; yet you see how this world goes.

GLOUCESTER

145 I see it feelingly.

|Justice|

LEAR

What, art mad? A man may see how this world goes with no eyes. Look with thine ears. See how yond *judge* justice rails upon yond simple thief. Hark, in thine ear: change places and, handy-dandy, which is the justice, which is the thief?

150 Thou hast seen a farmer's dog bark at a beggar?

GLOUCESTER

Ay, sir.

how do we judge when something is just and right •*depends on your position*

LEAR

And the creature run from the *beggar* cur? *rude word for a dog* There thou might'st behold the great image of authority: a dog's obeyed in office. Thou rascal beadle, *enforces the law* hold thy bloody hand! ** image of authority*

155 Why dost thou lash that whore? Strip thy own back;

Thou hotly lusts to use her in that kind

For which thou whip'st her. The usurer hangs the cozener.

Through tattered clothes great vices do appear;

Robes and furred gowns hide all. Plate *money* sin with gold,

160 And the strong lance of justice hurtless breaks; *repetition of injustice (money)*

Arm it in rags, a pigmy's straw doth pierce it.

None does offend, none, I say, none; I'll able 'em:

Take that of me, my friend, who have the power

To seal th' accuser's lips. Get thee glass eyes,

see things that don't exist.

165 And like a scurvy politician seem

To see the things thou dost not. Now, now, now, now!

Pull off my boots. Harder, harder — so.

realisation

138–9 *I . . . it:* I would not believe that what I am seeing could take place if someone else gave me an account of it. Unfortunately, it is taking place, and my heart is breaking at the sight

141 *What . . . eyes?* Would you have me read with empty eye-sockets?

142 *are . . . me?* is that what you mean?

145 *I . . . feelingly:* a pun: he means both (a) I keenly appreciate the way of the world; and (b) being blind, I can see the way of the world only by feeling

147–9 *Look . . . the thief:* since you cannot see, your ears will inform you of the corruption of the judicial system. Look at how the justice of the peace abuses the humble thief. Then a whispered bribe ('Hark, in thine ear') causes the justice to change his verdict. There is no moral distinction between the thief who is charged and the one who judges him

149 *handy-dandy:* take your pick

152–3 *And . . . office:* a beggar running from a dog is an image of the real meaning of authority: anything that wields power, even a dog, will be obeyed

154–7 *Thou . . . whip'st her:* the parish constable ('beadle'), his hand bloody from whipping the prostitute, should himself be whipped since he eagerly desires to commit the same offence with her as he is whipping her for

157 *The . . . cozener:* the great cheating moneylender ('usurer'), in his role as magistrate, sentences the petty thief ('cozener') to death

158–9 *Through . . . all:* all vices appear great when looked at through the tattered clothes of the poor, whereas the fur-trimmed robes and gowns of judges and magistrates conceal all their crimes

159 *Plate:* clothe in plate armour. Lear's idea is that gold is the criminal's most powerful defence against justice; it helps rich people to avoid legal punishment for their crimes

160 *hurtless:* without hurting the criminal or sinner

161 *a pigmy's straw:* the weakest possible weapon. The poor must face the full rigours of the law

162 *None . . . 'em:* no criminal will be found guilty; as king I'll vouch for the innocence of all criminals

163–4 *Take . . . lips:* Lear hands an imaginary royal pardon to Gloucester, which will make him secure against prosecution

164–6 *Get . . . not:* get yourself a pair of spectacles and like a despicable trickster ('scurvy politician') put on a show of seeing what you really cannot see

166–7 *Now . . . so:* Lear, exhausted by his attack on abuses, may be sitting down to get relief

EDGAR [aside]

O matter and impertinency mixed;

Reason in madness!

LEAR

If thou wilt weep my fortunes, take my eyes.　　　　170

I know thee well enough: thy name is Gloucester.

Thou must be patient; we came crying hither:

Thou know'st the first time that we smell the air

We wawl and cry. I will preach to thee: mark.

Takes his floral crown from his head.

GLOUCESTER

Alack, alack the day!　　　*pesimistic view on the world.*　　175

LEAR

When we are born, we cry that we are come

To this great stage of fools. This a good block:

It were a delicate stratagem to shoe

A troop of horse with felt; I'll put't in proof,

And when I have stol'n upon these son-in-laws,　　180

Then, kill, kill, kill, kill, kill, kill!

albany + cornrdil

stage: acting or pretending.
false place.

168–9　*O . . . madness!* this is one of the major paradoxes of the play. Edgar sees Lear's mad speeches as a compound of sense ('matter') and irrelevant nonsense ('impertinency'). In fact, they contain much greater wisdom and more sound judgement than anything found in Lear's officially sane utterances. Hence the paradox of 'reason in madness': the mad Lear has achieved depths of sanity inaccessible to him in his more 'rational' days

174　*wawl:* howl, bawl
mark: pay attention

→ *mad : philosophical reflection.*
• *fake, nothing real, no point*
• *when we are born we realise it.*

177　*block:* a mould for a felt hat. Lear may be referring to a hat he imagines he is holding or he may be admiring the floral crown he was wearing

179–81　*I'll . . . kill:* I'll put the idea to the test, steal up on my victims (Albany and Cornwall) and slaughter them. Perhaps the actor playing Lear destroys the floral crown as he repeats the word 'kill'

• *Regan / Goneril (false, pretending to like him) two-faced = not even good actors*

If thou wilt weep my fortunes,
take my eyes.

LEAR, Act 4, Scene 6, 170

184 *No . . . prisoner?* Lear imagines he is to be captured and imprisoned. Lear may be responding with fear to the word 'daughter' (line 183). A summons from any one of them might induce him to beg for merciful treatment

185 *natural . . . fortune:* a man born to be the victim of fortune's mockery

187 *I . . . brains:* I am troubled with madness

188 *No . . . myself?* Are there no followers to rescue me? Am I all alone?

189–91 *Why . . . dust:* this sad spectacle would cause a man to melt into tears, to weep so profusely that his tears would water gardens and keep the dust of autumn down

192 *I . . . bridegroom:* still imagining himself a captured monarch, he thinks of a death sentence. The word 'die' has sexual implications, hence the reference to a bridegroom

193 *jovial:* cheerful, merry

196 *Then . . . in't:* then all is not lost

196–7 *Come . . . sa:* Lear is challenging his imagined captors to catch him: if ('and') they are to capture him, they will have to run, like hounds after a hare ('sa' is a hunting call to urge the hounds forward)

200–1 *general . . . to:* the two ('twain') refers to Adam and Eve as well as to Goneril and Regan. The curse is that called down upon nature by the transgression of Adam and Eve

202 *gentle:* noble

202 *speed:* God speed (a polite greeting)

203 *Do . . . toward?* Have you any news of an impending battle?

204 *Most . . . vulgar:* I am sure that the news of this battle is commonly known ('vulgar')

205 *Which . . . sound:* who can hear

Enter GENTLEMAN, with ATTENDANTS.

GENTLEMAN
O here he is! [*to EDGAR*] Lay hand upon him, sir.

[*to LEAR*] Your most dear daughter—

LEAR
No rescue? What, a prisoner? I am even

185 The natural fool of fortune. Use me well:

You shall have ransom. Let me have surgeons;

I am cut to the brains.   *Lear is mad — get me a doctor too.*

GENTLEMAN
                    You shall have any thing.

LEAR
No seconds? All myself?

Why, this would make a man a man of salt,

190 To use his eyes for garden water-pots

Ay, and laying autumn's dust.

I will die bravely, like a smug bridegroom. *double meaning — sexual innuendo*

What! I will be jovial. Come, come; I am a king.

Masters, know you that?

GENTLEMAN
195 You are a royal one, and we obey you.

LEAR
Then there's life in't. Come and you get it, you shall get it

by running. Sa, sa, sa, sa.

Exit, running.

GENTLEMAN
A sight most pitiful in the meanest wretch,

Past speaking of in a king! Thou hast a daughter

200 Who redeems nature from the general curse

Which twain have brought her to.

EDGAR
Hail, gentle sir!

GENTLEMAN
                    Sir, speed you: what's your will?

EDGAR
Do you hear aught, sir, of a battle toward?

GENTLEMAN
Most sure and vulgar. Everyone hears that

Which can distinguish sound.

EDGAR

But, by your favour,   205

How near's the other army?

GENTLEMAN

Near, and on speedy foot; the main descry

Stands on the hourly thought.

EDGAR

I thank you, sir: that's all.

GENTLEMAN

Though that the queen on special cause is here,

Her army is moved on.

EDGAR

I thank you, sir.   210

Exit GENTLEMAN.

GLOUCESTER *repeated idea of him not wanting to kill himself anymore.*

You ever-gentle gods, take my breath from me.

Let not my worser spirit tempt me again

To die before you please!

EDGAR *fourth character ?*

Well pray you, father.

GLOUCESTER

Now, good sir, what are you?

EDGAR

A most poor man, made tame to fortune's blows,   215

Who, by the art of known and feeling sorrows,

Am pregnant to good pity. Give me your hand,

I'll lead you to some biding.

GLOUCESTER

Hearty thanks;

The bounty and the benison of heaven

To boot, and boot!

Enter OSWALD.

OSWALD *here to kill Gloucester*

A proclaimed prize! Most happy!   220

That eyeless head of thine was first framed flesh

To raise my fortunes. Thou old unhappy traitor,

Briefly thyself remember; the sword is out

That must destroy thee.

mean → he is blind.
cannot defend himself
hanus act

207–8	*Near . . . thought:* the other army is near, and advancing rapidly on foot; the main part of that army is hourly expected to come into view
207	*descry:* sight of a distant object
211–13	*You . . . please!* Gloucester is leaving it to the gods to choose the time of his death, and praying that the evil spirit who, he imagines, tempted him to suicide will not again tempt him to die before the time appointed by the gods
213	*father:* this was a common form of address from the young to the old. Edgar keeps talking to Gloucester without being recognised by the latter as his son
215	*made . . . blows:* beaten into submission by the cruel blows of fortune
216–17	*Who . . . pity:* Edgar has observed the grief of others ('known' their sorrows) and experienced his own (the 'feeling sorrows' are the ones he has had to endure); he is therefore inclined to pity those in distress
217	*pregnant:* disposed, receptive
218	*biding:* resting place
218–20	*Hearty . . . and boot!* in addition to offering Edgar his sincere thanks, Gloucester prays that the generosity ('bounty') and blessing ('benison') of heaven may help him to further reward
220	*To . . . boot:* in addition and to your benefit
220	*A proclaimed prize!* an outlaw with a price on his head *Most happy!* most fortunate for me
223	*Briefly thyself remember:* think of your sins, and repent, in the short time you have left

224–5 *Now . . . to't:* Gloucester welcomes the chance to die at Oswald's hand, which is 'friendly' because it is to send him to the death he longs for

225 *peasant:* Oswald casts Edgar in a role the latter immediately begins to act out by adopting peasant speech

226 *published:* proclaimed. There is irony in Gloucester's status as 'a published traitor'; circumstances have made him a fugitive just as he made Edgar one

227–8 *Lest . . . thee:* in case you are also branded as an outlaw for helping him

229 *Chill . . . 'casion:* I shall not let go, sir, without further reason

231–5 *go . . . with you:* get on your way, and let poor people pass. If I were to allow a swaggering bully like you to kill me, I would have died a fortnight ago. Do not come near the old man; keep away, I warrant you, or I shall test whether your head or my cudgel is the harder. I shall be plain with you

232 *zwaggered:* bullied

234 *costard:* the name of an apple, humorously applied to the head

237 *Chill . . . foins:* I shall pick your teeth, sir. I care nothing for your rapier thrust ('foins')

244 *serviceable:* useful in an evil sort of way

245–6 *As . . . desire:* as willing to cater for the vices of your evil employer as she could possibly wish you to be

245 *duteous:* obedient

GLOUCESTER   → *wants to die he just won't do it himself*

Now let thy friendly hand

Put strength enough to't. [*EDGAR intervenes*]
invites him to kill him.

OSWALD

225   Wherefore, bold peasant,

Darest thou support a published traitor? Hence,

Lest that th' infection of his fortune take

Like hold on thee. Let go his arm.

EDGAR   → *just, loyal behavior.*
→ *saving his DAD for the second time*
→ *natural behavior [proper bond]*

Chill not let go, zir, without vurther 'casion.   *puts on accent.*

OSWALD

230   Let go, slave, or thou diest.

EDGAR

Good gentleman, go your gate, and let poor volk pass. And
'chud ha' bin zwaggered out of my life, 'twould not ha' bin
zo long as 'tis by a vortnight. Nay, come not near th' old
man; keep out, che vor' ye, or ice try whither your costard

235   or my ballow be the harder. Chill be plain with you.

OSWALD

Out, dunghill!

EDGAR

Chill pick your teeth, zir. Come; no matter vor your foins.

They fight, and EDGAR knocks him down.

OSWALD

Slave, thou hast slain me. Villain, take my purse.

If ever thou wilt thrive, bury my body,

240   And give the letters which thou find'st about me

To Edmund, Earl of Gloucester. Seek him out

Upon the English party. O untimely death!

Death! [*he dies*]

EDGAR   *servant/villain*

I know thee well: a serviceable villain,

245   As duteous to the vices of thy mistress

As badness would desire.

GLOUCESTER

What, is he dead?

EDGAR

Sit you down, father; rest you —

Let's see these pockets. The letters that he speaks of

May be my friends. He's dead. I am only sorry

He had no other deathsman. Let us see.   250

Leave, gentle wax; and manners blame us not;

To know our enemies' minds we rip their hearts,

Their papers is more lawful. [*reads the letter*]

'Let our reciprocal vows be remembered. You

have many opportunities to cut him off; if your will   255

want not, time and place will be fruitfully offered.

There is nothing done if he return the conqueror,

then am I the prisoner, and his bed my gaol; from

the loathed warmth whereof deliver me, and supply

the place for your labour. *Sexual imagery.*   260

Your wife, so I would say —

Affectionate servant, *·should be focusing on*

Goneril.' *defending Britian from France.*

O undistinguished space of woman's will! *Sexist*

A plot upon her virtuous husband's life,   265

And the exchange my brother! Here, in the sands,

Thee I'll rake up, the post unsanctified

Of murderous lechers; and in the mature time

With this ungracious paper strike the sight

Of the death-practised duke. For him 'tis well   270

That of thy death and business I can tell.

GLOUCESTER

The King is mad; how stiff is my vilde sense,

That I stand up, and have ingenious feeling

Of my huge sorrows! Better I were distract;

So should my thoughts be severed from my griefs,   275

And woes by wrong imaginations lose *wishes he was*

mad like Lear

The knowledge of themselves. *so he wouldn't feel*

this grief.

Drum far off.

EDGAR

                                    Give me your hand,

Far off, methinks, I hear the beaten drum.

Come, father, I'll bestow you with a friend.

Exeunt.

---

250 *deathsman*: executioner. It is not clear whether Edgar is sorry that he had to kill anyone, even Oswald, or he is sorry that Oswald did not meet a more gruesome death

251 *Leave, gentle wax*: Edgar gently forces open the wax seal on the letter

251–3 *manners ... lawful*: the opening of other people's letters is a gross violation of manners. On the other hand, we do not hesitate to torture enemies to the point of death in order to discover their secrets, so ripping open their letters has to be morally more justified (i.e. it is more lawful to rip open their papers than their hearts)

254 *reciprocal vows*: mutual promises of devotion

255 *cut him off*: kill Albany

255–6 *if ... not*: if you are not lacking in determination

257 *done*: achieved

258–60 *from ... labour*: deliver me from the hateful intimacy of Albany's bed, and fill his place there as a reward for your efforts, and as an outlet for your amorous activities

264 *O ... will*: how immeasurable is the extent of woman's lust

267–8 *Thee ... lechers*: I'll give you a shallow, unsanctified grave (not in holy ground), you messenger ('post') for lustful murderers. Edgar is talking about covering Oswald with a thin layer of sand

268 *in ... time*: when the time is ripe

269 *ungracious paper*: evil letter

270 *death-practised*: whose death is being plotted

271 *business*: mischievous activity

272–4 *how ... sorrows!* how stubbornly sound my vile faculties are, that they enable me to retain an acute consciousness of my great miseries

274–7 *Better ... themselves*: it would be better for me if I were insane ('distract'). If I were, I would not be conscious of my sorrows, and these sorrows would not register their pain in my mind because they would lose themselves in insane fantasies

279 *father*: old man
bestow: lodge

Key points

In this moving scene Shakespeare brings the fortunes of the mad Lear and the blinded Gloucester to a simultaneous climax.

- The early part of this scene is devoted to Gloucester's regeneration. Gloucester's intention is to cast off the miseries of his life by suicide. He wants to do this to avoid quarrelling with the gods. Edgar deceives Gloucester into thinking that having supposedly thrown himself over a steep cliff and lived to tell the tale, his miraculous survival is the will of the gods.

- In the face of all the horrors that have befallen him and those he loves, Edgar is still able to preserve a cheerful faith in providential justice, in the miraculous works of 'the clearest gods' (line 74).

- With the 'side-piercing sight' (line 85) of Lear, seemingly madder than ever, and in a fantastic costume of wild flowers, Edgar's optimism is once again undermined.

- Lear's violent denunciations of various kinds of human corruption, particularly female sexual depravity, may be more than simply a symptom of his madness and diseased imagination. The behaviour of Goneril and Regan could understandably lead Lear to curse nature generally, and female nature in particular.

- Paradoxically, Lear's insanity offers the listener inspired insights into unpleasant realities. With all the fervour of an overpowering preacher, he exposes the gross abuses perpetrated by those in authority. His two great speeches (lines 106–29 and 146–66) address the corruption of human nature and of human institutions: hypocrisy, abuse of privilege, social inequalities, the degradation of some human beings by others, the link between lust and sadism, and how money is a criminal's best defence against justice.

- Lear's hatred of life encompasses the natural world: human adultery is mirrored in the behaviour of animals ('The wren goes to't, and the small gilded fly does lecher in my sight'; lines 110–11).

- Lear explores new depths of nihilism in his terrible lines about the absurdity of human life ('When we are born, we cry that we are come to this great stage of fools'; lines 176–7). There is no need to take these words as expressing Lear's (or Shakespeare's) considered view of life. They must be interpreted in context, as the outcome of Lear's despair.

- The key to Lear's 'madness' in this scene is that it goes along with a profound insight into the realities of everyday life. This is recognised by Edgar, who sees in Lear's mad speeches a compound of sense ('matter') and irrelevant nonsense ('impertinency'); Edgar rightly describes this as 'reason in madness' (lines 168–9). The mad Lear has achieved a degree of sanity unavailable to him in his more 'rational' days.

- The second part of the scene ends with an optimistic reference to Cordelia, whose role will be to restore, or redeem, Lear's sense of whatever is good in nature after Goneril and Regan have, because of their unnatural crimes, brought him to curse nature.

- Meanwhile, Gloucester has reconciled himself to the will of the 'ever-gentle gods', hoping that they will not permit his 'worser spirit' to tempt him with suicide again (lines 211–13). Gloucester may not try to take his own life, but he would still be happy to have someone else do it for him. Indicating his reluctance to live any longer, he invites Oswald's 'friendly hand' (line 224), perhaps as an instrument of the gods, to kill him.

- Oswald's mission is to kill Gloucester and raise his own fortunes as a result. Instead, Edgar kills Oswald, who, to the last, remains Goneril's faithful steward. With his dying breath, Oswald asks that her letter to Edmund be delivered. This letter provides Edgar with useful information.

Useful quotes

> Why I do trifle thus with his despair
> Is done to cure it.
>
> (Edgar, lines 33–4)

> Plate sin with gold,
> And the strong lance of justice hurtless breaks;
> Arm it in rags, a pigmy's straw doth pierce it.
>
> (Lear, lines 159–61)

> When we are born, we cry that we are come
> To this great stage of fools.
>
> (Lear, lines 176–7)

> Thou hast a daughter
> Who redeems nature from the general curse
> Which twain have brought her to.
>
> (Gentleman, lines 199–201)

> You ever-gentle gods, take my breath from me.
> Let not my worser spirit tempt me again
> To die before you please!
>
> (Gloucester, lines 211–13)

> I know thee well: a serviceable villain,
> As duteous to the vices of thy mistress
> As badness would desire.
>
> (Edgar, lines 244–6)

Questions ?

1 Discuss Edgar's plan to cure Gloucester of his despair. Do you think his plan is a good one? Explain your answer.

2 What is the explanation for Lear's views on women? Is there anything in the play to justify these remarks?

3 Comment on Edgar's idea of 'reason in madness' (line 169) in relation to this scene.

4 Lear sees the world as 'this great stage of fools' (line 177). What makes him reach this despairing conclusion? Does it take something more than the behaviour of Goneril and Regan towards him to account for it? Explain your answer.

5 Gloucester goes through various changes of outlook and mood in the course of this scene. Describe these changes, saying what you think causes them.

6 Edgar characterises Oswald as 'a serviceable villain, as duteous to the vices of thy mistress as badness would desire' (lines 244–6). What exactly does Edgar mean here? Is he giving a full and fair account of Oswald's character? Support your answers to these questions by reference to the text of the play.

7 Three characters in this scene – Lear, Gloucester and Edgar – express their views on the suffering that human life entails, and on the meaning that this suffering has for them. Comment on ways in which the views of these three characters differ from each other, and what they have in common.

8 Imagine you are a newspaper reporter. Write a short report on the meeting of Lear and Gloucester.

9 It has been said that while Lear and Gloucester experience things, Edgar preaches about them. Agree or disagree with this comment, basing your arguments on the text of the play.

10 If you were directing a performance of *King Lear* (for stage or screen), how would you depict Lear in this scene? Consider issues such as costume, hair, make-up, props, voice and movement in your answer.

ACT 4 ✝ Scene 7

Plot summary

Cordelia and Kent are reunited. A sleeping Lear is carried in. Cordelia prays for his recovery. He awakes and thinks he must be in heaven. When he realises he is not, he asks for forgiveness. The battle between the French and British forces is about to begin.

O look upon me, sir,
And hold your hand in benediction o'er me.

CORDELIA, Act 4, Scene 7, 58–9

A tent in the French camp.

Enter CORDELIA, KENT and GENTLEMAN.

CORDELIA

Justice

O thou good Kent, how shall I live and work

To match thy goodness? My life will be too short

And every measure fail me.

KENT

To be acknowledged, madam, is o'er-paid.

All my reports go with the modest truth;   5

Nor more nor clipped, but so.

CORDELIA

                                        Be better suited.

These weeds are memories of those worser hours:

I prithee, put them off.

KENT

                                        Pardon, dear madam,

Yet to be known shortens my made intent.

My boon I make it that you know me not   10

Till time and I think meet.

CORDELIA

Then be't so, my good lord.

[*to GENTLEMAN*] How does the King?

GENTLEMAN

Madam, sleeps still.

CORDELIA

O you kind gods,   *madness.*   15

Cure this great breach in his abused nature!

Th' untuned and jarring senses, oh, wind up,

Of this child-changed father.

his children have changed him into the

GENTLEMAN *man he is now*

                                        So please your majesty

That we may wake the King? He hath slept long.

CORDELIA

Be governed by your knowledge, and proceed   20

I' the sway of your own will. Is he arrayed?

GENTLEMAN

Ay, madam: in the heaviness of sleep

We put fresh garments on him.

---

2 *My ... short:* this is a grim irony as Cordelia does not realise just how short her life will be

3 *every ... me:* whatever I measure out to you by way of reward will be inadequate (because your goodness is immeasurable)

5–6 *All ... so:* all the reports I have given to you about Lear and about my service to him conform to ('go with') the exact ('modest') truth, being neither exaggerated ('more') nor understated ('clipped'), but accurate. Kent is implying that the rewards suggested by Cordelia in lines 1–3 would have been deserved only if he had done more

6 *suited:* dressed. Kent is still in the clothes he wore to disguise himself as Caius

7 *These ... hours:* these clothes ('weeds') will only remind you of bad times gone by

9–11 *Yet ... meet:* to be publicly recognised at this stage ('yet') would frustrate the plan I have made ('my made intent'). The favour ('boon') I ask of you is that you pretend not to know my true identity until I decide that the time is right ('meet'). Why Kent has to adopt this strategy is not made clear

16 *this ... nature:* this great, gaping wound in his natural powers. The wound is his deluded ('abused') mind

17 *Th' ... up:* Lear's disordered mind is here compared to an instrument whose strings are slack and therefore incapable of producing harmony. When the strings are tightened, harmony is restored

18 *child-changed:* changed for the worse by the conduct of his children

21 *I' ... will:* as you yourself wish or decide *arrayed:* dressed in his royal robes

22 *in ... sleep:* when he was in a deep sleep

Be by, good madam, when we do awake him;

I doubt not of his temperance.

CORDELIA

Very well.

GENTLEMAN/DOCTOR

Please you, draw near. — Louder the music there!

Enter LEAR (clad in royal robes) asleep in a chair carried by SERVANTS.

CORDELIA

O my dear father! Restoration hang

Thy medicine on my lips, and let this kiss

Repair those violent harms that my two sisters

Have in thy reverence made!

KENT

Kind and dear princess!

CORDELIA

Had you not been their father, these white flakes

Did challenge pity of them. Was this a face

To be opposed against the warring winds?

To stand against the deep dread-bolted thunder?

In the most terrible and nimble stroke

Of quick, cross-lightning? To watch, poor perdu,

With this thin helm? Mine enemy's dog,

Though he had bit me, should have stood that night

Against my fire. And wast thou fain, poor father,

To hovel thee with swine and rogues forlorn,

In short and musty straw? Alack, alack!

'Tis wonder that thy life and wits at once

Had not concluded all. — He wakes; speak to him.

GENTLEMAN

Madam, do you; 'tis fittest.

CORDELIA

How does my royal lord? How fares your majesty?

LEAR

You do me wrong to take me out o' the grave.

Thou art a soul in bliss; but I am bound

Upon a wheel of fire, that mine own tears

Do scald like molten lead.

CORDELIA

Sir, do you know me?

LEAR

You are a spirit, I know. Where did you die?   50

CORDELIA

[*to GENTLEMAN*] Still, still far wide.

GENTLEMAN

He's scarce awake: let him alone awhile.

LEAR

Where have I been? Where am I? Fair daylight?

I am mightily abused. I should e'en die with pity,

To see another thus. I know not what to say.   55

I will not swear these are my hands. Let's see:

I feel this pin-prick. Would I were assured

Of my condition!   · they should be in different places

CORDELIA   she = good   he = bad

O look upon me, sir,

And hold your hand in benediction o'er me.

LEAR falls to his knees.

You must not kneel.

LEAR

Pray, do not mock me.   60

I am a very foolish fond old man,

Fourscore and upward, not an hour more nor less,

And, to deal plainly,

I fear I am not in my perfect mind.

Methinks I should know you and know this man,   65

Yet I am doubtful; for I am mainly ignorant

What place this is; and all the skill I have

Remembers not these garments, nor I know not

Where I did lodge last night. Do not laugh at me,

For, as I am a man, I think this lady   70

To be my child Cordelia.

CORDELIA

[*weeps*] And so I am, I am.

LEAR

Be your tears wet? Yes, faith. I pray, weep not.

If you have poison for me, I will drink it.

---

50 *You are ... die?* this line depends on the Doomsday context created by lines 46–9. With a whole world of men and women rising from their graves, it is natural for one to wonder where another died

51 *far wide:* Lear's mind is still wandering; he has not returned to sanity

54 *abused:* deluded, uncertain. Lear is not sure that Cordelia is real

55 *thus:* deluded and bewildered like myself

57 *pin-prick:* as Lear pricks his hand with a pin, and feels the sensation, he can justifiably hope that his madness is abating. In Shakespeare's time there was a theory that the power of touch was adversely affected by madness

59 *benediction:* blessing

· alliteration 'foolish → soft sound.   fond '

61 *fond:* silly, doting   ✱contrast.

62 *Fourscore:* eighty

65 *this man:* Kent (disguised as Caius)

66 *mainly:* completely

74 *If ... it:* this is Lear's blunt way of expressing his guilt and his repentance

*he expects rough justice.
  *punishment.

– She had every right to punish him
– other sisters didn't and yet did.

77 *No cause:* Cordelia is as reluctant as she was in Act 1 to express her feelings in high-sounding language

78 *your own kingdom:* Britain, over which you are still king

80 *rage:* delirium

82 *To ... lost:* to make him re-live his distressing experiences, and so fill in the time he has lost through insanity

84 *Till further settling:* until he has become somewhat calmer, more settled

85 *walk:* retire, withdraw

88 *Holds it true:* has it been confirmed

91 *conductor:* leader

justice (Lear expects punishment)

75 I know you do not love me, for your sisters
Have, as I do remember, done me wrong.
You have some cause; they have not.

CORDELIA

No cause, no cause.

LEAR
Am I in France?

KENT

In your own kingdom, sir.

LEAR
Do not abuse me.

GENTLEMAN
Be comforted, good madam. The great rage,
80 You see, is killed in him; and yet it is danger
To make him even o'er the time he has lost.
Desire him to go in; trouble him no more
Till further settling.

CORDELIA
85 Will't please your highness walk?

LEAR
You must bear with me. Pray you now, forget
and forgive. I am old and foolish.

Exeunt all but KENT and GENTLEMAN.

GENTLEMAN
Holds it true, sir, that the Duke of Cornwall was so slain?

KENT
90 Most certain, sir.

GENTLEMAN
Who is conductor of his people?

KENT
As 'tis said, the bastard son of Gloucester.

GENTLEMAN
They say Edgar, his banished son, is with the Earl of Kent in Germany.

KENT

Report is changeable. 'Tis time to look about. The powers   95

of the kingdom approach apace.

95   *look about:* be on guard, be careful
95–6   *The ... kingdom:* the British forces
96   *apace:* swiftly

GENTLEMAN

The arbitrament is like to be bloody. Fare you well, sir.

Exit.

97   *arbitrament:* decisive battle
like: likely

KENT

My point and period will be throughly wrought,

Or well or ill, as this day's battle's fought.

Exit.

98–9   *My ... fought:* depending on the outcome of today's battle, the purpose and end of my life will be completely worked out ('throughly wrought'), whether for good or ill. Kent means that the battle will decide whether his work is to have a good or bad conclusion

Key points

This scene is divided into two parts. The reunion of Cordelia and Kent anticipates the reunion of Lear and Cordelia.

- Lear awakens from a deep, restorative sleep to a new life. His regeneration comes about as he is exposed to the influence of Cordelia, who represents what is good in human nature, and to the healing powers of sleep, curative herbs and music.

- Lear had been driven to madness by his unbearable sense of an overwhelming evil in every aspect of nature. In this scene he is restored to sanity when confronted by natural goodness and benevolence.

- Lear's recognition of Cordelia, and her response, are the most moving and memorable things in this scene, and in the play as a whole. All this is done in the briefest of exchanges and the simplest words (lines 69–72).

- Lear repents, in violent, exaggerated tones, for what he has done to her: 'If you have poison for me, I will drink it' (line 74). Cordelia's reassurance that she has 'no cause' (line 77) against him is also exaggerated (since she has some cause), but it is exaggerated in the direction of total forgetfulness on her part of whatever wrong

was done to her. She is unconscious of any feelings but her love for her father and her desire to restore him to health.

- Shakespeare handles the reconciliation of Lear and Cordelia with exquisite tact. In Act 1, Scene 1 Cordelia could not express her deepest feelings in rhetorical flourishes as her sisters could. She is still sparing in her speech, but her few simple words carry an immense weight of conviction and significance: 'And so I am, I am. … No cause, no cause' (lines 72, 77). She still cannot heave her heart into her mouth.

- One of the darker implications of the play is that the happiness engendered in this scene cannot endure. It will be all too quickly destroyed before the evil forces relinquish their power over the universe of the play.

- The whole scene provides a remarkable contrast to the turmoil, agitation, cruelty and hatred of previous scenes. The calm, loving reconciliation of this scene, however, is followed by further scenes of turmoil in Act 5.

Useful quotes

O thou good Kent, how shall I live and work
To match thy goodness? My life will be too short
And every measure fail me.

(Cordelia, lines 1–3)

O you kind gods,
Cure this great breach in his abused nature!
Th' untuned and jarring senses

(Cordelia, lines 15–17)

O my dear father! Restoration hang
Thy medicine on my lips, and let this kiss
Repair those violent harms that my two sisters
Have in thy reverence made!

(Cordelia, lines 27–30)

? Questions

1 Describe Lear's feelings as he recovers consciousness.

2 Discuss the symbolism in this scene.

3 Do Cordelia's qualities of character and outlook make her unique? Name the character whose qualities most resemble those exemplified in Cordelia. Explain your answers with reference to the text.

4 'Louder the music there!' (line 26) Describe the function of music in this scene and suggest what type of music would be appropriate.

Scene 1

- Edgar, still disguised as Poor Tom, meets his blinded father.
- Gloucester, intent on suicide by throwing himself from the cliffs at Dover, wants Edgar to lead him there.

Scene 2

- Oswald reveals that Albany is a changed man and cannot accept that Lear and Cordelia are the enemy, that Gloucester is a traitor and that Edmund is loyal and honest.
- Goneril expresses her ardent love for Edmund.
- Albany condemns Goneril as a barbarous, degenerate woman, and Regan as no better.
- Cornwall's death is revealed, causing Goneril to worry that Regan, now a widow, might want to marry Edmund.
- Albany expresses a determination to avenge Gloucester's blinding.

Scene 3

- We learn of Cordelia's grief when she read about her father's sufferings.
- Kent describes the shame that prevents Lear from wanting to reunite with Cordelia.

ACT 4 ✟ Key moments

Scene 4

- Lear, as mad as the vexed sea, and crowned like a festival king with weeds, is wandering through the countryside, singing aloud – Cordelia orders a search for him.
- It is hoped that sleep and natural herbal remedies will cure Lear's troubled mind.

Scene 5

- Regan, distracted with jealousy, wants to know what Goneril has written in a letter to Edmund.
- Oswald, loyal steward to Goneril, will not let Regan open the letter.
- Regan wants Goneril to know that she cannot have Edmund.
- Regan asks Oswald to kill Gloucester if he meets him.

Scene 6

- Edgar is able to persuade Gloucester that, in attempting suicide, he has fallen a great height, but has had his life preserved by the just gods.
- Lear launches a series of violent condemnations of corruptions rampant in human society, with special emphasis on female depravity and the power of money to corrupt the administration of justice.
- Lear runs away from a group of people trying to apprehend him on Cordelia's behalf.
- Oswald, attempting to carry out Regan's order to kill Gloucester, is slain by Edgar, who finds an incriminating letter from Goneril to Edmund on Oswald's body.

Scene 7

- Cordelia is reunited with Kent.
- Lear has been restored to sanity, and Cordelia and Lear are reconciled.

ACT 4 ✟ Speaking and listening

1 In groups of four, assign the roles of two production team members and two actors playing Gloucester and Edgar. Imagine you are meeting to discuss the staging of Gloucester's apparent suicide attempt (Act 4, Scene 6, lines 1–81). Identify the difficulties of staging this episode and discuss how they might be overcome.

2 Having assigned the part of Lear, divide into groups of three to agree a list of questions and to choose one member from each group to interview him. The purpose of the interview will be to get Lear to explain his strong views on women, on immoral behaviour and on the corruption he sees at the heart of the justice system, all expressed in Act 4, Scene 6, lines 106–66. He might be asked to explain the origin of these views, and when he first came to hold them.

ACT 5 ✝ Scene 1

Plot summary

The developing jealousies and suspicions involving Goneril and Regan in their lust for Edmund now threaten to disrupt the fragile unity of Lear's enemies. Regan suspects Edmund and Goneril of sleeping together. Goneril's grim aside indicates her determination not to allow Regan to take Edmund from her. Albany affirms that he is going into battle to repel foreign invasion rather than to oppose Lear. His position does not please Goneril and Regan, and underlines the fragmentation of Lear's enemies, but they agree to fight together. Edgar (still in disguise) makes his way into the British camp and gives Albany Goneril's letter to Edmund. He says he will return later if the herald's trumpet sounds. Edmund, in soliloquy, reveals his heartless, cynical attitude to the two women fighting over him. He also reveals his determination to benefit from the hoped-for elimination of Albany by Goneril when the battle is over, and his plan to have Lear and Cordelia murdered.

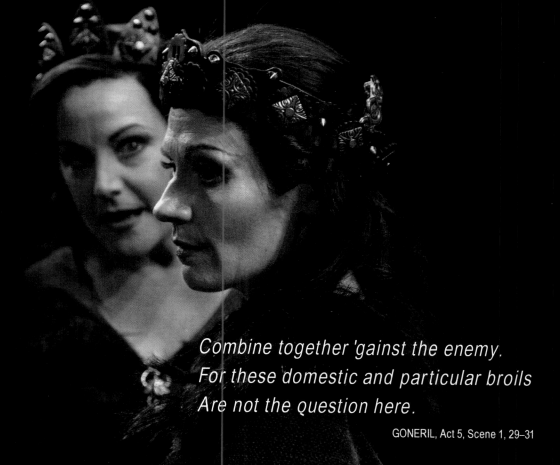

Combine together 'gainst the enemy.
For these domestic and particular broils
Are not the question here.

GONERIL, Act 5, Scene 1, 29–31

The British camp near Dover.

Enter, with drum and colours, EDMUND, REGAN, OFFICERS, GENTLEMEN, and SOLDIERS.

EDMUND

Know of the duke if his last purpose hold,

Or whether since he is advised by aught

To change the course. He's full of alteration

And self-reproving. Bring his constant pleasure.

OFFICER goes out.   paradox for Albany.

REGAN

Our sister's man is certainly miscarried.   5

EDMUND
                                  suspected.
'Tis to be doubted, madam.

REGAN

                        Now, sweet lord,

You know the goodness I intend upon you:

Tell me, but truly, but then speak the truth,

Do you not love my sister?

EDMUND

                        In honoured love.

REGAN

But have you never found my brother's way   10

To the forfended place?

EDMUND

                        That thought abuses you.

REGAN

I am doubtful that you have been conjunct

And bosomed with her, as far as we call hers.

EDMUND

No, by mine honour, madam.

REGAN

I never shall endure her. Dear my lord,   15

Be not familiar with her.

EDMUND

                        Fear me not:

She and the duke her husband—

1–4	*Know . . . pleasure:* find out from Albany if his intention to join Regan and myself against Lear and Cordelia still stands, or whether he has been induced by any new considerations to change his plans. His mind is constantly changing, and he is overcome by scruples and self-criticism. Bring me news of his final, firm decision
5	*Our . . . miscarried:* Oswald must have come to some harm
6	*doubted:* feared, suspected
7	*goodness:* favour *intend upon you:* mean to show you, mean to confer upon you
9	*honoured:* honourable
10	*brother's:* Albany's
11	*forfended:* forbidden. The 'forfended place' is Goneril's bed, which is forbidden to Edmund as long as Albany lives
11	*abuses:* dishonours, does no credit to
12	*doubtful:* suspicious
12–13	*conjunct . . . hers:* 'conjunct' and 'bosomed' can suggest that Edmund has been merely in Goneril's confidence – 'of her bosom' means 'in her confidence'. By adding 'as far as we call hers', Regan is suggesting that the Edmund–Goneril relationship is more than one of shared confidences; it is an intimate physical one in which Edmund is Goneril's ('hers') in every sense
14	*by mine honour:* this is one of the many ironies involving Edmund. If Regan knew the truth about his intentions, she would find this reference to his 'honour' most inappropriate
15	*endure her:* put up with her as your lover
16	*familiar:* overly intimate *Fear me not:* you have no reason to distrust me

19 *loosen:* unbind, break up

20 *well be-met:* well met (a common greeting)

22–3 *With . . . out:* Lear has joined Cordelia in the company of others whom the harshness of our rule has forced into opposition

23–4 *Where . . . valiant:* I have never been able to fight bravely for a cause that I could not fully support

25–7 *It . . . oppose:* Albany wants everybody to understand that Lear and his friends are not to be regarded as national enemies or conspirators, and that the French invasion is not Lear's responsibility. The King of France is their enemy as an invader; not as Lear's agent. Albany is saying: the French invasion is my concern because a foreign invasion is a threat to Britain. I am not prepared to accept that the invasion is prompting Lear and his friends to oppose our state; their opposition to our rule is founded on their just and serious grievances

28 *Why . . . reasoned?* What is the point of this talk about our motives for fighting?

29–31 *Combine . . . here:* let us unite against the common enemy; this is neither the time nor the place to discuss our national and personal differences

32–3 *Let's . . . proceeding:* in that case ('then'), having consulted our most experienced officers (the 'ancient of war'), let us decide how we should organise ourselves for battle

36 *convenient:* appropriate, fitting

Enter, with drum and colours, ALBANY, GONERIL and SOLDIERS.

GONERIL [*aside*]
I had rather lose the battle than that sister
Should loosen him and me.

ALBANY
20 Our very loving sister, well be-met.
Sir, this I hear: the King is come to his daughter,
With others whom the rigours of our state
Forced to cry out. Where I could not be honest,
I never yet was valiant. For this business,
25 It touches us as France invades our land,
Not bolds the King, with others — whom, I fear,
Most just and heavy causes make oppose.

EDMUND
Sir, you speak nobly.

REGAN
                                    Why is this reasoned?

GONERIL
Combine together 'gainst the enemy.
30 For these domestic and particular broils
Are not the question here.

ALBANY
Let's then determine with th' ancient of war
On our proceeding.

EDMUND
                                    I shall attend you
Presently at your tent.

REGAN
                                    Sister, you'll go with us?

GONERIL
35 No.

REGAN
'Tis most convenient. Pray go with us.

GONERIL [*aside*]

O, ho! I know the riddle. [*aloud*] I will go.

As they are exiting, enter EDGAR (disguised).

EDGAR   5th disguise

[*to ALBANY*] If e'er your grace had speech with man so poor,

Hear me one word.

ALBANY

[*to his OFFICERS*] I'll overtake you.

Exeunt all but ALBANY and EDGAR.

       Speak.   40

EDGAR

Before you fight the battle, ope this letter.

If you have victory, let the trumpet sound

For him that brought it; wretched though I seem,

I can produce a champion that will prove

What is avouched there. If you miscarry,   45

Your business of the world hath so an end,

And machination ceases. Fortune love you!

ALBANY

Stay till I have read the letter.

EDGAR

       I was forbid it.

When time shall serve, let but the herald cry,

And I'll appear again.

ALBANY

      Why, fare thee well.   50

I will o'er-look thy paper.

Exit EDGAR.

Enter EDMUND.

EDMUND

The enemy's in view; draw up your powers.

Here is the guess of their true strength and forces

By diligent discovery; but your haste

Is now urged on you.

ALBANY

      We will greet the time.   55

Exit.

---

37 *O ... go:* Goneril finds a hidden meaning ('riddle') behind Regan's words. She knows that Regan wants to keep a close eye on her dealings with Edmund. This will be possible if Goneril goes with Regan and Edmund to the Council of War

40 *overtake you:* catch you up

41 *ope this letter:* open this letter (the one from Goneril to Edmund that Edgar found in Oswald's possession in Act 4, Scene 6)

44 *champion:* one who fights in single combat on his own behalf, on behalf of somebody else or on behalf of a cause
45 *avouched there:* declared in the letter
45–7 *If ... ceases:* if you lose ('miscarry') the battle, your worldly activity will be at an end, and as far as you are concerned, all plots and intrigues will also be at an end
47 *machination:* intrigue, plotting (against Albany)

49 *herald:* an officer employed to convey challenges and marshal the combatants in a tournament

51 *o'er-look:* peruse, read
thy paper: the letter you have given me

52 *powers:* troops
53 *guess:* estimate
54 *By diligent discovery:* arrived at after a painstaking reconnaissance
54–5 *but ... you:* your present urgent business requires your immediate attention (and will not allow you much time to look at my report of the enemy's strength)
55 *greet the time:* welcome the opportunity or occasion (to do battle)

EDMUND

To both these sisters have I sworn my love;

Each jealous of the other, as the stung

Are of the adder. Which of them shall I take?

Both? One? Or neither? Neither can be enjoyed

60   If both remain alive. To take the widow

Exasperates, makes mad, her sister Goneril;

And hardly shall I carry out my side,

Her husband being alive. Now then, we'll use

His countenance for the battle, which being done,

65   Let her who would be rid of him devise

His speedy taking off. As for the mercy

Which he intends to Lear and to Cordelia,

The battle done, and they within our power,

Shall never see his pardon; for my state

70   Stands on me to defend, not to debate.

Exit.

57 *jealous:* suspicious

62–3 *And . . . alive:* I shall find it extremely difficult to fulfil my side of the bargain with Goneril, seeing that her husband is alive. Edmund's side of the bargain is to satisfy Goneril's lust; in return, she will advance his worldly prospects. There is an alternative meaning here. 'Carry out my side' can mean 'win my game', which in Edmund's case is now the crown

64 *His . . . battle:* Albany's authority, while the battle is being fought

65–6 *devise . . . off:* engineer a speedy death for him

68–9 *The . . . pardon:* when the battle is over, and Lear and Cordelia are under our control, they will not live to see the pardon Albany has in mind for them

69–70 *for . . . debate:* if I am to maintain my position, I am obliged to defend it actively, and not spend time discussing questions of right and wrong

Key points

This scene focuses on the deadly conflict of jealousy and passion between Goneril and Regan. It contrasts with the final scene of Act 4, in which we witnessed the love of Lear and Cordelia.

- This scene brings the breach between Goneril and Regan into the open. In Act 1, Scene 1 they were united in their hypocritical deception of their father and in the advancement of their own interests at his expense. As the action progressed they appeared able to combine a rational, calculating attitude with a passion for brutality. After Cornwall's death, however, with Regan free to marry Edmund and Goneril planning Albany's death to enable her to do the same, lustful jealousy displaced rational calculation. The consequences are exhibited in this scene.

- The mutual hatred of Goneril and Regan, engendered by the fierce desire of each for Edmund, is, in its own way, as deep as the love exhibited in the previous scene. The difference is that the forces motivating Goneril and Regan are negative and destructive, in contrast to the positive, creative impulses underlying the Lear–Cordelia relationship.

- The scene also reveals the contrast between Edmund's attitude to the two rival sisters and their attitude to him. He remains as rational and level-headed as ever, indifferent to the agonising torments of passionate jealousy that Goneril and Regan are suffering over him.

- Edmund's soliloquy displays his ruthless attitude. It also reveals the problem he has created for himself, and for which he can find no immediate solution. He has sworn his love to each of these jealous sisters, but when he speculates on choosing between them, his cynical mind is baffled ('Which of them shall I take? Both? One? Or neither? Neither can be enjoyed if both remain alive'; lines 58–60).

- It is significant that Goneril, in her letter, urged Edmund to kill her husband ('You have many opportunities to cut him off'; Act 4, Scene 6, lines 254–5). Edmund, however, would prefer to leave this task to Goneril herself. Indeed, although Edmund is responsible for the physical suffering and/or death of other characters, he never carries out these acts himself.

- It should be observed that Albany does not want anyone to think that the French invasion is prompting Lear and his supporters to oppose the British state. Instead, he believes that Lear's party has serious and just reasons for opposing the rulers of Britain, as distinct from opposing the state itself.

Useful quotes

> *Now, sweet lord,*
> *You know the goodness I intend upon you:*
> *Tell me, but truly, but then speak the truth,*
> *Do you not love my sister?*
>
> (Regan, lines 6–9)

> *I never shall endure her. Dear my lord,*
> *Be not familiar with her.*
>
> (Regan, lines 15–16)

> *For this business,*
> *It touches us as France invades our land,*
> *Not bolds the King, with others — whom, I fear,*
> *Most just and heavy causes make oppose.*
>
> (Albany, lines 24–7)

> *The battle done, and they within our power,*
> *Shall never see his pardon*
>
> (Edmund, lines 68–9)

? Questions

1 'In this scene personal relationships are of more pressing importance than political affairs.' Do you agree with this statement? Support your answer by referring to the text of the play.

2 What is Albany's attitude to the French invasion? How does this present him with a problem? How does he propose to deal with this problem?

3 Does Edmund agree with Albany on this issue? Support your answer with evidence from the text of the play.

4 Describe the atmosphere of this scene. Support your answer by referring to the text of the play.

5 Is there any indication as to how the play will end? Make a list setting out the plans and hopes of each of the major characters at this point in the play, and consider whether you expect each of them to succeed. When you reach the end of the play, you can update this list with the actual outcome for each character.

ACT 5 † Scene 2

Plot summary

Edgar leaves his father under a shady tree with a promise of hope and comfort; Gloucester prays for him. The battle between the French and British forces takes place off stage. Edgar returns quickly with the cruellest tidings: the French army has lost the battle and Cordelia and Lear have been taken prisoner. Gloucester sinks into the blackest despair, and Edgar has to persuade him to move to a safer place.

No further, sir; a man may rot even here.

GLOUCESTER, Act 5, Scene 2, 8

A field between the two camps.

*Alarum within. Enter, with drum and colours, LEAR,
CORDELIA, and SOLDIERS, over the stage; and exeunt.*

Enter EDGAR and GLOUCESTER.

EDGAR

Here, father, take the shadow of this tree

For your good host. Pray that the right may thrive.

If ever I return to you again,

I'll bring you comfort.

GLOUCESTER

                Grace go with you, sir!

Exit EDGAR.

Alarum and retreat within. Re-enter EDGAR.

EDGAR

Away, old man! Give me thy hand; away!   5

King Lear hath lost; he and his daughter ta'en.

Give me thy hand; come on.

GLOUCESTER

No further, sir; a man may rot even here.

EDGAR

What, in ill thoughts again? Men must endure

Their going hence, even as their coming hither;   10

Ripeness is all. Come on.

GLOUCESTER

                    And that's true too.

Exeunt.

---

2 *Alarum:* call to arms. The French side marches across and off the stage (to battle)

2 *For . . . host:* as a pleasant place of shelter for you
right: just, true

4 *comfort:* relief, joy. Edgar's characteristically buoyant optimism will again be immediately shattered. The 'comfort' he promises Gloucester is ironically converted to the dismal news of the defeat and capture of Lear and Cordelia

retreat within: the French army is retreating, off stage

6 *ta'en:* taken prisoner

8 *No further . . . here:* I do not want to go any further; this is as good a place to rot as any other

9 *ill thoughts:* evil, unworthy reflection
9–11 *Men . . . is all:* Edgar is rebuking Gloucester for seeing death merely as a matter of rotting away passively. He is saying: we must endure the ache and pain of our birth and equally the harsh ordeal that terminates in death. What is really important is that we should be prepared to wait for the time fixed for our death, to live out our lives to the end
11 *Ripeness:* maturity

Key points

The fluctuating moods of the play, its constant reversals, its juxtaposition of joy and sorrow, hope and despair, affirmation and negation, are all captured in miniature here

- Shakespeare disposes of the outward, 'public', action (i.e. the battle) with extraordinary economy and rapidity. The crucial battle, on which the destinies of the main characters depend, is not depicted on stage. Instead, the outcome is conveyed in the stark stage direction, 'Alarum and retreat within', and in Edgar's report, 'King Lear hath lost; he and his daughter ta'en' (line 6).

- The play contains many episodes that appear to underline the futility of looking to the heavenly powers for help, pity or the alleviation of human suffering. These episodes highlight the ironic contrast between the hopes nourished by belief in divine goodness and the apparent indifference or blindness of the gods to such hopes. Here, Edgar urges Gloucester to 'pray that the right may thrive', assuring

him that 'if ever I return to you again, I'll bring you comfort' (lines 2–4). He returns only to lead his father away; his prayers have not been answered, the battle has been lost and Lear and Cordelia are captives.

- Gloucester's moods continue to fluctuate. The news of the battle plunges him into what Edgar calls 'ill thoughts' (line 9). He wants to stop moving and die where he is. Once more, Edgar has to restore his will to go on with another of his inspirational sayings ('Men must endure their going hence, even as their coming hither; ripeness is all'; lines 9–11). Gloucester's comment on this ('And that's true too', line 11) suggests that defeatism and endurance are held in equilibrium; each as valid as the other. No final affirmation, it seems, can be made.

Useful quotes

If ever I return to you again,
I'll bring you comfort.

(Edgar, lines 3–4)

King Lear hath lost; he and his daughter ta'en.

(Edgar, line 6)

? Questions

1 In what way might this scene be regarded as a miniature version of the play as a whole?

2 Is Edgar helpful to Gloucester in this scene?

3 Edgar appeared naïve in Act 1, Scene 2. Now he feels able to give advice to his father, which the latter accepts. Account for Edgar's arrival at the level of understanding shown in this scene.

4 Describe how Shakespeare handles the battle in this scene. If you were creating a theatre or film version of the play, how would you deal with the battle?

ACT 5 ✝ Scene 3

Plot summary

Lear and Cordelia are imprisoned, on the orders of Edmund. With characteristic unselfishness, Cordelia is concerned for Lear, not for herself. Lear foresees a future in which the two of them are united in prison, enjoying their time together and safe from their enemies. Edmund instructs his Captain to follow them to prison and gives him a note on what to do with them. The orders are not specified, but their sinister significance is clear.

Albany asks Edmund to hand the prisoners over to him. When he refuses to comply, Albany sharply rebukes the upstart Edmund. Regan defends Edmund's right to equality with Albany, since he has led her army and acted on her behalf. Goneril argues that Regan is not the source of Edmund's status. Regan feels ill and is led away. Albany arrests Goneril and Edmund on a charge of high treason. A challenge is issued to anyone who can prove Edmund's treason by means of a trial by combat. Edgar, in disguise, emerges and defeats Edmund, who is fatally injured. Albany publicly exposes the dealings of Goneril and Edmund. Goneril runs off stage. Edgar reveals his identity and gives an account of his last encounter with Gloucester. A Gentleman enters with a bloody knife and reports that Goneril has poisoned Regan and killed herself.

It takes Kent's arrival to remind those on stage of the absence of Lear and Cordelia. Edmund, moved by the thought that he has been loved, determines to perform a good deed before he dies. His good impulse comes too late, however, as Lear enters with the hanged Cordelia in his arms. Kent reveals his true identity. Lear dies in the hope that Cordelia is still alive and can be saved. Albany wants Edgar and Kent to help him rebuild the kingdom. Kent declines. Edgar calls for an honest response to the events that have occurred.

The British camp near Dover.

Enter, in conquest, with drum and colours, EDMUND; LEAR and CORDELIA, as prisoners; CAPTAIN and SOLDIERS.

EDMUND

Some officers take them away: good guard,

Until their greater pleasures first be known

That are to censure them.

CORDELIA

caring cordelia   We are not the first

Who with best meaning have incurred the worst.

5 For thee, oppressed King, I am cast down;

Myself could else out-frown false fortune's frown.

[*to EDMUND*] Shall we not see these daughters and these sisters? *worried about her father.*

LEAR → *finally realised that family is the most important thing.*

No, no, no, no. Come, let's away to prison;

We two alone will sing like birds i' the cage;

10 When thou dost ask me blessing, I'll kneel down

And ask of thee forgiveness. So we'll live,

And pray, and sing, and tell old tales, and laugh

At gilded butterflies, and hear poor rogues

Talk of court news; and we'll talk with them too,

15 Who loses and who wins, who's in, who's out;

And take upon us the mystery of things,

As if we were God's spies. And we'll wear out,

In a walled prison, packs and sects of great ones

That ebb and flow by the moon.

EDMUND *reminder that it won't be as easy.*   Take them away.

LEAR

20 Upon such sacrifices, my Cordelia,

The gods themselves throw incense.

Have I caught thee?

He that parts us shall bring a brand from heaven, ← *heavenly only power that will split them up*

And fire us hence like foxes. Wipe thine eyes;

25 The good years shall devour them, flesh and fell,

Ere they shall make us weep;

We'll see 'em starved first. Come.

Exeunt LEAR and CORDELIA, guarded.

Margin notes (left column):

1 *good guard:* make sure they are well guarded

2–3 *Until . . . them:* until those in higher authority, whose function it is to pass sentence ('censure') on them, make their wishes known

5–6 *For . . . frown:* Cordelia is dejected ('cast down') for Lear's sake; her concern is for his welfare. If she had to think only of her own fate, she would defy fickle ('false') fortune to do its worst

6 *else:* otherwise

7 *daughters . . . sisters:* Goneril and Regan. There is bitter sarcasm in Cordelia's words

8–24 *Come . . . foxes:* Lear has reached the peak of his religious awareness, and feels in harmony with the wishes and purposes of the gods. He thinks of Cordelia and himself as partakers in privileged knowledge imparted by the heavens

ideal retirement

13 *gilded butterflies:* this is probably a reference to empty-headed, brightly dressed courtiers

13–14 *poor . . . news:* wretched individuals pitied by Lear because of their interest in so insignificant a thing as the news at court. Lear and Cordelia will share an interest in higher things

15 *Who loses . . . out:* which courtiers have fallen from favour, and which ones have replaced them

16 *And . . . things:* assume responsibility for explaining the mysteries of existence

17 *God's:* this is the play's only direct mention of God in the Christian sense

17–19 *we'll . . . moon:* in our secure prison we'll outlast the plots ('packs') and factions ('sects') of those in authority, whose fortunes vary from month to month

20–1 *Upon . . . incense:* even the gods bow in reverence before such sacrifices as those being made by Lear and Cordelia, who have renounced the world

22 *caught:* achieved union with

23–4 *He . . . foxes:* those who part us will be forced to burn us out with fire from heaven, just as foxes are driven from their dens by fire

reassure

23 *brand:* a piece of burning wood, a torch

25–6 *The . . . weep:* our enemies will be utterly destroyed before they will again bring tears to our eyes. The animal natures of Regan and Goneril are suggested in 'flesh and fell' ('fell' is animal skin)

EDMUND

Come hither, captain; hark.

Take thou this note. Go follow them to prison.

One step I have advanced thee; if thou dost   30

As this instructs thee, thou dost make thy way

To noble fortunes. Know thou this, that men

Are as the time is; to be tender-minded

Does not become a [sword]. Thy great employment

Will not bear question; either say thou'lt do't,   35

Or thrive by other means. *be fired.*

CAPTAIN

                    I'll do't, my lord.

EDMUND

About it; and write happy when thou hast done.

Mark, I say, instantly; and carry it so

As I have set it down.

CAPTAIN

I cannot draw a cart nor eat dried oats;   40

If it be man's work, I'll do't.

Exit.

Flourish. Enter ALBANY, GONERIL, REGAN, and SOLDIERS.

ALBANY

Sir, you have showed today your valiant strain,

And fortune led you well. You have the captives

Who were the opposites of this day's strife.

I do require them of you, so to use them   45

As we shall find their merits and our safety

May equally determine.

EDMUND

                  Sir, I thought it fit

To send the old and miserable King

To some retention and appointed guard;

Whose age had charms in it, whose title more,   50

To pluck the common bosom on his side,

And turn our impressed lances in our eyes

Which do command them. With him I sent the queen,

My reason all the same; and they are ready

Tomorrow, or at further space, t' appear   55

Where you shall hold your session. At this time

---

28 *hark:* listen

29 *this note:* we later discover that this is a warrant, signed by Edmund and Goneril, for the murder of Lear and Cordelia

31–2 *make . . . fortunes:* become a nobleman

32–3 *men . . . is:* the behaviour of men is decided by the circumstances ('time') in which they find themselves

33–4 *to . . . sword:* in time of war there is no room for mercy (it is not appropriate to a soldier)

34–5 *Thy . . . question:* this major assignment I am giving you cannot be discussed or debated. Edmund is reluctant to express in plain words his instructions covering the murder of Lear and Cordelia

37 *About it:* get on with it, go and do it
write happy: describe yourself as happy

38–9 *carry . . . down:* arrange the business exactly according to my written instructions

40–1 *I . . . do't:* I am not a horse and I am not prepared to work or eat like a slave, but I will undertake manly duties

42 *your valiant strain:* the brave spirit you have inherited from your ancestors

44 *the opposites:* our enemies

45–7 *so . . . determine:* my counsellors and I ('we') will deal with ('use') them according to their deserts, without putting our own safety at risk. We will make our decision on the case ('determine' it) impartially and justly. It is worth remarking that Albany is not proposing to pardon Cordelia and Lear, but to judge them

49 *To . . . guard:* to a place of confinement or custody under a duly appointed guard

50–3 *Whose . . . them:* Lear's old age, and still more his title and rights, will win the affections of ('charm') the hearts of the common people, and turn our conscripted soldiers ('impressed lances') against us ('our eyes') who control them

53 *queen:* Cordelia

55 *at further space:* at a later time

56 *session:* trial

58-9 *the best ... sharpness*: even the worthiest causes may be looked upon unfavourably in the heat of the moment by those who are smarting from the wounds they have sustained at their hands. Edmund is implying that if Lear and Cordelia were to be tried by their enemies in the recent battle, while these enemies were still grieving over their losses, they might not get a fair trial. Edmund's real purpose here is to gain time while his agent murders Lear and Cordelia

61 *a fitter place*: a more appropriate place than this military camp

61-3 *Sir ... brother*: if you will pardon my saying so, sir, I regard you as a subordinate in this war, not as a brother-in-law. Albany's rebuke is heavy with irony given that he is now aware of Edmund's relationships with Goneril and Regan

63-8 *That's ... brother*: the title of brother-in-law ('brother') is the one it pleases me to honour Edmund with. Before you spoke so harshly to him, you might have consulted my wishes. After all, he commanded our forces, and acted as my deputy; his status as my immediate subordinate makes him entitled to be regarded as your brother-in-law

63 *list*: desire, please

68 *hot*: fast

69-70 *In ... addition*: Edmund's status owes more to his personal qualities than to any title ('addition') you can confer on him

70-1 *In ... best*: the privilege of rank I have conferred on him makes him equal to the best

72 *That ... you*: even if he were your husband, you could not say more for him (i.e. Edmund would become Albany's equal only through acquiring Regan's power by marrying her)

73 *Jesters ... prophets*: this is a variation of the proverb: there's many a true word spoken in jest

74 *That eye ... asquint*: Regan's jealousy has distorted her vision and her judgement

76 *From ... stomach*: angrily

76-8 *General ... me*: Regan offers herself and all her worldly possessions to Edmund

77 *patrimony*: what she has inherited from her father

78 *the walls is thine*: Regan may be thinking of herself as a fortress willingly yielding itself to the besieger Edmund

79 *Witness the world*: let the world take note

80 *Mean ... him?* Do you intend to take Edmund as your mate? The question is cruelly ironic, since at this point Goneril knows that Regan, whom she has poisoned, will not live long enough to enjoy anything

We sweat and bleed; the friend hath lost his friend,
And the best quarrels in the heat are cursed
By those that feel their sharpness;
The question of Cordelia and her father 60
Requires a fitter place.

ALBANY
                          Sir, by your patience;
I hold you but a subject of this war,
Not as a brother.

REGAN
                          That's as we list to grace him.
Methinks our pleasure might have been demanded
Ere you had spoke so far. He led our powers, 65
Bore the commission of my place and person,
The which immediacy may well stand up
And call itself your brother.

GONERIL
                          Not so hot!
In his own grace he doth exalt himself
More than in your addition.

REGAN
                          In my rights, 70
By me invested, he compeers the best.

ALBANY
That were the most if he should husband you.

REGAN
Jesters do oft prove prophets.

GONERIL
                          Holla, holla!
That eye that told you so looked but asquint.

REGAN
Lady, I am not well; else I should answer 75
From a full-flowing stomach. [*to EDMUND*] General,
Take thou my soldiers, prisoners, patrimony;
Dispose of them, of me; the walls is thine.
Witness the world that I create thee here
My lord and master.

GONERIL
                          Mean you to enjoy him? 80

ALBANY

The let-alone lies not in your good will.

EDMUND

Nor in thine, lord.

ALBANY

Half-blooded fellow, yes. *illigitamate*

REGAN

[*to EDMUND*] Let the drum strike, and prove my title thine.

ALBANY

Stay yet; hear reason. Edmund, I arrest thee

On capital treason, and, in thine attaint,   85

[*points to GONERIL*] This gilded serpent. For your claim, fair
   sister,

I bar it in the interest of my wife.

'Tis she is sub-contracted to this lord,

And I, her husband, contradict your banns.

If you will marry, make your loves to me;   90

My lady is bespoke.

GONERIL

              An interlude! *lighthearted;*

ALBANY

Thou art armed, Gloucester, let the trumpet sound.

If none appear to prove upon thy person

Thy heinous, manifest and many treasons,

There is my pledge. [*throws down his glove*]

             I'll make it on thy heart,   95

Ere I taste bread, thou art in nothing less

Than I have here proclaimed thee.

REGAN

                Sick, O sick!

GONERIL [*aside*]   *cruelty.*

If not, I'll ne'er trust medicine.

EDMUND

There's my exchange. [*throws down his glove*]

            What in the world he is

That names me traitor, villain-like he lies.   100

Call by thy trumpet. He that dares approach,

On him, on you — who not? — I will maintain

My truth and honour firmly.

---

81 *let-alone:* veto

82 *Half-blooded fellow, yes:* Albany, reminding
Edmund that he is an illegitimate child, tells him
that he (Albany) has the power to prevent a union
between Edmund and Regan

83 *Let . . . thine:* prove victorious in combat with
Albany, and retain the sovereign powers I have
conferred on you

84 *Stay . . . reason:* wait a moment; listen to my
argument

85 *capital:* punishable by death

85–6 *in . . . serpent:* I also arrest Goneril, the outwardly
beautiful but inwardly corrupt creature who has
provided the evidence against you. Edmund's
'attaint' (or impeachment) is possible only because
of Goneril's incriminating letter

86–91 *For . . . bespoke:* as for your claim, my beautiful
sister-in-law, to marry Edmund, I exclude it from
consideration because of my wife's rights in the
matter. It is she who, having been pledged to
Edmund before you were, has the prior claim to
him, and I, her husband, acting on her behalf,
overrule your announced intention to marry
Edmund. If you wish to marry, propose to me; I am
free to marry because my wife is already pledged
('bespoke') to Edmund

88 *sub-contracted:* betrothed or engaged to one man
(Edmund) while still married to another (Albany)

91 *An interlude!* What a farce! An interlude was a
light-hearted piece performed between the acts of
medieval miracle and morality plays

94 *heinous:* odious, highly criminal
manifest: obvious, evident

95 *pledge:* a token (here, a glove) to be taken up by
the person prepared to accept the challenge to
combat

95–7 *I'll . . . thee:* I shall not eat again until I have
demonstrated, by piercing you to the heart, that
you are in no respect less than the traitor I have
already called you

98 *medicine:* poison

99 *exchange:* a technical term for the token (here, a
glove) thrown down in reply to a challenge
What . . . is: whatever worldly rank or title he may
hold

100 *villain-like:* like a slave

101 *Call . . . trumpet:* call in the trumpeter

101–3 *He . . . firmly:* I will justify ('maintain') my truth
and honour in the most determined way against
('on') you or anybody else who dares approach to
challenge me

104-6 *Trust ... discharge:* you will have to depend on your unaided valour ('single virtue') because the soldiers you led, who were recruited ('levied') in my name, have been disbanded, also in my name

108 *convey:* carry

111 *quality or degree:* nobility or high rank
lists: rolls

113 *manifold traitor:* traitor in many ways

117 *purposes:* intentions

* standing up for
his father and the country

119 *quality:* degree of nobility. Only a challenger of noble origin is acceptable

120-1 *Know ... canker-bit:* Edmund's treasonable conspiracy has destroyed my good name and forced me to give up my identity
canker-bit: withered, as if eaten by the canker-worm

ALBANY

                              A herald, ho!
Trust to thy single virtue, for thy soldiers,
105   All levied in my name, have in my name
Took their discharge.

REGAN
My sickness grows upon me.

ALBANY
She is not well; convey her to my tent.

REGAN is led away.

Enter a HERALD.

Come hither, herald. Let the trumpet sound,
110   And read out this.

A trumpet sounds.

HERALD
[*reads*] 'If any man of quality or degree within the lists of the army will maintain upon Edmund, supposed Earl of Gloucester, that he is a manifold traitor, let him appear by the third sound of the trumpet. He is bold in his defence.'

First trumpet sounds.

HERALD
115   Again!

Second trumpet.

HERALD
Again!

Third trumpet.

Trumpet answers within.

Enter EDGAR (armed).

ALBANY
Ask him his purposes, why he appears
Upon this call o' the trumpet.

HERALD
                              What are you?
Your name? Your quality? And why you answer
This present summons?

EDGAR — doing the right thing.

120   Know, my name is lost:
By treason's tooth bare-knawn and canker-bit;

irony.

Yet am I noble as the adversary

I come to cope.

ALBANY

              Which is that adversary?

EDGAR

What's he that speaks for Edmund, Earl of Gloucester?

EDMUND

Himself: what say'st thou to him?

EDGAR

                      Draw thy sword,   125

That, if my speech offend a noble heart,

Thy arm may do thee justice; here is mine: [*draws his sword*]

Behold, it is the privilege of mine honours,

My oath and my profession. I protest,

Maugre thy strength, place, youth and eminence,   130

Despite thy victor-sword and fire-new fortune,

<u>Thy valour and thy heart, thou art a traitor,</u>

<u>False to thy gods, thy brother and thy father;</u>

Conspirant 'gainst this high illustrious prince, Albany

And, from th' extremest upward of thy head   135

To the descent and dust below thy foot,

A most <u>toad-spotted traitor</u>. Say thou 'No',

This sword, this arm and my best spirits are bent

To prove upon thy heart, whereto I speak,

Thou liest.

EDMUND

              In wisdom I should ask thy name;   140

But since thy outside looks so fair and warlike,

And that thy tongue some say of breeding breathes, *you sound noble.*

What safe and nicely I might well delay

By rule of knighthood, I disdain and spurn.

Back do I toss these treasons to thy head,   145

With the hell-hated lie o'er-whelm thy heart,

Which, for they yet glance by and scarcely bruise,

This sword of mine shall give them instant way,

Where they shall rest for ever. Trumpets, speak.

Alarums. They fight. EDMUND falls.

---

has to be equal status.
| duel = status |

123 *cope:* match in combat

125–7 *Draw . . . justice:* prepare to fight, so that if any of the charges I am bringing against you are unjustified, you may prove them false in battle

127–9 *here . . . profession:* look at my sword ('mine'); my honour, the oath I swore when I became a knight, and my knighthood itself ('my profession') all entitle me to the privilege of drawing this sword against an adversary and of having my challenge answered

129 *protest:* state formally, declare

130 *Maugre:* in spite of
     place: position of power
     eminence: advantage, superiority

131 *victor-sword:* recent success in battle
     fire-new fortune: newly acquired status as army commander and Earl of Gloucester. 'Fire-new' means 'newly minted' (like a coin)

132 *heart:* courage

134 *Conspirant . . . prince:* a conspirator against Albany

135–6 *from . . . foot:* from the top ('extremest upward') of your head to the sole of your foot

137 *toad-spotted traitor:* stained ('spotted') with treason as a toad is spotted with venom or poison

138 *bent:* directed

140 *In . . . name:* it would be prudent of me to find out who you are, since I am not obliged to fight an opponent of lesser rank than myself

142 *And . . . breathes:* and because the quality of your speech provides some evidence that you are a man of breeding
     say: flavour, taste (also, perhaps, 'assay' or proof)

143–4 *What . . . spurn:* I scornfully dismiss and reject the idea of avoiding this encounter by resorting to caution (being 'safe') and a strict interpretation of the rules (acting 'nicely'), although the code of knighthood allows me to so do

143 *delay:* avoid

145–9 *Back . . . ever:* I throw your accusations back at your head and heart, but since ('for') my retort is merely verbal, it glances off your armour without doing you any real harm. However, my sword will thrust your accusations directly and urgently into your heart, where they will remain, and thus mark you out as the real traitor
     Alarums: skirmishes

150 *Save him:* the reference is to the wounded Edmund. We can only speculate as to why Albany desires to spare Edmund's life at that moment but it may be to confront him with the evidence for his crimes (see line 156)

151 *practice:* treachery

153 *opposite:* opponent
vanquished: defeated

154 *cozened and beguiled:* cheated and deceived

154 *dame:* woman

155 *this paper:* the letter from Goneril to Edmund, found by Edgar in Oswald's possession
Hold, sir: Albany again intervenes to keep Edmund alive

157 *tearing:* presumably Goneril snatches at the letter in an attempt to tear or destroy it

158–9 *Say ... for't:* even if I do know all about the letter, I make the laws, not you, who are merely my consort. So who is in a position to bring me to trial ('arraign me') for what I have done?

ALBANY

150 [*to EDGAR, who is about to kill EDMUND*] Save him, save him!

GONERIL

This is practice, Gloucester:

By the law of arms thou wast not bound to answer

An unknown opposite. Thou art not vanquished,

But cozened and beguiled.

ALBANY

manhood back
. contrast   Shut your mouth, dame,

155 Or with this paper shall I stop it. [*to EDGAR*] Hold, sir;

[*to EDMUND*] Thou worse than any name, read thine own evil.

[*to GONERIL*] No tearing, lady: I perceive you know it.

GONERIL

Say if I do, the laws are mine, not thine.

Who can arraign me for't?

ALBANY

Most monstrous! O!

[*to EDMUND*] Know'st thou this paper?   160

EDMUND

Ask me not what I know.

Exit GONERIL.

ALBANY

Go after her; she's desperate, govern her.

Exit an OFFICER.

EDMUND

What you have charged me with, that have I done;

And more, much more; the time will bring it out.

'Tis past, and so am I. But what art thou   165

That hast this fortune on me? If thou'rt noble,

I do forgive thee.

EDGAR

Let's exchange charity.

I am no less in blood than thou art, Edmund;

If more, the more th' hast wronged me.

My name is Edgar, and thy father's son.   170

The gods are just, and of our <u>pleasant vices</u>

Make instruments to plague us:

The dark and vicious place where thee he got,

Cost him his eyes.   *punished for his crimes.*   •karma.

*[handwritten: → Gloucester • protecture = Edgar. *cost him his eyes. | Justice]*

EDMUND

Th' hast spoken right. 'Tis true;

The wheel is come full circle; I am here.   175

ALBANY

[*to EDGAR*] Methought thy very gait did prophesy

A royal nobleness. I must embrace thee.

Let sorrow split my heart if ever I

Did hate thee or thy father.

EDGAR

Worthy prince, I know't.

ALBANY

Where have you hid yourself?   180

How have you known the miseries of your father?

---

161   *Ask ... know:* it is unclear whether Edmund refuses to answer out of defiance, or as a show of chivalry towards Goneril

162   *desperate:* in a state of despair
govern: restrain, control

164   *more, much more:* Edmund is probably referring to his order for the deaths of Lear and Cordelia

166   *That ... me:* who gained this victory over me

166–7   *If ... thee:* in his first soliloquy (Act 1, Scene 2, lines 1–22), Edmund showed his contempt for breeding; here, he recognises its claims with an absurd touch of snobbery

167   *charity:* forgiveness

168–9   *I ... me:* I am no less well-bred than you are; if my legitimacy makes me nobler than you, then you have wronged me all the more

171–4   *The ... eyes:* heavenly justice ensures that those vicious deeds that give us pleasure become instruments of torture to punish us; the dark sinful deed that led to your conception also led to the darkness of our father's blind condition

175   *The ... here:* the illegitimate Edmund began life at the lowest point of fortune's wheel. It carried him to the top, but now that the wheel has completed its turn, he is at the bottom once more, his life ebbing away

176   *Methought ... prophesy:* it seemed to me that your very bearing indicated

EDGAR

By nursing them, my lord. List a brief tale;

And when 'tis told, O that my heart would burst!

The bloody proclamation to escape

185 That followed me so near — O our lives' sweetness,

That we the pain of death would hourly die

Rather than die at once — taught me to shift

Into a madman's rags, t'assume a semblance

That very dogs disdained; and in this habit

190 Met I my father with his bleeding rings,

Their precious stones new lost; became his guide,

Led him, begged for him, saved him from despair;

Never — O fault! — revealed myself unto him

Until some half-hour past, when I was armed;

195 Not sure, though hoping, of this good success,

I asked his blessing, and from first to last

Told him our pilgrimage; but his flawed heart —

Alack, too weak the conflict to support —

'Twixt two extremes of passion, joy and grief,

Burst smilingly.   *Gloucest died*
              heart attack.   ● overjoyed.

EDMUND   *→ divine justice   ✱ wanted to die =*
                                    now doesn't ↑
200   This speech of yours hath moved me,   *dies.*

And shall perchance do good. But speak you on;

You look as you had something more to say.

ALBANY

If there be more, more woeful, hold it in;

For I am almost ready to dissolve,

Hearing of this.

EDGAR

205   This would have seemed a period

To such as love not sorrow; but another

To amplify too much would make much more

And top extremity.

Whilst I was big in clamour, came there in a man,

210 Who, having seen me in my worst estate,

Shunned my abhorred society; but then, finding

Who 'twas that so endured, with his strong arms

He fastened on my neck and bellowed out

As he'd burst heaven, threw him on my father,

182–200 *List . . . smilingly:* the whole speech is a single suspended sentence, much of it recording matters already familiar to the audience, but nevertheless conveying two vital items of information concerning Edgar's revelation of his identity to Gloucester, and the death of the latter

184 *The . . . escape:* my desire to escape the death sentence

185 *That . . . near:* which put my life in imminent danger

185–7 *O . . . once:* the fact that we would rather suffer pains equal to those of death every hour than die and rid ourselves of all pain serves to show that life is sweet

187 *shift:* change

188 *t'assume a semblance:* to take on a likeness

189 *habit:* outfit

190–1 *bleeding . . . lost:* eyeless sockets resembling rings without jewels

193 *fault:* sin, error

194 *some half-hour past:* a half-hour ago

195 *good success:* successful outcome (the defeat of Edmund)

196 *I . . . blessing:* the wronged Edgar asks the father who has wronged him to bless him (just as the wronged Cordelia asked a blessing from her erring father; Act 4, Scene 7, line 59)

197 *our pilgrimage:* our journeys together. 'Pilgrimage' has obvious religious overtones, suggesting salvation after a period of trial and suffering

197–200 *his . . . smilingly:* his shattered heart, alas too weak to endure ('support') the conflict between joy (at his reconciliation with Edgar) and grief (at the horrors he has experienced), burst in a sudden surge of happiness

201 *But . . . on:* although Edmund knows that urgent action is needed to save Lear and Cordelia, he is prepared to listen further to Edgar

204 *dissolve:* burst into tears

205–8 *This . . . extremity:* my account of Gloucester would have convinced those who do not enjoy dismal stories that the limit of sorrow had been reached. Another story like that one would, by adding new sorrows to already excessive ones, pass beyond tolerable limits

209 *big in clamour:* uttering loud cries of grief
a man: Kent

210 *worst estate:* poorest state (when Edgar was Poor Tom)

211 *Shunned . . . society:* avoided my repulsive company

212 *that so endured:* who had lived as Poor Tom

213 *fastened on:* threw his arms around

214 *As he'd:* as if he would
threw him: threw himself

Told the most piteous tale of Lear and him   215

That ever ear received; which in recounting,

His grief grew puissant, and the strings of life

Began to crack. Twice then the trumpets sounded,

And there I left him tranced.

ALBANY

                        But who was this?

EDGAR

Kent, sir, the banished Kent; who in disguise   220

Followed his enemy King, and did him service

Improper for a slave.

Enter GENTLEMAN (with a bloody knife).

GENTLEMAN

Help, help, O help!

EDGAR

                What kind of help?

ALBANY

                          Speak, man!

EDGAR

What means this bloody knife?

GENTLEMAN

                    'Tis hot, it smokes!

It came even from the heart of — O she's dead!   225

ALBANY

Who dead? Speak, man.

GENTLEMAN

Your lady, sir, your lady! And her sister

By her is poisoned; she confesses it.

EDMUND

I was contracted to them both. <u>All three</u>

<u>Now marry</u> in an instant.

EDGAR

                  Here comes Kent.   230

Enter KENT (no longer in disguise).

ALBANY

Produce the bodies, be they alive or dead.

Exit GENTLEMAN.

[Handwritten margin notes: "Gonerie has killed herself with a knite." and "married in death"]

216 *received:* heard

217 *puissant:* powerful

217–18 *the strings . . . crack:* his heart began to break. This is a clear indication of the imminent death of Kent

219 *tranced:* senseless

221 *his enemy King:* the king who was hostile to him

222 *Improper for:* beneath the dignity of

224 *smokes:* steams with fresh blood

225 *O she's dead!* at this point, the audience may expect this statement to refer to Cordelia

227 *Your lady:* Goneril, your wife

229–30 *I . . . instant:* I was engaged to both of them; all three of us are now to be united in death

231 *Produce:* exhibit

tension has been overarching, now released

This judgement of the heavens, that makes us tremble,

Touches us not with pity. [*to KENT*] O, is this he?

The time will not allow the compliment

Which very manners urges.   *·divine justice*

KENT

235   I am come

To bid my King and master aye good night.

Is he not here?

ALBANY

                          Great thing of us forgot!

Speak, Edmund, where's the King? And where's Cordelia?

The bodies of GONERIL and REGAN are brought in.

See'st thou this object, Kent?

KENT

Alack, why thus?

EDMUND   *pity.*

240   Yet Edmund was beloved.

The one the other poisoned for my sake,

And after slew herself.

ALBANY

Even so. Cover their faces.

EDMUND

dying. I pant for life. Some good I mean to do

245   Despite of mine own nature. Quickly send —

Be brief in it — to the castle, for my writ

Is on the life of Lear and on Cordelia.

Nay, send in time.   *good*

ALBANY

                          Run, run, O run!

EDGAR

To who, my lord? Who hath the office? Send

250   Thy token of reprieve.

EDMUND

Well thought on. Take my sword,

Give it the captain.

EDGAR

                          Haste thee, for thy life.

Exit OFFICER.

232–3   *This . . . pity:* the action of the gods in bringing about the deaths of Edmund, Goneril and Regan arouses fear rather than pity. Albany believes that the gods dispense just punishment to the wicked

234–5   *The time . . . urges:* the dire emergency ('time') in which we find ourselves will not allow us to observe the normal ceremonial courtesies that mere ('very') good manners should dictate

236   *To . . . night:* to say a final farewell to Lear. We must assume that he is thinking of saying farewell to Lear with his own last breath, not suspecting that Lear will die before he does
aye: for eternity

237   *Great . . . forgot!* Lear and Cordelia have been forgotten. This would have been unthinkable at the start of the play and is perhaps symbolic of their loss of power in Britain

239   *object:* sight (the bodies of Goneril and Regan)

240   *Yet:* in spite of everything
Edmund was beloved: it is significant that as the bodies of Goneril and Regan are put on display, Edmund's sole thought is of himself. His primary emotion is self-satisfaction, but it may be misplaced as the feelings Goneril and Regan had for him were probably motivated more by lust than by love

244   *I . . . life:* Edmund is nearing death
244–8   *Some . . . time:* that Lear and Cordelia may be spared now seems a real possibility
246   *brief in it:* quick about it
246–7   *my . . . of:* I have ordered the deaths of

249   *my lord:* Edgar is addressing Albany
office: commission
250   *token of reprieve:* sign that they are not to be killed

EDMUND

[*To ALBANY*] He hath commission from thy wife and me

To hang Cordelia in the prison, and

To lay the blame upon her own despair   255

That she fordid herself.

255–6   *To . . . herself:* to make it look like she had killed
        herself in despair

256   *fordid:* destroyed

ALBANY

The gods defend her! — Bear him hence awhile.

EDMUND is borne off.

*Enter LEAR, with CORDELIA in his arms, followed by OFFICER
and others.*

257   *The gods defend her!* Albany's fervent prayer
      followed immediately by the entry of Lear bearing
      the dead Cordelia is the cruellest of all the ironies
      in the play. Again, a hopeful sentiment gets a
      bleakly negative answer; the gods do nothing to
      defend Cordelia

LEAR   *onomatopeia.*

Howl, howl, howl! O you are men of stones!   *realism*
                                              where is god?

Had I your tongues and eyes I'd use them so

That heaven's vault should crack. She's gone for ever.   260

I know when one is dead and when one lives.   *REF*
                                              to see
She's dead as earth. Lend me a looking-glass;   *better*

If that her breath will mist or stain the stone,

Why, then she lives!

260   *heaven's vault:* the sky

260–4   *She's . . . she lives!* Lear is unable to accept the
        unbearable truth that Cordelia is dead

262   *looking-glass:* mirror

263   *stone:* mirror

KENT

                    Is this the promised end?
                        Doomsday

EDGAR

Or image of that horror?

264–5   *Is this . . . horror?* Is this Doomsday, that day of the
        final dissolution of the earth? Or simply a spectacle
        representing that terrible event? Kent's 'promised
        end' is one of three references to the end of the
        world in the play. See also Lear's first speech in the
        storm (Act 3, Scene 2, lines 1–9) and Gloucester's
        'This great world shall so wear out to naught' (Act
        4, Scene 6, lines 132–3)

ALBANY

                    Fall, and cease.   265

265   *Fall, and cease:* fall, heaven, and let things
      end. Albany, overcome by the spectacle of the
      heartbroken Lear and the dead Cordelia, prays that
      Doomsday may indeed come, and that all things
      on earth may come to an end

LEAR

This feather stirs! She lives! If it be so,

It is a chance which does redeem all sorrows   *• denial*
                                               • internal
                                               * torture*
That ever I have felt.   *• madness*
                                               → tragic hero.
                                               (suffering)

267   *redeem:* compensate me for. This is one of the
      many words with a specifically Christian meaning
      introduced by Shakespeare into his 'pagan' play

KENT

                    O my good master!

LEAR

Prithee, away!

EDGAR

                    'Tis noble Kent, your friend.

LEAR   *• reacted*
                                               * earlier*
A plague upon you, murderers, traitors all!   270

I might have saved her! Now she's gone for ever!

270–1   *A . . . her!* Lear curses those around him as
        murderers for having distracted his attention for a
        moment; in that moment, he imagines, he might
        have saved Cordelia's life

Sexist

→Goneril/Regan

277 *falchion:* a curved broad sword, with the edge on the convex side. The adjective 'biting' is appropriate, since the point faced inwards

278 *him:* the 'slave' who was hanging Cordelia; the younger Lear would have prolonged this man's agony by making him skip

279 *these . . . me:* the troubles of my old age prevent me from being the swordsman I once was

280 *I'll . . . straight:* I'll be able to recognise you in a moment

281–2 *If . . . behold:* as Lear and Kent look at each other, they each see a person who has experienced good and then bad fortune

283 *dull sight:* sad spectacle

285 *Caius:* this is the first indication that Kent's assumed name has been Caius

287 *He'll strike:* he'll strike a blow in defence of his master

289 *I'll . . . straight:* I'll attend to that [Kent's business] in a moment. Lear's mind is returning to Cordelia

290 *That . . . decay:* who from the beginning of the change ('difference') and decline ('decay') in your fortunes

292 *Nor . . . else:* I am really Kent, and not anyone else

293 *fordone:* destroyed

294 *desperately are dead:* have died in a state of despair, so that their souls are lost, without hope of salvation

Cordelia, Cordelia, stay a little! Ha!

What is't thou say'st? Her voice was ever soft,

Gentle and low, an excellent thing in woman.

275 I killed the slave that was a-hanging thee.

OFFICER
'Tis true, my lords, he did.

LEAR
                                    Did I not, fellow?

I have seen the day, with my good biting falchion,

I would have made him skip. I am old now,

And these same crosses spoil me — Who are you?

280 Mine eyes are not o' the best, I'll tell you straight.

KENT
If fortune brag of two she loved and hated,

One of them we behold.

LEAR
This is a dull sight. Are you not Kent?

KENT
The same, your servant Kent.

285 Where is your servant Caius?

LEAR
He's a good fellow, I can tell you that;

He'll strike, and quickly too. He's dead and rotten.

KENT
No, my good lord. I am the very man—

LEAR
I'll see that straight.

KENT
290 That from your first of difference and decay

Have followed your sad steps.

LEAR
                                    You are welcome hither.

KENT
Nor no man else. All's cheerless, dark and deadly.

Your eldest daughters have fordone themselves,

And desperately are dead.

> *All's cheerless, dark and deadly.*
>
> KENT, Act 5, Scene 3, 292

LEAR

                Ay, so I think.

ALBANY

He knows not what he says, and vain is it   295

That we present us to him.

EDGAR

                    Very bootless.

Enter MESSENGER.

MESSENGER

Edmund is dead, my lord.

ALBANY

                       That's but a trifle here.

You lords and noble friends, know our intent:

What comfort to this great decay may come

Shall be applied. For us, we will resign,   300

During the life of this old majesty,

To him our absolute power:

[*to EDGAR and KENT*] You to your rights

With boot and such addition as your honours

Have more than merited. All friends shall taste   305

The wages of their virtue, and all foes

The cup of their deservings. O see, see!

295–6 *vain ... him:* we would be wasting our time presenting ourselves to him

296 *bootless:* fruitless, useless

297 *but a trifle:* not important

299 *this great decay:* Lear, now merely a noble ruin, a piece of decayed royalty

300 *we will resign:* Albany's proclamation means that Lear will die a king

304 *with ... addition:* with such additional titles of honour
     boot: something given in addition
     honours: noble deeds

307 *O see, see!* Albany's optimistic vision of virtue rewarded is displaced by a grim spectacle – perhaps Lear collapses beside Cordelia, or is struggling to pick her up

308 *my poor fool:* this is commonly taken to refer to Cordelia – 'fool' being a term of endearment, Cordelia having just been hanged, and the remainder of the speech referring exclusively to her. However, some commentators contend that it is the Fool

312 *undo this button:* if the button is at Lear's throat, he is suffocating and wants it loosened; if it is at Cordelia's throat, perhaps he thinks that it is her clothes (or the noose) preventing her from breathing

313–14 *Do . . . there!* several critics have argued, on the strength of these lines (which are not found in the Quarto version), that Lear dies in an ecstasy of joy, thinking he detects signs of life in Cordelia

315–18 *Break . . . longer:* Kent suggests that Lear's death is due to a broken heart. As Edgar vainly tries to prolong Lear's life, Kent begs him to let Lear enjoy the merciful release of death

317 *the . . . world:* the world has been a rack to Lear. The 'rack' was an instrument of torture on which the victim was stretched

318 *Stretch . . . longer:* this suggests both torturing Lear for a longer period of time, and stretching him out to a greater extent

319–20 *The . . . life:* he lived longer than the normal biblical span of years allotted to men (i.e. three score and ten – seventy)

322–3 *Friends . . . realm:* if taken literally, he is offering to renounce his own powers, and to make Edgar and Kent ('you twain') joint rulers of the kingdom. Albany may even remove the crown from his head, thus repeating Lear's action in Act 1, Scene 1. It is also possible, however, that he is simply asking Kent and Edgar to be his counsellors

323 *the . . . sustain:* prevent the further disintegration of a society already torn apart by violence

324–5 *I have . . . no:* Kent is refusing Albany's offer of a share in the government of Britain; he cannot, he says, long outlive his master, Lear, who is calling to him from another world

326 *The . . . obey:* we must recognise the fact that this is a time of national sorrow and act responsibly

327 *Speak . . . say:* Edgar may be referring to the love-test of Act 1, Scene 1, in which Cordelia chose to voice her true feelings, rather than say what she was expected to say

328–9 *The . . . long:* these lines convey the impression that while those who remain will not suffer to the same extent as those who have gone, they are also of lesser stature than their predecessors

LEAR

And my poor fool is hanged! No, no, no life!

Why should a dog, a horse, a rat have life,

310 And thou no breath at all? Thou'lt come no more;

Never, never, never, never, never.

Pray you undo this button. Thank you, sir.

Do you see this? Look on her! Look, her lips!

Look there! Look there! [*he dies*]

EDGAR

He faints. My lord, my lord!

KENT

Break heart; I prithee break.

EDGAR

315   Look up, my lord.

KENT

Vex not his ghost. O let him pass. He hates him

That would upon the rack of this tough world

Stretch him out longer.

EDGAR

He is gone indeed.

KENT

The wonder is he hath endured so long.

320 He but usurped his life.

ALBANY

Bear them from hence. Our present business

Is general woe. [*to KENT and EDGAR*] Friends of my soul, you twain,

Rule in this realm, and the gored state sustain.

KENT

I have a journey, sir, shortly to go.

325 My master calls me; I must not say no.

EDGAR

The weight of this sad time we must obey;

Speak what we feel, not what we ought to say.

The oldest hath borne most: we that are young

Shall never see so much, nor live so long.

Exeunt with a dead march.

Key points

This bleak but fast-moving final scene features the deaths of many of the play's main characters. It is characterised by violence, disappointment, grief and sorrow.

- The first movement of this scene (lines 1–27) appears to mark a paradoxical triumph for Lear and Cordelia. Defeated in battle and now in captivity, Lear can only contemplate the future with delight. He and Cordelia will exchange blessings and forgiveness in prison, where he imagines they will have a mysterious union with the gods, and view mere worldly affairs with detachment.

- By this stage in the play, however, we have learned that hopes of a better future tend to be disappointed. There is already a shadow over Lear's idyllic vision of the future: Edmund's determination, expressed at the end of Act 5, Scene 1, that neither Lear nor Cordelia shall enjoy Albany's pardon. As Lear and Cordelia leave the stage for prison, Edmund is indeed arranging their murder with one of his officers.

- The brightest hopes of Lear and Cordelia are exposed as mere illusions. Fate, working through Edmund and his Captain, has a different, darker end in store for them than the one Lear has joyfully envisaged. Cordelia's words will prove ironically apt: 'We are not the first who with best meaning have incurred the worst' (lines 3–4).

- The arrival of Albany, who demands to be given control of the prisoners, seems to hold out the promise that Lear and Cordelia may, after all, be spared. However, Albany's lack of urgency proves fatal to their chances of survival. Instead of insisting on the immediate handing over of the captives, he allows a diversionary argument to develop between Goneril and Regan arising out of their feelings for Edmund.

- The prospects of a reprieve for Lear and Cordelia progressively diminish. The audience is acutely conscious of this. Even when the Gentleman arrives with the bloody knife, and everyone might well think that it is the blood of Lear or Cordelia, there is still no move to rescue them.

- Edgar's appearance in the role of heroic warrior and avenger of wrong leads to a dramatic reversal of the hopes of the confident, calculating Edmund, who seemed to have had everything under control. Edmund was on the winning side for the great battle, whereas Edgar was on the losing side, but Edgar's loss and Edmund's victory are quickly reversed in single combat between the two.

- Before, he dies, Edmund speaks one of his most memorable lines: 'The wheel is come full circle; I am here' (line 175). The image of the wheel of fortune sums up Edmund's career, which started at the bottom, rose to the top and, as the wheel completes its turn and he lies dying on the ground, is again at the bottom.

- Edmund offers conditional forgiveness to Edgar for killing him ('If thou'rt noble, I do forgive thee'; lines 166–7). This indicates Edmund's sense of his own importance: he would be reluctant to forgive an adversary for killing him in single combat unless his opponent happened to be a nobleman.

- Notice that as Edgar agrees to forgive Edmund in return, he cannot resist drawing a moral lesson from all that has transpired and tells Edmund that Gloucester's blindness was an illustration of the principle that 'The gods are just, and of our pleasant vices make instruments to plague us: the dark and vicious place where thee he got, cost him his eyes' (lines 171–4). Edgar's verdict does not do much credit to the gods – it is hardly 'just' to respond to human wrongdoers by inventing instruments of torture to plague them with.

- Edgar's severe 'poetic justice' depends on the argument that if Edmund had not been born then Gloucester would not have lost his eyes, but this ignores the fact that what actually cost Gloucester his eyes was his humane and virtuous intervention on Lear's behalf. This is a compelling irony.

- The part played by Edgar in this scene proves disastrous for Lear and Cordelia. Unaware that Edmund has arranged to have them speedily murdered, Edgar embarks on a long-winded account: first of how he attended to his father's needs, revealed his identity to him, asked his blessing and witnessed his death, and then of his encounter with Kent.

- Edmund, looking at the dead bodies of Goneril and Regan, is greatly moved by the fact that two women loved him so much that one poisoned the other and then slew herself. His feeling of self-satisfaction in the contemplation of the extent to which he, who loved nobody but himself, was able to attract such devotion, takes practical form in a decision to defy his own natural instinct by doing some good. His attempt to do good by cancelling the order to have Lear and Cordelia hanged comes too late.

- In a play full of cruel ironies, Albany's prayer, 'The gods defend her!' (line 257), followed as it is by the harrowing stage direction, 'Enter Lear, with Cordelia in his arms', is the cruellest of all.

- Some of the circumstances surrounding Lear's death scene are disputed, because some of his comments are ambiguous. The most celebrated of these ambiguities is: 'And my poor fool is hanged!' (line 308). The question at issue is whether Lear is referring to the Fool or to Cordelia. The Fool's last words in the play were spoken in Act 3, Scene 6 ('And I'll go to bed at noon'; line 82). It is difficult to explain why he should turn up to witness the hanging of Cordelia and be hanged as well. However, if Lear is not referring to the Fool, the latter is the only one of the characters whose fate is unknown. As a reference to Cordelia, the term would make sense, since it was a common term of endearment, and Cordelia has just been hanged.

- A more significant question is whether Lear dies thinking Cordelia is still alive. Those who think this is the case can point to the fact that it is suggested by the text (lines 263–4 and 266–8), particularly his final words: 'Do you see this? Look on her! Look, her lips! Look there! Look there!' (lines 313–14).

- Lear's last words may suggest that he dies joyfully in the belief that Cordelia is still alive, but Kent's comment on his death suggests that whatever concessions there are to optimism are fleeting

and fragile ('Vex not his ghost. O let him pass. He hates him that would upon the rack of this tough world stretch him out longer'; lines 316–18).

- Kent's dramatic career has had as its ultimate purpose the joyful reunion of Lear and Cordelia, and his own final revelation of himself (as Kent, not Caius) to the King who banished him. The 'promised end' (line 264) he talks about, and which he must now witness, is not the outcome he hoped for. It is a painful conclusion and Kent offers the only possible comment: 'All's cheerless, dark and deadly' (line 292).

- In contrast, Albany's proposals involving rewards for friends and punishments for enemies (lines 305–7) seem irrelevant. The fate of Lear and Cordelia suggests that in the world of this play, virtuous characters do not get justice; on the contrary, they are exposed to extreme suffering.

- This scene also shows that evil characters are not exempt from justice, and that evil does not ultimately prevail. Evil, as manifested in Edmund, Goneril and Regan, is shown to be self-destructive; for example, lust and jealousy lead Goneril to poison Regan and kill herself.

- The restoration of order at the end of this tragedy comes at a terrible price: the innocent Cordelia has been hanged, Lear's belated hopes of a happy retirement were shattered prior to his death, Kent is preparing for imminent death, and the few who remain at the close are absorbed in the 'cheerless, dark and deadly' (line 292) atmosphere of the most harrowing ending in any Shakespeare play.

- The text is by no means clear on what the future holds for Britain. One interpretation, a pessimistic one, is that Albany repeats Lear's initial error and renounces the kingship he has just inherited when he tells Kent and Edgar to 'rule in this realm, and the gored state sustain' (line 323). This would be an irresponsible act at a time when a single ruler would be better able to restore order and provide strong rule.

- When Kent refuses to be involved in ruling the kingdom, the remaining possibilities are joint monarchy under Albany and Edgar, or single rule under one of these men. The text gives us no indication as to which of these options becomes a reality, and so leaves a vital question about Albany's character unanswered.

Useful quotes

For thee, oppressed King, I am cast down;
Myself could else out-frown false fortune's frown.

(Cordelia, lines 5–6)

We two alone will sing like birds i' the cage;
When thou dost ask me blessing, I'll kneel down
And ask of thee forgiveness.

(Lear, lines 9–11)

The good years shall devour them, flesh and fell,
Ere they shall make us weep;
We'll see 'em starved first.

(Lear, lines 25–7)

Know thou this, that men
Are as the time is; to be tender-minded
Does not become a sword.

(Edmund, lines 32–4)

Witness the world that I create thee here
My lord and master.

(Regan, lines 79–80)

Edmund, I arrest thee
On capital treason, and, in thine attaint,
This gilded serpent.

(Albany, lines 84–6)

The gods are just, and of our pleasant vices
Make instruments to plague us:
The dark and vicious place where thee he got,
Cost him his eyes.

(Edgar, lines 171–4)

The wheel is come full circle; I am here.

(Edmund, line 175)

but his flawed heart –
Alack, too weak the conflict to support –
'Twixt two extremes of passion, joy and grief,
Burst smilingly.

(Edgar, lines 197–200)

I was contracted to them both. All three
Now marry in an instant.

(Edmund, lines 229–30)

Yet Edmund was beloved.
The one the other poisoned for my sake,
And after slew herself.

(Edmund, lines 240–2)

This feather stirs! She lives! If it be so,
It is a chance which does redeem all sorrows
That ever I have felt.

(Lear, lines 266–8)

Vex not his ghost. O let him pass. He hates him
That would upon the rack of this tough world
Stretch him out longer.

(Kent, lines 316–18)

The weight of this sad time we must obey;
Speak what we feel, not what we ought to say.
The oldest hath borne most: we that are young
Shall never see so much, nor live so long.

EDGAR, Act 5, Scene 3, 326–9

? Questions

1 Describe Lear's new vision of life as expressed early in this scene. Do you think it has any reality or substance?

2 'In this scene hope turns to despair.' Describe how this happens. At the end of the play, are you left with any hope?

3 How can one account for the fact that Lear and Cordelia are forgotten until the last moments of this scene? Base your answer on the evidence of the text of the play.

4 Some critics tend to blame Albany and Edgar for what happens to Lear and Cordelia. Do you think this blame is deserved? Give reasons for your answer.

5 The play has a 'cheerless, dark and deadly' (line 292) ending, according to Kent. Do you think it would have been a better play if Shakespeare had allowed Lear and/or Cordelia to survive? Explain your answer.

6 Edgar sums up his father's fate in the words: 'The gods are just, and of our pleasant vices make instruments to plague us: the dark and vicious place where thee he got, cost him his eyes' (lines 171–4). What exactly is Edgar saying here? Do you think he is giving a true account of Gloucester's fate? Explain your answer by reference to the text of the play.

7 In what ways does Gloucester's death prepare us for Lear's? Do you think that Lear's death is likely to have a greater emotional effect on an audience than Gloucester's? Give reasons for your answer.

8 Goneril asks Regan 'Mean you to enjoy him?' (line 80), despite the fact that, as we later learn, Regan is dying because Goneril has poisoned her. What does this detail reveal about Goneril's character?

9 Edmund declares his intention to do some good 'despite of mine own nature' (line 245). What does he mean here? What prompts his impulse to do good?

10 Albany is a more impressive character in this scene than he was in earlier scenes. What are the factors that have led to the emergence of this new Albany? Has his transformation gone far enough to satisfy the audience?

11 What does this scene tell us about the way in which love and loyalty are rewarded? Base your answer on the text of the play.

12 A few moments before Lear dies, Albany declares: 'All friends shall taste the wages of their virtue, and all foes the cup of their deservings' (lines 305–7). Is this a fair summary of what happens in the play? Refer to the text of the play in support of your answer.

ACT 5 † Key moments

Scene 1

- The conflict between Goneril and Regan over Edmund continues to grow.
- Edgar gives Albany the incriminating letter that Oswald was bringing from Goneril to Edmund, and promises Albany that if the British forces are victorious he will produce a champion who can prove the contents of the letter.
- Edmund admits that he has sworn his love to both Regan and Goneril. He expects that Goneril will see to it that Albany is murdered; he proposes to kill Lear and Cordelia once he takes power.

Scene 2

- Edgar places his father under the shade of a tree while he goes to find out about the battle. He quickly returns to announce that the French forces have lost and that Lear and Cordelia have been captured.

Scene 3

- Lear and Cordelia are taken away to prison, and Edmund gives instructions as to their fate.
- Goneril and Regan argue publicly over Edmund.
- Albany arrests both Edmund and Goneril on a charge of capital treason.
- Regan is led away, having been poisoned by Goneril.
- Edgar challenges Edmund to single combat, and wins. A desperate Goneril leaves the scene and kills herself with a knife.
- Edmund, moved by the realisation that two women loved him, tries, too late, to reverse the order he gave to have Lear and Cordelia hanged.
- A heartbreaking ending ensues, with Cordelia dead in Lear's arms, the speedy death of Lear, the seemingly imminent death of Kent, and only Albany and Edgar left to sustain the state.

ACT 5 † Speaking and listening

1 Your teacher assumes the part of Lear. In small groups, agree a list of questions to ask 'Lear' about his role during the course of the play. Select a leader to pose your questions. Each group takes it in turn to ask a question. For example: Why did you insist on bringing an army of followers with you to be housed at the expense of Goneril and Regan?

2 In groups, select a moment from the play that you consider to be particularly significant. Assign roles and portray this moment as though it is a photograph or film freeze-frame. The other groups must identify the moment that you have created. The class should then discuss why that moment is significant and comment on how your group has presented it.

Social, cultural and intellectual contexts

*K*ing Lear should be set in the legendary pre-history of Britain, a remote and primeval world. The original story on which it is mainly based is set in 750 BC. However, *King Lear* is firmly grounded in early seventeenth-century England, and it is likely that Shakespeare's audiences saw *King Lear* as a play with considerable topical significance.

It is not surprising that Shakespeare made no attempt to create an ancient British setting for his play, since there is no reliable history of those times. Shakespeare would have had to rely on legendary accounts, such as those reported in chronicles, which often have little or no basis in known fact. Indeed, the King Lear who is the subject of Shakespeare's play was possibly a creature of Celtic legend, and his story belongs to a well-known category in European folklore.

Monarchy

One of the earliest performances of the play was at the royal court of King James I on 26 December 1606. James (who was James VI of Scotland) had inherited the English throne three years earlier.

James I (1566–1625)

James was revered as the first monarch to rule over the whole of Britain and embodied the unity of the island. Lear, in contrast, is seen to divide Britain and set in train a series of tragic events. For Shakespeare's audience, *King Lear* offered a worrying insight into what life would be like under a king who allowed himself to be governed by his whims and passions, and was not wise and prudent like James I.

One of the play's central events, the death of a king, cannot have the same resonance for twenty-first-century playgoers or readers as it had for those of the early seventeenth century. Attitudes to monarchs have changed considerably. For example, it was believed that the king was God's anointed deputy on earth. His person was sacred. The overthrow or murder of the king was an offence not only against humanity, but against God. This should be remembered when evaluating the actions of some of the characters in the play.

Shakespeare's contemporaries were taught to believe that the king was the ultimate source of sustenance for all his subjects. This meant that the king's death involved each of his subjects, even the most insignificant, in a massive process of destruction. In *King Lear*, there is a sense that Lear's demise anticipates the end of the world. For example, when Kent sees Lear with the dead Cordelia in his arms, he asks rhetorically, 'Is this the promised end?', to which Edgar replies, 'Or image of that horror?' (Act 5, Scene 3, lines 264–5).

Natural order

King Lear presupposes a worldview and a world order now long obsolete. The key to right living was the preservation of authority, order, hierarchy and degree.

In common with his contemporaries, Shakespeare imagined the universe, the world of nature and the world of human beings as an ordered structure. The order prevailing in the heavens was thought to be duplicated on earth, with the king corresponding to the sun. The essential condition of social harmony and happiness was the natural subordination of the lower to the higher: of the subject to the king, the child to the parent. When these duties were violated, as they are by many characters in *King*

Lear, such unnatural behaviour leads to social disintegration.

Gloucester is troubled by the occurrence of an almost total eclipse of the sun (one actually occurred on 2 October 1605 while the play was being written) and partial eclipse of the moon (one occurred on 27 September 1605). In Gloucester's view, human nature is adversely affected by such eclipses, being scourged by a cooling of love, a falling off in friendships and a severing of family bonds (see Act 1, Scene 2, lines 97–107). In other words, disorder in the heavens is mirrored by disorder within human society. According to this view, the eclipses affected Lear's judgement and triggered the chaotic events of the play. Lear breached natural order and harmony by breaking up his kingdom and renouncing his daughter. This act of political and human destructiveness led to his own mental breakdown, which is mirrored by a furious storm.

Astrology

In Shakespeare's day, astrology was part of the general structure of belief among all classes of English society.

Fundamental to astrology is the belief that astrologers can foretell future events by observing the positions of the stars and the planets. People who could afford it had their children's horoscope cast at birth. The predictions of astrologers were recorded in books known as almanacs, which, in Shakespeare's time, were regularly consulted by the common people, as well as by aristocrats.

Gloucester is the main character in *King Lear* to take astrology seriously, assuming as he does that heavenly bodies influence happenings on earth: 'These late eclipses in the sun and moon portend no good to us' (Act 1, Scene 2, lines 97–8). Kent, however, marvelling at the fact that Lear has children so different as Goneril and Regan on the one hand, and Cordelia on the other, thinks that the explanation must lie in stellar influence: 'It is the stars, the stars above us govern our conditions' (Act 4, Scene 3, line 32–3).

One character who has no time for astrology is Edmund, who dismisses his father's belief in it as a sign of his folly or stupidity. Edmund finds it absurd that human beings should blame their misdeeds on the sun, moon and stars, making no allowance for their own free will.

Religion

Although the play officially has a pagan setting, and the characters belong to a pre-Christian period of history, much of what they say and do is measured against Christian values and practices.

Many references in the play have their sources in the Christian scriptures. The most striking of the Christian allusions in the play is to Cordelia as a Christ-like figure, 'who redeems nature from the general curse which twain [Adam and Eve – or Goneril and Regan] have brought her to' (Act 4, Scene 6, lines 200–1).

Alongside these Christian elements, Shakespeare introduces a range of Greek and Roman gods. For example, Lear swears by Apollo and Jupiter, and Kent by Juno. Lear is also familiar with figures from more primitive religious cults, disowning Cordelia 'by the sacred radiance of the sun, the mysteries of Hecate and the night' (Act 1, Scene 1, lines 105–6).

Class system

The political and social settings of *King Lear* are again based on the circumstances prevailing in the England of Shakespeare's time, with its rigid class structures and extreme social inequalities.

Shakespeare did not mind peopling ancient Britain with seventeenth-century noblemen: dukes, earls and knights.

The main characters in the play belong to the highest tiers of English society. Lear is a king, his three daughters are princesses, and two of their husbands are dukes. Cordelia becomes Queen of France. Gloucester is an earl; as is Kent. All of this should mean that the social setting of the play is a privileged, aristocratic one, and to some extent it is.

Royalty and the aristocracy are seen to use their privileges, one of which is to treat their social inferiors with contempt. When Oswald fails to show due deference to Lear, the latter showers abuse on him: 'Call the clotpoll back … Where's that mongrel?' (Act 1, Scene 4, lines 43, 45). The aristocratic Kent (in disguise) treats Oswald with more extreme contempt, calling him a base servant who eats scraps left over after meals and 'nothing but the composition of a knave, beggar, coward, pander' (Act 2, Scene 2, lines 13, 18–19). After Regan has killed the servant who fatally wounded Cornwall, the latter calls out to: 'Throw this slave upon the dunghill' (Act 3, Scene 7, lines 95–6).

Kent attacks Oswald

The most memorable episodes in the play, however, reveal social settings that are far from royal or aristocratic. This focus is made possible when two characters, Kent and Edgar, disguise themselves and lose their identities. Kent takes on the role of Caius, Lear's servant, and Edgar pretends to be a beggar recently discharged on licence from a London mental hospital. Further layers of underprivileged society unfold when the mad Lear and the blinded Gloucester, especially the former, speak passionately of a range of social injustices done to the poor by those with power.

Kent, who has long enjoyed the sheltered life of a courtier before taking on the role of servant to an unemployed king, soon experiences the disadvantages attaching to his new way of life. After he has insulted and beaten Oswald, and offended Cornwall, he is put in the stocks. This punishment is usually reserved, as Gloucester remarks, for 'basest and contemn'd wretches' who have been found guilty of petty crimes such as theft; Kent calls the stocks a 'shameful lodging' (Act 2, Scene 2, lines 136, 165). Shakespeare's early audiences would have well understood what Gloucester and Kent were talking about. Vagabonds and beggars without licences to beg – a large element of society at the time – were liable to be set in the stocks for three days and nights on bread and water.

Through his disguise as a Bedlam beggar, Edgar exposes another cruel feature of the social setting of *King Lear*: the attitude to the insane and the treatment of those deemed to suffer from mental illness. Because Edgar appears so often in the play as Poor Tom o'Bedlam, and goes into such detail about the torments suffered by the kind of person whose part he is playing, the plight of the wretched people of the earth is a prominent theme in *King Lear*.

Edgar gives a graphic account of the way of life of the sham lunatics, or real ones, who wandered about the countryside. Poor Tom 'swallows the old rat and the ditch-dog, drinks the green mantle of the standing pool … is whipped from tithing to tithing and stocked, punished and imprisoned' (Act 3, Scene 4, lines 123–5). These details are not attributable to Shakespeare's imagination. A 1572 law passed by the English parliament covering the punishment of

Kent in the stocks

vagabonds such as Bedlam beggars prescribed that they were to be whipped publicly from one parish ('tithing') to another and put in the stocks.

Shakespeare also used Lear's madness as an opportunity for a passionate critique of social inequality, injustice, poverty and discrimination. It is only after Lear is exposed at the height of the storm 'to feel what wretches feel' (Act 3, Scene 4, line 34) that he is inspired to condemn the gross inequalities between rich and poor that prevail in the kingdom he ruled for so long and to which he himself, as he acknowledges, turned a blind eye: 'O I have ta'en too little care of this!' (lines 32–3).

Lear has to experience what it is like to be without shelter before he can wonder how the 'houseless heads and unfed sides' (line 30), the poor people of the kingdom, dressed as they are in rags, can protect themselves from the harsh weather. Lear's remedy is that those enjoying excessive wealth should distribute their surplus among those in need (line 35).

Gloucester, on the verge of suicide, feeling compassion for Edgar as Poor Tom, gives him his purse as a gesture of solidarity with the poor people of the kingdom. Like Lear, Gloucester pleads for a fairer division of resources, praying that the heavenly powers will ensure this.

Gloucester's comments on this issue closely resemble Lear's. The latter wanted those with too much to 'shake the superflux' (Act 3, Scene 4, line 35) to those with too little, while Gloucester's demand is that 'distribution should undo excess and each man have enough' (Act 4, Scene 1, lines 69–70). These social reformist views, delivered so emphatically, suggest a social setting for the play in which extremes of wealth and poverty are widely prevalent.

Legal system

The 'Poor Tom' episodes draw attention to another notable feature of the social system that operates in *King Lear*. The law is hardest on those social classes already disadvantaged by their economic circumstances. It imposes the most extreme and degrading penalties for relatively trivial offences, the worst of these being poverty, which is the main motive for vagrancy and begging.

In his madness, Lear also exposes the flaws and corruption at the heart of the seventeenth-century justice system. He recognises that the legal system operates in such a way as to defend the interests of the wealthy members of society and to grind the faces of the poor. This idea forms the basis of one of the most impressive speeches in the play, when Lear is at his most eloquent (Act 4, Scene 6, lines 146–66).

What makes this speech so memorable is that Lear, instead of making general comments on a corrupt legal system, provides concrete instances of how discrimination works in practice. For example, we have the image of a beadle, or village constable, lashing the back of a prostitute, while at the same time wanting to commit a similar offence with her to the one he is punishing her for; thus eliciting from Lear the comment that the punisher himself should be punished.

Lear's illustration of judicial absurdity, where 'the usurer hangs the cozener' (line 157) is the most telling of all. In these five words, Shakespeare identifies a major illness affecting not only the administration of justice but society in general. The cozener is a petty thief. The usurer here is a corrupt moneylender who charges excessive rates of interest but who is also a magistrate. The moneylender, in his role as a magistrate, sentences the petty thief to death by hanging, but Lear implies that it is the moneylender who deserves hanging more than the petty thief does. This example helps to support Lear's complaint that the crimes of poor people are visible through the holes in their ragged clothes, while the fur-trimmed gowns of people like the magistrate conceal their much greater crimes.

Anachronisms

The mingling of pagan, classical and Christian elements and the confusion of various social, political and cultural settings mean that the play is full of anachronisms (that is, it shows people, events and things in a historical context in which they did not exist – they belong to a different time).

Clearly Shakespeare was not concerned about preserving a consistent and credible historical background. He was much more interested in those fundamentals of human character, motive and behaviour that are independent of all periods of history.

The limits of this confusion are reached, appropriately enough, during Lear's mad phase. This produces episodes of absurd comedy. The Fool provides an extreme example of this in his Utopian vision of society. Imagining a time when justice is the main feature of the legal system, the Fool ends his speech with the line: 'This prophecy Merlin shall make; for I live before his time' (Act 3, Scene 2, lines 94–5). Merlin, King Arthur's magician, is reputed to have flourished in the sixth century AD and Lear in the eighth century BC.

Lear associates Poor Tom, who wears only a blanket, with the classical philosophers who were supposed to live poorly and dress sparingly. First, he calls Tom a 'learned Theban', a Greek philosopher or scientist of a relatively low rank, but later thinks more highly of him, calling him 'good Athenian' (Act 3, Scene 4, lines 145, 168). Offering to engage Tom as one of his hundred knights, Lear tells him he will need new clothes. He remembers a line from one of the odes of the Roman poet Horace which, translated, means, 'My boy, Persian attire and I don't agree'. Lear's version is: 'I do not like the fashion of your garments. You will say they are Persian, but let them be changed' (Act 3, Scene 6, lines 76–8). Lear, the eighth-century BC British king, is referring to philosophers and poetry from well after his time. Indeed, Lear knows the Latin term for hysteria (*'Hysterica passio'*; Act 2, Scene 4, line 55) over seven centuries before the Romans invaded Britain.

Aristotle (384–322 BC), ancient Greek philosopher and scientist

Genre

King Lear is a tragedy. In works that we call tragic, certain features seem to recur with unfailing regularity, and these features may be considered to be the essential elements of the genre. In tragedies we see the random interaction of external forces (such as fate, chance or accident) and human weakness (such as vice, lack of awareness or stupidity). The result threatens the well-being of the individual and of society.

The tragic aspect of this play arises from what happens within Lear as the events unfold. It is the development of Lear's understanding of himself and his plight, and his sharing of this with the audience, that lifts the play to a higher plane.

The **essential** elements of **tragic drama:**

- Tragic drama focuses on a single individual, whom we call the **tragic hero** or the tragic protagonist. The tragic hero, in this case Lear, should enjoy the good will of the audience.

- In Shakespearean tragedy the hero is invariably **a man of status**, an eminent individual who is engaged in great events. Lear is King of Britain and a commanding presence.

- The tragic hero must be motivated by a serious purpose or undertake a **serious course of action**. Lear's serious purpose is to abdicate his throne and to retire happily in the care of Cordelia.

- Through that purpose or action, the tragic hero **inevitably** meets with grave physical and/or spiritual **suffering**. The direction of his career in the play is always **from prosperity to adversity**. Lear starts out as a strong ruler, but has lost everything he holds dear by the close of the play.

- The hero's passage from good to bad fortune is the result of some initial and fundamental human error. This may be a false step, a miscalculation or a defect of character. Such a defect is generally described as the hero's **tragic flaw**. Lear's division of the kingdom between two evil daughters is foolish and prompted by pride and vanity, but it is not wicked.

- External factors also have a part to play. In Shakespearean tragedy it is difficult to avoid the impression that **fate** is working against the hero from the beginning. Whatever Lear may do, he is in some sense a doomed man. The influence of order, justice and reason is extremely limited.

- The tragic hero's situation is organised in such a way that he has **no chance of a happy outcome**. It is the tragic dramatist's task to ensure that the tragic hero's activities are inseparable from disaster. If the forces supporting Lear had won the battle, allowing Lear to spend the remainder of his life in the care of Cordelia, the necessary tragic ending would be absent.

- The **audience must be persuaded to identify with the tragic hero** in his sufferings. He must remind us strongly of our humanity, so that we can see him as in some way standing for us. He must be vulnerable to extreme suffering, as Lear clearly is, and we should feel some degree of **pity and fear** in response to what happens to him. Lear's suffering is partly physical, but mainly mental and spiritual: his obsessive focus on filial ingratitude disturbs the balance of his mind.

- For the hero, **recognition** is the essential tragic experience. It occurs when he finally understands his character and situation. Recognition is not simply Lear's knowledge of what has happened to him; it also involves a new awareness of the unalterably fixed pattern he has created for himself through his deeds. He recognises his initial blindness to the villainous natures of Goneril and Regan, and to the reality of Cordelia's love for him. He gains a profound sense of his own folly and a desire for forgiveness. This implies recognition on his part that he must share the burden of responsibility for what he has helped to bring about.

- The tragic hero grows in stature, and in the audience's estimation, as he **faces up to his destiny** and confronts it. Lear's last speeches reflect his increased self-awareness; and his blindness and ignorance die with him.

- Shakespearean tragedy depicts **first the violation, and then the restoration, of order** and health in society. Goneril, Regan, Cornwall and Edmund, the agents of social and moral disorder, involve 'good' characters (Cordelia and Edgar), as well as the less good Gloucester, as victims of their corrupt schemes. As the play reaches its conclusion, a semblance of order is restored. The villainies are exposed, and Albany and Edgar will rebuild the wounded state.

In *King Lear*, the gap between the tragic hero's initial error and its consequences is appallingly wide. Once Lear rashly decides to banish Cordelia and Kent, he sets a chain of events in motion beyond the power of human beings to control. His acts of senile foolishness precipitate the collapse of an entire social order. The bonds of nature, as well as those of society, break apart, and human beings prey upon and torment each other 'like monsters of the deep' (Act 4, Scene 2, line 51). The tragic hero and those involved with him drift helplessly towards their doom.

We are asked to imagine a social and moral order so fragile and vulnerable that a single breach of its fabric can allow the forces of ruin and disorder to enter, as an army might pour through a breach in a city wall. Once these forces have gained entry, they are not subject to control. Established codes of behaviour and conventions collapse. Children betray their parents and parents betray their children. Humane values wither. Cruelty becomes rampant. Unnatural acts are committed. The elements erupt in the rage and fury of the storm scenes, and the mind of Lear collapses.

Innocence offers no protection from disaster and suffering. The saintly Cordelia fares no better than her bestial sisters, and the reformed Gloucester is blinded as a consequence of a virtuous impulse. However, it is through profound suffering that Lear achieves *recognition*, an understanding of the truth about himself and his relation to others. Suffering alone, without recognition (or self-knowledge), is not fully tragic.

General vision and viewpoint

The vision or worldview implicit in *King Lear* is largely the outcome of its status as high tragedy. Tragedy involves an exploration of the worst things that can happen to human beings. While our moral sense and our sense of justice may wish for a happy outcome – Lear and Cordelia reunited and able to enjoy life after their suffering – these expectations cannot be met in tragedy.

In tragedy, human happiness and well-being are painfully short-lived and fragile. They are always vulnerable to hostile forces lurking to destroy them. These forces can be found within the tragic characters, or outside them. The evil forces precipitating tragic events and outcomes are mainly within characters. The external forces generally operate to multiply and intensify the disasters unleashed by perverted human effort. The result is tragic suffering for the innocent and guilty alike.

Medieval wheel of fortune

In *King Lear*, the tragic action has its primary impulse in the almost unfathomably evil tendencies motivating Edmund, Goneril, Regan and Cornwall. Shakespeare's tragic world is such that it can appear futile to look for rational explanations for these tendencies.

Lear remarks: 'Is there any cause in nature that make these hard-hearts?' (Act 3, Scene 6, lines 74–5). One answer to Lear's question is that nature, human and non-human, is deeply flawed, subject to the curse originally called down by Adam and Eve and renewed through the evil conduct of Goneril and Regan (see Act 4, Scene 6, lines 200–1).

Shakespeare's vision is not of a world entirely controlled, from start to finish, by the agents of evil. They may set terrible events in motion, and influence their course, but they do not enjoy unmitigated triumph. Evil runs its course, causes its devastation, destroys much that is good, but ultimately defeats its own purposes. Edmund, Goneril and Regan are destroyed by over-ambition and unaccustomed surges of emotion.

At the end of the play, a few good survivors are left to restore order and to re-affirm the decencies of life. This outcome does little to compensate for the suffering inflicted, particularly on Lear, Cordelia and Gloucester.

It can be argued that Shakespeare's tragic vision gives us a glimpse of a world in which the poison of evil can be expelled only after massive devastation, a process that shows no regard for good or evil.

If we consider the good and evil forces operating in the world of *King Lear* simply in terms of the impulses motivating characters, it is possible to make credible assumptions about what Shakespeare may have thought of as constituting fundamental good and fundamental evil in human beings.

The play shows the confrontation of unbounded egotism and selfless, loving service:

- The evil characters in *King Lear* are all ruthless individuals, with a deep contempt for social bonds or obligations, and a wilful blindness to the rights and needs of others. Extreme egotism dictates their actions: whatever serves their selfish purposes is good, whatever hinders them is evil. Gloucester and Edgar are obstacles to Edmund's advancement, so they must be destroyed. Lear is an inconvenient, troublesome guest, so Goneril and Regan deny him hospitality.

- The good characters are loyal to social and family obligations, and care for those in need of being helped. Edgar and Cordelia were wronged by their fathers, but return to offer them unconditional love and support, and sustain them through harrowing experiences.

There is much reason for pessimism in *King Lear*, as in every other tragedy, but we must not overlook the play's optimistic aspects. Great suffering is depicted in the play, but its positive effect is to facilitate the moral and spiritual development of the sufferers. Lear and Gloucester become better men. Suffering teaches them compassion for others, enhances their spiritual awareness and leads them to recognise their errors.

The world of *King Lear* contains some good and honest human beings. The positive values of the play are exemplified by Lear, Cordelia, Gloucester, Edgar, Kent, Cornwall's servant and, towards the end, Albany. Cordelia is as profoundly good as Goneril and Regan are profoundly evil. Edgar's selfless kindness to his father counterbalances Edmund's destructive hatred.

At the heart of the most terrible scene of the play, the blinding of Gloucester, Shakespeare inserts an episode that illustrates decent human values. When Cornwall has put out the first of Gloucester's eyes, one of his servants, sacrificing his own life in the act, draws his sword in outraged protest and gives Cornwall a wound that soon proves fatal.

Later, Albany fearfully contemplates the terrible consequences for society if Goneril's savage inhumanity is not stopped, picturing humans preying on humans like predatory monsters. But this is not how things end in *King Lear*. Decent humanity asserts itself heroically in the face of all that the evil characters can do. Kent, Cordelia and Edgar exhibit heroic virtue, while Lear comes to learn the meaning of love to which he was blind at the beginning. Only by ignoring such optimistic indications can we attribute a facile pessimism to Shakespeare's vision of the tragic world.

*Lear's daughter Regan and
Gloucester's son Edmund*

There are many close parallels between the sub-plot (Gloucester – Edgar – Edmund) and the main plot (Lear – Cordelia – Goneril – Regan). For example:

- Both fathers fail to recognise the true natures of their children. Lear, in his blind folly, believes the dishonest speeches of Goneril and Regan and banishes the honest Cordelia. The credulous Gloucester is tricked by the unscrupulous Edmund into disowning the honest Edgar.

- Lear is cast adrift by the children he treated generously, and helped and forgiven by the one he deeply wronged. Gloucester is betrayed by the son he favoured, and consoled by the one he outlawed.

- Gloucester and Lear have somewhat similar deaths. Gloucester dies in a mood compounded of joy and woe, following his reconciliation with Edgar. Lear, perhaps, dies in the false belief that Cordelia may still be alive. The death of each father, primarily from exhaustion, is seen as a release from the tortures of the cruel world.

- The good child in each plot exhibits constant, unflinching love, which is the supreme positive value of the play.

- Even individual passages have close resemblances. In the storm, Lear feels sympathy for the poor in their houseless condition and suggests that the wealthy should 'shake the superflux to them and show the heavens more just' (Act 3, Scene 4, lines 35–6). Gloucester arrives at much the same insight. Meeting the naked beggar Poor Tom, he understands the need for a fairer sharing of the world's wealth: 'So distribution should undo excess and each man have enough' (Act 4, Scene 1, lines 69–70).

- The father in each plot develops morally and spiritually through intense suffering. Each is wiser, and better, at the end than he was at the beginning. Each has been brought to recognise his shortcomings, and to appreciate the value of love.

- Gloucester's transformation is announced, like Lear's, at the centre of the play (Act 3, Scene 3).

- The suffering of Lear differs from that of Gloucester both in kind and in degree. Gloucester, the sensual sinner, is deprived of one of his senses, his sight, and suffers deeply in the knowledge of what he has done to Edgar. Lear is punished on a larger scale, and his punishment is more complex. He undergoes a process of moral education, passes through a phase of mental derangement, which involves a paradoxical acquisition of wisdom, and then faces the supreme agony of Cordelia's death, just as he has learned to love her with all his heart.

- Lear overcomes his fierce pride when he kneels to Cordelia, pities others and assumes a new humility and gentleness. He appears more sensible and reasonable in his madness than he was in his sanity, achieving what Edgar calls 'reason in madness' (Act 4, Scene 6, line 169). After his physical blinding, Gloucester recognises that he was morally and spiritually blind for much of his life: 'I stumbled when I saw' (Act 4, Scene 1, line 19).

- The meeting between Lear and Gloucester (Act 4, Scene 6) is the symbolic climax of the play, bringing the two plots together.

- The events in one plot exert an influence on the events in the other; consider, for example, Gloucester's decision to help Lear.

- Edgar acts as chorus and commentator on the events of both plots. He is one of the 'judges' at the mock-trial of Goneril and Regan, and a witness to the meeting of Lear and Gloucester.

- Edmund, too, plays a key role in both plots. He becomes involved in a love triangle with Goneril and Regan and is directly responsible for the murder of Cordelia, with fatal consequences for Lear.

- The 'realistic' sub-plot helps to reinforce our willingness to accept the fairy-tale nature of the main plot.

Characters

All accounts of dramatic characters and their relationships, including those given here, should be received with caution. It is seldom possible to give a definite account of any character or relationship in *King Lear* or any other Shakespearean play.

Portrayals on stage

Stage productions and film versions of *King Lear* reveal that the text is open to a variety of interpretations of characters, motives and actions.

Directors and actors have approached *King Lear* from different angles and with varying objectives, with the result that no two productions provide us with quite the same overall impression, particularly of the characters. Audience members who know the text well will often notice that what they see on stage or screen does not match the impressions they formed from their reading.

Staging of Act 1, Scene 4 in the Abbey Theatre's 2013 production of King Lear

Interpretations of Lear himself differ widely. One director, for example, may see Lear as an overwhelmingly sympathetic character with the best of intentions who, being senile and increasingly tired, wants to hand power over to the next generation, and to be taken care of by his favourite daughter, Cordelia. All he wants in addition is that Cordelia give him a verbal demonstration of her exceptional love for him. This director may decide that Cordelia's response is unreasonable, needlessly hurting her father's feelings, humiliating him in public and shattering his hopes for a happy future. The production will stress this point of view and tend to present Lear as a pathetic, if angry, victim.

Another director may decide that Lear is the primary cause of his own misfortunes because he brings matters to a head. Such a production will stress Lear's lack of self-control and his violent, savage outbursts of temper. The director might focus on Lear's stay with Goneril in Act 1, Scene 4, and accept as fact Goneril's remarks that Lear's knights are treating her palace like a tavern or brothel. To make this convincing, the audience could be given a glimpse of Lear's knights being drunk and disorderly, singing loudly and destroying Goneril's property. Lear could also be seen bullying her servants, and acting as if he were master of the palace, not its guest. Goneril would then look like a victim of Lear's irresponsible conduct, giving her, and Regan, some justification for reducing his entourage.

A different director could decide that Goneril's comments on Lear's knights are unfounded, and that Lear's defence of them as men who preserve proper standards of behaviour and live up to their reputations as men of honour represents the truth. This director might show Lear's knights speaking quietly and observing perfect table manners. Such a favourable presentation of Lear and his followers would portray Goneril in a less than flattering light.

The above comments show that in performance at any rate there is great scope for differing interpretations of characters without doing violence to the text.

Lear

hot-tempered
rash
changeable
self-willed
self-centred
unreasonable
unbalanced
self-pitying
foolish
victim
obsessive
caring
insightful
repentant
pitiable

Lear begins the play as an almost superhuman figure, marking out the map like a god, and making his pronouncements with complete authority and power:

Come not between the dragon and his wrath …
The bow is bent and drawn, make from the shaft …
Nothing: I have sworn; I am firm.

(Act 1, Scene 1, lines 118, 139, 241)

Shakespeare's great achievement is that he can take a man at the height of his powers and of at least eighty years of age and still develop and expand his character and experiences.

It is interesting to dwell on Lear's motives for abdicating. He makes it clear that he has made an irreversible decision to retire as king, and to pass the worries and duties of monarchy on to members of the next generation, those with the strength to govern, which he now lacks. It is suggested that Lear feels that he is not far from death, and sees no point in trying to cope with running a kingdom. If this is the case, it is natural that he should want to step back and ensure a smooth succession.

It is clear that Lear has planned for his future after retirement. He has decided that Cordelia will have the best share of the kingdom, and that he will spend his last years in her care. His mistake is to link his division of the kingdom to a silly demand for a show of public affection from his daughters, obviously expecting that Cordelia will provide him with the most impressive declaration of love. When Cordelia refuses to play the role he has planned for her, Lear is driven into a corner.

From that moment, everything starts to go wrong. He loses control of himself, and of events, and in a sudden rage tells Cornwall and Albany to divide Cordelia's share between them, thus depriving Cordelia of her dowry and making her less attractive to suitors. He makes a further rash decision to spend the rest of his time with Goneril and Regan, a month with one, a month with the other, and to bring with him one hundred knights, whose upkeep, as well as his, will have to be paid for by them.

The most obvious feature of Lear's character, and the dominant one from the beginning, is his arrogant self-will, which has been nourished by a long career of absolute power. The slightest opposition sends him into a towering rage. Those who question him are exposed to extreme forms of retaliation. It is not enough for him to banish Kent, he also threatens him with capital punishment. He not only withdraws his favour from Cordelia, he also acts as if he has never known her.

These traits remain evident after his abdication, when he abandons himself to the charity of Goneril and Regan. Indeed, his impatience, lack of self-control and arrogance may even increase. Faithful followers are treated with scant consideration: he threatens the Fool whenever the latter ventures some unpalatable truth about his present condition, and makes little of the disguised Kent's offer of faithful service. He flies into a childlike rage when he does not get his own way: he strikes Goneril's gentleman, and insults her steward, Oswald. His curses on Goneril are fearsome.

Shakespeare takes considerable pains to underline Lear's brutality, bitterness, fickleness, ferocity, egotism, self-pity and vindictiveness. Early in the play, Goneril and Regan provide a cynical, though reasonably accurate, account of their father's character and motivation. This is one instance where it is intended that we see things from their point of view. They comment on his hot-headedness ('the best and soundest of his time hath been but rash'; Act 1, Scene 1, line 288). They feel that age has further weakened his already poor judgement and note that his angry nature can break out in 'unconstant starts' (line 293).

The entire tendency of the play, however, is to cause the reader or spectator to discount Lear's failings and to regard him with compassion, sympathy and understanding. All the characters we admire look on Lear's situation from Lear's point of view, and this is clearly what Shakespeare wants us to do. We are compelled to see Lear as a man 'more sinned against than sinning' (Act 3, Scene 2, line 59). His faults and failings are not the things we are invited to concentrate on.

Shakespeare is concerned less with the personal weakness of his main character than with the monstrous insult offered by Goneril, Regan and their associates to some of the most sacred human values: fatherhood, old age and kingship. In this sense Lear becomes a majestic figure strongly raging against the storm. As his opportunities for positive action become more and more limited, his mental and emotional horizons expand.

Lear's movement from pride, egotism and spiritual blindness to understanding, insight and love is, perhaps, the real significance of the play. In the first two acts he worries only about the extent to which his suffering affects *him*. In the storm, he begins to generalise from his own suffering to those of other people, as his imagination awakens to the plight of classes and individuals hitherto beneath or beyond his notice. The first sign of this expanding consciousness is his show of sympathy for the Fool in Act 3, Scene 2.

Lear begins to think of needs that are common to all of humanity. It also dawns on him that his long neglect of the unfed, ragged poor is a cause for shame. His desire to share whatever vile amenities are available is evidence of a growing sense on his part of the need for identification with his people. His prayer on behalf of the poor and the homeless represents genuine pity for others.

Lear also acquires a growing desire for knowledge. Paradoxically, it is during his mad phase that he learns fundamental truths denied to him while he was sane. Poor Tom o'Bedlam, dressed only in a blanket, becomes for Lear a compelling image of the true nature of humanity reduced to its basic essentials. Lear's quest for truth is temporarily and comically centred on this 'philosopher', whom he regards as a Theban and Athenian oracle, and from whom he enquires about such great traditional mysteries as the cause of thunder.

Lear's lunacy is allowed to co-exist with his deepest insights. Like Gloucester's blindness, Lear's madness becomes a positive value. *Because* he is mad, Lear is set free from conventional restraints and limitations, and sees the defects of society from a new perspective.

When Lear meets Gloucester in Act 4, Scene 6, he expresses some of these new insights, providing a disturbing analysis of reality and appearance, justice and authority, law and the exercise of power, corruption in high places, social inequalities, and the blinding power of flattery.

When he is reunited with Cordelia, Lear acknowledges his guilt and exhibits an unprecedented humility. By the beginning of Act 5, Lear has transcended mere worldly concerns, and can now welcome the prospect of joining with Cordelia in a quest for the ultimate truth.

Lear's progress is not an altogether simple movement from human folly to piety. Indeed, it would be misleading to suggest that he is converted during the course of the play from a proud, fierce egotist to a patient, suffering Christian. Cordelia's death marks another turning point, not alone in Lear's fortunes, but in his emotional and spiritual history.

The closing minutes of Act 5, after Lear enters with Cordelia in his arms, suggest that his regeneration has not, after all, been complete or final:

> *A plague upon you, murderers, traitors all! …*
> *I killed the slave that was a-hanging thee …*
> *I have seen the day, with my good biting falchion,*
> *I would have made him skip.*

(Act 5, Scene 3, lines 270, 275, 277–8)

In response to Cordelia's death, Lear exacts speedy revenge, killing the perpetrator. This reaction is exactly what we would have expected from him in the opening scene. In addition, Albany restores Lear's royal powers and authority moments before his death, allowing Lear to die a king once more.

Edgar

naïve
deceived
victim
humiliated
actor
pitiable
moralist

good-natured
charitable
unselfish
noble
forgiving
kind
optimistic
heroic

Lear, who is given 22 per cent of the lines in the play, has by far the biggest part; Edgar and Kent come next, getting 11 per cent each.

Edgar is the most puzzling character in the play. There are those who suggest that he is not really a character at all, and that the name Edgar covers a variety of roles rather than a stable personality. One can identify at least five different Edgars:

(a) the simple-minded victim of Edmund's schemes

(b) the Bedlam beggar

(c) the peasant (as pictured here)

(d) the chivalrous champion who dares Edmund to single combat

(e) the chorus or commentator on the action.

Edgar and Kent stand apart from the other characters in the play in that both are forced by circumstances to adopt a false identity in order to remain alive. Edgar's role as a Bedlam beggar marks the lowest point in his fortunes. He takes on a humiliating disguise so close to that of a wild beast that he becomes no better than nothing at all, or as he himself puts it, 'Edgar I nothing am' (Act 2, Scene 3, line 21).

Edgar imagines himself into a more desirable role when he assumes the character of a poor but sane peasant who speaks a rustic dialect and saves Gloucester's life by killing Oswald (Act 4, Scene 6). His next part marks a significant improvement: he becomes the nameless knight who, having challenged and overcome Edmund, is at last able to regain his true identity and become co-ruler with Albany, or, in some accounts, sole ruler, of the kingdom of Britain.

Those who wonder about Shakespeare's intentions with regard to Edgar ask how one is to believe that the foolish, pitiful figure of his first few scenes can become the impressive, authoritative one who lends distinction to the close of the play. The commonest explanation is to see change in Edgar in terms of the kind of moral development exhibited in other characters: Lear, Gloucester, Cordelia and Albany. Edgar must then be understood as one who learns from his experiences and from exposure to suffering (his own and that of others).

It is best, however, not to look too closely at Edgar's 'personality', or the lack of it, but to emphasise his functions as a commentator and as the spokesperson for the play's more optimistic moods. He embodies much of the religious feeling of the play, as can be seen from his numerous pronouncements on the relations of the gods with men.

Edgar has a deep and cheerful faith in the ultimate triumph of goodness, and in the benevolence of the powers who govern people's destiny on earth. He is the one who can see beyond temporary changes in human fortune to some grand design.

Edgar's function with regard to Gloucester is to save him from despair. For example, in response to Gloucester's black indictment of the gods as no better than boys who kill flies for sport, he says:

> *Therefore, thou happy father,*
> *Think that the clearest gods, who make them honours*
> *Of men's impossibilities, have preserved thee.*
> (Act 4, Scene 6, lines 73–5)

It is possible, at times, to find Edgar's moral stance a bit chilling and stern. For example, his verdict on his dead father, delivered to the dying Edmund, is:

> *The gods are just, and of our pleasant vices*
> *Make instruments to plague us:*
> *The dark and vicious place where thee he got,*
> *Cost him his eyes.*
> (Act 5, Scene 3, lines 171–4)

Moralising comes naturally to Edgar, but he is, on the whole, a compassionate moralist, feeling deeply for his father, acting as his guide and tutor, and repaying evil with kindness and sympathy.

Those who see *King Lear* as a Christian play with a pagan setting can point to Edgar's Christian behaviour, attitudes and comments. A striking instance is his treatment of the dying Edmund: 'Let's exchange charity' (Act 5, Scene 3, line 167).

Many commentators find Edgar's buoyant optimism somewhat irritating in the context of a play in which there is little warrant for hopeful comment. Certainly Edgar's optimistic moral pronouncements are at times brought into ironic conflict with such bleak realities as the sight of his blinded father.

There is uncertainty as to Edgar's position at the end of the play: is he sole ruler of Britain, joint ruler with Albany or simply an advisor to Albany? One version has it that the play comes to an end with the transfer of power from Lear's family, as represented by the king's son-in-law Albany, to Gloucester's family in the person of Edgar. Two arguments support this version. One is that Shakespeare has gradually been developing Edgar's character and stature to the point where he ends up as the only person fit to reign. Another is that he speaks the final lines, reserved as a rule in Shakespeare's tragedies for the surviving character of the highest rank.

For modern actors and directors, the role (or roles) of Edgar can present difficulties. The actor is given a great deal to say, much of which is not easy for today's audience to understand. Some of his material consists of references to things that are no longer topical or relevant. Those who have studied the text in detail have a clear advantage over those who have not. A common solution is to cut Edgar's lines, so that the actor can work harder on making the lines he does speak more comprehensible to the audience.

Kent

honest
observant
insightful
truthful
blunt
cranky
loyal

forgiving
brave
unselfish
loving
faithful
humane
heroic

Kent's honest nature and blunt manner of speaking mean that he must endure harsh punishment. Nevertheless, his loyalty and devotion to Lear remain strong throughout the play.

One of Kent's most significant utterances occurs in the first scene of the play, when he intervenes with Lear on Cordelia's behalf. Kent is appalled by Lear's erratic behaviour as well as by the injustice of his treatment of Cordelia. He cannot refrain from expressing his anger and horror at what Lear is doing: 'be Kent unmannerly, when Lear is mad. What wouldst thou do, old man?' (Act 1, Scene 1, lines 141–2).

It is important to recognise Kent's physical and moral courage here. He is confronting a monarch who has long been used to exercising absolute power, unquestioning obedience and flattering modes of address. The one thing Lear does not want to hear at this point is the unpleasant truth that he has made a blunder.

Kent's willingness to tell the truth, even when this is unpleasant or unpopular, is a central feature of his character. Like Cordelia, he finds flattery repulsive. In standing for plain truth and honesty he takes his place with the other two representatives of these qualities in the play: Cordelia and the Fool.

Disguised as Caius, Kent is still prepared to challenge the fearsome Cornwall with an unflattering comment, and ends up being severely punished and humiliated as a result. In the process, he reveals an important truth about himself:

> Sir, 'tis my occupation to be plain.
> I have seen better faces in my time
> Than stands on any shoulder that I see
> Before me at this instant.

(Act 2, Scene 2, lines 86–9)

Kent shares another quality with Cordelia and the Fool: he embodies the ideas of loyalty and service to an extreme degree. Nothing that happens can deflect him from his role as a totally loyal follower of Lear, whose sufferings he feels intensely, even though Lear has humiliated him by banishing him from the kingdom.

Kent's loyalty and loving concern are touchingly expressed when he tries to persuade Lear to shelter from the storm: Lear asks, 'Wilt break my heart?' and Kent answers, 'I had rather break mine own' (Act 3, Scene 4, lines 4–5). His description of himself in the final scene of the play is very apt. As he tells Lear, he is one 'that from your first of difference and decay have followed your sad steps' (Act 5, Scene 3, lines 290–1).

Kent also plays a key part in maintaining contact between those loyal to Lear's cause in Britain and the advance guard of the French invading force preparing to come to his aid. One of his functions is to represent Cordelia in her absence and to keep her before our minds. He also gets Lear to Dover to join Cordelia in the French camp there.

Kent's love for Lear gives his life its focus, its direction and its meaning. He has no vocation but to serve his master and to suffer on his behalf. Even though he is 'a gentleman of blood and breeding' (Act 3, Scene 1, line 40), he is prepared to sacrifice his own comforts and well-being to look out for Lear. His great reward, and perhaps the only one he seeks, is to receive a small token of half-recognition at the end from the demented Lear. Kent is heartbroken at Lear's death, and will not survive him long, nor does he want to: 'I have a journey, sir, shortly to go. My master calls me' (Act 5, Scene 3, lines 324–5).

The play presents a bleak picture of human nature. Without characters like Kent, this picture would be even more grim and more depressing. One way of looking at the play is to see it as enacting a great struggle between good and evil forces. Some of the characters reach profound depths of evil, both in outlook and conduct. They are not, however, fully representative of the general vision of human nature in the play. Against their extreme evil is the counterbalancing presentation of heroic virtue in characters such as Kent.

Kent does not represent the triumph of goodness, because goodness does not triumph in the tragic world of *King Lear*. He does, however, affirm human values and decency. Kent's best testimonial is pronounced by Edgar, since it conveys the essence of his mission throughout the play:

> *Kent, sir, the banished Kent; who in disguise*
> *Followed his enemy King, and did him service*
> *Improper for a slave.*

(Act 5, Scene 3, lines 220–2)

Goneril and Regan

wicked

hypocritical

selfish

unprincipled

ruthless

murderous

cruel

violent

merciless

uncaring

brutal

lustful

jealous

treacherous

heartless

While they have much in common, Lear's two evil daughters cannot quite be classified together as indistinguishable partners in evil and are different in some significant aspects of character.

Goneril, the elder, is the more active of the two in the pursuit of crime. She plots and commits murder and adultery. She has the more forceful character and, as far as one can judge, fears nothing or nobody in this world or the next. She pays no heed to Lear's curses, and, significantly, she is the only one of the major characters who never mentions the gods. Her suicide, following her exposure and the collapse of her schemes, is undertaken without hesitation or any sign of inner turmoil.

Regan is meaner and weaker in character than Goneril, and her wickedness is not on as grand a scale as Goneril's. She resorts to telling a lie about Edmund's intentions towards Gloucester, something Goneril would scorn doing. The thought that Edmund and Goneril may be lovers troubles her so much that she becomes incoherent and confused in her speech, and is reduced to trying to blackmail Oswald into allowing her to read Goneril's letter to Edmund.

On the other hand, it is the 'weaker' Regan who becomes the more violent in cruelty, turning more savage than even Cornwall, her merciless husband. She jeers at the blinded Gloucester, telling him with relish that his favoured son has betrayed him; and kills the servant who attacks Cornwall.

An important quality of mind that Goneril and Regan have in common is that they are rationalists and realists, totally unhampered by any moral sense or family feeling. Their primary aim is to satisfy their own ambitions and desires.

These shrewd, practical and, within limits, effective operators have no time for sentiment, and fail to see why Lear should want to enjoy the outward symbols of status. They are prepared to use his old age as a justification for taking these away from him. In their logical scheme of things, old age has no use or function, and old men are superfluous nuisances.

Goneril, in particular, exhibits considerable cunning in bringing about Lear's humiliation. She acts to bring trouble to a head and gets things over with quickly and ruthlessly. She uses her staff to provoke a conflict with her father. She then complains to Lear in a righteous tone about the behaviour of his followers. Regan's dishonesty follows a similar pattern. She is mistress of the technique of guilt by association: when Gloucester comments on Edgar's supposed treachery, she asks about Edgar's links to Lear's knights.

Lear touches on an essential characteristic of both daughters when he wonders about Regan's conduct: 'let them anatomise Regan, see what breeds about her heart. Is there any cause in nature that make these hard-hearts?' (Act 3, Scene 6, lines 73–5).

Hardness of heart is a mild term for what Goneril and Regan exhibit as they grow in power. When they hear of Gloucester's defection, they react spontaneously with brutal directness. Regan's 'hang him instantly' is met with Goneril's 'pluck out his eyes' (Act 3, Scene 7, lines 4–5).

It is appropriate that some of the more repulsive images of the play are used in connection with the two women, and with Goneril in particular. She is a kite; her ingratitude has a serpent's tooth; she has a wolfish face; in her sharp-toothed unkindness she is like a vulture attacking her father. Albany sees her as a gilded serpent; Gloucester as having the fangs of a boar.

Goneril and Regan are effective in serving their own interests up to a point. There are hints in their wild dealings with Gloucester that they may be beginning to lose control. However, the real turning point is reached when their strongest weapons – coolness and calculation – are destroyed by desire and jealousy. The passion they both feel for Edmund cannot be controlled in the same way that their other activities could.

Their intense rivalry over Edmund causes Goneril and Regan to behave rashly and even foolishly. There is a fundamental irony in the fate of the two women, particularly in the fact that they, who could entertain no particle of feeling for the aged father who loved them, should be destroyed by a consuming passion for an egotistical monster who cares nothing for either of them.

Regan and Cornwall

Do Goneril and Regan have any credible motive for their treatment of their father, apart from their heartless natures? From Lear's point of view, nothing can excuse what they have done to their 'old kind father, whose frank heart gave all' (Act 3, Scene 4, line 20). However, Goneril and Regan might question the circumstances under which he 'gave all' to them. A careful reading of the abdication scene (Act 1, Scene 1) can lead one to conclude that they have reason to complain about the conditions Lear attaches to the division of the kingdom.

Lear lays it down that he will live with each of his two remaining daughters in turn for a month until he dies; that he will keep a personal retinue of one hundred knights at the expense of his daughters and their husbands; and that he will keep the name of king with all the formal marks

of respect due to a monarch, but without the power and authority of kingship, which will belong to Albany and Cornwall. He devises these conditions on the spur of the moment – since he cannot spend his retirement in Cordelia's care, he is obliged to think of an alternative arrangement.

It is important to note that none of those who will be affected by this arrangement (Goneril, Regan, Cornwall, Albany) gives any sign of agreeing to it. Lear thinks that because he has announced it, all present must have accepted its terms. It is not an arrangement he can legally enforce, since he is no longer king.

What must Goneril and Regan feel about these conditions? Lear's reference to one hundred knights is quite misleading: as Goneril points out when she is entertaining them it is in fact 'a hundred knights and squires' (Act 1, Scene 4, line 228). Thus, with each knight accompanied by a squire, Lear's hundred is really two hundred. And then the knights and squires will be accompanied by their servants, making a total of three or four hundred; in effect a private army.

This reality may explain why Goneril and Regan want to reduce the number of Lear's knights. They already know how volatile Lear can be, and it is not unreasonable for them to be worried. Until they reduce, drastically, the numbers at Lear's command, he has it in his power to take back by force everything he has given them, and to reassume his authority as king.

Goneril and Regan cannot have failed to notice how quickly Lear forgets that he no longer holds sway as king. Within minutes of his abdication, he imposed an extraordinary sentence of banishment on Kent, using language that indicated he was still king in every sense of the word (see Act 1, Scene 1, lines 162–75).

Goneril is given, or gives herself, another motive for wanting to reduce Lear's train of followers. She is severely critical of the behaviour of his knights and squires, the Fool, and Lear himself. She accuses them of riotous and unruly activities, of being debauched and of mistreating members of her staff. Their gluttony and drunken behaviour have infected the manners of her court to such an extent that immediate action is called for, especially since Lear has shown himself willing to sanction these abuses of her hospitality.

Lear's response to Goneril's angry accusations, rebukes and threats is to accuse her of lying. His defence of his followers, however, proves futile. Goneril's version of their behaviour is accepted without question by Regan.

How convincing are Goneril's accusations? One indication that there may be some substance to them is found in Act 1, Scene 4, lines 1–87. Lear clearly expects everyone to continue treating him as a king: 'Let me not stay a jot for dinner; go get it ready' (line 8). When Oswald, on Goneril's instruction, refuses to come to him when called, Lear calls him a few offensive names, and then abuses him further when he does appear. When Oswald objects, Lear strikes him; and Kent, with Lear's warm approval, trips him up.

In fairness to Lear, we have to bear in mind that Goneril has been hoping that Oswald will provoke Lear into violent action. However, when she does launch her verbal assault on Lear, it is not entirely based on his treatment of Oswald. She makes it clear that she has already spoken to Lear about the trouble he and his followers have been causing (Act 1, Scene 4, lines 192–3).

Of course, Goneril and Regan have every reason to paint Lear and his followers in the worst possible light, given that their ultimate objective is to rid themselves of any responsibility for the maintenance of their father, who has become surplus to their needs and generally a nuisance (and potential threat). Hence their readiness to expose him to the violence of the storm.

It seems more than likely that if Shakespeare had visualised Lear's knights as Goneril describes them, he would have provided some specimens of the kind to make her accusations credible. There is also the point that Albany, who shares the palace with Goneril, shows no awareness of riotous knights or of the disorder in which they were supposed to have been involved.

I cannot think my sister in the least
Would fail her obligation. If, sir, perchance
She have restrained the riots of your followers
'Tis on such ground, and to such wholesome end,
As clears her from all blame.

REGAN, Act 2, Scene 4, 137–41

Gloucester

insensitive
superstitious
gullible
irresponsible
easy-going
good-natured
cautious
unheroic
loyal
humane
suffering
depressed
suicidal
repentant
transformed

One of Gloucester's main functions is to serve as a parallel to Lear. Like Lear, he is betrayed by a child he loves, and supported by another he unjustly rejects. His sufferings may be traced to human folly and injustice, and, like Lear's, these sufferings purify his character and enlighten him. He dies a better man than he was when we first met him.

There are parallels of character and temperament, too. Like Lear, Gloucester is credulous, hasty and affectionate. Nevertheless, the personality of Gloucester is built on a very much smaller scale than Lear's. He has nothing of the latter's tempestuous force and energy. He is the kind of man one might encounter anywhere in fiction or, indeed, in the real world: sensual, careless of the moral code, easy-going and prone to deceit.

One aspect of Gloucester's behaviour is difficult to credit: the ease with which he falls victim to Edmund's deception. Few people would be so gullible. Shakespeare is asking us to allow him the fact of the deception, just as we have allowed him Lear's unlikely partition of the kingdom. Such a starting point is necessary to get the story going.

There are strong indications that Gloucester is not a man of firm moral purpose. His flippant attitude to his 'fault' in fathering the illegitimate Edmund places him as an irresponsible libertine, as does the fact that Edmund is younger than Edgar, which implies that he was conceived through adultery. On the other hand, Gloucester is pleasant, good-natured and affable.

It is only when prosperous times change to bad, when multiple suffering strikes, that the 'new' Gloucester begins to emerge. He tries at first to fight against the facts of his predicament. Rather than be conscious of his sorrows, he would choose madness like Lear's.

Gloucester's conversion from benevolent, helpless neutrality to tentative support for Lear is not exactly heroic; he tries to conceal his actions and asks Edmund to cover for him while he helps the king. The irony here is that by confiding in Edmund he is ensuring not his safety but his destruction, blinding and casting out of doors.

The essential feature of Gloucester's dramatic career is his transformation from a weak, erratic sensualist into an impressive witness to the power of filial love and to the triumph of duty and loyalty over self-interest. Like Lear, Gloucester attains a higher conception of himself and of human destiny through appalling suffering and worldly failure.

Gloucester's development through suffering elicits from him a profoundly religious response. His astrological superstition is the nearest he gets to a sense of the supernatural before he is made to endure torture and deprivation. His real transformation begins during the scene in which he is blinded by Cornwall.

The extremity of his suffering causes him to call on the gods for help. He prays for Edgar and asks forgiveness for his own sins. Before he casts himself down to what he thinks will be his death, he kneels and prays to the gods and renounces the world. After he has been saved from death (by Edgar) his sense of heavenly goodness deepens. It is surely worth remarking that after all he has suffered, Shakespeare makes him utter this prayer:

> *You ever-gentle gods, take my breath from me.*
> *Let not my worser spirit tempt me again*
> *To die before you please!*

(Act 4, Scene 6, lines 211–13)

It is, paradoxically, through his own pain and sorrow and his awareness of the misery of others that Gloucester is at last made aware of 'the bounty and the benison of heaven' (Act 4, Scene 6, line 219).

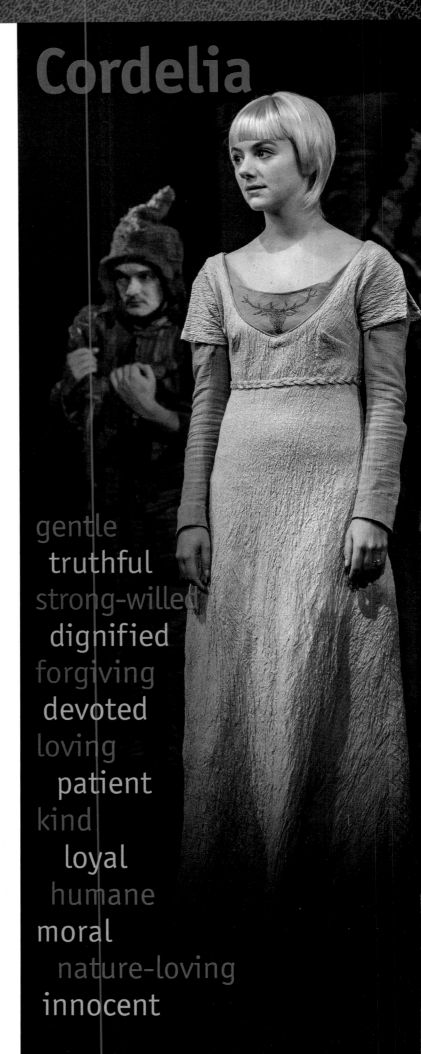

Cordelia

gentle
truthful
strong-willed
dignified
forgiving
devoted
loving
patient
kind
loyal
humane
moral
nature-loving
innocent

Cordelia appears in only four of the twenty-six scenes of the play, and speaks only one hundred lines. Her influence on the overall effect of the play, however, is out of all proportion to this small contribution.

Cordelia can be misunderstood. She is not to be seen as a totally meek, saintly sufferer, or as a passive victim. Close resemblances can be found between her and her father. She has inherited his pride and, like him, she can be obstinate and unyielding. In the opening scene, she responds to his pride (in wanting public declarations of love) with her own pride (that he already knows that she loves him and she is too honest to engage in excessive flattery).

There is one main line of development in her character: by the end, pride, though still evident, is submerged in love. A detail in the reconciliation scene (Act 4, Scene 7) tells us much about her character. While her father is still asleep, she can address him eloquently and in a way that leaves us in no doubt about her love for him. But when he is awake, she finds it difficult to express her love, and speaks only in monosyllables.

For many in the audience, her very presence in the play goes far in the direction of counterbalancing the evil represented by her sisters and their allies. She can be eloquent at times, but her characteristic feature, emphasised more than once, is silence or quietly economical speech. Lear remembers her voice as having been 'soft, gentle and low' (Act 5, Scene 3, lines 273–4).

Cordelia recognises her inability to find words to express her deepest feelings: 'Unhappy that I am, I cannot heave my heart into my mouth' (Act 1, Scene 1, lines 87–8). Her motto is 'love, and be silent' (Act 1, Scene 1, line 58). All she can manage by way of verbal reaction to Kent's letter informing her of Lear's condition is the repetition of a few words, and then she goes off 'to deal with grief alone' (Act 4, Scene 3, line 32). Her reticence during the reconciliation scene is again characteristic ('And so I am, I am', 'No cause, no cause'; Act 4, Scene 7, lines 72, 77). Her response to Lear's final speech in this scene is one of tearful silence.

Cordelia's integrity and strong principles are in marked contrast to the corrupt and dishonourable natures of her sisters. Indeed,

Kent wonders how Goneril and Regan could be children of the same parents as Cordelia:

> It is the stars,
> The stars above us govern our conditions;
> Else one self mate and make could not beget
> Such different issues.

(Act 4, Scene 3, lines 32–5)

The unattractive side to Cordelia's character emerges during the first scene of the play. Her father wants, and needs, the assurance of her devotion lovingly expressed. Instead, he gets from her a cold, uninspiring formula describing filial duty and stressing legalism rather than love. Her self-righteous pride, which she later regrets, precipitates the catastrophe.

Just as Lear's abdication can be seen as a withdrawal from responsibility, Cordelia's refusal to co-operate in his childish love-test also amounts to a withdrawal from responsibility. The combined withdrawal of Lear and Cordelia, through pride and self-will, allows power to pass into the hands of Goneril and Regan.

In the thematic scheme of the play, Cordelia is the embodiment of a concept of nature totally opposed to that represented by Edmund, Goneril, Regan and Cornwall. For her, the natural bond between parent and child becomes of central importance. Her absolute fidelity to this is her most obvious claim to our attention and admiration.

Cordelia upholds the principles on which civilised life must ultimately depend. Her role in this regard is as 'a daughter who redeems nature from the general curse which twain have brought her to' (Act 4, Scene 6, lines 199–201). The surface meaning of these lines is that Cordelia, through her selfless charity with regard to her erring father, has corrected the gross imbalance in nature that Goneril and Regan brought about. There is, however, a case to be made for seeing a second meaning, not incompatible with the first, in these lines. This would involve making Cordelia a Christ-like figure, with a redemptive function, and finding in 'the twain' a reference to Adam and Eve.

Albany

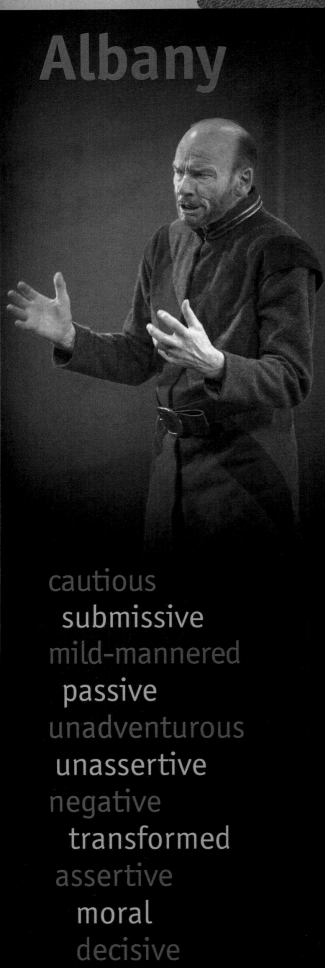

cautious
submissive
mild-mannered
passive
unadventurous
unassertive
negative
transformed
assertive
moral
decisive

Albany is one of those characters (Lear and Gloucester are other examples) who develop in moral stature during the course of the action. There are two distinct phases in Albany's career in the play.

At first, Albany is under the sway of his strong-minded wife, Goneril. Such, indeed, is her dominance that he is unable to act independently of her will, however differently he may feel from her.

He does not appear to *want* to be cruel to Lear, and is almost certainly telling the truth when he protests that he does not know the reason for Lear's violent rage. On the other hand, there is a strong hint that he is less than enthusiastic about Lear's stay at his house; the Knight tells Lear that the 'abatement of kindness' he has observed appears 'in the duke himself also and your daughter' (Act 1, Scene 4, lines 54–6).

When Lear does decide to leave, Albany makes a half-hearted stand against Goneril's proceedings, only to be brushed aside contemptuously. A little later, Goneril gives her frank assessment of her husband's character:

> *This milky gentleness and course of yours*
> *Though I condemn not, yet, under pardon,*
> *You are much more at task for want of wisdom*
> *Than praised for harmful mildness.*

(Act 1, Scene 4, lines 329–32)

She regards him as an inoffensive, negative, dull-spirited man, wanting to leave well enough alone. His motto seems to be: 'Striving to better, oft we mar what's well' (Act 1, Scene 4, line 334).

Albany casts aside his timidity and begins to exert a moral authority that justifies Oswald's 'never man so changed' (Act 4, Scene 2, line 3) as a description of his new persona. Goneril can no longer put him in his place; her heaped insults now fail to intimidate him or even greatly impress him. He answers her in something like her own kind of language: his hands 'are apt enough to dislocate and tear [her] flesh and bones' (lines 66–7).

The 'new' Albany, who recoils in horror from what has been done to Gloucester by Regan, Goneril and Cornwall, seems quite a different character from the earlier one. It appears that there has come a point when his passive nature said enough is enough and he was spurred into action. Goneril has made herself intolerable to him, and he is also determined to avenge Gloucester's wrongs.

At the opening of Act 5, Albany must make a difficult choice. A battle is imminent between the British forces, under his leadership, and an invading French army, of which Cordelia is a part. This army has come to assist Lear and his supporters, who have been suffering at the hands of Goneril, Regan, Cornwall and Edmund. Albany is aware of the evil practices of all four. On the one hand, he sees it as his patriotic duty to take arms against an army of foreign invaders, although this will involve him in an alliance with people he despises. On the other, he will not accept that Lear and his friends are opposing the British state. He argues that they have just cause to oppose those who are ruling the state.

It is clear that Albany requires a good deal of persuasion from Goneril to commit himself to battle. As Oswald observes, Albany sets forth only after making a great deal of fuss ('with much ado'; Act 4, Scene 5, line 2). The only conclusion one can draw from this is that Albany is uncertain of his duty. His full thinking on the matter is left unspoken.

More than half of all Albany's speeches are delivered in the closing scene. Albany, formerly hesitant, is now in command. He orders Edmund to hand over those he has taken prisoner in battle, including Lear and Cordelia, so that he himself can decide their fate. When Edmund tries to stake his claim, Albany immediately and firmly rebukes him, asserting his supreme authority.

After a further challenge from Edmund, Albany puts him in his place as a 'half-blooded fellow' (Act 5, Scene 3, line 82), and then arrests him and Goneril on a charge of capital treason on the evidence of the incriminating letter supplied by the disguised Edgar. He also acts decisively in dismissing the soldiers Edmund has levied. Edgar's intervention to face Edmund in single combat saves Albany from having to do so himself.

With the deaths of Regan, Goneril and Edmund, it appears that Albany's difficulties have been resolved. His army has defeated the foreign invader, he is reconciled with Edgar and he has reason to hope that Lear and Cordelia will be saved. He has also confronted the wrongs done by his wife in the kingdom over which he can now claim to be sole ruler, the one remaining figure of authority.

However, Albany's conduct during the concluding phase of the action is extremely puzzling. Instead of taking decisive control of the state as he is entitled to do, he does two curious things. The first is to echo what Lear did, with such disastrous results, at the beginning of the play. Albany decides to resign and give away his power to Lear while he remains alive, even though he sees Lear, at this stage, as merely a noble ruin: 'this great decay' (Act 5, Scene 3, line 299). This strange decision is set at naught when Lear dies almost immediately after Albany makes it.

Next, Albany does something even more unexpected. He looks around to find a replacement for Lear, and settles on two, as Lear had done when he divided the kingdom between Cornwall and Albany. He turns to the other two survivors, Kent and Edgar, apparently inviting them to be joint rulers of the kingdom in his place: 'Friends of my soul, you twain, rule in this realm, and the gored state sustain' (Act 5, Scene 3, lines 322–3).

What makes this invitation so surprising is that Albany, of all the characters, must be intimately aware of the enormity of the problems Lear set in train by doing what he is now proposing. This makes him a second Lear, anxious to shed the burdens of responsibility and to pass these on to others. It also makes him appear as if he has learned nothing from what happened to Lear.

Kent declines Albany's invitation to share power with Edgar, being physically and mentally exhausted and knowing that he has not long to live. Where does this leave Albany? The text of the play does not provide an answer to this question. Some commentators speculate that Albany and Edgar share power between them. Others suggest that one of them will be sole ruler. In the absence of textual guidance, speculation takes over.

Another interpretation of the ending focuses on Albany's invitation to Edgar and Kent to rule in Britain and sustain the state and requires us not to take it literally, but instead to assume that Albany is merely asking Edgar and Kent to assist him in ruling Britain by serving as his counsellors or advisors. Those who advance this interpretation find it impossible to imagine that Albany, having experienced the terrible consequences of Lear's division of the kingdom, would repeat Lear's mistake by dividing it again.

The Fool

truth-teller
commentator
wise
blunt
critical
hard-hitting
sane
comic
sincere
loyal
devoted

In creating this character, Shakespeare accepted the convention that the Fool is understood to speak the truth and that he knows the truth not because he has superior reasoning powers, but because he is gifted with inspired intuition. Shakespeare's audiences would have understood that the stage-Fool was not a fool at all, but, on the contrary, the mouthpiece of sanity and wisdom. When discussing the part played by the Fool in the play, we have to bear in mind that convention.

One of the Fool's most profound insights is that when good and evil forces are in contention, as they are in *King Lear*, and when the battle between those two forces is waged by intellect alone, no decision is possible. However, when heartfelt, instinctive judgement becomes involved, the decision is immediate. The Fool receives his wisdom not only through his mental faculties, but also through his senses and through his heart.

Only the Fool realises from the beginning that Lear, once he has given away his kingly power, can no longer count on the artificial relationships (with his two hypocritical daughters, for example) that his former status made possible. When Lear asks, 'Dost thou call me fool, boy?' The Fool responds, 'All thy other titles thou hast given away; that [folly] thou wast born with' (Act 1, Scene 4, lines 138–40).

In the course of the play, the Fool functions as a kind of chorus, providing a shrewd commentary on Lear's foolish act in giving all to his daughters. The point of this commentary is that Lear is foolish and the Fool is wise. For example, after Goneril has rebuked him, Lear thinks Regan will be kind to him; but the Fool's instinct tells him that the second daughter will prove no better than the first.

The Fool is also a dramatic character, pining away after Cordelia's departure for France, and totally loyal to Lear in good as well as bad times. When the storm breaks, and Lear is 'contending with the fretful elements', Kent asks who is with him, to be told: 'None but the fool, who labours to out-jest his heart-strook injuries' (Act 3, Scene 1, lines 4, 16–17).

One of his more amusing jests comes when Lear, looking at the half-naked Edgar wrapped in a blanket, and obsessed with his own daughters' ingratitude, wonders: 'Has his daughters brought him to this pass? Couldst thou save nothing? Wouldst thou give 'em all?' To which the Fool wryly remarks: 'Nay, he reserved a blanket, else we had been all shamed' (Act 3, Scene 4, lines 60–2).

It is reasonable to wonder why the Fool makes his last appearance in the play soon after the halfway stage, with the cryptic comment, 'And I'll go to bed at noon' (Act 3, Scene 6, line 82). It is sometimes suggested that because 'bed' can mean 'grave' the Fool is referring to his premature death. On the other hand, the Fool's final line may be simply a witty reply to Lear's 'We'll go to supper i' the morning' (line 81).

The Fool's last words may express his determination to depart from the action with its course half-run. Two scenes earlier, he has foretold that bodily suffering will adversely affect the minds of Lear, Kent and himself: 'This cold night will turn us all to fools and madmen' (Act 3, Scene 4, line 74). By the end of that scene, Lear has lost his grip upon reality, and the Fool sees that he can do nothing more to help him. His role of driving out Lear's sorrows by the force of his witticisms is obsolete. Now that Lear can receive only physical help, the Fool has good reason to fade out of the play.

Another explanation for the Fool's withdrawal from the action may be that Lear, in his disturbed state, is in a position to take on the role the Fool has been filling up to this point: telling uncomfortable and unpopular truths. Now that Lear has begun in earnest to tell such truths about himself (as the Fool has been doing), and about the hypocrisies and evils of society, the play has no need for a professional truth-teller and so the Fool is superfluous.

It seems surprising that Shakespeare, having given the Fool such a significant part in the action, should not provide a clue to his ultimate fate. However, it is possible that he has, in fact, provided such a clue, even a clear indication, in the last scene of the play. After Cordelia has been hanged, Lear exclaims: 'And my poor fool is hanged!' (Act 5, Scene 3, line 308). It is commonly assumed that Lear is referring here to Cordelia, since 'fool' could be a term of endearment, and Cordelia has just been hanged. But there is no certainty that Lear is not referring to the Fool, to whom the remark seems equally appropriate.

Given the Fool's affection for Cordelia, and his loyalty to her, it is reasonable to assume that, if he reached Dover, he would have made contact with her and attached himself to her, and even shared her fate. To make the Fool the subject of Lear's comment would be artistically satisfying, and in tune with the symbolic significance of both the Fool and Cordelia, the former standing for reason, the latter for love. Shakespeare's audience would have appreciated, and understood, the horror involved in the revelation that reason and love were strangled by the same hangman's halter.

There is also a practical explanation for the Fool's disappearance, to do with casting. In the kind of theatre Shakespeare wrote for, female characters were played by boy-actors, and a boy-actor also played the part of the Fool. For reasons of economy, or due to problems of casting, the same boy-actor could be used to play both the Fool and Cordelia, meaning they could never be on stage at the same time.

In *King Lear*, the Fool does not come on stage until Cordelia has left for France, and by the time she returns to the action, he has become lost to view. If, as Lear may be suggesting, the Fool is hanged, the only way we can know this is by way of report from one who has witnessed his death, in this case Lear himself. If the same actor is playing both Cordelia and the Fool, it is impossible to produce the Fool's body on stage as evidence of his death, since Cordelia's body has already been carried on stage by Lear.

Edmund

lively
clever
ruthless
self-centred
ambitious
charming
quick-witted
unprincipled
disloyal
self-seeking
heartless
plausible
hypocritical
immoral
cynical

Edmund is one of the more interesting 'personalities' of the play. He is endowed by Shakespeare with singular force and energy. He has a distinctive point of view and attitude to everybody and everything around him, and a highly individual mode of expression. He is one of the most evil of all Shakespeare's characters. He is totally amoral, devoted exclusively to his own interests and prepared to destroy anything or anybody that might interfere with these.

There is, however, a significant contrast between Edmund and Lear's evil daughters. In Edmund's case, one is compelled to acknowledge a certain superficial attractiveness, a range of interesting attitudes, a liveliness of mind and a real (if perverted) sense of humour. His positive qualities include a considerable strength of will, an excellent presence and enough charm and plausibility of manner to impress a variety of observers, including Goneril and Regan.

Edmund's 'wit' is, of course, exercised at the expense of his credulous father and noble brother; the first a man of limited intellect to begin with, the second an incredibly naïve victim. Edmund's 'attractiveness' lies partly in his difference from these pitiful dupes, whose behaviour early in the play is somewhat embarrassing.

Edmund is a rational, cynical observer of the follies and superstitions of other men, particularly Gloucester. He is very much the 'modern' man, with no time for traditional values or the accepted view of things. He is an atheist. He denies any relationship between the planets and his own destiny. He refuses to accept the central notion of an organic universe, with all the bonds and relationships that this implies. He recognises no ties between himself and others, no obligations on his own part. Edmund thus rejects the scheme of values represented by Cordelia and, later in the play, by Albany.

Edmund has no principles of any kind, nor does he pretend to have any. He places no value on anybody else. The claims of blood-relationship, friendship and loyalty mean nothing to him. He looks on others either as the means of helping him to make his way in the world, or as hindrances to his advancement, and he acts accordingly.

His attitude to the two women who come closest to him, Goneril and Regan, illustrates both his total heartlessness and his cynical humour:

> *To both these sisters have I sworn my love;*
> *Each jealous of the other, as the stung*
> *Are of the adder. Which of them shall I take?*
> *Both? One? Or neither? Neither can be enjoyed*
> *If both remain alive.*
>
> (Act 5, Scene 1, lines 56–60)

Edmund never allows himself to be distracted from his aims, his ultimate one being the crown. He takes his chances as they come. He is master of the technique of plausible lying, most evident in his undoing of Edgar; his consummate hypocrisy is demonstrated as he talks of loyalty while he betrays his father to Cornwall.

Shakespeare provides various subtle touches in his portrait of Edmund. For example, as he advances in the world he becomes a snob: 'If thou'rt noble,' he tells the masked Edgar, 'I do forgive thee' (Act 5, Scene 3, lines 166–7). He finally exposes himself to ridicule and humiliation when he begins to regard himself as Albany's equal, and tries to patronise him ('Sir, you speak nobly'; Act 5, Scene 1, line 28). Albany, however, is more than a match for him here, and firmly puts him in his place.

Perhaps the ultimate sign of Edmund's unworthiness as a human being is his belated gesture in attempting to save Lear and Cordelia, and his motives for the attempt. It is only after Goneril confesses to poisoning Regan and then takes her own life that Edmund, believing that he was loved, thinks of saving Lear and Cordelia:

> *Yet Edmund was beloved.*
> *The one the other poisoned for my sake*
> *And after slew herself …*
> *I pant for life. Some good I mean to do*
> *Despite of mine own nature.*
>
> (Act 5, Scene 3, lines 240–5)

It is worth noticing that in the presence of the dead bodies of those he supposes loved him, he says nothing about them but thinks only of himself. Even at this late hour of his life he enjoys the luxury of being 'loved' in so extreme and dramatic a fashion. There is a note of sentimental vanity and self-congratulation in his closing utterance. It is also characteristic of him that he talks impressively about *meaning* to do good, and that his only real effort in this direction comes too late to be of any use.

We can only speculate about his motives for wanting to save Lear and Cordelia. One suggestion is that he is moved by Edgar's account of their father's death. Another is that, surrounded as he is at this point by 'good' characters, he takes on some of their qualities. Yet another view is that, having lost everything he cared for (his own life and worldly position), he can perform this dramatic gesture to impress the onlookers without any loss to himself. There is also the possibility that we are to take Edmund's last gesture as suggesting that even the most morally depraved people sometimes display unaccustomed virtue in special circumstances.

It is interesting to note that Shakespeare makes Edmund a less guilty figure than his counterpart in Philip Sidney's *Arcadia*, from which Shakespeare derived him. In *Arcadia*, it is the Edmund-figure who tears out his father's eyes. In *King Lear*, however, Edmund is not present when the cruel deed is performed by Cornwall. In fact, Edmund always leaves the violent acts to others – instructing the Captain to kill Cordelia and Lear, and deciding that Goneril will have to get rid of Albany herself.

It should also be noted that Edmund is not a motiveless villain. His vindictive and envious attitude to the two members of his own family may be accounted for in terms of his illegitimate birth and status as an outcast (we see Gloucester's insensitive attitude towards him in the opening scene). Knowing that the nature of his birth makes him 'stand in the plague of custom' (Act 1, Scene 2, line 3), he exacts a terrible price for his social and legal disabilities from the society with which he is at odds.

Cornwall

vicious
heartless
cruel
inhuman
ruthless
violent
vindictive
authoritarian
ambitious
corrupt
unjust
merciless
wicked

Cornwall is a character who lacks any redeeming feature. He and his wife, Regan, for whom he is an ideal partner, perpetrate one of the two most appalling acts in the play: the blinding of Gloucester (the other, arranged by Edmund, is the hanging of Cordelia).

Cornwall combines cruelty with cowardice. His courage manifests itself only when Goneril arrives at the castle and supports him and Regan against Lear. Gloucester is blinded, on the suggestion of Goneril, because he has tried to relieve the sufferings of Lear, and because Edmund has told Cornwall that Gloucester is in sympathy with the French invasion and its aims. Cornwall is particularly angry that Gloucester, whose patron he is, has betrayed him.

When Gloucester expresses the hope that he will live to see the swift vengeance of heaven descend on Goneril and Regan, Cornwall proceeds with his own act of vengeance: 'See't shalt thou never … upon these eyes of thine I'll set my foot' (Act 3, Scene 7, lines 64–5).

Cornwall has put out one of Gloucester's eyes, with Regan demanding that he pluck out the other, when one of their servants fatally wounds him. Cornwall nevertheless completes the task of blinding Gloucester, taunting him as he does so: 'Out, vile jelly! Where is thy lustre now?' (Act 3, Scene 7, lines 82–3).

Although seriously wounded, Cornwall has time for two further cruel gestures, ordering his servants to turn the blind Gloucester, 'that eyeless villain' (line 95), out of doors, and inflicting a final indignity on the servant who wounded him: 'Throw this slave upon the dunghill' (lines 95–6), thus denying him a proper burial. The motive for this final gesture of contempt for a fellow human being is to be found in Cornwall's deeply felt embarrassment that he has been challenged, and fatally wounded, by a mere servant; a feeling shared by Regan: 'A peasant stand up thus!' (line 79).

From the point of view of the plot, the most significant event in Cornwall's life is his death. This leaves the way open for a series of new developments in the relationships between some of the main characters. Regan, now a widow, decides that she has a better claim on Edmund than Goneril has, because she is free to re-marry. The bitter rivalry between the two sisters, initiated by Cornwall's death, will lead to their deaths as well as Edmund's.

Oswald

capable
efficient
loyal
dutiful
responsible
much-abused
ambitious
mercenary

Oswald is Goneril's steward, which means that he is no ordinary servant. He is an important and valued official at the court of Albany and Goneril. He is literate and experienced and highly capable. Stewardship was a respectable calling, and seen as a means of reaching high office in the state. The status of a steward also depended very much on the status of the person employing him. It follows that Shakespeare's audiences would have expected Goneril, a princess married to a duke, to have a steward of high social rank.

Oswald acts as chief officer in Goneril's household, responsible for the management of her estates and keeping her accounts. He has a supervisory role over all her domestic servants, officers and attendants, and must be obeyed by them in all things. It is natural that he should also demand respect from the people he encounters in the course of his duties performed on Goneril's behalf.

This expectation explains his shocked responses to his treatment at the hands of Lear and Kent, both of whom roundly abuse him. Lear calls him a 'clotpoll' (blockhead, fool) and a 'mongrel', a 'slave', a 'whoreson dog' and a 'cur' (Act 1, Scene 4, lines 43, 45, 47, 74, 75). Oswald deals with these offensive remarks as a gentlemen would: 'I am none of these, my lord, I beseech your pardon' (line 76). When Lear strikes him, Oswald maintains his dignity: 'I'll not be strucken, my lord' (line 78).

Later, when Oswald meets Kent/Caius, whom he does not recognise, he greets the latter with the utmost politeness. Kent, thinking of Oswald simply as Goneril's servant and therefore as an enemy of Lear, subjects him to a vile litany of abuse. When Kent offers to engage him in a duel, Oswald sensibly declines. In these encounters, Oswald the steward behaves much more like a gentleman than does Kent the earl.

Oswald's relationship with Goneril is quite close. As her steward, it is his duty to offer her advice in all serious matters and to keep all her secrets. Their intimacy in this regard is shown in his comments to her on the changed attitude of her husband, Albany (Act 4, Scene 2, lines 3–11). He speaks as if he is her close confidant, privy to her domestic affairs.

Goneril employs him as her personal ambassador to Regan, who in turn tries to use him as her ambassador to Goneril, asking him to convey a hostile, threatening message (Act 4, Scene 5, lines 34–5). Goneril can trust Oswald absolutely to keep her secrets, as he does when Regan tries to persuade him, and even tempt him, to let her open and read Goneril's letter to Edmund. After he has killed Oswald, Edgar takes a cynical view of this aspect of his role, when he calls him 'a serviceable villain, as duteous to the vices of thy mistress as badness would desire' (Act 4, Scene 6, lines 244–6).

Oswald's importance to Goneril, and the extent to which she depends on him, becomes clearer when his function as her confidential secretary is considered. Goneril tells Albany that she has written to Regan to tell her of the abuse that Lear has heaped upon her after she challenged him. It soon transpires that Oswald, not Goneril, has written the letter, on her instruction (Act 1, Scene 4, line 322–3).

Goneril then tells Oswald that he may supplement the letter he has written for her with 'reasons' of his own, so making the content of the letter more convincing to Regan (Act 1, Scene 4, lines 325–7). In contrast, Lear's messenger, Kent (disguised as Caius), is merely to deliver Lear's letter to Regan, and is warned not to comment on the recent events at Albany's palace, but to confine himself to questions arising from the content of the letter (Act 1, Scene 5, lines 1–3).

The most memorable comments made by other characters in the play on Oswald are extremely hostile: Lear's 'mongrel', Edgar's 'serviceable villain' and Kent's 'base, proud, shallow, beggarly' knave. These, however, are not impartial or objective comments, since they are made by people who dislike Oswald, not necessarily for what he is, but because he is Goneril's agent.

In that capacity, there is little to fault Oswald for. He does all he can to serve Goneril's interests. He is as loyal to her as Kent, for example, is to Lear. Besides, as Goneril's ambassador to Regan and Cornwall, he is more effective than Kent is as Lear's messenger to them. Kent arrives first, but Oswald's letters are the ones that Regan and Cornwall read first and act upon (Act 2, Scene 4, lines 29–36).

One aspect of Oswald's conduct is impossible to condone. He is prepared, in order to gain promotion, to fall in with Regan's suggestion that he should kill Gloucester if he encounters him. When he finds Gloucester, he declares: 'That eyeless head of thine was first framed flesh to raise my fortunes' (Act 4, Scene 6, lines 221–2). He fails to carry out this task only because Edgar kills him first.

Oswald, on the point of death, remains loyal to Goneril and to his duty at a time when he has nothing to gain from this. His last thought is of the safe delivery of Goneril's letter to Edmund, which she has entrusted to him. It is, however, a nice irony that it is Oswald's fidelity to her interests that leads Edgar to discover the evidence of Goneril's adulterous relationship with Edmund, which in turn brings about the downfall of both these characters.

Summary charts

The following chart shows the social hierarchy of characters in *King Lear*

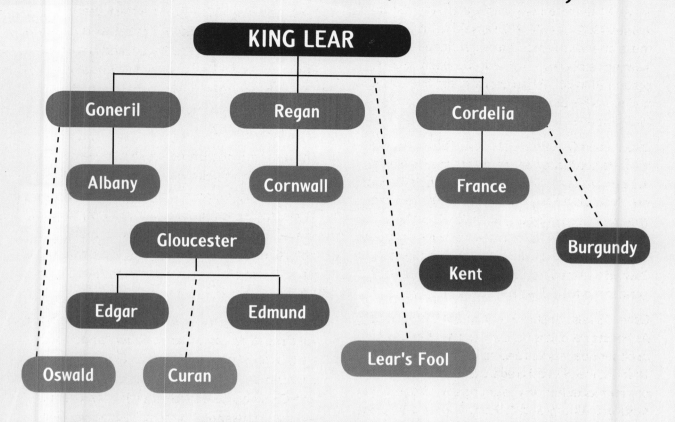

KING LEAR

Goneril — Albany

Regan — Cornwall

Cordelia — France

Gloucester — Edgar, Edmund

Kent

Burgundy

Lear's Fool

Oswald   Curan

Knights, Gentlemen, Captain, Officers, Soldiers, Herald, Messengers, Attendants, Servants, Old Man

Political factions in *King Lear*

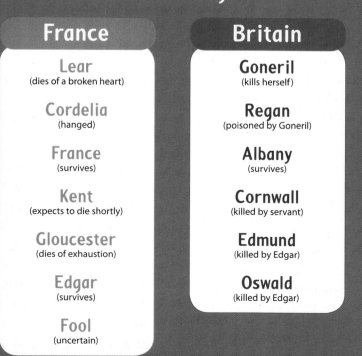

France	Britain
Lear (dies of a broken heart)	**Goneril** (kills herself)
Cordelia (hanged)	**Regan** (poisoned by Goneril)
France (survives)	**Albany** (survives)
Kent (expects to die shortly)	**Cornwall** (killed by servant)
Gloucester (dies of exhaustion)	**Edmund** (killed by Edgar)
Edgar (survives)	**Oswald** (killed by Edgar)
Fool (uncertain)	

The following chart illustrates the main interactions between the characters during the play.

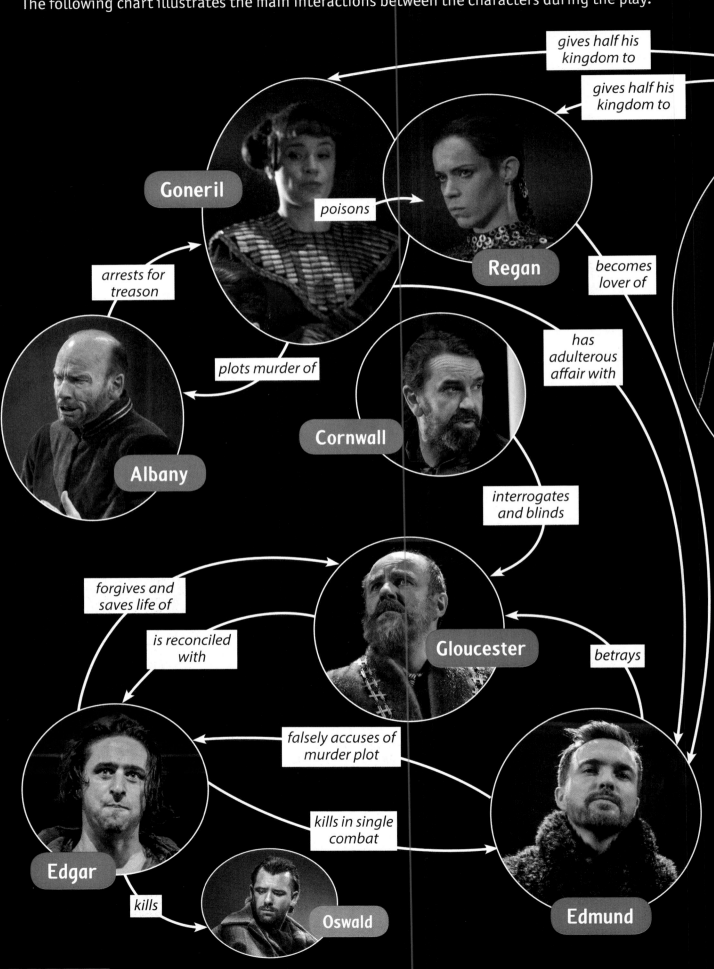

gives half his kingdom to

gives half his kingdom to

Goneril

poisons

Regan

becomes lover of

arrests for treason

has adulterous affair with

Albany

Cornwall

plots murder of

interrogates and blinds

forgives and saves life of

Gloucester

betrays

is reconciled with

falsely accuses of murder plot

Edgar

kills in single combat

kills

Oswald

Edmund

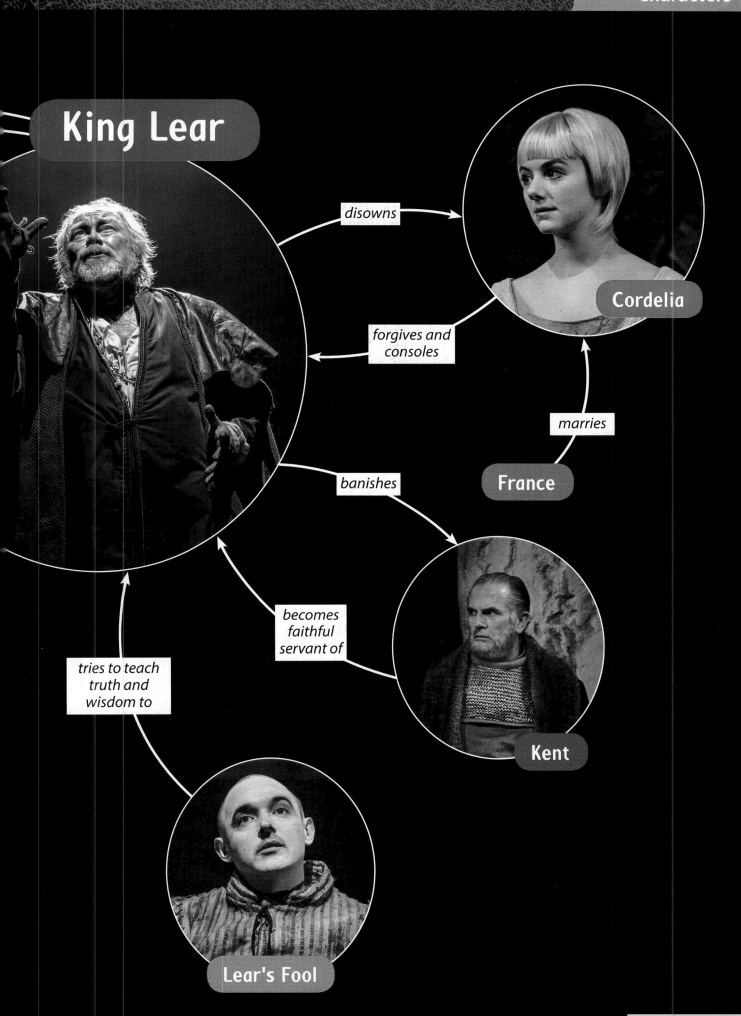

King Lear

disowns → Cordelia

forgives and consoles ←

marries

banishes

France

becomes faithful servant of

Kent

tries to teach truth and wisdom to

Lear's Fool

Relationships

Many of the characters in *King Lear* belong to one of two complementary categories: those who exploit and those who are exploited. The relationships between Lear and his two evil daughters, between Gloucester and Edmund, and between Edmund and Edgar are largely exploitative.

Lear's decision to quantify love and to grade the rewards on offer to his daughters in terms of the weight of their expressed affections permits Goneril and Regan to exploit his need to feel loved. Their declarations of love are totally insincere, but achieve the desired effect, which is enhanced when Cordelia's refusal to flatter Lear induces him to divide her share of the kingdom between them. Having thus exploited him for their own ends, they quickly disown him.

Edmund the exploiter

Edmund is the ultimate exploiter, looking on everybody else as an instrument of his own profit and advancement.

His father and brother are gullible enough to be deceived by his cunning stratagems. Edmund revels in his power to manipulate them: 'A credulous father, and a brother noble, whose nature is so far from doing harms that he suspects none' (Act 1, Scene 2, 167–9). Since Edmund cannot benefit from the social and legal systems and inherit lands 'by birth', he decides to destroy his next of kin and gain their lands 'by wit' (line 171).

Edmund pretends that Edgar wants him to kill their father. His scheming works, and Gloucester determines to take legal measures to make him capable of inheriting, even though his illegitimacy is an obstacle to this. Gloucester's reward is to find his humane gesture in support of Lear exploited by Edmund to deprive him of his title and possessions. Edmund betrays his father to the merciless Cornwall, knowing, as he tells himself, that this 'must draw me that which my father loses' (Act 3, Scene 3, lines 21–2). For his betrayal of his father he is made Earl of Gloucester by Cornwall.

Edmund, however, has greater ambitions. His ultimate aim is to be the sole ruler of the kingdom. This involves him in a complex love triangle with Goneril and Regan. The jealous passion of the two sisters for him, and their murderous rivalry for his affection, permit him to exploit them for a while as a means to his own advancement. He can do this all the more effectively because he has no feeling for either, having no emotional attachment to anybody other than himself.

Edmund hopes to use Goneril to kill her husband, Albany, after he has used Albany's authority to win the battle against the forces fighting for Lear. At the same time he hopes that either Goneril or Regan will kill the other, thus leaving him free to possess the survivor and the whole kingdom.

Edmund's relationship with the rest of the characters, characterised by a total absence of concern for them as persons and an exclusive

This weaves itself perforce into my business.

EDMUND, Act 2, Scene 1, 15

focus on them as means to his own ends, may be credibly explained in terms of the stigma attached to his illegitimacy, and his resentment at his father's insensitivity and lack of respect and consideration for him. How Edmund might have related to others had these circumstances been different may be guessed at from his changed outlook after Goneril and Regan have died for love of him. His grateful recognition that he was loved, in however grotesque a fashion, prompts his single generous, humane impulse: 'I pant for life. Some good I mean to do despite of mine own nature' (Act 5, Scene 3, lines 244–5).

Lear the loved

The great loving relationship of the play involves Lear and Cordelia. It is clear in the opening scene that she is the daughter on whom he relies for his future happiness, but that his emotional well-being depends on her public expression of love for him: the more fulsome the better.

The temporary breach in the Lear–Cordelia relationship comes about through pride on both sides. Her faintly self-righteous pride in her own frankness and honesty prevents her from conveying her real feelings for him in the way he wants these expressed. His offended pride at this failure converts his love to anger and even to hatred.

Despite the immense wrongs she suffers at his hands, Cordelia's love for Lear remains constant and absolute: it is one of the supreme positive values of the play. When she re-enters his life after her banishment, her sole concern is for his welfare and restoration to health. When her forces are defeated in battle, she can face her own fate with an even mind, but cannot come to terms with his: 'For thee, oppressed King, I

am cast down; myself could else out-frown false fortune's frown' (Act 5, Scene 3, lines 5–6). Lear enjoys the consolation of Cordelia's love and forgiveness before they die, and learns to love her unconditionally.

Lear is loved unconditionally by two other characters: Kent and the Fool; just as Gloucester enjoys the selfless devotion of Edgar. The Fool's role is to be at Lear's side, to express his love and concern for his master by trying to show him the error of his ways, and to try to alleviate his sorrows by means of appropriate witticisms. His service to Lear is exclusively one of love. Lear takes this for granted. Only when Lear himself is exposed to the elements does he seem to become aware of the Fool as a person with needs and feelings.

Kent's great love for Lear is the single motivating force in his life. His view of their relationship is expressed during his passionate intervention on behalf of Cordelia:

> *Royal Lear,*
> *Whom I have ever honoured as my king,*
> *Loved as my father, as my master followed,*
> *As my great patron thought on in my prayers—*
>
> (Act 1, Scene 1, lines 135–8)

The fact that he is banished by Lear for his effort to help him see the truth makes no difference to his loyalty and love. If he cannot serve Lear, his life will have no meaning, so he disguises himself as Caius and offers himself in that persona as a new servant, ready to perform all kinds of tasks for Lear. Being Lear's faithful servant and watching out for his interests represents total fulfilment for Kent. On the whole, Lear takes Kent's fidelity and loyal service for granted, but lack of recognition plays no part in Kent's view of this relationship; thoughtlessness of himself and indifference to his own fortunes are the chief marks of his character throughout. Even after Lear's death, Kent feels he must follow him.

I have a journey, sir, shortly to go.
My master calls me; I must not say no.

KENT, Act 5, Scene 3, 324–5

Milk-livered man!

GONERIL, Act 4, Scene 2, 51

Albany and Goneril

The Albany–Goneril relationship evolves significantly throughout the course of the play. It is never an equal one. Albany owes his position to his marriage to Goneril, who uses this fact to bully and humiliate him.

At first Albany appears indecisive and weak-minded. He does not fully approve of Goneril's treatment of Lear, but when he intervenes apologetically on Lear's behalf, Goneril can show only a dismissive contempt. She is the dominant, masterful partner in the relationship, from time to time expressing misgivings about her husband's passive nature, feeling that his civilised attitudes, his 'milky gentleness' and 'harmful mildness' (Act 1, Scene 4, lines 329, 332) fall far short of the iron-willed determination she thinks necessary in times of strife.

Goneril's comments to Edmund, with whom she establishes an adulterous relationship, sufficiently explain her view of her dominant position. Albany will attend to household duties as she goes to war: 'I must change arms at home, and give the distaff into my husband's hands' (Act 4, Scene 2, lines 17–18).

As Goneril sinks further into depravity, Albany's inner spirit asserts itself, and the nature of their relationship changes radically. Her verbal abuse no longer impresses him, and he subjects her to some of his own. Exposure to Goneril's influence, in particular to her savage, animal nature, brings Albany's primitive impulses into play. If his self-control and sense of propriety did not overrule his instincts, his hands would be ready, he tells her, 'to dislocate and tear thy flesh and bones' (Act 4, Scene 2, lines 66–7), which makes her dismissive comment on his 'manhood' appear oddly inappropriate.

Hero, heroine and villain

The world of *King Lear* exhibits remarkable extremes of good and evil. This is partly a function of the primitive, fairy-tale quality of the play, which is most evident in the opening scene with its ritual love-test, and one good and two evil daughters. The main plot and the sub-plot are each founded on the same contrast between the children of one father, as demonstrated in the combat between Edgar and Edmund in the closing scene.

The immense moral difference between Cordelia and Edgar on the one hand, and Goneril, Regan and Edmund on the other, raises interesting and important questions about the influence of heredity on the development of human character.

The mysterious fact that so much good and so much evil can co-exist in Lear's family leads Kent to dismiss the notion of hereditary influence in favour of the theory that character must be conditioned by planetary influences:

> It is the stars,
> The stars above us govern our conditions;
> Else one self mate and make could not beget
> Such different issues.

(Act 4, Scene 3, lines 32–5)

Evil is embodied in Edmund, Goneril, Regan, Cornwall and Oswald. The distinguishing marks of these villains are their extreme attachment to self and to selfish interests, their exploitation of others, their rejection of natural bonds and of the claims of kinship, their abandonment of civilised standards, and their ready indulgence in savage cruelty.

The extremes of evil are counterbalanced by the goodness in Cordelia, Kent, Edgar, the Fool and Cornwall's servant. This group of heroic characters (joined by Gloucester and Albany as the play progresses) seeks to do good. They show kindness, civility, charity and concern for others, and recognise the obligations of society and family.

Heroes and heroine

Each of the good characters is governed by an instinctive sense of service and duty.

Love for the parent or master is for them more than a matter of emotion; it is primarily a matter of self-sacrifice in the performance of duties deriving from the natural bond between characters. This is how we are to see **Edgar's** service to his father. When Albany asks how he has known Gloucester's miseries, there can only be one answer: 'by nursing them', I 'led him, begged for him, saved him from despair' (Act 5, Scene 3, lines 182, 192).

Edgar's goodness is sustained by a deep religious faith, on which his interpretation of life and its duties is based. He looks to 'the clearest gods' (Act 4, Scene 6, line 74) for inspiration. His services to his father and his ability to feel and offer sympathy and support are made possible through his belief that the higher powers are ultimately benevolent, that human beings need never despair.

In the same way, **Kent's** attachment to Lear is one in which love means not easy sentiment but service immeasurably beyond the call of duty. This is clear from his final summary of the purpose of his life: 'I am the very man ... that from your first of difference and decay have followed your sad steps' (Act 5, Scene 3, lines 288–91).

Cordelia's heroic, self-forgetful service to Lear is motivated not by love alone, but also by a sense of duty and the obligations of a daughter to a father.

The heroic activities of the good characters involve care for their family, their employers, the vulnerable in society and the state as a whole. The real heroism of the play is found not in military success but in the often thankless performance of numerous unspectacular duties based on a clear consciousness of what is right and wrong.

Villains

It is relatively easy to classify the characters of the play as good and evil, heroes and villains, although when one comes to consider the evil ones, gradations and discriminations come into question.

Oswald is the least important and the easiest to classify. Edgar can only describe him in terms of his capacity for evil-doing: he is 'a serviceable villain, as duteous to the vices of [his mistress, Goneril] as badness would desire' (Act 4, Scene 6, lines 244–6). If we can regard a strong sense of duty to even so evil a mistress as Goneril as a virtue, then we cannot dismiss Oswald as an utterly evil character. He stoutly resists Regan's request to let her open Goneril's letter to Edmund, and his dying concern is that the letter be safely delivered.

In contrast, **Cornwall** exhibits no redeeming quality to balance his dedication to wickedness. His chief contribution to the plot is to perpetrate one of its most extreme horrors: the blinding of Gloucester. He combines cowardice with cruelty; for example, he becomes bold with Lear only when Goneril arrives to support him and Regan (Act 2, Scene 4, lines 195–6). On the scale of evil, however, he does not fully rank with Goneril, Regan or Edmund since, unlike them, he does not direct his savagery at members of his own family.

Edmund is a conventional figure, the stock villain of melodrama, who characterises himself as an evil, amoral individual, with treacherous designs on his closest relatives. He does not appear to harbour either affection or dislike for anybody. His single controlling impulse is to make his way in the world, to get his hands on Edgar's inheritance, then to supplant his father, and then to become king. He sees two categories of people: those who can help him to achieve these ambitions, and those who may hinder him. He uses those in the first category, and eliminates those in the second. Unimpeded by emotion, he proceeds rationally and mechanically. He thinks of the torture of his father without qualm of conscience. He regards morality as an artificial convention imposed by society that may be ignored by those it does not suit.

Despite these frightening attributes, Edmund is, in respects, an attractive villain. He has courage, liveliness, a sardonic sense of humour and an imposing personality. He is redeemed from absolute villainy at the end, being moved to attempt his one kind and disinterested act by two circumstances: the story of his father's death and the fact that he was loved by two women. It is significant that his impulse to do good comes too late to be effective. While his 'attractive' qualities do something to make us less conscious than we might otherwise be of his profoundly evil nature, he remains one of the most monstrous of all Shakespeare's villains.

A greater depth of evil is reached by **Goneril** and **Regan**. In Shakespeare's time gender roles and attributes were rigidly defined, and, in a play so strongly focused on unnatural dealings, it is significant that two of the three female characters fail to display any characteristically female qualities such as kindness, pity, concern or gentleness. Instead, they outdo the male

characters in cruelty and primitive savagery. Their general tendency is indicated in their suggested punishment for Gloucester. Regan's 'hang him instantly' is met with Goneril's 'pluck out his eyes' (Act 3, Scene 7, lines 4–5).

There can be no doubt that Goneril is the most complete manifestation of evil in the play. Amongst other things, she commits adultery with Edmund, poisons her sister, plots to murder her husband, and co-signs the warrant with Edmund to have Cordelia hanged in prison. Regan is also monstrous but lacks Goneril's energy, courage and strength of character.

The two sisters are ruined in the end by their own villainy. This fate is deeply ironic. Like Edmund, they thrive on rational calculation, which allows them to deal successfully with Lear. They lose control of their destinies when their rationality is clouded by their mutual passion for Edmund. It is a satisfying turn of fate that two women who could entertain no feeling for the father who loved them should be destroyed by an all-absorbing passion for a man who has no feeling for either of them.

Imagery and themes

In *King Lear*, various sequences of imagery give us a sense of the world that Shakespeare sought to represent and the central themes he wanted to explore. Actions and imagery are closely dependent on each other in this play. The imagery flows from the circumstances of the drama, reflecting, for example, the mental and physical suffering of Lear and the violent world in which he lives.

Torture Nature Animals
Madness and reason
Justice Appearance and reality
Sight and blindness
Power

Characterisation through imagery

Imagery, or its absence, can influence our response to certain characters. For the purposes of this discussion, the characters may be divided into two groups: those associated with Lear, including the Fool, Edgar and Kent, and those opposed to him, including Edmund, Goneril, Regan, Cornwall and Oswald.

Lear and his allies

The imagery we associate with Lear is not merely decorative or used for the purpose of making meaning clearer. In his great speeches in Act 3, Scene 2 and Act 4, Scene 6, for example, Lear uses image after image to convey deeply personal visions. The Fool, Edgar and Kent also speak a language rich in imagery.

As the action progresses, Lear loses contact with the world around him. His words and images are used less as a means of communication with other characters than as a means of exposing what is going on within himself. His speeches take on the character of a monologue. When he does not speak to himself, he speaks to the elements, to nature and to the heavens.

Forsaken by human beings, Lear turns to non-human powers. In his tremendous speeches on the heath, his imagery invokes the elemental forces that surge through the play with an irresistible force:

> *Blow, winds, and crack your cheeks! Rage, Blow! ...*
> *You sulph'rous and thought-executing fires,*
> *Vaunt-couriers of oak-cleaving thunderbolts,*
> *Singe my white head!*
>
> (Act 3, Scene 2, lines 1–6)

> *Let the great gods,*
> *That keep this dreadful pudder o'er our heads,*
> *Find out their enemies now.*
>
> (Act 3, Scene 2, lines 48–50)

We cannot expect the Fool to compete with Lear's range of cosmic imagery, nor would it be desirable that he should replicate the gigantic dimensions of the ideas and feelings that Lear's images convey. On the contrary, the Fool's role is to bring Lear's actions and fantasies within the scope of everyday reality. He achieves this through the use of commonplace images. When, for example in Act 1, Scene 4, he wants to remind

Lear of his folly in dividing the kingdom, he uses the simile of an egg: Lear has divided the egg and given away both halves (the two crowns).

Edgar's language, particularly after he begins to play the role of madman, is full of imaginative references to the natural world, as Lear's is. When he says that he is prepared to 'outface the winds and persecutions of the sky' (Act 2, Scene 3, lines 11–12), his words anticipate Lear's in the next scene when he chooses 'to wage against the enmity of the air' (Act 2, Scene 4, line 206).

Kent habitually conveys his thoughts through images. For example, his life is a pawn to wage against Lear's enemies; he asks Lear to kill his physician and to bestow his fee 'upon the foul disease' (Act 1, Scene 1, lines 151–2, 159–60).

Lear's enemies

The relative absence of imagery from the speeches of Goneril, Regan, Edmund and Cornwall distinguishes them in a significant way from the characters associated with Lear. While the imaginative speech-patterns of the 'good' characters tell us a lot about their natures and their roles, the unimaginative speeches of the 'bad' ones reflect their dispositions also.

All four are limited in outlook and consequently in language. They are rational and speak deliberately and without much elaboration. They use the language of ruthless and efficient operators with well-defined goals, and everything they have to say is directed at achieving these. Their language, with the occasional exception of Edmund's, does not reveal what is taking place within their minds, as imaginative language might. Instead, they state their aims and how they intend to put these into practice.

Their characters are substantially reflected in their inability to use creative imagery. Goneril,

Edmund and Regan are calculating and largely unemotional. They have no relationship either to nature or to the gods. Their talk is of possession and calculation, of gain and loss in commercial terms. For example: Lear is asked to 'disquantity' his train (Act 1, Scene 4, line 236), to dismiss half of it, then half again, then all.

Animal imagery

The play's animal imagery leaves the most lasting impression. The imagination is filled with pictures of wild and menacing creatures, ravenous in their appetites, cruel in their instincts: the wolf, the boar, the tiger, the vulture, the serpent, the sea-monster. The underlying emphasis in such imagery is on the vileness of which humanity is capable.

It is mainly Goneril and Regan who are seen in terms of repulsive animal images. Lear is convinced that Regan, when she hears how he has been mistreated by Goneril, will 'flay' the latter's 'wolfish visage' with her nails (Act 1, Scene 4, lines 295–6). Filial ingratitude is as if 'this mouth should tear this hand for lifting food to't' (Act 3, Scene 4, lines 15–16). Gloucester tells Regan he has sent Lear to Dover:

> Because I would not see
> Thy cruel nails pluck out his poor old eyes;
> Nor thy fierce sister in his anointed flesh
> Stick boarish fangs.

> (Act 3, Scene 7, lines 53–6)

Albany tells Goneril that she and Regan are 'tigers, not daughters' (Act 4, Scene 2, line 41). It is also Albany who declares that if the bestial cruelty of Goneril and Regan is not checked, the human world may become like that of the wild beasts: 'Humanity must perforce prey on itself, like monsters of the deep' (Act 4, Scene 2, lines 50–1).

Such animal images suggest that the worst representatives of humanity threaten to destroy human values since they live by the law of the jungle. As well as savage wolves and other predators, the imagery features darting serpents; a sharp-toothed vulture; stinging adders; gnawing rats; and whipped, whining, mad and biting dogs.

Edgar, as Poor Tom, uses animals as emblems of sin: 'hog in sloth, fox in stealth, wolf in

greediness' (Act 3, Scene 4, line 87). When Lear looks at the almost naked Edgar, disguised as a Bedlam beggar, the very nature of man is defined in terms of animal imagery: 'Thou art the thing itself! Unaccommodated man is no more but such a poor, bare, forked animal as thou art' (Act 3, Scene 4, lines 98–100).

There is a close association between the animal images and the pervasive suggestion of bodily pain and suffering in the play.

Violence and bodily torture

The play is overshadowed by one image-pattern, which flows naturally from the physical and mental suffering of Lear in particular. This pattern focuses on the human body in anguished movement: beaten, scourged, dislocated, flayed, gashed, tortured and broken on the rack.

Many of the images involving pain and violence are metaphors for mental torture. Lear pictures himself as a man tortured by an engine beating at the gate (his head) that let his folly in. He complains that Goneril has struck him with her tongue. His heart will 'break into a hundred thousand flaws' (Act 2, Scene 4, line 280). Gloucester's 'flawed heart' will finally 'burst smilingly' (Act 5, Scene 3, lines 197–200). Kent would like to crush Oswald into mortar. Albany tells Goneril that if he followed his instinct he would 'dislocate and tear' her 'flesh and bones' (Act 4, Scene 2, lines 66–7).

Death can be seen as a welcome release from torture, which is almost the permanent condition of Lear and Gloucester. As Lear is dying, Kent appeals to those who would like to keep him alive:

> *O let him pass. He hates him*
> *That would upon the rack of this tough world*
> *Stretch him out longer.*

(Act 5, Scene 3, lines 316–18)

This image of the world as a torture chamber darkens the closing moments of the play. Earlier, when Lear imagined himself in some kind of afterlife, he still felt pain: 'I am bound upon a wheel of fire, that mine own tears do scald like molten lead' (Act 4, Scene 7, lines 47–9).

Violent images are complemented by patterns of verbs and nouns conveying an atmosphere of destructive cruelty. Gloucester's response to Edmund's 'revelations' about Edgar is full of agitated images. Within the space of ten lines we find: scourged, falls off, cracked, falls from bias, mutinies, machinations, ruinous disorders, discord (Act 1, Scene 2, lines 99–107). Gloucester himself is subjected to cruel and violent treatment in Act 3, Scene 7 (lines 27–93); he is bound to a chair, plucked by the beard, has his beard 'ravished' from his chin, feels like a bear tied to a stake and must 'stand the course', has his eyes gouged out and is 'thrust out at gates'.

Nature

No Shakespeare play is so consistently devoted to a single, central theme as *King Lear* is to the exploration of the meaning of the concept 'nature'. Explicit references to nature and ideas associated with it (natural, unnatural, monstrous and so on) are very numerous and occur in every scene.

Nature is central to the events of the play and the behaviour of the characters. It can be the force that inspires kindly impulses in a person, or the devastating power of a storm, or the created world seen as an orderly system operating according to well-defined laws.

Lear disowns his one loyal and loving daughter in favour of two who will turn savagely on him.

Gloucester makes a similar mistake, believing that the utterly treacherous Edmund is his 'loyal and natural boy' (Act 2, Scene 1, line 85) and disowning the devoted Edgar as an unnatural monster. Each parent severs the bond of nature with animal-like ferocity; then, with grim irony, invokes nature as a reason for doing so. Lear argues that Cordelia is 'a wretch whom nature is ashamed almost t'acknowledge hers' (Act 1, Scene 1, lines 208–9). Gloucester argues that Edgar is an 'unnatural, detested, brutish villain' (Act 1, Scene 2, line 71).

Lear and Gloucester, who act from brute instinct and in blindness, commit mortal sins against nature. The rest of the play is mainly concerned with the terrible revenge that nature will take on these two offenders. Lear and Gloucester will each pay a price that bears little proportion to their initial error.

Each will be largely cut off from the kindness, generosity and protection that human beings naturally afford each other. They will be

forced to wander in a storm, one of the great Shakespearean symbols of disorder. They will learn the lessons of their folly through pain and suffering. Gloucester, paradoxically, must be blinded in order to see. Lear, paradoxically, must be driven to madness to achieve an understanding of himself and his acts.

Nature as a force for good

Contrasting characters hold radically differing positions on the meaning of the term 'nature'. For some it is a benevolent force, keeping all created things in proper harmony.

For this group, living in accordance with nature involves obligation: loyalty, affection, kindness, observance of rank and place. Cordelia, Kent and Edgar are faithful to this view of nature; as are Lear and Gloucester, although it must be said that initially they both show an imperfect awareness of natural obligation.

When Lear expresses his desire for Cordelia's exclusive love, she tells him that the law of nature imposes other obligations, for example to a husband, of which he takes no account. Gloucester's (apparently) extra-marital liaison, the result of which is Edmund, suggests his defective view of the loyalty required on entering into marriage, one of the most fundamental of all natural relationships.

Nature as a force for bad

Nature has quite a different meaning for Edmund, Goneril, Regan and Cornwall. For them, it does not involve any consideration of duty, kinship or filial obligation. Instead, it is about rampant, heartless individualism.

Goneril, Regan and Edmund place a heavy emphasis on filial love when they seek to impress their parents; but their actions involve a total rejection of the obligation of natural affection.

Edmund's first soliloquy is an address to nature as a goddess, but this nature is a force encouraging him to disregard all obligation to others and to pursue his own interests with single-minded determination. In practice, this means ignoring, and even infringing on, the rights of others, including his father, whose life Edmund is prepared to sacrifice for his own benefit.

Similarly, Goneril and Regan are prepared to allow Lear to lose his reason and risk his life in order to avoid the inconvenience of housing and providing for him. Goneril's unnatural behaviour finally takes a more extreme form: she and Edmund sign the document ordering the execution of Lear and Cordelia, and she also poisons Regan.

Such violation of humane standards and of natural bonds leads Albany to conclude that, if the heavenly powers do not intervene to chastise the offenders, human relationships will be like those of wild animals: 'Humanity must perforce prey on itself, like monsters of the deep' (Act 4, Scene 2, lines 50–1).

Meanings of 'nature'

'Nature' is one of the key terms of the play. It is used with a wide range of meanings and in a variety of contexts, ranging from the pre-civilised, brutish condition of mankind, through an object of pagan worship, to the bonds that unite families and human beings in general.

Here are some examples of the widely varying meanings of the term 'nature' in the play:

- The primitive conditions of mankind before human society began to evolve.

> *Allow not nature more than nature needs,*
> *Man's life is as cheap as beast's.*
>
> (Act 2, Scene 4, lines 262–3)

- The innocence before the fall (in the biblical sense) corrupted it.

> *Thou hast a daughter*
> *Who redeems nature from the general curse*
> *Which twain have brought her to.*
>
> (Act 4, Scene 6, lines 199–201)

- The primitive universal object of pagan worship; a goddess personifying the forces that create the phenomena of the natural world.

> *Thou, nature, art my goddess; to thy law*
> *My services are bound.*
>
> (Act 1, Scene 2, lines 1–2)

- Human nature or the human race.

> *... nature finds itself scourged ...*
>
> (Act 1, Scene 2, line 99)

- As character, disposition, the sum total of personal qualities.

> *A tardiness in nature*
> *Which often leaves the history unspoken*
> *That it intends to do*
>
> (Act 1, Scene 1, lines 231–3)

- The natural affection between relatives, in this case filial affection.

> *Thou better know'st*
> *The offices of nature, bond of childhood ...*
>
> (Act 2, Scene 4, lines 173–4)

- Bodily constitution, vital functions, natural powers.

> *We are not ourselves*
> *When nature, being oppressed, commands the mind*
> *To suffer with the body.*
>
> (Act 2, Scene 4, lines 103–5)

- Natural impulse (as opposed to the traditional norms of society).

> *Who in the lusty stealth of nature ...*
>
> (Act 1, Scene 2, line 11)

Madness and reason

Madness is explored from several points of view in *King Lear*, and mainly through three characters: Lear, Edgar and the Fool. Lear's madness is real; Edgar's is a pretence, since he is taking on the role of a madman to conceal his identity; and the Fool's is an essential part of his role as a vessel of wisdom, which constantly emerges in his apparently insane comments on Lear's folly.

The madness of the storm, the professional madness of the Fool, the feigned madness of Edgar and the actual madness of Lear all exemplify the collapse of society and the break-up of the universe itself under the impact of ingratitude and treachery. During the storm scenes, Kent is the only wholly sane character around Lear.

Edgar

Edgar's feigned madness is a function of his disguise as a Bedlam beggar, a pauper lunatic released on licence from Bethlehem hospital, an asylum for the insane in London. Former inmates of this institution roamed the land begging for a living at cottages and farmhouses.

Edgar's assumption of this role allows Shakespeare to extend the range of social comment associated with Lear's madness. Edgar's account of the life of a Bedlam beggar gives a grim picture of the brutal treatment inflicted on the unfortunates who were judged insane by contemporary society: 'whipped from tithing to tithing and stocked, punished and imprisoned' (Act 3, Scene 4, lines 124–5).

In acting out the madman's role, Edgar precipitates Lear's madness.

Lear

Lear's madness may be studied from a number of angles. It may be seen simply as a psychological phenomenon, and as revealing Shakespeare's understanding of abnormal mental life. Lear's madness, or what would now perhaps be called his nervous breakdown, represents the collapse of a highly strung, volatile personality, which is deprived of its identity and its grasp of objective reality. His indulgence in emotional violence and rage has led to nervous exhaustion.

At the heart of his mentally disturbed state is his obsession with the ingratitude of his daughters. This filial ingratitude drives him beyond the boundaries of reason. It also sustains him in that state until his mind is eventually healed. Shakespeare dramatises this obsession in Act 3, Scene 4. It preoccupies his mind exclusively, so that he is convinced that no evil can befall anybody except through the agency of ungrateful daughters. Thus, when he encounters Edgar, as Poor Tom, dressed only in a blanket, he assumes that he has been deprived of his possessions by his daughters.

Lear's madness is also a symbol of a chaotic world in which norms have disintegrated. This process is symbolised by the storm that forms the background to his violent outbursts. The storm is the projection on the macrocosm (the universe) of the tempest in the microcosm (the human mind).

Lear's madness reflects the tragic pattern of the play: through the process of suffering, he achieves recognition and self-knowledge. This is one of the play's great paradoxes: deprived of his reason, Lear develops an imaginative awareness of evil, a knowledge of himself and of his erring ways not available to him in his rational days.

Edgar is struck by the fact that the lunacy of Lear is compatible with the most profound insight. He marvels at the understanding of injustice achieved by a raving lunatic: 'O matter and impertinency mixed; reason in madness!' (Act 4, Scene 6, lines 168–9).

The following are the main stages in Lear's madness, which is induced by a series of shocks:

- He is rebuffed by Cordelia.
- Goneril's attacks make him pretend not to know her and not to know himself.
- He begins to realise how much he has wronged Cordelia.
- He fully recognises his folly, in Act 1, Scene 5.
- His first serious premonition of insanity: 'O let me not be mad, not mad, sweet heaven!' (Act 1, Scene 5, line 38).
- He finds Kent in the stocks. This insult to his royal dignity causes the first physical symptoms of hysteria.
- He is rejected by Regan.
- His premonition of madness becomes more acute: 'O fool, I shall go mad!' (Act 2, Scene 4, line 281).
- He identifies with the storm, a sign that reason has been overthrown by passion.
- He is on the verge of madness when he invites the storm to destroy the seeds of matter (life): 'all germens spill at once' (Act 3, Scene 2, line 8).
- Entering the hovel (out of concern for the Fool), the burdens he has had to bear prove too much for him: 'My wits begin to turn' (Act 3, Scene 2, line 66).
- He crosses the borderline between sanity and madness when he encounters Poor Tom, who is a living embodiment of naked poverty – apparently, what Lear has feared to become.

- Exposure to the elements and physical exhaustion hinder his recovery from the shocks he has endured.
- He is soon trying to identify himself with 'unaccommodated man' (Act 3, Scene 4, line 99) by tearing off his clothes.
- He enters a more extreme state of madness – a psychotic state in which thought and emotions are so impaired that contact is lost with external reality.
- He is now dominated by a fixed idea or obsession: the belief that all the evils in the world have been caused by ungrateful daughters.
- He becomes delusional, as evidenced by the mock-trial in Act 3, Scene 6.
- Just as he begins to take a much-needed rest, Gloucester arrives with a litter to transport him to Dover, and so he must be wakened and moved.
- He roams the countryside 'as mad as the vexed sea, singing aloud, crowned with rank fumiter and furrow-weeds …' (Act 4, Scene 4, lines 2–3). The whole tableau marks a reversion to childhood.
- Lear recovers his wits at the end of Act 4. His cure comes with sleep, natural herbs, music, Cordelia's love, and finally with his confession and kneeling to her.

Sight and blindness

The theme of sight and blindness is introduced very early in the play, after Lear has failed to see through the flattery of Goneril and Regan or to recognise the honesty of Cordelia.

Lear, blinded by anger, orders Kent out of his sight (Act 1, Scene 1, line 153). Kent suggests that Lear's vision is defective and invites him to 'see better' (line 154) – if Lear could see the situation through his (Kent's) eyes, then he would face reality. The morally blind Lear then swears by Apollo (line 156), which is ironic because Apollo is the ancient Greek god of light.

The theme is taken up in the second scene, when Edmund pretends that the document he has been reading contains 'nothing', and Gloucester replies, 'come, if it be nothing, I shall not need spectacles' (Act 1, Scene 2, line 34–5). The irony of this remark is completed most dramatically by the blinding of Gloucester in Act 3, Scene 7, which marks the symbolic climax of the blindness theme.

Lear and Gloucester are the two characters whose careers in the play are best summed up in terms of sight and blindness. Lear progresses from an unwillingness to see the truth, through a period of gradual enlightenment, to a strong desire to face reality.

In Gloucester's case, following his blinding, the Old Man refuses to abandon him, remarking 'You cannot see your way' (Act 4, Scene 1, line 17). Gloucester replies by summing up his career in terms of sight and blindness: 'I have no way, and therefore want no eyes; I stumbled when I saw' (lines 18–19). Gloucester thinks that suicide will relieve him from his misery and that as his road through life is about to end, he does not need eyesight. And anyway, when he could see, he blundered ('stumbled') into error and wickedness. He goes on to speak of Edgar: 'Might I but live to see thee in my touch, I'd say I had eyes again!' (lines 23–4). What he means here is that although he can only touch Edgar, not see him, there is a sense in which he does see him: that is, he at least sees the truth about him.

The sight theme is taken up again in Gloucester's prayer that the heavens might act to ensure a better division of the world's goods: 'Let the superfluous and lust-dieted man that slaves your ordinance, that will not see because he does not feel, feel your power quickly' (lines 66–8). Gloucester is not merely calling down the anger of the heavens on evil-doers. He is also describing his old self. He was 'lust-dieted', he showed contempt for divine laws, and he would not see because he did not feel. Now that he does feel, he understands himself as he never did before.

When Gloucester had eyes, he used them badly. Just as he was achieving real insight, he was blinded. His loss of outward sight has facilitated this insight.

During the meeting of Lear and Gloucester in the countryside near Dover, the sight and blindness theme comes into strong focus. Lear makes a cruel comment on Gloucester's blindness: 'Dost thou squiny [squint] at me?' and addresses him as 'blind Cupid', whose image was commonly displayed at the doors of London brothels (Act 4, Scene 6, lines 134–5). Lear is suggesting that Gloucester's lechery has led to his blindness, an idea later repeated by Edgar to Edmund in reference to their father: 'The dark and vicious place where thee he got, cost him his eyes' (Act 5, Scene 3, lines 173–4).

The mad Lear asks the blind Gloucester to read a document he (Lear) has written. Gloucester wonders how he is expected to read without eyes ('Were all the letters suns, I could not see') and Lear tells him that he can still 'see' the state of the world by using his other senses: 'Look with thine ears. See how yond justice rails upon yond simple thief' (Act 4, Scene 6, lines 137, 146–8). Lear is telling Gloucester that his ears will tell him how unjust the judicial system is.

Lear finds it difficult to abandon the sight and blindness theme because the blind Gloucester's presence keeps reminding him of it. He hands an imaginary pardon to Gloucester that will put him above the law, and then tells him to get a pair of spectacles ('glass eyes') and, like a disreputable trickster ('scurvy politician'),

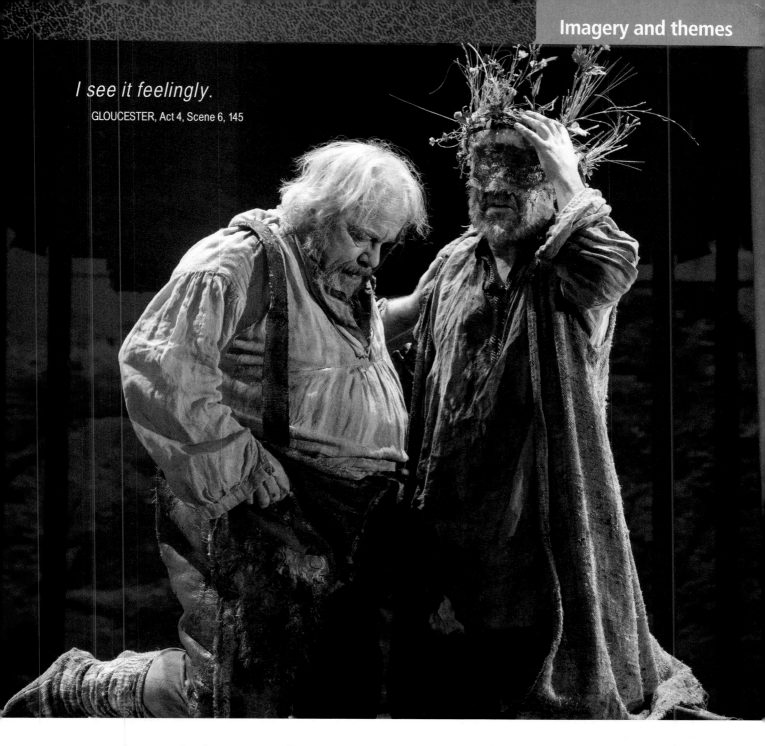

I see it feelingly.

GLOUCESTER, Act 4, Scene 6, 145

pretend to see what he cannot really see (Act 4, Scene 6, lines 164–6). Finally he tells Gloucester that if the latter wants to weep he is welcome to take his (Lear's) eyes for the purpose of shedding tears (line 170).

In the sight pattern, a late scene can echo an earlier one. For example, Lear can hardly recognise Kent physically in the final scene, just as he could not recognise (or see) Kent's moral rightness and so ordered him out of his sight in the first scene; Lear confesses, 'Mine eyes are not o' the best' (Act 5, Scene 3, line 280).

The comments of one character can also echo or anticipate those of another. In Act 1, Scene 4

Lear, discussing Goneril's true nature, asks questions about himself: 'Does any here know me? . . . Does Lear walk thus? Speak thus? Where are his eyes?' (lines 213–14). This anticipates Gloucester's insight after his blinding: 'I stumbled when I saw' (Act 4, Scene 1, line 19).

These cross-references emphasise the theme that those with the best of eyesight can fail to see the reality beneath surface appearances. In the opening scene Lear was unable to distinguish between appearances and realities in relation to his daughters and Kent. In his madness, however, he displays depths of insight that were denied to him when he was sane.

Appearance and reality

The contrast between appearance and reality is announced and developed at the beginning of the play.

Lear is utterly deceived by what is said and what is meant by both his two evil daughters and his one good one; while Gloucester falls into a parallel error in the case of the hypocritical Edmund and the innocent Edgar. Both fathers learn from their errors.

Clothing

Clothing imagery is often used in *King Lear* to illustrate this key theme.

At the centre of the action, Lear stresses the function of clothing as a symbol of class and wealth, as a means of concealing perversions of justice, and of helping the rich to enjoy privileges denied to the poor:

> Through tattered clothes great vices do appear;
> Robes and furred gowns hide all. Plate sin with gold,
> And the strong lance of justice hurtless breaks;
> Arm it in rags, a pigmy's straw doth pierce it.
>
> (Act 4, Scene 6, lines 158–61)

Lear has learned much by the time he makes this pronouncement. His initial error was to take appearances at face value, to confuse outward show with inward reality. Both Cordelia and Kent suffer because they refuse to conceal their true feelings. Cordelia is disowned and banished. Kent has to resort to disguise and takes on a new identity as Caius.

Edgar is also forced to assume a disguise, although his case is more extreme as he must become Poor Tom, a Bedlam beggar, to survive. There is much emphasis on Tom's nakedness, on the 'unaccommodated man' (Act 3, Scene 4, line 99) bereft of clothing and other aids to dignity. Lear tries to tear off his clothes to be like him.

There is a symbolic appropriateness in the fact that Lear runs about in the storm 'bare-headed' (Act 3, Scene 2, line 59). In the storm scenes he reduces himself to the level of the poorest of his subjects. He is as defenceless and unprotected as they are in facing the elements. He can therefore make a speech of compassion without condescension:

> Poor naked wretches, wheresoe'er you are
> That bide the pelting of this pitiless storm,
> How shall your houseless heads and unfed sides,
> Your looped and windowed raggedness, defend you
> From seasons such as these?
>
> (Act 3, Scene 4, lines 28–32)

Images of clothing take on further symbolic value as Lear's sanity is restored. The Gentleman tells Cordelia that 'in the heaviness of sleep we put fresh garments on him' (Act 4, Scene 7, lines 22–3). The new garments, his royal robes, symbolise the new Lear, a king once more, as Cordelia's first greetings to him suggest: 'How does my royal lord? How fares your majesty?' (line 45).

Justice

The theme of justice has two aspects in *King Lear*: cosmic and human.

Divine justice

In its cosmic aspect, justice is directly linked to the constant emphasis by characters on the gods. Characters talk about 'the gods' rather than 'God' for two reasons. The first is that the play is set in pagan times. The second is that a law passed in 1606 forbade God to be invoked in the singular, out of respect for the name. When we are discussing 'the gods' in *King Lear*, it is best to think of the term as referring to the mysterious powers that control the world and what happens to people who inhabit it, the 'secret cause' of all things.

Anyone reading or watching the play is bound to be struck by the frequency with which the gods are called upon or discussed. Some characters take a positive view of the gods as good, benevolent and just in their dealings with human beings and as seeing to it that good will prevail over evil. Some express the view that the gods care so little for human welfare that they make sport of human suffering and seem to enjoy inflicting pain. Some exhibit conflicting views on the gods, sometimes seeing them as friends of humanity, sometimes as enemies. And others appear totally indifferent to the gods, or fail to recognise their existence.

In the early part of the play, Kent takes a friendly view of the gods as sources of kindness to humans, Cordelia for example, for whom he prays that 'the gods to their dear shelter take thee' (Act 1, Scene 1, line 178). However, the view of the gods as agents of punishment and revenge, rather than of justice, is much more common. Lear associates them with his own anger and desire for revenge. He curses Goneril, praying that 'all the stored vengeances of heaven fall on her ingrateful top!' (Act 2, Scene 4, lines 158–9). On the heath, he thinks of the gods as angry beings who inflict a deadly storm on humanity and pursue their enemies (Act 3, Scene 2, 48–58).

Edgar is the outstanding example of a character who expresses a consistent faith in the justice and benevolence of the gods, in addition to the belief that good will prevail over evil.

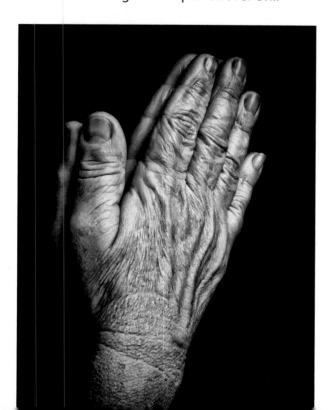

He undergoes punishment and physical and mental suffering that he does not deserve when, having been unjustly made an outlaw, he is forced to flee his home. In spite of this, he preaches endurance and trust in divine providence, and leads both Gloucester and Lear to follow his example.

Like Edgar, Gloucester undergoes overwhelming suffering, the worst of which (his blinding) is certainly not deserved and results from an act of kindness on his part. When he defies Cornwall, Goneril and Regan by offering Lear shelter from the storm, Kent remarks, 'The gods reward your kindness!' (Act 3, Scene 6, line 5). But he is not rewarded by the gods: instead, his eyes are gouged out. This experience is bound to test Gloucester's faith in divine justice. However, just after Cornwall blinds him, he calls upon the 'kind gods' to forgive him for the wrong he has done to Edgar, and to bring prosperity to the latter (Act 3, Scene 7, line 91).

In the next scene Gloucester lapses into despair and sees the gods as cruel beings who enjoy torturing victims like him: 'As flies to wanton boys are we to the gods. They kill us for their sport' (Act 4, Scene 1, lines 36–7). This is not Gloucester's final word on divine justice, however. When Edgar saves him from despair, he feels able to affirm the benevolence of the gods: 'You ever-gentle gods … Let not my worser spirit tempt me again to die before you please!' (Act 4, Scene 6, lines 211–13).

Lear, Gloucester, Cordelia and Edgar endure extreme suffering. They do not deserve to suffer to the extent that they do. Their prayers to be relieved of this suffering are not given favourable answers. It appears that the gods do not hear them, or simply ignore or disregard them. For example, as Edgar hastens to save Cordelia's life in prison, Albany's prayer, 'The god's defend her!' (Act 5, Scene 3, line 257), is immediately followed by the arrival of Lear with Cordelia dead in his arms.

The play certainly exposes the folly of thinking that the operations of providence (or 'the gods') should conform to human expectations. Does all this mean that in *King Lear* the gods are content to preside over a universe in which good and innocent people suffer unjustly at the hands of the wicked? Is the play simply a depiction of divine injustice and malice towards humanity, or should we see the suffering endured by the 'good' characters as a positive, redeeming thing?

There can be little doubt that it is only when Lear and Gloucester are subjected to the most tormenting experiences – spiritual, psychological and physical – that their better natures find expression. Selfishness and arrogance in both men give way to compassion and concern for others; they learn patience and humility. The self-regarding Lear learns through his own suffering and deprivation to feel and share the needs of the deprived. The soft, self-indulgent Gloucester is made strong and heroic

Human justice

Justice, or the lack of it, in human society is a major theme in *King Lear*. In the opening scene, by virtue of his power as king, Lear is the first agent of justice and dispenses it energetically. His idea of justice is that it should be allocated according to merit rather than need. However, his thoroughly mistaken assessment of merit exposes his defects as an agent and dispenser of justice. Goneril and Regan satisfy his sense of merit by resorting to insincere expressions of love. The honest, loving Cordelia fails the test, and her sisters get her share of the kingdom as well as their own.

Lear then proceeds with unfair acts of vengeful justice against Cordelia and Kent. Their punishment is quite out of proportion to their offence: in Cordelia's case telling him the truth and refusing to flatter him, and in Kent's case pointing out his folly in disowning and disinheriting Cordelia. Furthermore, when he banishes Kent from the kingdom on pain of death, he is no longer king and chief magistrate, having handed these powers to Albany and Cornwall. As Lear lacks the legal power to pass sentence on Kent, this is an abuse of justice.

In a parallel development, Gloucester violates a basic principle of justice by accepting without question Edmund's false evidence against a totally innocent Edgar, who is forced to flee to save himself from death at the hands of Gloucester's patron Cornwall. The moral development of Lear and Gloucester is intimately associated with the deeper understanding they acquire, through their

after he has experienced adversity. True human goodness shows itself in these two characters mainly in response to, or as a result of, their suffering. In this way, the events of the play amount to a partial, if mysterious, vindication of divine justice.

Furthermore, the events of the play show that although evil is allowed to triumph for a time and cause inexplicable suffering, it carries the seeds of its own destruction and ultimately proves self-defeating. This point is made by the cases of Regan and Goneril, whose eventual hatred, suspicion and jealousy of each other result in their deaths.

own experience of injustice, of more ethically acceptable concepts of justice.

When Lear gives up his crown, and with it the power to dispense justice, he, for the first time in his life, is simply a subject. He is then governed by a system of justice devised and administered by people (his daughters) who are hostile to his welfare, just as he has unwittingly shown himself hostile to the welfare of Cordelia and Kent.

Now that he is no longer exercising the functions of a judge, Lear can take an objective view of the legal system. He can feel and express an emotional and spiritual identification with the problems of fellow-sufferers of injustice. In much of Act 3 there is considerable emphasis, on Lear's part, on the theme of justice, and on the fair distribution of the world's goods in particular. When he is pelted by the pitiless storm, Lear wonders how the ill-clothed poor can contend with such conditions. He admits that in the days of his prosperity he paid insufficient attention to such questions.

Lear argues passionately for distribution of wealth based on true need (and not on false merit, which marked his actions in the opening scene). He has evolved an advanced theory of justice that would require the rich to dispose of their surplus wealth to help the poor, and to 'shake the superflux to them' (Act 3, Scene 4, line 35). After his blinding, Gloucester arrives at a similar insight: he wishes that providence would ensure that the wealthy should see to the needs of the deprived, so that 'distribution should

undo excess and each man have enough' (Act 4, Scene 1, lines 69–70).

The place of punishment in the justice system occupies Lear in the absurd version of a trial in Act 3, Scene 6. In this mock-trial, a fake madman (Edgar), a professional Fool and Kent sit on the bench as justices. Lear takes the role of prosecutor, charging Goneril and Regan for their cruelty to him. Lear's arrangements for the trial entirely undermine the normal procedures in a court of justice. Before it begins, he decides on a suitable penalty to be imposed on the defendants, which means that whatever happens in the hearing, Goneril and Regan will be found guilty. This comic version of a trial foreshadows events in the next scene, when Gloucester is tried and punished as a traitor. Both trials make a mockery of justice.

As in the mock-trial, the sentence in Gloucester's case precedes the trial itself. Even before Gloucester's capture, Cornwall pronounces on his guilt, telling Edmund that the 'revenges we are bound to take upon your traitorous father are not fit for your beholding' (Act 3, Scene 7, line 7–8). Cornwall makes it clear that the proceedings are merely a formality, since they cannot pass a sentence on Gloucester 'without some form of justice' (line 24). Cornwall and Regan act as judges, prosecutors, interrogators, torturers and executioners of the grim sentence.

Lear later examines the flaws and contradictions at the heart of the justice system (Act 4, Scene 6). In his mad state, he understands these at a depth not available to him when he was sane. He concludes that official justice is necessarily divorced from morality and that fairness plays no part in its operations; for example:

- There is no moral distinction between the thief and the justice of the peace who abuses him from the bench, since the justice will acquit the thief on payment of a bribe and thus become a second thief.

- Rich people have the resources to buy immunity from punishment for their crimes, while the poor must pay in full.

- The king, as chief magistrate, can intervene to prevent the prosecution of criminals.

Lear's analysis of justice and its subversion of money, power and privilege strikes one of the most pessimistic notes in the play.

Power

Lear, aged 'fourscore and upwards', has enjoyed a very long spell of uninterrupted power, and the corrupting effects of this on his character and actions are evident in the opening scene. The habits associated with the exercise of absolute power have become a fixed part of his character. He is arrogant, rash and unreasonable. Above all, he is unable to listen to advice or to tolerate opposition to his wishes.

Lear is evidently so used to getting his own way and imposing his will that his automatic response to any challenge to his authority is a bout of violent rage. His curses and threats are followed by cruelly unjust punishment for the honest offenders who oppose his whims (see Act 1, Scene 1, lines 118, 150, 153, 157, 162–75, 229–30).

Kent's attempt to reason with Lear is answered with a threat to his life ('The bow is bent and drawn, make from the shaft'; Act 1, Scene 1, line 139). Lear's extreme exercise of power is revealed in his sentence of banishment on Kent, who has just reminded him that he has, in the cases of Goneril and Regan, yielded his power to those willing to flatter him. Having just invested the treacherous flatterers with his power, he still acts as if he has retained it and makes Kent the victim of a massive abuse of power that he is no longer entitled to exercise.

The deadliest side effect of Lear's conditioning by absolute power is that it blinds him to his own limitations: his poor judgement and his tendency to treat people as means to an end, to be used to minister to his self-esteem rather than to value them as persons with their own views and qualities. Like most tyrants, he is assured of the total rightness he does, as if he feels that supreme authority confers superior judgement.

Lear's sudden and total shedding of his power shows how mistaken his decision is. By transferring power to Goneril and Regan and their husbands, he falls under their control. They use their new power to destroy his happiness and his sanity. The Fool has a clearer understanding of the mechanisms of power than Lear has. Without power, Lear becomes a non-entity; as the Fool tells him: 'I am better than thou art now: I am a fool, thou art nothing' (Act 1, Scene 4, lines 181–2).

Lear had not realised how much his personal identity was bound up with his role as king and the power this conferred. Man and role were essentially the same. Loss of power means loss of identity and substance, so that, as a powerless former monarch, he becomes, in the Fool's words, merely 'Lear's shadow' (line 218).

Lear learns painfully how loss of power can be quickly translated into loss of privilege and status. Forgetting that he is no longer king, he issues arrogant commands to Goneril's attendant ('Let me not stay a jot for dinner; go get it ready'; Act 1, Scene 4, line 8). When his commands are ignored, he explodes in a rage: 'Where's that mongrel?', 'Why came not the slave back to me when I called him' (lines 45, 47). This display of unconcern for Lear has been contrived by Goneril.

It is only when Lear becomes temporarily insane that he begins to understand how defectively he exercised his royal powers when these were at their height, particularly in regards to the poorest of his subjects. On the heath in the storm, he is willing to share the miseries of 'houseless poverty' endured by the 'poor naked wretches' of whose plight he has previously taken 'too little care' (Act 3, Scene 4, lines 26–36).

Those who inherit Lear's power, particularly Goneril, Regan and Cornwall, believe that once in legal possession of the privileges it confers, they are free to abuse these powers with impunity. This view is articulated by Goneril in the closing scene. When Albany confronts her with evidence of her conspiracy with Edmund to murder him, she responds by telling him that the power she has inherited from her father places her beyond his reach or the scope of the law: she can do as she pleases ('the laws are mine, not thine. Who can arraign me for't?'; Act 5, Scene 3, lines 158–9).

Thus, as Goneril sees it, power makes her the sole proprietor of the legal system, which is to be exploited by her for personal goals. The possession of power corrupts the holder, sometimes absolutely. It becomes an instrument of tyranny and terror, to be exercised without morality or pity. The fate of Gloucester, whose offence is that he tries to help the distressed Lear, shows what happens when power is disjoined from sympathy and humane feelings.

In *King Lear* the struggle for power, as well as its exercise, appears inseparable from profound evil. Decisive ruthlessness is the necessary means to attain power. Tender, human feelings disqualify and disable the power-seeker. Edmund, for example, operates on the principle that its achievement justifies whatever means he finds necessary. He is prepared to destroy his brother's prospects of inheriting, to betray his father to the merciless Cornwall and to exploit the emotions of Goneril and Regan with a view to making himself king. Goneril, too, is prepared to do anything to increase her power.

By giving away his kingdom, Lear gave away the greater part of his identity. When he loses the rest of his possessions, including his rights of residence, maintenance and retainers, he is forced to shed everything else that made up his identity. In the eyes of two of his daughters, Lear was only what he had: property and power. When he loses the first and sheds the second, what is he then? The answer, as the Fool recognises, is nothing, since having is the essence of being, at least in the world of *King Lear*.

By divesting himself of all he has, Lear becomes a non-being. He remains in that situation until the final movement of the play, when he is restored to a sense of his true identity by Cordelia. He is also restored to absolute power in the final moments of his life, when it is clear that he will never enjoy this power or savour his true identity as king. Within minutes, he is dead.

Exam tips

Read all the questions carefully, making sure that you understand what is being asked in each, then choose the one that you are best prepared to answer. Underline the key words in the question.

Prepare a brief list of the points you want to make and determine the structure of your answer. Make sure that you deal equally with all the elements in the question.

It is essential that you support your answer with suitable reference to the play. In order to do this you must be thoroughly familiar with the details of the plot, as well as with the characters and their actions.

Good answers include brief, relevant quotations to enhance your analysis of the play. There is no need for lengthy quotations; short ones can make the point just as well and leave more space and time for making further points.

From the beginning to the end of your answer it is essential to stay with the exact terms of the question you are dealing with. Remember that marks are awarded for making relevant points clearly and economically, with the support of reference and quotation.

A good way to ensure that you stick to the question is to mention the key term(s) of the question in your introduction, conclusion and at suitable intervals throughout your answer. This reminds the examiner, and yourself, that you are dealing consistently with the issue you have been asked to address.

Students occasionally provide long summaries of the plot or accounts of characters that may, or may not, touch on the issues raised in the question. Other students write long introductions dealing with matters that they are not being asked to discuss. These ramblings will not earn marks.

Know in advance how much time you will give to each question and stick to this plan.

It is desirable to devote a separate paragraph to each new point you make. This makes it easier for you to structure your answer properly and for the examiner to follow your argument.

Bring your answer to a clear conclusion, perhaps referring back to the question and summarising your main argument.

Ordinary Level exam questions on *King Lear* comprise three shorter and one longer question (see examples opposite). Questions may deal with:

- Significant scenes and what happens in these.
- The motives of characters for behaving as they do.
- Your opinion of individual characters.
- Reasons for what happens to the characters.
- Choosing a character you would like to play and giving reasons for your choice.
- Assessing the play's merits as an exciting, moving drama, or its drawbacks as a painful, agonising experience for audiences and readers.
- How a particular scene might be staged.
- Imagining yourself interviewing one of the characters on his or her conduct at some moment in the play.

Suppose you are asked to choose a character you would like to play and to explain your choice, and you choose Edmund. All you have to do is give a number of reasons for wanting to play Edmund. What you must not do is set about summarising Edmund's character. That is not what the examiner wants to know. Instead, what he or she wants to know is why you have chosen to play Edmund.

Start your answer by giving your first reason for wanting to play Edmund. For example: *My first reason for wanting to play Edmund is that this is the most enjoyable role for an actor as it is full of variety, action and excitement.* You might support this point by adding an appropriate quotation from the play, such as: *As Edmund says himself, 'Let me, if not by birth, have lands by wit'.*

Higher Level exam questions on *King Lear* may:

- Deal with a major theme or issue in the play, for example madness or the clash of good and evil.

- Involve discussion of one character or a particular scene.

- Require a discussion of imagery and/or symbolism, such as storm and tempest.

- Ask for your response to the play and reasons for enjoying or not enjoying it.

Two of these topics will appear on the paper and you will be asked to deal with one of them.

> **Remember that the highest marks are obtained by students who deal directly with the question asked and who make their points in a logical sequence. They make a series of relevant points, clearly, and back them up with suitable references to the text and with brief and appropriate quotations.**

Past papers

It is worth looking at past exam papers to familiarise yourself with the types of question asked. The following questions on *King Lear* were part of the 2006 and 2010 Leaving Certificate exams.

Ordinary Level Paper 2, 2006

Answer **all** of the questions.

1 In the opening scene of the play Lear says:

'Tell me, my daughters, …

Which of you shall we say doth love us most … ?'

(a) Describe King Lear's reaction when Cordelia refused to take part in the Love Test he organised for his daughters at the start of the play.

(b) In your opinion did Cordelia do the right thing in refusing to take part? Explain your view.

2 Apart from the Love Test, what do you think was the most important moment in the play? Give reasons for your answer, supporting them by reference to the text.

3 Answer **ONE** of the following:

(i) The most important lesson the play teaches us is that:

  - *Young people have a duty to respect their elders, no matter what*
  - *People are not to be trusted*
  - *Everybody makes mistakes*

Choose **one** of the above statements and explain how the play teaches you that lesson.

OR

(ii) Imagine that the Fool kept a diary of the time he spent with King Lear. Write out **two** entries he might make about his experience during that time.

OR

(iii) Your local library is holding an event called *My Favourite Play* where readers explain what they particularly liked about their chosen play. You are to take part and you choose to introduce *King Lear* to the audience. Write the talk you would give.

Ordinary Level Paper 2, 2010

Answer **all** of the questions.

1 (a) How does Cordelia upset her father at the beginning of the play?

(b) Do you think that King Lear was wise to banish Kent? Explain your answer.

2 Do you like Edmund? Explain your answer with reference to the text.

3 Answer **ONE** of the following:

(i) Based on your reading of the play, write a piece beginning with one of the following statements:

– this is a story about foolishness

– this is a story about love.

OR

(ii) *'Sisters! Sisters! Shame of ladies!'*

This is Cordelia's comment on her sisters, Goneril and Regan. Describe the character and conduct of the two sisters. Support your answer with reference to the play.

OR

(iii) Which of the characters would you like to play in your school's production of *King Lear*? Give reasons for your choice. Support your answer with reference to the play.

Higher Level Paper 2, 2006

Answer **one** of these questions:

(i) 'In the play *King Lear,* the stories of Lear and Gloucester mirror one another in interesting ways.'

Write a response to this view of the play, supporting your answer by reference to the text.

OR

(ii) 'Reading or seeing *King Lear* is a horrifying as well as an uplifting experience.'

Write a response to this view, supporting the points you make by reference to the play.

For a possible answer to question (ii), see Sample essays, pp. 291–2.

Higher Level Paper 2, 2010

Answer **one** of these questions:

(i) 'In *King Lear* honour and loyalty triumph over brutality and viciousness.'

Write your response to this statement supporting your answer with suitable reference to the text.

OR

(ii) 'In *King Lear* the villainous characters hold more fascination for the audience than the virtuous ones.'

Discuss this statement with reference to at least one villainous and one virtuous character. Support your answer with suitable reference to the text.

Note that if you are asked to discuss a statement of opinion, as in the 2010 questions above, you are not necessarily expected to agree with the opinion quoted. You may, for example, decide that, in answering question (i), you will argue that brutality and viciousness triumph over honour and loyalty. Or if you choose question (ii), you may opt to argue in favour of the idea that the virtuous characters hold more fascination for the audience than the villainous ones, or even that the villainous and virtuous characters are equally fascinating.

Matters are different in the 2006 questions above because the statements made are both true. In answering such questions you must demonstrate the truth of the statements with appropriate reference to the text. In the case of (ii), you could also refer to a stage or screen production of the play.

Examination-based questions

The following lists give examples of the types of question that could be asked about *King Lear* in the Leaving Certificate exam.

Suitable for Ordinary Level

1 Why does Cordelia refuse to declare her love for her father in the way her sisters do?

2 In your opinion, why does Lear become so angry with Cordelia?

3 Do you approve of Lear's behaviour in the first scene of the play?

4 Give your opinion of the conduct of Goneril and Regan in the first scene.

5 Which of the characters in *King Lear* would you like to play? Explain why you would like to play this character.

6 Write an account of how Edmund manages to deceive Gloucester into thinking that Edgar wants to have him murdered.

7 Describe Gloucester's response to what Edmund tells him about Edgar.

8 Edgar decides to disguise himself as a mad beggar. Why, in your opinion, does he choose this particular disguise?

9 Imagine that Edgar keeps a diary of his adventures as a beggar. Write out two entries he might make describing his most memorable moments.

10 Based on what Edgar has to say during the play, give a summary of the life of a Bedlam beggar.

11 What are Edmund's reasons for turning Gloucester against Edgar? What does he hope to gain from doing this?

12 Do you believe Goneril when she tells Oswald that Lear and his knights are misbehaving? What does she want Oswald to do about this?

13 Explain why Kent wants to be Lear's servant. What makes Lear pleased to accept him?

14 The Fool has a big part in the first half of the play. What purpose does he serve? Is he of any help to Lear? Explain.

15 Goneril does not like the Fool. Suggest possible reasons for this.

16 Does Lear give Goneril any excuse for wanting to act against him? Explain your answer.

17 After his quarrel with Goneril, why does Lear want to get in touch with Regan? Does this move do him any good? Give reasons for your answer.

18 *King Lear* tells us a number of things about human beings, and how they treat each other. For example: (a) many people are vicious and cruel to others; (b) few people are to be trusted; (c) people tend to act from selfish motives. Choose *one* of these statements and explain how the play illustrates its truth.

19 Gloucester pays a heavy price for trying to do good. What is the good he tries to do and what price does he pay?

20 Pick out one scene from *King Lear* that you found enjoyable. Write a brief account of the scene, drawing attention to some of its enjoyable features.

21 Before he confronts the storm, Lear calls his daughters 'unnatural hags'. Suggest why he uses this term to describe Goneril and Regan. Do you think Lear is justified in describing them thus? Explain your answer.

22 If you were asked to select the most evil character in *King Lear*, which one would you choose? Give reasons for your choice.

23 Which character in *King Lear* do you admire most? Mention the qualities displayed by this character that appeal to you.

24 It is often noticed that Lear says more sensible things when he is mad than he does when he is sane. What can we learn from his 'mad' speeches?

25 'The good characters in *King Lear* suffer much more than the evil ones.' Agree, or disagree, with this comment, giving reasons for doing so.

26 The evil characters in *King Lear* have one thing in common: they all pursue their own interests at the expense of everyone else. Choose two such characters, showing how each behaves in this way.

27 Mention one quality that 'good' characters like Cordelia, Kent and Edgar have in common. Show how each of the three puts this quality to use.

28 Describe the scene in which Lear is reunited with Cordelia after he begins to be restored to health. What does this episode tell you (a) about Lear and (b) about Cordelia?

29 In your opinion, what is the most painful episode in the play? Describe this episode, and say why you have chosen it.

30 Why, do you think, does Edmund decide to try to save Cordelia? Why does he delay so long in revealing his decision to have her killed?

31 For much of the play Goneril and Regan are friends and allies. Then they become deadly enemies. Describe the way in which this change happens.

32 Describe what happens when Kent meets Oswald outside Gloucester's castle. What is your opinion of Kent's behaviour towards Oswald? Suggest reasons why he behaves as he does.

33 Do you feel sympathy for Oswald at any time during the play? Give reasons for your answer.

34 The scene in which Gloucester is blinded marks a major turning point in the fortunes of many of the characters. (a) Mention the characters, apart from Gloucester, whose fortunes are most affected by what happens here. (b) Explain how the lives of the characters you mention are about to be changed.

35 From the following statements, choose *one* which, in your opinion, best describes what the play is about: (a) it is a play about love; (b) it is a play about power; (c) it is a play about evil. Give reasons for your choice.

36 *King Lear* is one of Shakespeare's most popular plays, and is still performed throughout the world. Do you think it has anything important to say to modern audiences? Give reasons for your answer by referring to your experience of studying and/or watching the play in performance.

37 In your opinion, why do both Goneril and Regan fall in love with Edmund? How does Edmund feel about them? Support your answers by referring to the text of the play.

38 How important is Edgar's role in the play? Support your answer by reference to the text.

39 Select one theme from *King Lear* that caused you to think deeply and explain why. Support your answer with reference to the text.

40 Lear describes himself as 'a man more sinned against than sinning'. Do you agree with his judgement of himself? Base your answer on his conduct in the play.

Suitable for Higher Level

1 'The madness of Lear is a positive thing, because it frees him from the conventional attitudes of society, and opens his mind to truths about people, and about society, that he has previously ignored or been blind to.' Write your response to this statement, supporting your answer with appropriate reference to the text.

2 'In *King Lear*, evil prevails and does its harm for much of the time, but ultimately proves to be self-destructive.' Comment on how this pattern works through the course of the play.

3 'In *King Lear*, intentions may be good, or not seriously harmful, but they produce painful results, unforeseen, yet logical.' Respond to this statement, supporting your comments with reference to the text.

4 Lear's arrogance and selfishness are major facets of his character, and have a significant influence on the course of the tragedy. Discuss.

5 Discuss the various ways in which Cordelia, Kent and the Fool help to sustain Lear.

6 Examine the role of Edgar in the play.

7 'Lear's progress is from pride, arrogance and absolute power towards humiliation, deprivation, madness and self-knowledge.' Trace this progress through the course of the play, by reference to the text.

8 There are interesting parallels between Lear's story and Gloucester's. Comment on these parallels, referring to the text in support of the points you make.

9 In his plays, Shakespeare seldom presents characters who are either wholly good or wholly evil. Is *King Lear* an exception to this? Support your answer by reference to the text.

10 '*King Lear* is a tragedy in which the brightest hopes and expectations of the characters, whether these characters are good or bad, are continually dashed.' Discuss this view, with reference to the characters and events of the play.

11 Give an account of the events of the play from Goneril's *or* Regan's point of view. Your account should try to justify the attitudes and actions of your chosen character.

12 *King Lear* focuses our attention on the positive values of loyalty and love. Explore Shakespeare's treatment of these values.

13 'In *King Lear*, Shakespeare uses imagery to considerable effect in evoking atmosphere, in developing thematic patterns, and in the portrayal of characters by giving them distinctive voices.' Discuss this statement, supporting your answer with suitable reference to the text.

14 '*King Lear* offers valuable insights into issues of power and authority.' Discuss this view, supporting your answer with suitable reference to the text.

15 'By the close of the play, we have gained a variety of useful insights into Lear's mind, which help us to understand his complex character.' Discuss this view, supporting your answer with suitable reference to the play.

16 'Corruption, both in people and in society, is a major theme of *King Lear*.' Write a response to this statement, referring to the text in support of your answer.

17 'Different versions of justice feature largely in *King Lear*: Lear's "trial" of his three daughters in the opening scene; Cornwall's and Regan's trial and punishment of Kent and their interrogation and blinding of Gloucester; Lear's mock-trial of Goneril and Regan; and the trial by combat featuring Edgar and Edmund. We also have Lear's and Gloucester's comments on the injustice of the legal system and of society in general, and questions are raised about heavenly justice.' Discuss the ways in which this theme is treated in the play, supporting your points with suitable reference to the text.

18 'Suffering of various kinds is experienced by almost every character in *King Lear*.' Explore this idea, referring to the text in support of your answer.

19 Which character in the play do you find the most interesting? Explain your choice with appropriate reference to the text.

20 If you were asked to nominate the most evil character in the play, which one would you select? Give reasons for your choice, with suitable reference to the text.

21 'Power tends to corrupt.' Would this, in your opinion, make a suitable motto for the play? Give reasons for your answer, supporting these by reference to the text.

22 'Lear's ridiculous love-test and Cordelia's refusal to go along with it have terrible consequences for the two of them and for the rest of the characters.' Explore this point of view, supporting your answer by reference to the text.

23 The play combines elements of high tragedy, comedy, horror, farce and fairy tale. Comment on Shakespeare's use of these elements, supporting your comments by reference to the text.

24 'Conflict is an essential element of drama, and features from start to finish in *King Lear*.' Comment on this statement, supporting your answer by referring to the text of the play.

25 'Shakespeare's *King Lear* shows us how weak and fallible human judgement can be.' Discuss this statement with the aid of suitable reference to the text.

26 'Lear is the author of his own misfortune.' Do you agree with this statement? Support your answer with the aid of suitable reference to the text.

27 'Lear is not a particularly likeable character, but the play encourages us to feel profound sympathy for him, and to take his side.' Discuss this view of Lear's character, supporting the points you make by reference to the text.

28 'Violence, whether of deed or speech, deception and betrayal govern the main relationships between characters in *King Lear*.' Write a response to this statement, supporting your views by reference to the play.

29 'The mood or atmosphere of *King Lear* is a very bleak one.' Discuss this view of the play with reference to the text.

30 'No character in *King Lear* is completely in control of his or her destiny.' Discuss this statement, supporting the points you make by referring to the text.

31 '*King Lear* has some powerfully dramatic scenes.' Choose one scene that you found particularly exciting, and say why you found it to be so. Support your answer by reference to the play.

32 'Of all the characters in the play, Cordelia is the one who most deserves our admiration.' Write a response to this view of Cordelia, supporting your points by reference to the text.

33 'In *King Lear*, we are presented with a powerful vision of evil.' Write a response to this statement, with support from the text.

34 Do the events of the play support Gloucester's claim: 'As flies to wanton boys are we to the gods. They kill us for their sport'? Your answer should be based on evidence from the play.

35 'Average humanity, the play insists, is not corrupted; it remains true to that nature which lifts man above the beasts.' Comment on this statement, basing your comments on what the play tells us about 'average humanity'.

36 'In *King Lear*, the wicked are punished and die a deserved death, but apart from that, justice is not done.' (a) Give your views on this verdict, supporting your arguments by reference to the play. (b) If justice is not done, how do you think might it have been done?

37 'By his early actions, Lear has earned our fierce disapproval, but in a rapid and apparently effortless way, Shakespeare turns this disapproval into profound sympathy for him.' Consider the ways in which Lear has earned the 'fierce disapproval' of the audience, and how disapproval turns into 'profound sympathy'.

38 'For over a century and a half after Shakespeare's death, his *King Lear*, when performed, was given a happy ending, which featured Lear's restoration to the throne and the marriage of Edgar to Cordelia. This was because it was widely felt that the play Shakespeare wrote was unnecessarily brutal and depressing, and too painful to watch.' Give your views on the issues raised by the above quotation in the light of your own experience of reading the play and seeing it in performance.

39 'What we get in *King Lear* is the truth about humanity: man at his worst and man at his best.' Discuss Shakespeare's presentation of the characters in the play in the light of this comment.

40 The Chorus in *Agamemnon*, by the Greek dramatist Aeschylus, twice speaks as follows: 'Zeus, who guided men to think, has laid it down that wisdom comes only through suffering'. Give your views on whether this insight could serve as a motto for what happens in *King Lear*.

Sample essays

Suitable for Ordinary Level

1 Does Lear deserve (a) sympathy, (b) blame or (c) both of these, for his behaviour in the opening scene of the play?

I would argue that Lear deserves a great deal of blame, and only a small degree of sympathy, for his behaviour in the opening scene. He is to be blamed for a number of the things he does.

The first of these, and the worst, is his decision to divide his kingdom between his three daughters. This decision is mainly responsible for the terrible things that soon follow, all the conflicts, all the sufferings, all the deaths.

The second action for which he deserves blame is his decision to base the division of the kingdom on a childish love-test, which means that the daughter who praises him most, and who claims to love him most, will be given the most desirable share of the kingdom.

What follows from this love-test shows Lear's very poor judgement. Cordelia is too honest to play his silly game, and she is deprived by him of her share of the kingdom. He then divides this between the two hypocritical sisters who flattered him, and who then proceed to plot against him. This conduct provides a third reason for blaming Lear.

My fourth reason for blaming Lear concerns his shocking verbal abuse of Cordelia. Because she disappoints him, he rejects and disowns her with amazing violence, launching a ferocious attack on her, featuring disgusting imagery, telling her that from now on he will give her no more help, or show her no more kindness, than he would to a cannibal.

My fifth reason concerns Lear's treatment of Kent when he tries to defend Cordelia. He banishes Kent from Britain in a fit of rage, and threatens him with death if he tries to return.

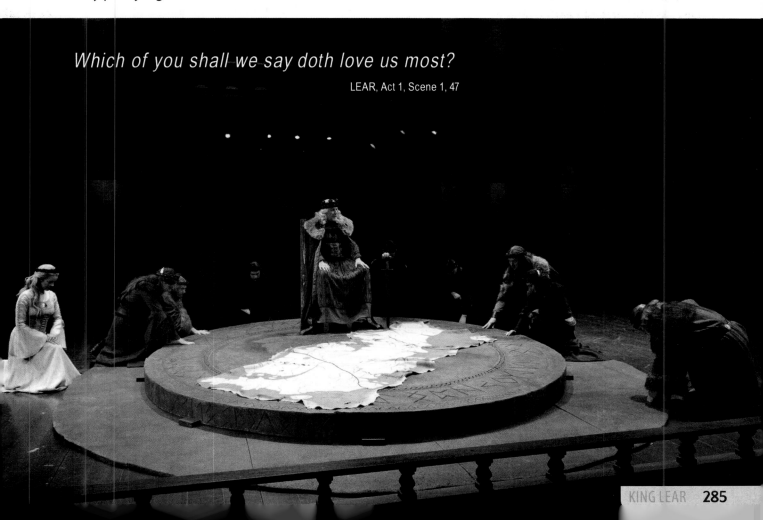

Which of you shall we say doth love us most?

LEAR, Act 1, Scene 1, 47

Lear then shows further public contempt for Cordelia when he leaves the stage with Burgundy, the man who has just refused to marry her. In this way, he leaves her to face the unkind comments of her sisters. His conduct here provides me with a sixth reason for blaming Lear.

Although it is hard to feel sympathy for Lear in this scene, it might be said in his defence that he feels disappointed and humiliated that his favourite daughter, Cordelia, in a public place, falls far short of what he hoped from her. He expected nothing more than a declaration of her strong feelings of love for him, but she denied him this and gave a cold and formal response instead. He started out looking forward to spending his final years with Cordelia, and ended up thinking that he would never see her face again.

Furthermore, Lear is an old man, used to being obeyed, and also a very proud, hot-tempered man, who resents not getting his way. Old men with backgrounds like Lear's can be difficult and changeable, and for this reason Lear might deserve our pity, if not our sympathy.

> 2 Gloucester pays dearly for helping Lear when the latter is sent out by his daughters into the storm. Briefly describe the scene where Gloucester is interrogated and punished by Cornwall and Regan.

The scene of Gloucester's interrogation and punishment is a room in his own castle. He has been captured by servants of Cornwall and Regan. Edmund has already told Cornwall of Gloucester's plan to help Lear, and also identified him as a collaborator with the French cause. If these allegations are true, he can be charged with treason, which is a hanging offence. This is why Regan calls for the death penalty ('Hang him instantly'), although Goneril wants him blinded ('Pluck out his eyes').

Gloucester is brought in and his ordeal begins. His arms are bound tightly and he is tied to a chair. Regan plucks his beard. This is a gesture of contempt, intended to humiliate him.

Then Cornwall and Regan interrogate Gloucester. The technique they use is designed to make him confess to treason, with as little delay as possible. They convince him that they already know what he has been up to ('we know the truth') by mentioning such details as letters from France, his association with traitors, and his sending Lear to safety. This breaks Gloucester's resistance. He reveals that he has sent Lear to Dover to prevent his savage daughters from plucking his eyes out and tearing at his flesh.

Having got the information they want, Cornwall sets about the task of blinding Gloucester. He puts out one of his victim's eyes by setting his foot upon it. Before he can satisfy Regan's demand that he remove the other eye, he is challenged by one of his own servants not to proceed with the punishment. A skirmish breaks out and Cornwall is fatally wounded by the brave servant. Regan attacks and kills this servant.

The physical torture of Gloucester continues as Cornwall has enough energy left to gouge out the other eye. His mental torture follows. When he expresses the hope that Edmund will avenge his blinding, Regan takes a special delight in telling him that Edmund is the one who has betrayed him. She follows this cruel act with another, when she instructs her servants to thrust Gloucester out of his own house so that he may 'smell his way to Dover'. Cornwall completes the picture of cruelty when he asks that the body of the servant who challenged him be thrown on the dunghill.

This scene gives a bleak picture of how the system of law can operate. Cornwall admits that Gloucester should be given some kind of trial. However, in this case, he is prepared to allow the primitive instinct of vengeance to dispense with law. Besides, since he and Regan are in authority, nobody can stop them from doing as they wish.

Although the scene is dominated by the savagery of Cornwall and Regan, their cruelties inspire three servants to pity Gloucester, to condemn the actions of those who have tormented him, and to do all they can to help him. They agree to follow him on his journey, and one fetches some flax and egg whites to apply to his face.

Be simple-answered, for we know the truth.

REGAN, Act 3, Scene 7, 42

3 Dysfunctional Royal Family: Lear and his daughters. Exclusive!

Using your knowledge of their behaviour in the play, write a report for a tabloid newspaper under the above headline.

High society in Britain is reeling today at news of a series of shocking events involving ex-King Lear and his family. Despite rumours, palace officials had kept details of these events secret until now. The *Daily Eclipse*, however, has uncovered the terrible facts and today brings you a glimpse of life behind palace doors.

When Lear ended his reign, we thought it was due to his very advanced age. It now appears that his mind was wandering. He called his court together to witness him divide the kingdom into three parts between Goneril, Regan and Cordelia. Courtiers were stunned when he then announced a love-contest between the three princesses.

The winner was to be the one who flattered him the most. Her prize would be the finest share of the kingdom. Amazingly, Goneril and Regan tied for first place, and Cordelia came nowhere! Cordelia simply refused to play the game. A furious Lear then disowned her.

Cordelia left for a new life overseas with husband-to-be, the King of France. There were great scenes of sadness at her departure, and Lear's Fool was said to be inconsolable. Goneril and Regan, who had hit the jackpot with half a kingdom each, were noticeably absent. It now seems that they were busy plotting against their father!

Lear, a pensioner of no fixed abode, wanted to stay at the palaces of his two remaining daughters. It was only then that these women showed their true colours.

The old king demanded to retain one hundred knights, with their squires and servants, to be fed and housed by Goneril and Regan. Sources close to the family say that Lear considered this a small price for them to pay in return for his generosity, whereas his thankless daughters disagreed.

The sisters were disgusted by Lear's followers, and balked at the cost of entertaining them. They could see no reason why he needed even one follower.

Under pressure from them, Lear became increasingly angry. He had a growing feeling that Britain, under its new rulers, was no country for old men. In various outbursts he accused them of ingratitude and called down terrible curses on their heads.

Observers say that Lear was powerless and felt extremely sorry for himself. In the end he stormed out, following an incident at Gloucester's castle. Calling his daughters 'unnatural hags', he galloped off in a raging temper into the violent tempest that caused such devastation last month. Shockingly, the evil sisters demanded that the castle doors be shut in case he returned.

Lear's experience at the hands of these daughters from hell drove him mad. Sources close to Edgar, Earl of Gloucester, have revealed that Lear ran wild on the heath, criticising women and the legal system, calling both of these corrupt. It seems that our former king was more aware of the issues facing our poorest people than we thought!

The evil sisters' united front soon crumbled when they both made a beeline for the bed of handsome bachelor Edmund, illegitimate son of the Earl of Gloucester. Following the murder of the Duke of Cornwall, Regan decided that marriage to Edmund would solve a lot of her problems. However, Goneril, tired of the Duke of Albany, was distraught at the prospect.

It has been confirmed that these events led to the recent failed French invasion of this nation. When Cordelia heard how her sisters had treated her father, she came to England with a French army to help him.

The invaders were defeated by our brave soldiers. Lear and Cordelia did not die in battle, as had been speculated, but were captured and condemned to death by Edmund and Goneril. Lear killed the soldier who hanged Cordelia, but then died soon afterwards of a broken heart.

The love triangle between Regan, Goneril and Edmund ended in the joining of all three in death. Goneril poisoned her love rival, Regan, and then knifed herself. Edmund was killed by Edgar in single combat.

Tomorrow's edition will feature further gruesome details of the intimate lives of this dysfunctional family. We will also carry exclusive eye-witness accounts of the hanging of Cordelia and the blinding of the Earl of Gloucester.

I am a man
More sinned against than sinning.

LEAR, Act 3, Scene 2, 58–9

Suitable for Higher Level

'Reading or seeing *King Lear* is a horrifying as well as an uplifting experience.'

Write a response to this view, supporting the points you make by reference to the play.

Based on my experience of studying *King Lear* and seeing it performed on stage, I agree that this play offers an experience that is both horrifying and uplifting. I propose to deal with these two elements separately.

When one is considering the horrifying aspects of *King Lear*, a distinction should be made between reading the play and seeing it performed. When I attended a performance of *King Lear* in the Abbey Theatre, I was struck by how the horrifying and painful elements had a much greater impact on me than they did when I read the text. This is not surprising, since watching a revolting act performed is bound to be more disturbing than reading or hearing about it.

The horrifying aspects of *King Lear* are not confined to the cruel and inhuman deeds done by some of the characters. The words these characters say can also be horrifying. To take one example, in the first scene of the play, when Cordelia 'cannot heave her heart into her mouth' and flatter Lear with false declarations of love, he reacts with a furious, and quite vicious, verbal assault on the daughter he has just called 'our joy' and now calls his 'sometime daughter', no more welcome in his sight than if she were a barbarous cannibal who eats her own children. A horrifying speech is then matched by a horrifying act: he renounces his blood relationship with Cordelia and deprives her of her share of the kingdom and of her dowry. Lear turns on Kent, who tries to defend Cordelia, with similar violence. Forgetting that he lacks the authority to do so, he passes a sentence of banishment on Kent, with death as the penalty if he tries to return.

It is soon Lear's turn to be victim, rather than perpetrator, of an unnatural and horrifying punishment. This time the agents of unnatural cruelty are Goneril and Regan. Their common desire is to banish Lear, whom they have come to think of as an unwanted burden, from their lives, just as Lear banished Cordelia from his. By giving away his kingdom, Lear lost all his power and became totally dependent on the good will of his daughters. The appalling, terrifying truth soon emerges. The two daughters to whom he has given his kingdom and entrusted his welfare, prove quite willing to allow him to risk his life and his sanity in a frightful thunderstorm rather than afford him the shelter of Gloucester's castle. Should Lear return to the castle, Goneril instructs Gloucester: 'My lord, entreat him by no means to stay.' Regan and her husband order Gloucester to shut his doors. It is harrowing to see Lear thoroughly humiliated, deprived of the company of his knights and of his self-esteem, by two daughters whom he now calls, with good reason, 'wicked creatures' and 'unnatural hags'.

The horrifying behaviour of Regan and Goneril to their father is replicated by that of Edmund to his father, Gloucester. Edmund, who has already contrived the banishment of his brother, Edgar, on a false charge, betrays his father to Cornwall for helping Lear. The scene depicting Cornwall's revenge on Gloucester explores new depths of horror: Gloucester is blinded by Cornwall in full view of the audience and with the hearty approval of Regan, who adds to the physical horror by telling Gloucester that his own son Edmund betrayed him.

The culminating act of horror is the hanging of Cordelia on the orders of Goneril and Edmund. Mercifully, this act is reported, not shown. Similarly, the suicide of Goneril occurs off stage, although the bloody knife with which she stabbed herself to death, after she admitted to poisoning Regan, is produced on stage. The hanged body of Cordelia is carried on stage by Lear, whose harrowing comments on the manner of Cordelia's death, and his attempts to prevent it, reinforce the horror of this 'cheerless, dark and deadly' scene: 'I might have saved her! Now she's gone for ever! … I killed the slave that was a-hanging thee.'

All these elements help to explain why, for over a century and a half, audiences found *King Lear* too distressing to watch, and why they insisted on a happy ending.

An account of the play would not be complete without mentioning the uplifting elements we encounter throughout. When we talk about uplifting elements, we should consider the play from a moral point of view, that is, in terms of the good and evil elements it presents. If the moral universe of *King Lear* could fairly be described as given over to evil, the play could not be described as uplifting, since evil is not, by definition, uplifting. However, it can be said that while some of the characters deserve to be called evil (Edmund, Goneril, Regan, Cornwall and, to an extent, Oswald), others (Cordelia, Kent and Edgar) are thoroughly good, and Gloucester, Albany and unnamed characters such as Cornwall's servants, who appear only briefly, display positive moral qualities.

Lear, the tragic hero, initially displays some notable moral weaknesses: he behaves unjustly to Cordelia and Kent and gives way too easily to rage and bad temper. He is self-centred and self-willed. After Act 1, however, he is the victim of evil rather than its perpetrator. Gloucester, as we learn from his encounter with Kent in the first scene, appears to have been morally lax and irresponsible, but develops in the course of the action into a somewhat heroic figure.

The uplifting elements in *King Lear* concern virtues such as truth, unselfishness, loyalty, willingness to help those in distress and, most notably, readiness to forgive those who have wronged us. I will look first at forgiveness in the play. Kent provides the earliest example. Lear wrongs Kent deeply for telling him the truth about his behaviour to Cordelia. Kent's response to being wronged is not only to forgive Lear but to disguise himself in order to serve him and to perform any number of difficult tasks for him. For Kent, Lear, no matter how he has ill-treated him, is still the master he loves.

Kent's behaviour throughout the play demonstrates a heroic sense of love and loyalty. Seeing these virtues in action is a profoundly uplifting experience. Edgar conveys a sense of this to Albany towards the end of the play, when he talks of 'the banished Kent; who in disguise followed his enemy King, and did him service improper for a slave'.

Edgar is another character who has suffered a grave wrong. Edmund led Gloucester to believe that Edgar wanted him murdered in order to inherit his estates. Gloucester responded by making Edgar an outlaw. Like Kent, Edgar returns good for evil. One of the most moving and uplifting experiences in the final scene is Edgar's account of his efforts on behalf of the father who had wronged him. He became his guide, begged for him, saved him from despair and suicide and, what he does not mention, saved him from being killed by Oswald. On his way to challenge Edmund, he had asked for his father's blessing. Another uplifting moment is Edgar's offer to exchange forgiveness with the dying Edmund: 'Let's exchange charity.'

Cordelia's conciliatory, comforting approach to her father on his restoration to sanity is another uplifting experience. She has forgotten the wrong Lear has done to her. All that concerns her is the suffering he has endured, and her need to 'repair those violent harms that my two sisters have in thy reverence made'. Lear is deeply conscious of his guilt, but she asks his blessing. When he tells her she has cause not to love him, she simply replies, 'No cause, no cause.' When he says 'Pray you, now, forget and forgive,' it is as if he has read her mind, because this is what she has done.

During the worst phases of the play Shakespeare does not forget to show the goodness ordinary human beings are capable of, even when their decent impulses can put their own welfare at risk. Two examples illustrate this. The cautious Gloucester, when his moral sense is roused by the dangers facing Lear, risks his own safety and goes to Lear's aid, enduring torture and blinding for his trouble. During the horrifying blinding scene, one of Cornwall's servants is killed in a brave attempt to interrupt Cornwall's terrible work, and other servants go to Gloucester's assistance after he has been turned out of his own house.

These and other inspiring episodes save the play from being an unrelieved chronicle of horrors, and lead me to conclude that *King Lear* offers an experience that is both horrifying and uplifting.